T0401047

EDUCATION IN A COMPETITIVE AND GLOBALIZING WORLD

YOUNG ADULTS WITH DISABILITIES

POST-HIGH SCHOOL OUTCOMES

EDUCATION IN A COMPETITIVE AND GLOBALIZING WORLD

Additional books in this series can be found on Nova's website
under the Series tab.

Additional E-books in this series can be found on Nova's website
under the E-book tab.

DISABILITY AND THE DISABLED-ISSUES, LAWS AND PROGRAMS

Additional books in this series can be found on Nova's website
under the Series tab.

Additional E-books in this series can be found on Nova's website
under the E-book tab.

YOUNG ADULTS WITH DISABILITIES

POST-HIGH SCHOOL OUTCOMES

DAVID F. MORRIS
AND
CHRISTOPHER B. ALLEN
EDITORS

Nova Science Publishers, Inc.
New York

Copyright © 2012 by Nova Science Publishers, Inc.

All rights reserved. No part of this book may be reproduced, stored in a retrieval system or transmitted in any form or by any means: electronic, electrostatic, magnetic, tape, mechanical photocopying, recording or otherwise without the written permission of the Publisher.

For permission to use material from this book please contact us:
Telephone 631-231-7269; Fax 631-231-8175
Web Site: http://www.novapublishers.com

NOTICE TO THE READER

The Publisher has taken reasonable care in the preparation of this book, but makes no expressed or implied warranty of any kind and assumes no responsibility for any errors or omissions. No liability is assumed for incidental or consequential damages in connection with or arising out of information contained in this book. The Publisher shall not be liable for any special, consequential, or exemplary damages resulting, in whole or in part, from the readers' use of, or reliance upon, this material. Any parts of this book based on government reports are so indicated and copyright is claimed for those parts to the extent applicable to compilations of such works.

Independent verification should be sought for any data, advice or recommendations contained in this book. In addition, no responsibility is assumed by the publisher for any injury and/or damage to persons or property arising from any methods, products, instructions, ideas or otherwise contained in this publication.

This publication is designed to provide accurate and authoritative information with regard to the subject matter covered herein. It is sold with the clear understanding that the Publisher is not engaged in rendering legal or any other professional services. If legal or any other expert assistance is required, the services of a competent person should be sought. FROM A DECLARATION OF PARTICIPANTS JOINTLY ADOPTED BY A COMMITTEE OF THE AMERICAN BAR ASSOCIATION AND A COMMITTEE OF PUBLISHERS.

Additional color graphics may be available in the e-book version of this book.

Library of Congress Cataloging-in-Publication Data

ISBN: 978-1-61942-159-2

Published by Nova Science Publishers, Inc. ✦ *New York*

CONTENTS

PREFACE

This book examines The National Longitudinal Transition Study-2 (NLTS2) funded by the U.S. Department of Education, which provides a unique source of information to help in developing an understanding of the experiences of secondary school students with disabilities nationally as they go through their early adult years. NLTS2 addresses questions about youth with disabilities in transition by providing information over a 10-year period about a nationally representative sample of secondary school students with disabilities who were 13 to 16 years old and receiving special education services in grade 7 or above. Information about these former secondary school students is examined to describe the experiences of young adults with disabilities in the postsecondary education, employment, independence, and social domains in their first 6-8 years out of high school.

Chapter 1 - Increasingly, researchers are contending that changes in the latter part of the 20th century and the early 21st century have prompted a reconsideration of the notion of adolescence - a developmental stage encompassing the years between 11 and 18 - being immediately followed by adulthood - a stage marked by "completion of schooling, movement from the parental household, entrance into the labor force, formation of partnerships, and the onset of childbearing and parenting". They suggest that, among other social shifts, an increasing emphasis on postsecondary education and the growing struggles postadolescents face in becoming economically self-sufficient elongate or postpone the transitions usually associated with adulthood. Recognizing this reality, a growing body of research is focusing on the period of "early adulthood," ages 18 through 34, as distinct from adolescence and full. The John T. and Catherine D. MacArthur Foundation Research Network on Transitions to Adulthood and Public Policy recently assembled an extensive collection of analyses of the social forces shaping the early adult period and the experiences that characterize it. After reviewing the available data, however, the authors concluded that a need remains to "pioneer research efforts aimed at understanding the new frontiers of early adult life".

Chapter 2 - Traditional social indicators of adolescents emerging into adulthood include living independently, earning a postsecondary degree, obtaining full-time employment, getting married, or becoming a parent. Although there has been a shift in the timing and sequence of adult transitions these core indicators have remained the same. As youth with disabilities leave high school and transition to adulthood, they are increasingly exposed to opportunities for postsecondary education, employment, and independent living. Current national policy mandates are holding schools and states more accountable for the postschool outcomes of youth with disabilities. The 2004 reauthorization of the Individuals With Disabilities Education Act (IDEA) highlighted the importance of improving the postschool outcomes of youth with disabilities by requiring schools to develop "measurable postschool goals in the areas of employment, education/training, and, if appropriate, independent living" and states to "report student postschool outcome performance".

In: Young Adults with Disabilities
Editors: David F. Morris and Christopher B. Allen

ISBN: 978-1- 61942-159-2
© 2012 Nova Science Publishers, Inc.

Chapter 1

THE POST-HIGH SCHOOL OUTCOMES OF YOUNG ADULTS WITH DISABILITIES UP TO 8 YEARS AFTER HIGH SCHOOL: A REPORT FROM THE NATIONAL LONGITUDINAL TRANSITION STUDY-2 (NLTS2)

United States Department of Education

EXECUTIVE SUMMARY

Increasingly, researchers are contending that changes in the latter part of the 20th century and the early 21st century have prompted a reconsideration of the notion of adolescence (e.g., Fussell and Furstenberg 2005)—a developmental stage encompassing the years between 11 and 18 (Hall 1904)—being immediately followed by adulthood—a stage marked by "completion of schooling, movement from the parental household, entrance into the labor force, formation of partnerships, and the onset of childbearing and parenting" (Furstenberg, Rumbaut, and Settersten 2005, p. 7). They suggest that, among other social shifts, an increasing emphasis on postsecondary education and the growing struggles postadolescents face in becoming economically self-sufficient elongate or postpone the transitions usually associated with adulthood. Recognizing this reality, a growing body of research is focusing on the period of "early adulthood," ages 18 through 34 (Furstenberg, Rumbaut, and Settersten 2005), as distinct from adolescence and full adulthood (e.g., Arnett 2001; Arnett 2002). The John T. and Catherine D. MacArthur Foundation Research Network on Transitions to Adulthood and Public Policy recently assembled an extensive collection of analyses of the social forces shaping the early adult period and the experiences that characterize it (Settersten, Furstenberg, and Rumbaut 2005). After reviewing the available data, however, the authors concluded that a need remains to "pioneer research efforts aimed at understanding the new frontiers of early adult life" (Settersten, Furstenberg, and Rumbaut 2005, p. 7).

The National Longitudinal Transition Study-2 (NLTS2) funded by the National Center for Special Education Research at the Institute of Education Sciences, U.S. Department of Education, provides a unique source of information to help in developing an understanding of the experiences of secondary school students with disabilities nationally as they go through their early adult years. NLTS2 addresses questions about youth with disabilities in transition by providing information over a 10-year period about a nationally representative sample of secondary school students with disabilities who were 13 to 16 years old and receiving special education services in grade 7 or above, under the Individuals With Disabilities Education Act (IDEA) in the 2000–01 school year. NLTS2 findings generalize to youth with disabilities nationally and to youth in each of the 12 federal special education disability categories in use for students in the NLTS2 age range. The study was designed to collect data on sample members from multiple sources in five waves, beginning in 2001 and ending in 2009.

This document uses information about these former secondary school students to describe the experiences of young adults with disabilities in the postsecondary education, employment, independence, and social domains in their first 8 years out of high school.

Much of the information reported in this document comes from young adults with disabilities themselves in the form of responses to either a telephone interview or a self-administered mail survey with a subset of key items from the telephone interview[1] conducted in 2009, as part of NLTS2's referred to as Wave 5. Data for young adults who fifth and final wave of data were reported by parents to be unable to respond to an interview or complete a questionnaire or who did not respond to interview or survey attempts were provided by parents. Data from the three sources were combined for the analyses reported here and subsetted to include only data for those who were known to be out of high school at the time of the Wave 5 data collection in 2009. In constructing variables that describe young adult's experiences since leaving high school, data from the Wave 2 through Wave 4 parent and youth telephone interviews and mail surveys (conducted in 2003, 2005, and 2007, respectively) also were used for young adults who were out of high school at the time of each data collection. When similar data items were available, comparisons were made between young adults with disabilities and the same-age young adults in the general population. The analyses approach used for the general population data bases mirrors the approach used for NLTS2 data. General population comparison data were taken from The National Longitudinal Survey of Youth, 1997 (NLSY97), 2005 data collection, from The National Longitudinal Study of Adolescent Health (Add Health), Wave 3 collected in 2001-2002, and from the Current Population Survey (CPS) 2009.[2] Comparison analyses of these weighted data included a subset of respondents who were out of high school at the time and were 21 to 25 years old.[3]

This report focuses on the subset of young adults with disabilities who were out of secondary school and 21 to 25 years old when telephone interviews were conducted with their parents and, whenever possible, with the young adults themselves in 2009. Young adults included in this report varied in the length of time they were out of high school, ranging from less than 1 month to 8 years post-high school. NLTS2 findings reported in this document use information collected from these young adults or parents to describe the experiences of young adults with disabilities in the postsecondary education, employment, independence, and social domains in their first 4 years out of high school. Findings are presented for young adults with disabilities as a whole and for those who differ in disability category, length of time out of high school, highest level of educational attainment, gender, parent's household income, and race/ethnicity.

This report is organized to provide information on young adults with disabilities in several key domains, including the following:

- Postsecondary education enrollment, educational experiences, and completion.
- Employment status and characteristics of young adults' current or most recent job.
- Productive engagement in school, work, or preparation for work.
- Residential independence; the prevalence of marriage and parenting; and aspects of their financial independence.
- Social and community involvement, including friendship activities and community participation in both positive and negative ways.

This executive summary presents all findings related to these key domains that are included in the full report for young adults with disabilities as a group as well as all differences between young adults who differ in their length of time since leaving high school, highest level of educational attainment, and demographic characteristics that are significantly different at at least the $p < .01$ level. Patterns of significant differences between disability categories are noted and illustrated by specific examples of significant findings.

Postsecondary Education

Over the course of a lifetime, an individual with a college degree will earn $1 million more on average than a worker with a high school diploma (U.S. Department of Commerce U.S. Census Bureau 2002). As the U.S. economy becomes progressively more knowledge based, attaining a postsecondary education becomes more critical (Carnevale and Desrochers 2003). For example, only 20 percent of workers needed at least some college for their jobs in 1959; by 2000, that number had increased to 56 percent (Carnevale and Fry 2000).

Along with their peers in the general population, young adults with disabilities are increasingly focusing on postsecondary education. Postsecondary education is a primary post-high school goal for more than four out of five secondary school students with disabilities who have transition plans (Cameto, Levine, and Wagner 2004). NLTS2 provides the opportunity to examine the postsecondary education experiences of young adults with disabilities who have been out of secondary school up to 8 years.

- Sixty percent of young adults with disabilities were reported to have continued on to postsecondary education within 8 years of leaving high school.
- Young adults with disabilities were more likely to have enrolled in 2-year or community colleges (44 percent) than in vocational, business, or technical schools (32 percent) or 4-year colleges or universities (19 percent).
- The mean time between leaving high school and enrolling in a postsecondary school was 7 months; however, the median was 3 months.
- Most students with disabilities were enrolled in postsecondary education programs on a consistent (77 percent), full-time (71 percent) basis.
- Postsecondary students who attended 2-year colleges were more likely to have been enrolled in an academic than vocational course of study (51 percent vs. 30 percent). Students at all types of colleges focused on a broad range of majors.
- To receive accommodations or supports from a postsecondary school because of a disability, students first must disclose a disability to their school. Sixty-three percent

of postsecondary students who were identified by their secondary schools as having a disability did not consider themselves to have a disability by the time they transitioned to postsecondary school. Twenty-eight percent of postsecondary students with disabilities identified themselves as having a disability and informed their postsecondary schools of their disability.

- Nineteen percent of postsecondary students who were identified as having a disability by their secondary schools were reported to receive accommodations or supports from their postsecondary schools because of their disability. In contrast, when these postsecondary students were in high school, 87 percent received some type of accommodation or support because of a disability.
- Postsecondary students who were given assistance because of their disability received a range of accommodations and supports from their schools. Additional time to complete tests was the most frequently received type of assistance, with 79 percent receiving this type of accommodation.
- Postsecondary students received help with their schoolwork beyond the support provided by schools because of their disability. Forty-four percent reported receiving some type of help, whether or not the assistance was related to their disability.
- Most students who received any type of help with their schoolwork reported that these supports were "very" or "somewhat" useful(88 percent) and that they "probably" or "definitely" (85 percent) were getting enough assistance.
- Forty-three percent of postsecondary students who had not received any type of help with their school work reported that it would have been helpful to have received assistance with school work.
- On average, students with disabilities who had been out of high school up to 8 years and had attended a 2-year or 4-year college had earned 59 semester credits. Those who had attended 2-year or community colleges had earned on average 23 semester credits, and those who ever had attended a 4-year college had earned 71 semester credits.
- Ninety percent of students with disabilities who were currently enrolled in postsecondary school reported that they were working toward a diploma or certificate.
- At the time of the Wave 5 interview, 41 percent of postsecondary students had graduated from their most recent postsecondary program; 31 percent had left their most recent postsecondary school prior to completing, and the remaining students still were currently enrolled in their postsecondary program at the time of the interview. Forty-one percent had completed their 2-year college programs, 57 percent had completed their vocational, business, or technical school programs, and 34 percent had completed their 4-year college programs.

Employment

Many adults consider employment a central component of their lives, providing not only economic benefits, but also a social network and a sense of worth as a productive member of society (Levinson and Palmer 2005; Rogan, Grossi, and Gajewski 2002). Indeed, employment has been linked to a range of positive outcomes, including financial independence and enhanced self-esteem (Fabian 1992; Lehman et al. 2002; Polak and Warner 1996). Given the importance of post-high school employment, preparation for employment is a primary focus of many transition services for secondary-school-age youth with disabilities, and achieving employment is the primary transition goal of the majority of secondary students with disabilities served under IDEA (Cameto, Levine, and Wagner 2004).

- Working for pay outside the home was an aspect of the post-high school experiences of a majority of young adults with disabilities. Ninety-one percent of young adults with disabilities out of high school up to 8 years reported having been employed at some time since leaving high school, holding an average of four jobs during that time.
- Among young adults with disabilities who had been out of high school 8 years, 67 percent worked full time at their current or most recent job.
- Wages of working young adults averaged $10.40 per hour, and 61 percent received at least one of the benefits investigated in NLTS2 (paid vacation or sick leave, health insurance, or retirement benefits).
- The average hourly wage of young adults with disabilities who were employed full time was significantly higher than that of young adults working part time ($11.00 vs. $9.00).
- Young adults working full time were more likely to receive employment benefits (paid vacation or sick leave, health insurance, and retirement benefits) than those working part time (77 percent vs. 31 percent).
- About 26 percent of working young adults reportedly had employers who were aware of their disability, and 7 percent reported receiving some kind of accommodation on the job, most often adaptations to assignments or supervisory arrangements.
- Approximately 88 percent of working young adults reported that they liked their job at least fairly well and 90 percent reported being treated pretty well by others at their job. Approximately 62 percent to 75 percent agreed that their job paid pretty well, offered opportunities for advancement, put their education and training to good use, and, among those employed 6 months or more, had thus far involved a raise or promotion.
- Despite positive feelings about their jobs, young adults with disabilities were more likely to have quit their last job (53 percent) than to have left for other reasons.

Productive Engagement in the Community

NLTS2 considered young adults with disabilities as being productively engaged in the community if they had participated in employment, education, and/or job training activities since leaving secondary school. Addressing this broader concept of engagement, rather than considering individual outcomes (employment or postsecondary education) separately, was encouraged by the advisory panel during the design of the initial NLTS; as a result, NLTS was one of the first studies to present a broader perspective on how young adults and young adults with disabilities could be productively engaged in their communities. The advisory panel for the current study continued to endorse that view of engagement. The importance of this broader view of what constitutes a successful transition is now incorporated in the current federal policy that requires states to collect data on "Indicator 14"—i.e., "the percent of young adults who had IEPs, are no longer in secondary school, and who have been competitively employed, enrolled in some type of postsecondary school, or both, within one year of leaving high school" (20 U.S.C. 1416(a)(3)(B)). The NLTS2 operationalization of this concept, as endorsed by the NLTS2 design advisory panel, is somewhat broader than Indicator 14, in that NLTS2 includes all forms of employment, not just competitive employment, and includes job training as a productive form of preparation for work, in addition to enrollment in postsecondary education.

- Ninety-four percent of young adults with disabilities who had been out of secondary school up to 8 years were reported to have been engaged in employment, postsecondary education, and/or job training during this post-high school period.
- Thirty percent had paid employment as their only mode of engagement since high school.
- Forty-two percent had been employed since leaving high school and also had been enrolled in postsecondary education.
- Nineteen percent had been employed and also involved in other activities, including job training.
- Postsecondary education was the only mode of engagement since high school for 3 percent of those with disabilities.

Household Circumstances of Out-of-High School Young adults with Disabilities

Markers on the path to adult responsibility typically have included financial and residential independence and self-sufficiency, marriage, and parenting (Arnett 2000; Chambers, Rabren, and Dunn 2009, Rindfuss 1991; Settersten 2006).

- Within 8 years of leaving high school, 59 percent of young adults with disabilities had lived independently (on their own or with a spouse, partner, or roommate), and 4 percent had lived semi-independently (primarily in a college dormitory or military housing).
- When young adults were asked about their satisfaction with their current living arrangement, 69 percent reported being satisfied with their residential arrangement.
- Twenty-nine percent of young adults with disabilities reported having had or fathered a child by the time they had been out of high school for up to 8 years. Twenty-two percent of males reported having fathered a child and 42 percent of females reported having had a child.
- Thirteen percent of young adults with disabilities were married.
- Fifty-nine percent of young adults with disabilities had a savings account, 59 percent had a checking account, and 41 percent had a credit card in their own name. Seventy-

four percent had annual individual incomes (or for those living with a spouse, household incomes) of $25,000 or less.

Social and Community Involvement of out-of-High School Young Adults with Disabilities

Social inclusion "rests on the principle that democratic societies are enriched by the full inclusion of their citizens in the ebb and flow of community affairs"(Osgood et al. 2005, p. 12). Consistent with this notion, the domains encompassed in an understanding of a successful transition to young adulthood for individuals with disabilities have long included living successfully in one's community (Halpern 1985; National Center on Educational Outcomes 1993). An important aspect of whether a young adult is living successfully in the community is the "adequacy of his or her social and interpersonalnetwork [which] is possibly the most important of all" aspects of adjustment for young adults with disabilities (Halpern 1985, p. 480).

- NLTS2 findings suggest that young adults with disabilities had active friendships—77 percent reported seeing friends outside of organized activities at least weekly.
- Fifty-four percent were reported to communicate by computer at least once a week, with 32 percent doing so once a day or more often.
- The participation rate in any one of three types of extracurricular activities—lessons or classes outside of school, volunteer or community service activities, and organized school or community groups—was 52 percent, rangi ng from 20 percent to 39 percent of young adults across the three types of activities.
- Eleven percent of young adults were reported never to see friends outside of organized activities, and 48 percent did not take part in any of the three types of extracurricular activities mentioned above.
- More than three-fourths (78 percent) of young adults with disabilities had driving privileges and 71 percent exercised civic participation through registering to vote.
- Several negative forms of community participation or involvement also characterized the out-of-high school experiences of some young adults with disabilities. For example, 11 percent reported having been in a physical fight in the past year and 17 percent reported carrying a weapon in the past 30 days.
- Fifty percent of young adults with disabilities reported at some time having been stopped and questioned by police for reasons other than a traffic violation, and 32 percent had been arrested. Seventeen percent had spent a night in jail and 18 percent were reported to have been on probation or parole.

Disability Category Differences

Disability category differences are apparent in many of the post-high school outcomes examined in this report. For example, youth with sensory impairments, emotional disturbances, mental retardation, or multiple disabilities were quite different from each other in their patterns of post-high school outcomes.

Youth with Sensory Impairments

- Young adults with visual or hearing impairments were more likely to attend postsecondary school (71 percent and 75 percent) than those with emotional disturbances, multiple disabilities, or mental retardation (53 percent, 33 percent, and 29 percent, respectively). In addition, young adults with visual or hearing impairments were more likely to have enrolled in a 4-year college or university (40 percent and 34 percent) than those with emotional disturbances, autism, other health impairments, multiple disabilities, or mental retardation (7 percent to 20 percent), and those with visual impairments also were more likely to have attended a 4-year college than those with learning disabilities, orthopedic impairments, or traumatic brain injuries (21 percent, 26 percent, and 19 percent, respectively).

- Young adults with visual or hearing impairments were more likely to have received accommodations and supports from their schools because of a disability (59 percent and 53 percent, respectively) than were young adults speech/language impairments, other health impairments, learning disabilities, emotional disturbances, or mental retardation (12 percent to 24 percent).

- Young adults with visual impairments were less likely to have been employed at the time of the interview than young adults with other health impairments, speech/language impairments, or learning disabilities (44 percent to 67 percent).

- Young adults with visual impairments were more likely to have disclosed a disability to their employers (75 percent) compared with young adults with learning disabilities, speech/language impairments, other health impairments, emotional disturbances, or traumatic brain injuries (19 percent to 30 percent).

- Young adults with hearing impairments were reported to be more likely communicate by computer at least daily (e.g., e-mail, instant message, or participate in chat rooms), than those with emotional disturbances, autism, or multiple disabilities to (21 percent to 51 percent).

- Young adults with visual impairments were more likely to have taken lessons or classes outside of formal school enrollment (38 percent) than were young adults with learning disabilities, mental retardation, other health impairments, or traumatic brain injuries (12 percent to 20 percent). They also had a significantly higher rate of participation in volunteer or community service activities (44 percent) than did young adults with speech impairments or mental retardation (26 percent and 19 percent, respectively). Young adults with visual impairments also were more likely to have belonged to an organized community or extracurricular group than young adults with emotional disturbances (51 percent vs. 32 percent).

Young Adults with Emotional Disturbances

- Young adults in several categories were more likely than those with emotional disturbances to have enrolled in 4-year colleges or universities, including those with speech/language impairments, hearing impairments, visual impairments, or orthopedic impairments (11 percent vs. 26 percent to 40 percent).

- Young adults with emotional disturbances who were enrolled in postsecondary programs were less likely than young adults in several other disability categoriesto have informed their schools of a disability, including those with orthopedic impairments, visual impairments, multiple disabilities, deaf-blindness, autism, or hearing impairments (27 percent vs. 59 percent to 76 percent).
- Involvement with the criminal justice system also was more common for young adults with emotional disturbances than those in many other categories. Overall, 75 percent of young adults with emotional disturbances had been involved with the criminal justice system at some point in their lives. Their rate of ever having been involved in the criminal justice system at all was significantly higher than the rates for those in all other disability categories (26 percent to 55 percent).
- Young adults with emotional disturbances were more likely to have been stopped by the police, other than for a traffic violation, in the past 2 years (43 percent) than young adults in all other categories except traumatic brain injury (4 percent to 21 percent).
- Young adults with emotional disturbances also had significantly higher rates of being arrested in the past 2 years (27 percent) than those in all other categories except traumatic brain injury (less than 1 percent to 12 percent). They were more likely to have spent a night in jailin the past 2 years (19 percent) than young adults with in all other categories except traumatic brain injury and other health impairment (less than 1 percent to 8 percent).
- Young adults with emotional disturbances also were more likely to have been on probation or parole in the past 2 years (15 percent) than young adults in all other categories except traumatic brain injury and other health impairment (less than 1 percent to 8 percent).

Young Adults with Mental Retardation or Multiple Disabilities

- Young adults with mental retardation or multiple disabilities were exceeded by young adults in several categories in their rate of enrollment in postsecondary education. Those with learning disabilities; speech/language impairments, hearing impairments, visual impairments, orthopedic impairments, other health impairments, or traumatic brain injuries were more likely to be enrolled in postsecondary education than those with multiple disabilities or mental retardation (61 percent to 75 percent vs. 33 percent and 29 percent, respectively). Young adults with emotional disturbances, autism or deaf-blindness (53 percent, 44 percent, and 57 percent, respectively) also significantly exceeded young adults with mental retardation in their rates of postsecondary enrollment.
- Students with multiple disabilities were more likely to receive accommodations or supports from their postsecondary schools because of a disability than were those with speech/language impairments, learning disabilities, or other health impairments (46 percent vs. 12 percent, 17 percent, and 15 percent, respectively).
- In the employment domain, young adults with mental retardation or multiple disabilities were less likely to have been employed at the time of the interview than young adults with other health impairments, speech/language impairments, learning

disabilities, or hearing impairments (39 percent and 39 percent vs. 57 percent to 67 percent).

- Young adults with mental retardation or multiple disabilities worked fewer hours per week on average (28 hours and 25 hours, respectively) than those with learning disabilities, emotional disturbances, speech/language impairments, or other health impairments (34 to 38 hours). Young adults with learning disabilities, speech/language impairments, hearing impairments, visual impairments, other health impairment, or emotional disturbances earned more per hour on average than their peers with mental retardation ($10.50 to $11.10 vs. $7.90).

- Young adults with mental retardation or multiple disabilities were more likely to report that their employers were aware of their disability than young adults with learning disabilities, speech/language impairment, or other health impairments, emotional disturbances, or traumatic brain injuries (60 percent and 72 percent vs. 19 percent to 30 percent).

- In terms of residential independence, young adults with multiple disabilities were less likely to have lived independently than those with learning disabilities, emotional disturbances, or speech/language impairments (16 percent vs. 65 percent, 63 percent, and 51 percent, respectively). In addition, they were less likely to be married than those with learning disabilities, emotional disturbances, speech/language impairments, or mental retardation (1 percent vs. 11 percent to 15 percent).

- In the social domain, 53 percent of young adults with multiple disabilities and 58 percent of those with mental retardation reported seeing friends informally at least weekly. This rate was exceeded by young adults with speech/language impairments, learning disabilities, other health impairments, visual impairments, traumatic brain injuries, hearing impairments, or emotional disturbances (75 percent to 84 percent). Youth with visual or orthopedic impairments, deaf-blindness, or multiple disabilities also were more likely than youth with mental retardation to have belonged to an organized community group, taken extracurricular lessons or classes, or taken part in volunteer service activities (47 percent vs. 62 percent to 67 percent).

- In the financial domain, young adults in most disability categories were more likely to have used several types of financial tools than were young adults with mental retardation. For example, compared with young adults with mental retardation, young adults with learning disabilities, speech/language impairments, hearing impairments, visual impairments, orthopedic impairments, or other health impairments were more likely to have savings account (42 percent vs. 63 percent to 67 percent), to have a checking account (29 percent vs. 63 percent to 74 percent),or a credit card (19 percent vs. 47 percent to 57 percent).

Differences in Experiences by Length of Time out of High School

Young adults with disabilities included in this report varied in their length of time out of high school, ranging from 1 month or less to 8 years post-high school. Twelve percent of young adults had been out of high school less than 3 years, 36 percent had been out from 3 up to 5 years, and 52 percent had been out of high school from 5 up to 8 years.

- Those who had been out of high school from 5 up to 8 years were more likely to receive paid vacation or sick leave (57 percent) and health insurance from their employer (53 percent) than those who had been out of high school for less than 3 years (27 percent and 32 percent, respectively).
- Young adults who were out of high school from 5 to 8 years or from 3 to 5 years were more likely to report having been engaged in employment, job training, or postsecondary education since high school than those who had been out of high school for less than 3 years (96 percent and 94 percent, respectively, vs. 85 percent).
- Young adults with disabilities out of high school from 5 to 8 years were more likely to report living independently than those out of high school for less than 3 years or (71 percent vs. 39 percent) and were more likely to live independently than those out of high school 3 to 5 years (48 percent).
- Young adults with disabilities out of high school from 5 to 8 years were more likely to report to have had or fathered a child than those out of high school for less than 3 years (36 percent vs. 18 percent).
- Marriage status differed significantly such that those out of high school from 5 up to 8 years were more likely to be married than those who left school for less than 3 years (17 percent vs. 3 percent).
- Those out of high school from 5 to 8 years were more likely to communicate by computer at least daily than those out of high school the shortest time (38 percent vs. 19 percent).
- Young adults out of high school from 5 to 8 years were more likely to be reported to have driving privileges than those who had been out of high school from 1 to 3 years (83 percent vs. 60 percent).

Differences in Experiences by Highest Level of Educational Attainment

Several post-high school outcomes varied by level of educational attainment. Those who had higher levels of educational attainment were more likely to experience several positive post-high school outcomes. In contrast, young adults who had left high school without finishing were significantly more likely to have experienced each of the various forms of criminal justice system involvement.

- High school completers were approximately three times as likely as their peers who did not complete high school to have enrolled in a postsecondary school (65 percent vs. 23 percent).
- Young adults who had received a postsecondary education degree or certificate were more likely to be employed at the time of the interview than those with lower levels of educational attainment (83 percent vs. 38 percent to 58 percent).
- Average hourly wages were significantly higher for young adults with disabilities who had completed a postsecondary education program than for those who had

completed high school or who had some postsecondary education ($12.50 vs. $9.80 per hour and $9.80 per hour).

- Young adults whose highest education level was high school completion were more likely than those whose highest education level was some postsecondary education to report that their education was put to good use (84 percent vs. 63 percent).

- Young adults with disabilities who had completed postsecondary education or training were significantly more likely to have lived independently than those for whom high school was their highest level of education (74percent vs. 50 percent).

- High school noncompleters were more likely to have had or fathered a child than young adults with disabilities who had earned a postsecondary degree or certificate (48 percent vs. 21 percent).

- Young adults with disabilities who had completed postsecondary education or training were more likely to have a savings account (78 percent), checking account (86 percent), or credit card (64 percent) than those who had not completed high school (25 percent, 25 percent, and 19 percent, respectively) and those for whom high school was their highest level of education (49 percent, 47 percent, 32 percent, respectively). In addition, young adults who had completed a postsecondary program were more likely to have had a checking account than those who had attended but not completed their postsecondary education (61 percent).

- High school completers were more likely to have had a savings or checking account than high school noncompleters (49 percent vs. 25 percent, 47 percent vs. 25 percent, respectively).

- High school noncompleters were more likely to report being in the lowest annual income category ($25,000 or less) than those who had completed a postsecondary program (83 percent vs. 59 percent).

- Young adults with a postsecondary degree or certificate had higher weekly rates of seeing friends than those for whom completing high school was their highest level of educational attainment (90 percent vs. 70 percent).

- Those who had completed a postsecondary education program were more likely than high school completers to have participated in a volunteer or community service activity (39 percent vs. 19 percent) and were more likely than high school noncompleters to have been a member of a community group (48 percent vs. 24 percent) and to have engaged in any of the forms of community participation investigated in NLTS2 (66 percent vs. 29 percent).

- Postsecondary education degree were more likely to have a driver's license (95 percent) and to have registered to vote (89 percent) than high school noncompleters (62 percent and 48 percent, respectively) or completers (66 percent and 60 percent, respectively).

- Young adults who had some postsecondary education and those who had earned a postsecondary degree or license were more likely to have taken part in at least one of the modes of community participation investigated in NLTS2 than those who had not completed high school (55 percent and 66 percent vs. 30 percent).

- Young adults with disabilities who had not completed high school were more likely to have had each of the various forms of criminal justice system involvement than those who had earned a postsecondary degree or had completed their high school education, including being stopped by police for other than a traffic violation (75 percent vs. 42 percent and 48 percent, respectively); having been arrested (59 percent vs. 22 percent and 32 percent), spending a night in jail (40 percent vs. 10 percent and 17 percent), or having been on probation or parole (39 percent vs. 10 percent and 19 percent).

Demographic Differences in Post-High School Experiences

Differences were apparent across young adults' gender, age, household income, and race/ethnicity for some post-high school outcomes but not for others.

Postsecondary school enrollment or completion rates; engagement in school, work, or training for work; and most aspects of independence, including residential arrangements, marital status, having driving privileges, and using personal financial management tools, were similar for young men and women with disabilities. However, some gender differences were apparent:

- Young men with disabilities worked on average 38 hours per week, whereas young women averaged 32 hours of work per week.
- Forty-two percent of young women with disabilities had had a child since high school, whereas 22 percent of young men with disabilities had fathered a child.
- Young men were more likely than young women to report carrying a weapon in the preceding 30 days (24 percent vs. 7 percent); to have been stopped by police other than for a traffic violation (58 percent vs. 37 percent); to have been arrested (39 percent vs. 21 percent); and to have been jailed overnight (21 percent vs. 9 percent).

Young adults with disabilities who came from households with different income levels were similar in several aspects of their post-high school experiences. For example, postsecondary enrollment and completion rates, social and community involvement, residential independence, and involvement in violence-related activities or with the criminal justice system did not differ significantly by the economic status of the households in which young adults with disabilities grew up. However, young adults from wealthier families[4] were more likely than their peers to experience several positive outcomes:

- Young adults with disabilities from parent households with incomes of more than $50,000, or $25,001 to $50,000 were more likely than those from households with incomes of $25,000 or less to have been employed at the time of the interview (71 percent and 65 percent vs. 44 percent).
- Those from households with incomes of more than $50,000 were less likely to have been fired from their most recent job than were those from household with incomes of $25,000 or less (4 percent vs. 20 percent).
- Compared with young adults with disabilities from households in the lowest income category ($25,000 or less), those in the highest income category (more than $50,000) were more likely to have a savings account (72 percent vs. 43 percent), checking account (70 percent vs. 40 percent), or a credit card (50 percent vs. 26 percent).

- Young adults who came from households in the highest income category were less likely to be in the lowest individual income category ($25,000 or less) than those from households in the lowest income category (68 percent vs. 87 percent).
- Young adults with disabilities from the lower and middle income categories were more likely to have had or fathered a child than those from families with household incomes of more than $50,000 (38 percent and 37 percent, respectively vs. 15 percent).
- Young adults with disabilities in the highest income group were more likely to be reported to have electronic communication at least daily than young adults from households in the lowest income group (37 percent vs. 20 percent), and young adults with disabilities from the upper income groups were more likely to have driving privileges than young adults from households with incomes of $25,000 or less (87 percent, respectively, vs. 67 percent).

Similarities and differences also were apparent for young adults with different racial/ethnic backgrounds.[5] There were no significant differences across racial/ethnic groups in the likelihood of being engaged in school, work, or preparation for work; in postsecondary school enrollment or completion; in social or community involvement; and in involvement in violence-related activities or with the criminal justice system. For post-high school outcomes that differed by race/ethnicity:

- African American young adults with disabilities were more likely to have had or fathered a child than White young adults with disabilities (26 percent vs. 45 percent).
- White young adults with disabilities were more likely to be married than African American young adults with disabilities (17 percent vs. 4 percent).
- White young adults with disabilities were more likely to have a checking account or credit card than African American young adults with disabilities (66 percent vs. 39 percent for checking account; 44 percent vs. 26 percent for credit card).
- White young adults with disabilities were more likely than their African American peers to have driving privileges (84 percent vs. 63 percent).

Comparisons with the General Population

When similar data items were available, comparisons were made between young adults with disabilities and same-age young adults in the general population. The analyses approach used for the general population data bases mirrored the approach used for NLTS2 data. Comparison data were taken from The National Longitudinal Survey of Youth, 1997 (NLSY97), 2005 data collection, The National Longitudinal Study of Adolescent Health, (ADD Health), Wave 3, collected in 2001-02, and the Current Population Survey (CPS) 2009.

The picture of young adults with disabilities presented in this report differed from that of young adults in the general population on several dimensions; for example:

- Young adults with disabilities were less likely to have enrolled in postsecondary programs than were their peers in the general population (60 percent vs. 67 percent).

- Young adults with disabilities were more likely to have attended a 2-year college (44 percent) or a postsecondary vocational, technical, or business school (32 percent) than their peers in the general population (21 percent and 20 percent, respectively). In contrast, those with disabilities were less likely than their peers in the general population to have attended a 4-year university (19 percent vs. 40 percent).
- Postsecondary completion rates of students with disabilities were lower than those of similar-aged students in the general population (41 percent vs. 52 percent).
- Young adults with disabilities who had attended 2-year colleges were more likely to have completed their 2-year college programs than were those in the general population (41 percent vs. 22 percent); however, they were less likely than their general population peers to have completed their 4-year college programs (34 percent vs. 51 percent).
- Young adults with disabilities earned an average of $10.40 per hour compared with $11.40 per hour for young adults in the general population.
- Young adults with disabilities were less likely to live independently than were their peers in the general population (45 percent vs. 59 percent).
- The marriage rate for young adults with disabilities was lower than that of their peers in the general population (13 percent vs. 19 percent).
- Young adults in the general population were more likely than young adults with disabilities to have a checking account (59 percent vs. 74 percent) or a credit card (41 percent vs. 61 percent).

Cautions in Interpreting Findings

Readers should remember the following issues when interpreting the findings in this report:

- The analyses are descriptive; none of the findings should be interpreted as implying causal relationships. Neither should differences between disability categories be interpreted as reflecting disability differences alone, because of the confounding of disability and other demographic factors.
- Data presented are combined young adults' self-reports and parent-reported data. If a Wave 5 youth interview/survey was completed, young adults' responses to the items were used in this report. If a youth interview/survey could not be completed for an eligible young adult, or if a young adult was reported by parents not to be able to participate in an interview/survey, parents' responses were used. For the subsample of out-of-high school young adults included in this report, the youth interview/survey was the source of data for post-high school outcomes for 65 percent of young adults, and the parent interview was the source for 35 percent of young adults. Combining data across respondents raises the question of whether parent and young adults' responses would concur—that is, would the same findings result if parents' responses were reported instead of young adults' responses. When both parents and young adults were asked whether the young adult attended community college, belonged to

an organized community group, currently works for pay, and worked for pay in the past 2 years, their responses agreed from 73 percent to 88 percent of the time

- It is important to note that descriptive findings are reported for the full sample of out-of-high school young adults; those findings are heavily influenced by information provided for young adults with learning disabilities, who constitute 63 percent of the weighted sample. Comparisons also were conducted between groups of young adults who differed with respect to disability category, high school-leaving status and timing, gender, race/ethnicity, and household income. These bivariate analyses should not be interpreted as implying that a factor on which subgroups are differentiated (e.g., disability category) has a causal relationship with the differences reported. Further, readers should be aware that demographic factors (e.g., race/ethnicity and household income) are correlated among young adults with disabilities, as well as being distributed differently across disability categories. These complex interactions and relationships among subgroups relative to the variables included in this report have not been explored.

- Several types of analyses were conducted for this report, including between-group means, between-group percentages, and within-subject percentages. Because of the weighted nature of NLTS2 data, equality between the mean values of the responses to a single survey item in two disjoint subpopulations was based on a test statistic essentially equivalent to a two-sample t test for independent samples using weighted data. Sample sizes for each group being compared were never less than 30. For a two-tailed test, the test statistic was the square of the t statistic, which then followed an approximate chi-square distribution with one degree of freedom, that is, an F (1, infinity) distribution.

- Although discussions in the report emphasize only differences that reach a level of statistical significance of at least $p < .01$, the large number of comparisons made in this report will result in some significant differences that are "false positives," or differences mistakenly determined to be significant when they are not (i.e., type I errors). Readers also are cautioned that the meaningfulness of differences reported here cannot be derived from their statistical significance.

This report provides the final national picture of the post-high school outcomes and experiences of young adults with disabilities represented in NLTS2 who had been out of high school up to 8 years, how these outcomes and experiences differed across disability categories and demographic groups, by school completion status and years out of high school, and, when data were available, how they compared with those of young adults in the general population.

1. YOUNG ADULTS WITH DISABILITIES: STUDY BACKGROUND AND METHODS

Increasingly, researchers are contending that changes in the latter part of the 20th century and the early 21st century have prompted a reconsideration of the notion of adolescence (e.g., Fussell and Furstenberg 2005)—a developmental stage encompassing the years between 11 and 18 (Hall 1904)—being immediately followed by adulthood—a stage marked by "completion of schooling, movement from the parental household, entrance into the labor force, formation of partnerships, and the onset of childbearing and parenting" (Furstenberg, Rumbaut, and Settersten 2005). They suggest that, among other social shifts, an increasing emphasis on postsecondary education and the growing struggles postadolescents face in becoming economically self-sufficient elongate or postpone the transitions usually associated with adulthood. Recognizing this reality, a growing body of research is focusing on the period of "early adulthood," ages 18 through 34 (Furstenberg, Rumbaut, and Settersten 2005), as distinct from adolescence and full adulthood (e.g., Arnett 2001; Arnett 2002). The John T. and Catherine D. MacArthur Foundation Research Network on Transitions to Adulthood and Public Policy recently assembled an extensive collection of analyses of the social forces shaping the early adult period and the experiences that characterize it (Settersten, Furstenberg, and Rumbaut 2005). After reviewing the available data, however, the authors concluded that a need remains to "pioneer research efforts aimed at understanding the new frontiers of early adult life" (Settersten, Furstenberg, and Rumbaut 2005).

The National Longitudinal Transition Study-2 (NLTS2) provides a unique source of information to help in developing an understanding of the experiences of secondary school students with disabilities nationally as they go through their early adult years. NLTS2 addresses questions about youth with disabilities in transition by providing information over a 10-year period about a nationally representative sample of secondary school students with disabilities who were receiving special education services under the Individuals with Disabilities Education Act (IDEA) in the 2000–01 school year. This document uses information about these former secondary school students to describe the experiences of young adults with disabilities in the postsecondary education, employment, independence, and social domains in their first 8 years out of high school. Specifically, this report addresses questions that reflect critical domains of young adulthood that are central to the purpose of IDEA as expressed in 20 U.S.C. 1400(d)(1)(A) to "prepare them [children with disabilities] for future education, employment, and independent living." These questions are the following:

- What is the pattern of enrollment in various kinds of postsecondary schools for young adults with disabilities? What are the characteristics of postsecondary education for young adults with disabilities (e.g., stability of enrollment, full- vs. part-time enrollment, field of study, receipt of services and supports)? What are the postsecondary school completion rates for young adults with disabilities who have ever enrolled in postsecondary programs?
- What are the employment experiences of young adults with disabilities (e.g., employment status, hours worked, types of jobs, accommodations received)? What reasons did young adults with disabilities report for having left their most recent jobs and what were the job search activities of those who were unemployed?
- How engaged are young adults with disabilities up to 8 years after high school in terms of involvement in postsecondary education, training, or employment?
- What are the household circumstances of young adults with disabilities after high school in terms of living arrangements, marriage and family formation, and economic circumstances?
- To what extent are young adults with disabilities involved in their communities in both positive (e.g., belonging to organized groups, doing volunteer/community

service activities) and negative (e.g., criminal justice system involvement) ways? What are the characteristics of the leisure and social lives of young adults with disabilities?

- How do the post-high school experiences of young adults with disabilities compare with those of their peers in the general population?
- How do post-high school experiences differ for young adults with disabilities in different disability categories and for those with different levels of educational attainment, length of time since leaving high school, and demographic characteristics?[6]

To address these questions, this report focuses on the subset of young adults with disabilities who were out of secondary school for up to 8 years and were 21 to 25 years old[7] when telephone interviews were conducted with their parents and, whenever possible, with the young adults themselves in 2009, during the fifth and final wave of data collection for NLTS2.[8]

Study Overview

NLTS2 is a 10-year-long study of the characteristics, experiences, and outcomes of a nationally representative sample of youth with disabilities who were 13 to 16 years old and receiving special education services in grade 7 or above on December 1, 2000. NLTS2 findings generalize to youth with disabilities nationally and to those in each of the 12 federal special education disability categories in use for students in the NLTS2 age range.[9] (Details of the NLTS2 design, sample, and analysis procedures are presented in appendix A.)[10] The study was designed to collect data on sample members from multiple sources in five waves, beginning in 2001 and ending in 2009.[11]

The NLTS2 sample was constructed in two stages, beginning in the 2000-2001 school year. The NLTS2 district sample was stratified to increase the precision of estimates, to ensure that low-frequency types of districts (e.g., large urban districts) were adequately represented in the sample, to improve comparisons with the findings of other research, and to make NLTS2 responsive to concerns voiced in policy debate (e.g., differential effects of federal policies in particular regions, districts of different sizes). Three stratifying variables were used: region, size (student enrollment), and community wealth. A stratified random sample of school districts was selected from the universe of approximately 12,000 that served students receiving special education in at least one grade from 7th through 12th grades. These districts were invited to participate in the study, with the intention of recruiting approximately 500 districts. For NLTS2 to be nationally representative of youth with disabilities who attended the most common types of publicly supported schools, the 77 state-supported "special schools"—i.e., those that primarily served students with hearing and vision impairments and multiple disabilities—were invited to participate.

The goal was to select from these districts and special schools a target sample of about 12,000 students. Extensive efforts to obtain consent to participate from eligible districts and the known universe of special schools resulted in 501 school districts and 38 special schools agreeing to participate in NLTS2. Analyses of the NLTS2 district sample revealed that it closely resembled to participate in NLTS2. Analyses of the NLTS2 district sample revealed that it closely resembled the universe of districts from which it was drawn on the sample's stratifying variables and on selected variables from the U.S. Department of Education's Office of Civil Rights database on the universe of school districts. Participating school districts and special schools provided rosters of students receiving special education services in the designated age range, from which the student sample was selected.

The roster of all students in the NLTS2 age range who were receiving special education services from each district and special school was stratified by primary disability category, as reported by the districts. Students then were selected randomly from each disability category. Sampling fractions were calculated that would produce enough students in each category so that, in the final study year, findings would generalize to most categories individually with an acceptable level of precision, accounting for attrition and for response rates to the parent/youth interview. A total of approximately 11,280 students[12] were selected and eligible to participate in NLTS2.

Table 1. NLTS2 data sources for post-high school experiences of young adults with disabilities included in this report

Source	Approximate number	Percent of young Adults included in this report
Total number of sample members with responses to Wave 5 survey known to be out of secondary school at the time of the Wave 5 data collection	4,810	100.0
Youth telephone interview	2,360	49.0
Youth mail questionnaire	760	16.0
Parent telephone interview	1,690	35.0
Number in Wave 5 report and out of school in Wave 4, with Wave 4 survey data coming from	3,980	83.0
Youth telephone interview	2,100	44.0
Youth mail questionnaire	330	7.0
Parent telephone interview	1,550	32.0
Number in Wave 5 report and out of school in Wave 3, with Wave 3 survey data coming from	2,080	43.0
Youth telephone interview	1,320	27.0
Youth mail questionnaire	160	3.0
Parent telephone interview	600	14.0
Number in Wave 5 report and out of school in Wave 2, with Wave 2 survey data coming from	860	18.0
Youth telephone interview	560	12.0
Youth mail questionnaire	50	<1.0
Parent telephone interview	250	5.0
Number in Wave 5 report with Wave 1 survey data		
Parent interview	4,660	97.0
High school transcript	3,630	75.0
School and school district student rosters	4,810	100.0

Data Sources for Young Adults with Disabilities

This section presents the multiple data sources used in this report to describe the post-high school experiences of young adults with disabilities at the time of the Wave 5 interview, who were known to be out of secondary school at the time of the Wave 5 data collection. Appendix A includes a description of the overall response rates for each wave of data collection.

Primary sources used in this report were the Wave 5 youth telephone interview and mail survey or the Wave 5 parent telephone interview, conducted in 2009.13 In addition, those variables that describe young adults' experiences since leaving high school were constructed on the basis of data from the Waves 2 through 4 (conducted in 2003, 2005, and 2007, respectively) youth telephone interviews and mail surveys or the Waves 2 through 4 parent telephone interviews for young adults who were out of high school at that time. School district rosters, high school transcripts, and the Wave 1 parent interview or mail survey also provided a small amount of the data used in this report. Each data source for young adults with disabilities is described briefly below and discussed in greater detail in appendix A.[14]

The data for this report were obtained on approximately 4,810[15] NLTS2 sample members with responses to the Wave 5 survey who were known to be out of high school at the time of the Wave 5 data collection in 2009 (table 1).

Young Adult/Parent Data

Wave 5 Data

Much of the information reported in this document comes from young adults with disabilities themselves in the form of responses to either a telephone interview or a self-administered mail survey with a subset of key items from the telephone interview.[16] Data for young adults who were reported by parents to be unable to respond to an interview or complete a questionnaire or who did not respond to interview or survey attempts were provided by parents. Data from the three sources were combined for the analyses reported here and subsetted to include only data for out-of-high school young adults.

Youth Telephone Interview

NLTS2 sample members who were eligible for a Wave 5 youth telephone interview were those (1) for whom working telephone numbers or addresses were available so that they could be reached by phone and (2) whose parents or guardians (referred to here as parents) had reported in the Wave 2 parent telephone interview (if interviewed at that time) or in later-wave parent interviews (if interviewed in later waves for the first time) that the young adult could answer questions about his or her experience by phone (a total of approximately 4,180 young adults).[17] At those times, after making the initial telephone contact with the parents of sample members and completing items intended only for parent respondents, parents were asked whether their children with disabilities were able to respond to questions about their experiences by telephone for themselves. Parents who responded affirmatively and whose sample children were younger than age 18 then were asked to grant permission for their children to be interviewed and told the kinds of questions that would be asked.[18] Parents of those 18 or older were informed of the kinds of questions that would be asked of the young adult, but permission was not requested because they were no longer minors. Interviewers obtained contact information for these young adults and attempted to complete telephone interviews with them.

Wave 5 telephone interviews were completed with approximately 2,410 young adults, 77 percent of the approximately 4,180 who were eligible.[19] Approximately 2,360 telephone interview respondents to the Wave 5 telephone interview were out-of-high school young adults, the focus of this report.

Youth Mail Survey

If parent respondents to the telephone interview indicated that their children with disabilities were not able to respond to questions about their experiences for themselves by telephone, interviewers asked whether they would be able to complete a mail questionnaire; young adults respondents also could request that they be sent a mail questionnaire, rather than respond to the phone interview. Mailing addresses were obtained for those sample members, and questionnaires were sent to the young adult. In addition, questionnaires were tailored to the circumstances of individual young adults. For example, if a parent indicated in the telephone interview that a young adult was employed, the questionnaire for that young adult contained a section on employment experiences, which was not included in questionnaires for young adults reported not to be employed. Questionnaires were returned by approximately 790 young adults, 40 percent of the approximately 2000 young adults who were mailed a survey. Approximately 760 mail questionnaire respondents were out-of-high school young adults who are part of the sample that generated the findings reported in this document.[20]

Parent/Guardian Interview

In addition to sample members who completed a telephone interview or mail survey, parents completed a telephone interview for sample members who did not respond for themselves either because they were reported not to be able to do so or because young adults who were reported to be able to respond could not be reached or refused to respond. In the latter case, parents were contacted to complete a subset of interview items that experience demonstrated could readily be answered by many parents (e.g., whether a young adult was employed or enrolled in postsecondary education). Approximately 1,690 young adults for whom parents were the sole respondents were out of secondary school and are included in the sample that forms the basis of this report. Out-of-high school young adults whose parents responded for them did not differ significantly in their disability category, age identified as having a disability, age when first special education services were received, health status, or most functional abilities, with one exception. Young adults whose parents responded for them were less likely to have been reported to have high functional abilities than were those who had responded for themselves (56 percent vs. 74 percent; appendix B provides detailed information regarding comparisons between these groups).

Wave 2 through Wave 4 Data

As mentioned previously, several variables that were created for this report indicate whether a young adult had had a particular experience "since high school" (e.g., postsecondary enrollment, employment and independent living arrangements). Seventeen percent of out-of-high school respondents (approximately 830 young adults) had left high school since the Wave 4 data collection; thus, Wave 5 data are all that are required to generate values for these variables for them. However, the remainder of the out-of-high school respondents (approximately 3,980 young adults) were already out of high school in Wave 2, 3, or 4. Thus, data from prior waves needed to be taken into account to generate values for variables measuring experiences "since high school." Prior-wave data also were used to determine whether young adults had completed high school or left without completing and the year in which they left. Wave 2 through Wave 4 data collection mirrored procedures followed for Wave 5. The Wave 4 youth telephone interview produced data for approximately 2,100 young adults included in the sample that forms the basis of this report, the mail questionnaire generated data for approximately 330 young adults, and parent interviews provided data for approximately 1,550 young adults, for a total of approximately 3,980 sample members. The Wave 3 youth telephone interview produced data for approximately 1,320 young adults included in the sample that forms the basis of this report, the mail questionnaire generated data for approximately 160 young adults, and parent interviews provided data for approximately 600 young adults, for a total of approximately 2,080 sample members. The Wave 2 youth telephone interview produced data for approximately 560 young adults included in the sample that forms the basis of this report, the mail questionnaire generated data for approximately 50 young adults, and parent interviews provided data for approximately 250 young adults, for a total of approximately 860 sample members.

Because of the relatively small percentage of young adults enrolled in postsecondary schools at the time of the Wave 5 interview, Wave 2 through Wave 4 data also were used to augment data for variables related to the postsecondary education experiences of students who had been enrolled in these types of schools in prior waves but not in Wave 5. Variables included those related to timing and intensity of enrollment, course of study, receipt of accommodations and supports, and postsecondary school completion. Including earlier wave data increased the sample size, enabling broader analyses of these variables, particularly analyses by disability category. For these variables, for young adults who did not have Wave 5 postsecondary school data but who were out of high school and enrolled in postsecondary school in an earlier wave, data from the most recent wave in which they had been enrolled in postsecondary education were combined with the responses of postsecondary attendees in Wave 5.

Wave 1 Data

The initial wave of NLTS2 data collection involved parent telephone interviews and a mail survey of parents who could not be reached by telephone. Data for two demographic items (gender and race/ethnicity) were drawn from these Wave 1 sources for 4,660 young adults with disabilities included in the sample that forms the basis of this report.

High School Transcripts

High school completion status and high school leave date were based on data from high school transcripts. Final high school transcripts were requested for all NLTS2 sample members. Transcript data were collected for approximately 3,630 young adults included in this report. For those for whom transcript data were not available, school completion status and leave dates were based on information from parent/youth interviews.

School and School District Student Rosters

Information about the primary disability category of NLTS2 sample members came from rosters of students in the NLTS2 age range receiving special education services in the 2000–01 school year under the auspices of participating school districts and state-supported special schools. Additionally, data on the racial/ethnic background of sample members were taken from this source when they were included on rosters. In the absence of roster data on youth's racial/ethnic background, data were taken from the Wave 1 parent interview or mail survey. The student rosters and the parent interview/mail survey provided similar racial/ethnic classifications.

Data Sources for Comparisons with Young Adults in the General Population

When similar data items were available, comparisons were made between young adults with disabilities and the same-age young adults in the general population. The analyses approach used for the general population data bases mirrored the approach used for NLTS2 data.[21] Comparison data were taken from:

- The National Longitudinal Survey of Youth, 1997 (NLSY97). This study includes a nationally representative sample of approximately 9,000 youth who were 12 to 16 years old as of December 31, 1996. Round 1 of the survey took place in 1997. In that round, both the eligible youth and one of each youth's interviews. Youth have continued to be interviewed annually. Comparison data were taken from the 2005 data collection for young adults who were 21 to 25 years old and out of high school at the time to match the sample of NLTS2 young adults included in this report. Calculations were made from public-use data available at http://www.nlsinfo.org/web-investigator/webgator.php. NLSY data collected in 2005 were the best match for NLTS2 2009 data because of the age of the young adults in both data sets at those time points, however readers should note the 4 year difference between the two data collection periods. Readers also should be aware that the population of young adults with disabilities in this age range differs from the general population of young adults in ways other than disability status (e.g., the population of young adults with disabilities is 64 percent male; see appendix B for further description of the population represented in NLTS2). In addition, there is a 4 year difference between NLTS2 data collected in 2009 and NLSY data collected in 2005.
- The National Longitudinal Study of Adolescent Health, Wave 3. Comparisons with the general population regarding financial independence, reported in chapter 5, are based on the public-use version of the National Institutes of Health, National Institute of Child Health and Human Development (NICHD), National Longitudinal Study of Adolescent Health (Add Health), Wave 3, a nationally representative study that explores health-related behaviors of adolescents in grades 7 through 12 and their outcomes in young adulthood. Wave 3 data were collected in 2001–02. Comparisons

included a subset of respondents who were 21 to 25 years old. The time period for Add Health Wave 4, collected in 2007–08 would have been a more appropriate comparison for the 2009 Wave 5 NLTS2 data; however, the items related to financial independence were not collected in Add Health Wave 4.

- Current Population Survey (CPS) 2009. Several items regarding the employment of young adults in the general population were taken from the Current Population Survey (CPS) 2009. The CPS is a monthly survey of 50,000 households conducted by the Bureau of the Census for the Bureau of Labor Statistics. The nationally representative sample included in this monthly survey was selected to represent the civilian noninstitutional population in the United States. Comparison data for this report were taken from the May 2009 data collection for young adults who were 21 to 25 years old and out of high school. Calculations were made from public use data available at http://www.census.gov/cps/, using the Data Ferret Web tool.[22]

Young Adults Included in the Report

The young adults with disabilities who are the focus of this report represent only a subset of young adults with disabilities who received special education services in secondary school in 2000–01, not the entire population. The full population to which the NLTS2 sample generalizes is a cohort of young adults who were 13 to 16 years old and received special education services in grade 7 or above in participating schools and school districts as of December 1, 2000. Weights for analyses reported in this document were calculated so that all young adults with disabilities who were out of secondary school and for whom a telephone interview or mail survey was completed or for whom parents responded to the second part of the parent interview generalize to all young adults with disabilities who were out of high school. Weights were computed adjusting for various youth and school characteristics used as stratifying or poststratifying variables. (See appendix A for additional information related to sample weighting.)

Analysis Approaches

Analyses reported in this document involve simple descriptive statistics (e.g., percentages, means) and bivariate relationships (i.e., cross-tabulations). All statistics were weighted to be representative of a larger population of young adults (as discussed earlier). These analysis approaches excluded cases with missing values; no imputation of missing values was conducted.[23]

Statistical tests examining differences between independent subgroups or between responses to different items given by the same group that involve categorical variables with more than two possible response categories were conducted by treating each of the possible response categories as separate dichotomous items.[24] For example, each of the four possible response categories to a question regarding satisfaction with the amount of services young adults received from their postsecondary school ("definitely getting enough," "probably getting enough," "probably not getting enough," and "definitely not getting enough") was treated as a separate dichotomous item. The percentages of young adults who gave each response were then compared across disability or demographic groups or across different questionnaire/interview items. This approach, rather than using scale scores (e.g., the average response for a disability group on a 4-point scale created by assigning values of 1 through 4 to the response categories), was adopted for two reasons: The proper scaling for the response categories was not apparent, and it was felt that reporting differences in percentages responding in each of the response categories would be more meaningful and easier for readers to interpret than reporting differences in mean values.

Rather than test for differences between all independent subgroups (e.g., young adults in different disability categories) simultaneously (e.g., using a $k \times 2$ chi-square test of homogeneity of distribution, where k is the number of disability groups), the statistical significance of differences between selected pairs of independent subgroups was tested. This approach was followed because the intent was to identify significant differences between specific groups (e.g., young adults with learning disabilities are significantly more likely than those with mental retardation to report that they had ever enrolled in a postsecondary school) rather than to identify a more general "disability effect"(e.g., the observed distribution across disability categories differs significantly from what would be expected from the marginal distributions) for the variable of interest.

The test statistic used to compare Bernoulli-distributed responses (i.e., responses that can be allocated into one of two categories and coded as 0 or 1) for two independent subgroups is analogous to a chi-square test for equality of distribution (Conover 1999) and approximately follows a chi-square distribution with one degree of freedom. However, because a chi-square distribution with one degree of freedom is the same as an F distribution with one degree of freedom in the numerator and infinite degrees of freedom in the denominator (Johnson and Kotz 1995), this statistic can be considered the same as an F value; it also can be considered "chi-squared."[25]

Tests also were conducted to examine differences in the rates at which young adults with disabilities as a whole provided specific kinds of self-representations (for example, the percentage of young adults who reported the help with schoolwork they received from postsecondary schools as "very useful" compared with the percentage who rated the sufficiency of the help as "definitely getting enough"), using an analogous one-sample statistic based on difference scores.[26] The test statistic follows a chi-square distribution with one degree of freedom for sample sizes of 30 or larger and, for similar reasons to those cited above, is considered roughly equivalent to an F (1, infinity) distribution.

Technical Notes

Readers should remember the following issues when interpreting the findings in this report:

- **Purpose of the report.** The purpose of this report is descriptive; as a nonexperimental study, NLTS2 does not provide data that can be used to address causal questions. The descriptions provided in this document concern the post-high school experiences of young adults with disabilities. No attempt is made to "validate" respondents' reports with information on their understanding of the survey items or with third-party information on their experiences (e.g., from employers or postsecondary education institutions). Further, the report does not attempt to explain why parents or young adults responded as they did or why responses differ for youth in different subgroups (e.g., disability categories).

- **Subgroups reported.** In each chapter, the descriptive findings are reported for the full sample of young adults; those findings are heavily influenced by information provided by young adults with learning disabilities, who constitute 63 percent of the weighted sample (see appendix B). Young adults with mental retardation, emotional disturbances, other health impairments, and speech/language impairments constitute 12 percent, 12 percent, 5 percent, and 4 percent of the weighted sample, respectively. The other seven categories together make up less than 6 percent of the weighted sample. Findings then are reported separately for young adults in each federal special education disability category in tables that are ordered by disability prevalence, as determined at the beginning of the study. Comparisons also were made between groups of young adults who differed with respect to years since leaving high school, highest level of educational attainment, gender, race/ethnicity, and parents' me. These bivariate analyses should not be interpreted as implying that a factor on which subgroups are differentiated (e.g., disability category) has a causal relationship with the differences reported. Further, readers should be aware that demographic factors (e.g., race/ethnicity and parents' household income) are correlated among young adults with disabilities, as well as being distributed differently across disability categories (e.g., young adults in the category of mental retardation are disproportionately likely to be African American, and those in the other health impairment category are disproportionately likely to be White relative to the general population; see appendix B, table B-4, for percentage of youth within each disability category, by demographic characteristics).[27] The complex interactions and relationships among subgroups relative to the other variables included in this report (e.g., postsecondary enrollment status) have not been explored.

- **Findings weighted.** NLTS2 was designed to provide a national picture of the characteristics, experiences, and achievements of youth with disabilities in the NLTS2 age range as they transition to young adulthood. Therefore, all the statistics presented in this report are weighted estimates of the national population of young adults who received special education in the NLTS2 age group and of each disability category individually who were out of high school.

- **Standard errors.** For each mean and percentage in this report, a standard error is presented that indicates the precision of the estimate. For example, a variable with a weighted estimated value of 50 percent and a standard error of 2.00 means that the value for the total population, if it had been measured, would, with 95 percent confidence, lie between 46 percent and 54 percent (i.e., within plus or minus 1.96 x 2, or 3.92 percentage points of 50 percent). Thus, smaller standard errors allow for greater confidence to be placed in the estimate, whereas larger ones require caution.

- **Combined young adult self-report and parent-report data.** If a Wave 5 youth interview/survey was completed, young adults' responses to these items were used in this report. If a youth interview/survey could not be completed for an eligible young adult or if a young adult was reported by parents not to be able to participate in an interview/survey, parent responses were used. For the subsample of out-of-high school young adults included in this report, the youth interview/survey was the source of data for post-high school outcomes for 65 percent of young adults, and the parent interview was the source for 35 percent of young adults who did not have a youth interview. Combining data across respondents raises the question of whether parent and young adult responses would concur—i.e., whether the same findings would result if parents' responses were reported instead of the young adult's responses. When both parents and young adults were asked whether the young adult attended community college, belonged to an organized community group, currently works for pay, and worked for pay in the past 2 years, their responses agreed from 73 percent to 88 percent of the time (analyses presented in appendix A).

- **Small samples.** Although NLTS2 data are weighted to represent the population, the size of standard errors is influenced heavily by the actual number of young adults in a given group (e.g., a disability category). In fact, findings are not reported separately for groups that do not include at least 30 sample members because groups with very small samples have comparatively large standard errors. For example, because there are relatively few young adults with deaf-blindness, estimates for that group have relatively large standard errors. Therefore, readers should be cautious in interpreting results for that group and others with small sample sizes and large standard errors.

- **Significant differences.** A large number of statistical analyses were conducted and are presented in this report. Because no explicit adjustments were made for multiple comparisons, the likelihood of finding at least one statistically significant difference when no difference exists in the population is substantially larger than the type I error for each individual analysis. To partially compensate for the number of analyses that were conducted, we have used a relatively conservative p value of $< .01$ in identifying significant differences. The text mentions only differences reaching at least that level of significance. If no level of significance is reported, the group differences described do not attain the $p < .01$ level. Readers also are cautioned that the meaningfulness of differences reported here cannot be inferred from their statistical significance.

Organization of the Report

This report is envisioned as an update of earlier NLTS2 reports based on data collected in Wave 3 (2005) and Wave 4 (2007) of the study, when young adults had been out of high school for up to 4 and 6 years, respectively.[28] The current Wave 5 (2009) report augments prior NLTS2 findings as more youth transitioned to early adulthood, were out high school longer (up to 8 years), and had increasing exposure to opportunities for postsecondary education, employment, and independent living. This report is organized to provide information on young adults with disabilities in several key domains. Chapter 2 describes the extent to which young adults with disabilities enrolled in any postsecondary education and their participation in 2- and 4-year colleges and vocational or trade schools specifically; features of their educational experience, such as their major field of study and support services they accessed, as well as their postsecondary education completion rates, also are presented. Chapter 3 considers the employment status of young adults with disabilities, including current employment and employment since leaving high school. Characteristics of young adults' most recent job also are described. Chapter 4 addresses the extent to which young adults with disabilities were productively engaged in school, work, or preparation for work after they left high school.

The household circumstances of young adults with disabilities are considered in chapter 5, including the extent to which young adults were living away from home, the prevalence of marriage and parenting, and aspects of their financial independence. Chapter 6 focuses on the social and community involvement of young adults with disabilities, including their friendship activities and community participation in both positive and negative ways, such as participation in extracurricular lessons or classes and organized group and volunteer activities and involvement in violence-related activities and with the criminal justice system.

Appendix A provides details of the NLTS2 design, sample, measures, and analysis approaches. Appendix B presents data on the characteristics of young adults with disabilities included in the out-of-high school sample.

The following chapters provide the final national picture from NLTS2 of the post-high school experiences of young adults with disabilities.

2. POSTSECONDARY EDUCATION

Over the course of a lifetime, an individual with a college degree will earn $1 million more on average than a worker with only a high school diploma (U.S. Department of Commerce 2002). As the U.S. economy becomes progressively more knowledge based, attaining a postsecondary education becomes more critical (Carnevale and Desrochers 2003). For example, only 20 percent of workers needed at least some college for their jobs in 1959; by 2000, that number had increased to 56 percent (Carnevale and Fry 2000).

Along with their peers in the general population, young adults with disabilities are increasingly focusing on postsecondary education. Postsecondary education is a primary post-high school goal for more than four out of five secondary school students with disabilities who have transition plans (Cameto, Levine, and Wagner 2004). In addition, youth with disabilities increasingly are taking rigorous academic courses in high school, including college-preparatory courses, such as a foreign language and science (Wagner, Newman, and Cameto 2004).

However, even when their high school programs prepare them for postsecondary education, students with disabilities can encounter a variety of challenges in the transition from secondary to postsecondary school. Postsecondary schools are guided by a legal framework of rights and responsibilities that is different from the framework governing secondary schools. When students leave high school, their education no longer is covered under the IDEA umbrella but instead is under the auspices of two civil rights laws—Section 504 of the Rehabilitation Act and the Americans with Disabilities Act (ADA) (Stodden, Jones, and Chang 2002; Wolanin and Steele 2004). Unlike high school, there is not a mandatory Individualized Education Program (IEP) process to identify and provide the supports students may need to succeed in the postsecondary school (Office for Civil Rights U.S. Department of Education 2007). In high school, IDEA places "the burden on the school to find and serve the student with an IEP. In higher education the burden is on the student, not the school, to find the appropriate services and navigate through higher education" (Wolanin and Steele 2004, p. 27).

This understanding of the challenges posed by the postsecondary school environment for young adults with disabilities raises the following questions:

- To what extent do young adults with disabilities enroll in postsecondary schools?
- How does their level of enrollment compare with that of their peers in the general population?
- What are the experiences of those enrolled in postsecondary schools, including the intensity of their enrollment and their course of study?
- To what extent do those who enroll receive supports and accommodations as part of their postsecondary education?
- What are the completion rates for students who enroll in postsecondary schools?

This chapter examines the postsecondary education experiences of young adults with disabilities who have been out of secondary school for up to 8 years. It focuses on participation in three types of institutions: 2-year or community colleges; postsecondary vocational, business, or technical schools; and 4-year colleges. The chapter begins with an examination of postsecondary education enrollment rates and continues with findings regarding the experiences of postsecondary students with disabilities, including their courses of study, receipt of accommodations and modifications, and rates of completion. These findings are presented for young adults with disabilities as a whole and for those who differ in length of time out of high school, high school completion status, disability category, gender, parents' household income, and race/ethnicity.

Postsecondary School Enrollment

Ensuring that students with disabilities have "access to and full participation in postsecondary education" has been identified as one of the key challenges in the future of secondary education and transition for such students (National Center on Secondary Education and Transition 2003, p. 1). Postsecondary education has been linked to increased earning potential for youth who continue their education after high school, even for those who have not earned a degree (Marcotte et al. 2005).

For young adults in the general population, "postsecondary enrollments are at an all-time high" (Ewell and Wellman 2007, p. 2). Of young adults with disabilities, 60 percent were reported to have continued on to postsecondary education within 8 years of leaving high school.[29] The percentage of similar-age young adults in the general population who had ever enrolled in postsecondary school was higher than that of young adults[30] with disabilities (67 percent, $p < .01$; figure 1).

Thirty-four percent of young adults with disabilities who were out of high school up to 8 years were reported to have been enrolled in a postsecondary program in the 2 yearsprior to the interview, and 15 percent were enrolled at the time they were interviewed. By both measures, young adults in the general population were more likely than young adults with disabilities to be enrolled. Approximately half (51 percent) of young adults in the general population had been enrolled in college in the 2 years prior to the interview, and 28 percent were enrolled at the time they were interviewed[31] ($p < .001$ for both comparisons).

Rates of enrollment varied by type of postsecondary program. Among young adults with disabilities, enrollment in 2-year or community colleges since leaving high school (44 percent) was more common than enrollment in postsecondary vocational, business, or technical schools (32 percent, $p < .001$), and enrollment in both of these categories of institutions was more common than enrollment in 4-year colleges or universities (19 percent, $p < .001$ for both comparisons; figure 2).

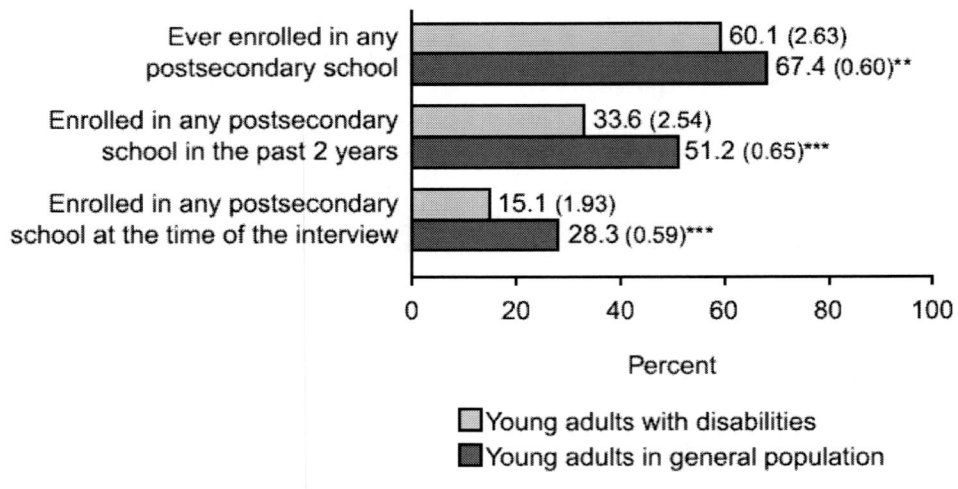

** $p < .01$, *** $p < .001$ for the difference between young adults with disabilities and young adults in the general population.

Note: Standard errors are in parentheses. Findings are reported for young adults with disabilities out of high school up to 8 years. NLTS2 percentages are weighted population estimates based on a sample of approximately 4,800 young adults with disabilities.

Source: U.S. Department of Education, Institute of Education Sciences, National Center for Special Education Research, National Longitudinal Transition Study-2 (NLTS2), Wave 5 parent interview and youth interview/survey, 2009; U.S. Department of Labor, Bureau of Labor Statistics, National Longitudinal Survey of Youth 1997 (NLSY97) 2005 youth survey, responses for 21- to 25-year-olds.

Figure 1. Postsecondary school enrollment of young adults with disabilities and young adults in the general population.

Young adults with disabilities were more likely than same-age young adults in the general population to have attended a 2-year college or a postsecondary vocational school at some point since leaving high school (44 percent vs. 21 percent and 32 percent vs. 20 percent, $p < .001$ for both comparisons). In contrast, young adults in the general population were more likely to have attended a 4-yearcollege (40 percent vs. 19 percent, $p < .001$). These patterns of differences also are found for enrollment in 2-year and 4-year institutions in the 2 years before the interview (22 percent vs. 12 percent at 2-year colleges and 11 percent vs. 32 percent at 4-year colleges, $p < .001$ for both comparisons) and for enrollment in 4-year institutions at the time of the interview (16 percent vs. 5 percent, $p < .001$).

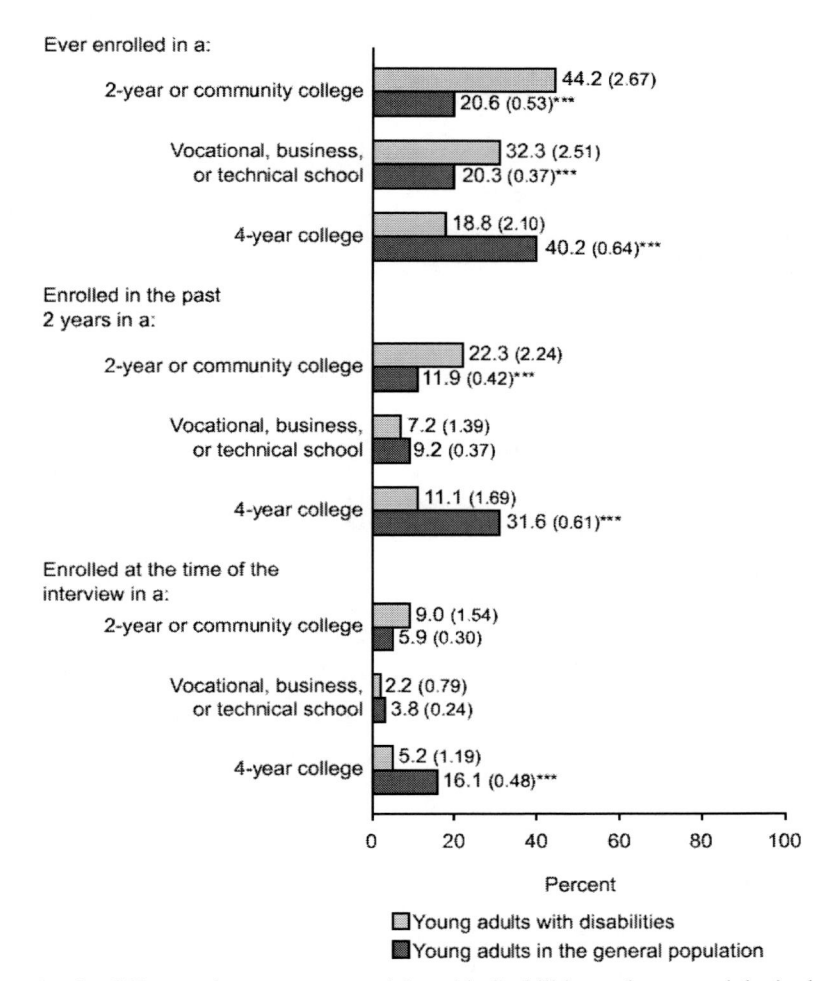

*** $p < .001$ for the difference between young adults with disabilities and young adults in the general population.

Note: Young adults who had enrolled in more than one type of postsecondary school were included in each type of school they had attended. Standard errors are in parentheses. Findings are reported for young adults with disabilities out of high school up to 8 years. NLTS2 percentages are weighted population estimates based on a sample of approximately 4,800 young adults with disabilities.

Source: U.S. Department of Education, Institute of Education Sciences, National Center for Special Education Research, National Longitudinal Transition Study-2 (NLTS2), Wave 5 parent interview and youth interview/survey, 2009; U.S. Department of Labor, Bureau of Labor Statistics, National Longitudinal Survey of Youth 1997 (NLSY97) 2005 youth survey, responses for 21- to 25-year-olds.

Figure 2. Postsecondary school enrollment of young adults with disabilities and young adults in the general population, by school type.

Table 2. Postsecondary school enrollment of young adults, by disability category

	Learning disability	Speech/ language impairment	Mental retardation	Emotional disturbance	Hearing impairment	Visual impairment	Orthopedic impairment	Other health impairment	Autism	Traumatic brain injury	Multiple disabilities	Deaf-blindness
	Percent											
Ever enrolled in:												
Any postsecondary school	66.8 (3.89)	66.9 (3.63)	28.7 (3.60)	53.0 (4.53)	74.7 (4.24)	71.0 (5.00)	62.0 (4.42)	65.7 (4.04)	43.9 (4.65)	61.0 (7.37)	32.8 (5.07)	56.8 (7.09)
2-year or community college	49.9 (4.13)	46.0 (3.84)	18.9 (3.12)	37.7 (4.40)	51.5 (4.88)	51.5 (5.52)	50.3 (4.56)	51.6 (4.25)	32.2 (4.38)	42.2 (7.47)	21.7 (4.45)	36.9 (6.91)
Vocational, business, or technical school	35.8 (3.96)	28.5 (3.48)	16.4 (2.94)	33.3 (4.28)	42.9 (4.84)	26.2 (4.84)	26.2 (4.08)	32.2 (3.98)	21.0 (3.82)	36.9 (7.30)	17.5 (4.10)	22.1 (6.21)
4-year college	21.2 (3.38)	32.5 (3.61)	6.7 (1.99)	10.8 (2.82)	33.8 (4.62)	40.1 (5.40)	26.1 (4.00)	19.6 (3.38)	17.4 (3.56)	18.5 (5.88)	7.4 (2.83)	23.7 (6.09)

Note: Young adults who had enrolled in more than one type of postsecondary school were included in each type of school they had attended. Standard errors are in parentheses. Findings are reported for young adults with disabilities out of high school up to 8 years. NLTS2 percentages are weighted population estimates based on samples that range from approximately 4,770 to 4,810 young adults with disabilities.

Source: U.S. Department of Education, Institute of Education Sciences, National Center for Special Education Research, National Longitudinal Transition Study-2 (NLTS2), Wave 5 parent interview and youth interview/survey 2009.

Almost one-third (31 percent) of young adults with disabilities had enrolled in more than one type of postsecondary institution since leaving high school (not in the table). In comparison, 29 percent reported having attended only one type of postsecondary school since high school.

Disability Differences in Postsecondary School Enrollment

Enrollment in postsecondary programs varied widely by disability category (table 2), with percentages ranging from 30 percent to 75 percent. Having ever enrolled was significantly more common among young adults in every disability category except one (multiple disabilities) than among young adults with mental retardation ($p < .01$ for all comparisons). In addition, such enrollment was significantly more common among young adults with learning disabilities (67 percent); speech/language, hearing, visual, orthopedic, or other health impairments (67 percent, 75 percent, 71 percent, 62 percent, and 66 percent, respectively); or traumatic brain injuries (61 percent) than among those with multiple disabilities (33 percent, $p < .01$ for all comparisons). Such enrollment also was more common among those with learning disabilities or speech/language, hearing, visual, orthopedic, or other health impairments than among those with autism (44 percent, $p < .01$ for all comparisons); and more common among those with hearing or visual impairments than among those with emotional disturbance (53 percent, $p < .01$ for all comparisons).

Consistent with the pattern for overall enrollment, percentages of young adults ever having enrolled in 2-year or community colleges were higher among those with learning disabilities (50 percent); speech/language, hearing, visual, orthopedic, or other health impairments (46 percent, 52 percent, 52 percent, 50 percent, 52 percent, respectively); traumatic brain injuries (42 percent); or deaf-blindness (37 percent) than among those with mental retardation (19 percent, $p < .01$ for all comparisons). Two-year or community college enrollment was also higher among those with learning disabilities or speech/language, hearing, visual, orthopedic, or other health impairments than among those with multiple disabilities (22 percent, $p < .01$ for all comparisons); and higher among those with learning disabilities or hearing, visual, orthopedic, or other health impairments than among those with autism (32 percent, $p < .01$ for all comparisons).

Similarly, ever having enrolled in a 4-year college was more common among young adults with learning disabilities (21 percent); speech/language, hearing, visual, orthopedic, or other health impairments (33 percent, 34 percent, 40 percent, 26 percent, and 20 percent respectively); or deaf-blindness (24 percent) than among young adults with mental retardation (7 percent, $p < .01$ for all comparison). Four-year college enrollment also was more common for young adults in all these categories except other health impairments and traumatic brain injuries than it was for young adults with multiple disabilities (7 percent, $p < .01$ for all comparisons). Young adults with speech/language, hearing, visual, or orthopedic impairments also were more likely than young adults with emotional disturbances (11 percent, $p < .01$ for all comparisons) ever to have attended a 4-year college. In addition, those with speech/language, hearing, or visual impairments were more likely than those with autism (17 percent, $p < .01$ for all comparisons); those with hearing or visual impairments also were more likely than those with other health impairments ($p < .01$ for both comparisons); and those with visual impairments also were more likely than those with learning disabilities, orthopedic impairments, or traumatic brain injury ($p < .01$ for all comparisons) ever to have enrolled in a 4-year college.

Young adults with learning disabilities (36 percent), emotional disturbances (33 percent), hearing or other health impairments (43 percent and 32 percent, respectively), or traumatic brain injury (37 percent) also were more likely than young adults with mental retardation (16 percent) or multiple disabilities (18 percent) to ever have been enrolled in vocational, business, or technical school ($p < .01$ for all comparisons). In addition, young adults with hearing impairments were more likely than those with autism (21 percent) to have attended these types of schools ($p < .01$)

Differences in Postsecondary School Enrollment by High School-Leaving Characteristics

Secondary school completers were more likely to have enrolled in postsecondary school than were noncompleters; 65 percent of completers had attended postsecondary school at some time since leaving high school up to 8 years earlier, compared with 23 percent of noncompleters ($p < .001$; table 3). Differences between high school completers and noncompleters were apparent for enrollment in both 2-year and 4-year colleges (48 percent vs. 13 percent and 21 percent vs. <1 percent, respectively, $p < .001$ for both comparisons) but not in vocational, business, or technical school.

Rates of enrollment in postsecondary school overall or in each type of postsecondary school did not differ significantly by length of time out of high school.

Demographic Differences in Postsecondary School Enrollment

As other studies have found for young adults in the general population (e.g., Corak, Lipps, and Zhao 2005), household income is related to the likelihood of enrolling in postsecondary school. Young adults with disabilities from households with incomes of more than $50,000 were more likely than those with household incomes of $25,000 or less ever to have been enrolled in postsecondary education (70 percent vs. 50 percent, $p < .001$;table 4).

Family income differences were apparent in enrollment at 2-year colleges. Young adults from wealthier parent households (those with incomes of more than $50,000) were more likely than those from lower-income parent households ($25,000 or less) to have ever enrolled in a 2-year college (53 percent vs. 33 percent, $p < .01$). In contrast, parents' household income was not significantly related to enrollment in vocational, business, or technical schools or 4-year colleges.

In the general population, females had higher 2-year and 4-year college enrollment rates than males (Peter and Horn 2005). In contrast to their peers in the general population, young adults with disabilities' postsecondary enrollment did not differ significantly by gender (60 percent for postsecondary males and 60 percent for females).

Rates of enrollment in postsecondary schools also did not differ significantly by race or ethnicity for young adults with disabilities. Sixty-two percent of Hispanic, 60 percent of African American, and 61 percent of White young adults with disabilities had ever enrolled in a postsecondary program.

Table 3. Postsecondary school enrollment of young adults with disabilities, by high-school-leaving status and years since leaving high school

	Completers	Non-completers	Less than 3 years	3 up to 5 years	5 up to 8 years
			Percent		
Ever enrolled in:					
Any postsecondary school	64.5 (2.74)	22.8 (6.85)	52.3 (6.21)	60.0 (4.62)	61.9 (3.61)
2-year or community college	48.0 (2.86)	12.7 (5.44)	37.5 (6.02)	42.1 (4.66)	47.2 (3.72)
Vocational, business, or technical school	34.7 (2.73)	12.3 (5.37)	24.4 (5.34)	33.2 (4.45)	33.4 (3.51)
4-year college	20.9 (2.33)	0.2 (0.73)	13.1 (4.20)	15.9 (3.41)	22.4 (3.10)

Note: Young adults who had enrolled in more than one type of postsecondary school were included in each type of school they had attended. Standard errors are in parentheses. Findings are reported for young adults with disabilities out of high school up to 8 years. NLTS2 percentages are weighted population estimates based on samples that range from approximately 4,770 to 4,810 young adults with disabilities.

Source: U.S. Department of Education, Institute of Education Sciences, National Center for Special Education Research, National Longitudinal Transition Study-2 (NLTS2), Wave 5 parent interview and youth interview/survey, 2009.

Postsecondary School Experiences

The findings reported thus far indicate that young adults differed in their rates of enrollment in postsecondary programs; those who were enrolled also differed in aspects of their schooling. This section shifts the focus from young adults' enrollment in postsecondary schools to the experiences of those who had enrolled in these types of programs, examining students' experiences related to timing and intensity of enrollment, postsecondary course taking, accommodations and supports, and completion rates.[32]

Timing and Intensity of Enrollment

Most students with disabilities who continued on to postsecondary school did so within 6 months of leaving high school.[33] Overall, 41 percent were reported to have enrolled in a postsecondary school within 2 months of leaving high school, 35 percent enrolled within 2.1 to 6 months, 14 percent enrolled within 6.1 to 12 months, and 10 percent waited longer than 1 year before continuing their education (figure 3). The mean time between high school leaving and first postsecondary enrollment was 7.4 months (0.97 SE). However, the median time between leaving high school and enrolling in a postsecondary school was 3 months.

Table 4. Postsecondary school enrollment of young adults with disabilities, by parents' household by income, and young adults' race/ethnicity and gender

	$25,000 or less	$25,001 to $50,000	More than $50,000	White	African American	Hispanic	Male	Female
	Percent							
Ever enrolled in:								
Any post-secondary school	50.2 (4.66)	58.3 (5.42)	70.3 (3.74)	60.6 (3.14)	59.6 (5.92)	61.7 (8.12)	60.0 (3.26)	60.2 (4.46)
2-year or com-munity college	33.1 (4.39)	45.2 (5.47)	53.1 (4.08)	43.7 (3.18)	44.4 (6.00)	49.5 (8.36)	43.2 (3.30)	46.0 (4.54)
Vocational, business, or technical school	32.6 (4.37)	28.5 (4.96)	36.0 (3.93)	30.7 (2.96)	34.9 (5.75)	37.9 (8.11)	35.1 (3.17)	27.4 (4.07)
4-year college	10.1 (2.81)	18.1 (4.23)	27.1 (3.63)	19.6 (2.55)	19.1 (4.72)	14.6 (5.90)	17.6 (2.53)	20.7 (3.69)

Note: Young adults who had enrolled in more than one type of postsecondary school were included in each type of school they had attended. Standard errors are in parentheses. Findings are reported for young adults with disabilities out of high school up to 8 years. NLTS2 percentages are weighted population estimates based on samples that range from approximately 4,770 to 4,810 young adults with disabilities.

Source: U.S. Department of Education, Institute of Education Sciences, National Center for Special Education Research, National Longitudinal Transition Study-2 (NLTS2), Wave 5 parent interview and youth interview/survey, 2009.

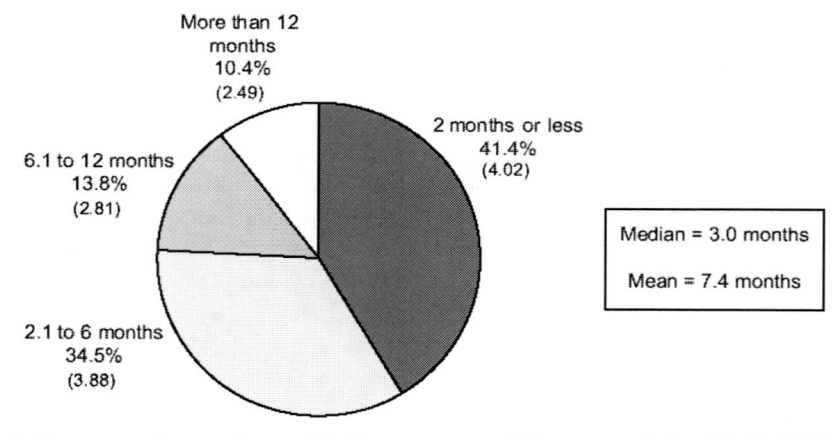

Note: Standard errors are in parentheses. Findings are reported for young adults with disabilities out of high school up to 8 years. NLTS2 percentages are weighted population estimates based on a sample of approximately 1,920 young adults with disabilities.

Source: U.S. Department of Education, Institute of Education Sciences, National Center for Special Education Research, National Longitudinal Transition Study-2 (NLTS2), Waves 2, 3, 4, and 5 parent interview and youth interview/survey, 2003, 2005, 2007, and 2009.

Figure 3. Months elapsed between high school leaving and first postsecondary school enrollment among young adults with disabilities ever enrolled in postsecondary school.

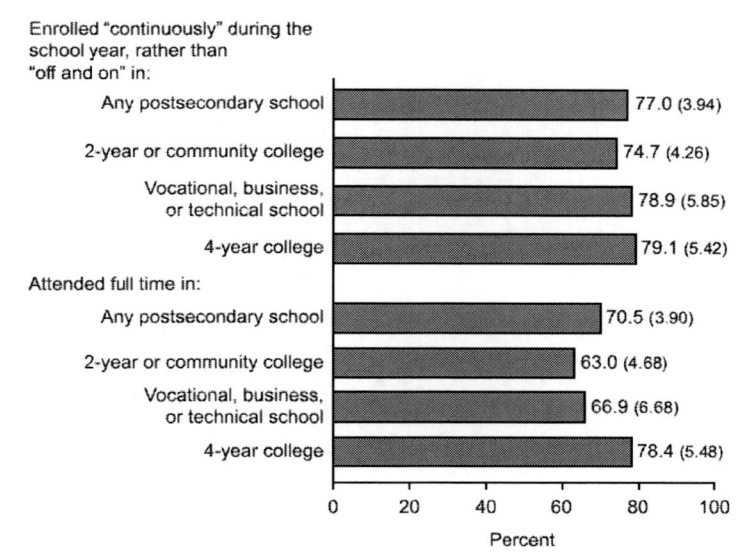

Note: Standard errors are in parentheses. Findings are reported for young adults with disabilities out of high school up to 8 years. NLTS2 percentages are weighted population estimates based on samples that range from approximately 1,760 to 2,100 young adults with disabilities.

Source: U.S. Department of Education, Institute of Education Sciences, National Center for Special Education Research, National Longitudinal Transition Study-2 (NLTS2), Waves 2, 3, 4, and 5 parent interview and youth interview/survey, 2003, 2005, 2007, and 2009.

Figure 4. Intensity of enrollment in postsecondary schools by young adults with disabilities ever enrolled in postsecondary school.

Students waited a mean time of 7.3 months (1.24 SE) to enroll in 2-year colleges; 14.3 months (2.53 SE) for vocational, business, or technical schools;and 12.5 months (2.58 SE) for 4-year institutions. Median values for the months between high school leaving and postsecondary school enrollment were 3 months for both 2- and 4-year colleges and 6 months for vocational, business, or technical schools. Differences in these high school-postsecondary school time gaps are not statistically significant.

Seventy-seven percent of young adults with disabilities who had ever been enrolled in postsecondary school were reported to have been enrolled steadily,[34] whereas 23 percent were reported to have taken classes some semesters or quarters but not others (figure 4).[35] Seventy-five percent of students at 2-year colleges; 79 percent of students at vocational, business, or technical schools; and 79 percent of students at 4-year institutions were reported to have been enrolled steadily during the school year.

Whether students attend postsecondary school full or part time may help shape their postsecondary experiences; for example, a report on community college student engagement suggested that full-time students were more likely to interact with faculty, academic advisors, or other students than their part-time peers (Inside Higher Ed 2006). Seventy-one percent of young adults with disabilities who ever had attended postsecondary institutions were reported to have attended full time.[36] These included 63 percent of students at 2-year colleges; 67 percent of students at vocational, business, or technical schools; and 78 percent of students at 4-year institutions.

Table 5. Intensity of enrollment of young adults with disabilities ever enrolled in a postsecondary program, by disability category

	Learning disability	Speech/ language impairment	Mental retardation	Emotional disturbance	Hearing impairment	Visual impairment	Orthopedic impairment	Other health impairment	Autism	Traumatic brain injury	Multiple disabilities	Deaf-blindness
Mean number of months between having left high school and began postsecondary school	6.6 (1.22)	6.9 (1.31)	10.0 (2.79)	11.0 (2.16)	5.6 (1.36)	4.8 (1.07)	7.7 (1.50)	9.8 (1.69)	5.8 (1.33)	9.2 (2.68)	10.5 (2.75)	8.4 (3.15)
Median number of months between having left high school and began postsecondary school	3.0	3.0	6.0	3.0	3.0	3.0	3.0	3.0	3.0	3.0	3.0	3.0
Percentage enrolled "steadily" during the school year rather than "off and on"	81.9 (4.96)	77.5 (4.78)	44.5 (12.89)	58.0 (7.48)	61.9 (8.22)	77.4 (6.07)	74.6 (5.32)	68.7 (5.75)	85.7 (6.50)	66.7 (10.28)	84.9 (7.33)	76.3 (10.03)
Percentage enrolled full time (12 or more credit hours)	73.6 (5.32)	76.6 (4.47)	45.5 (10.81)	58.8 (7.09)	71.1 (6.49)	81.5 (5.64)	74.7 (5.35)	63.3 (5.63)	72.8 (6.77)	72.5 (9.39)	72.4 (8.21)	64.6 (9.89)

Note: Standard errors are in parentheses. Findings are reported for young adults with disabilities out of high school up to 8 years. NLTS2 percentages are weighted population estimates based on samples that range from approximately 1,760 to 2,100 young adults with disabilities.

Source: U.S. Department of Education, Institute of Education Sciences, National Center for Special Education Research, National Longitudinal Transition Study-2 (NLTS2), Waves 2, 3, 4, and 5 parent interview and youth interview/survey, 2003, 2005, 2007, and 2009.

**Table 6. Intensity of enrollment of young adults with disabilities
ever enrolled in a postsecondary program, by high school-leaving status
and years since leaving high school**

	Completers	Non-completers	Less than 3 years	3 up to 5 years	5 years or more
Mean number of months between having left high school and began going to a postsecondary school	7.2 (0.97)	18.4 (5.35)	7.2 (2.79)	7.5 (1.67)	7.4 (1.30)
Median number of months between having left high school and began going to a postsecondary school	3.0	12.0	3.0	3.0	3.0
Percentage enrolled continu-ously during the school year rather than "off and on"	77.5 (3.98)	43.7 (22.15)	84.9 (9.10)	73.6 (7.33)	77.8 (5.17)
Percentage enrolled full time (at least 12 credit hours)	71.1 (3.95)	30.4 (17.80)	77.0 (9.35)	66.0 (7.35)	72.2 (5.08)

Note: Standard errors are in parentheses. Findings are reported for young adults with disabilities out of high school up to 8 years.NLTS2 percentages are weighted population estimates based on samples that range from approximately 1,760 to 2,100 young adults with disabilities.

Source: U.S. Department of Education, Institute of Education Sciences, National Center for Special Education Research, National Longitudinal Transition Study-2 (NLTS2), Waves 2, 3, 4, and 5 parent interview and youth interview/survey, 2003, 2005, 2007, and 2009.

Disability Differences in Timing and Intensity of Enrollment

The mean length of time between leaving high school and beginning a postsecondary program ranged from approximately 5 months for students with visual impairments to 11 months for students with multiple disabilities (table 5), with no significant differences between disability categories. Median values were 3 months for all disability categories except mental retardation, for which the median value was 6 months. Continuous enrollment during the school year was significantly more common among postsecondary students with learning disabilities (82 percent), autism (86percent), or multiple disabilities (85 percent) than among those with mental retardation (45 percent, $p < .01$ for all comparisons). In addition, full-time enrollment was significantly more common among postsecondary students with speech/language impairments (77 percent) or visual impairments (82 percent) than among those with mental retardation (46 percent, $p < .01$ for both comparisons).

Differences in Timing and Intensity of Enrollment by
High School-Leaving Characteristics

Timing and intensity of enrollment in postsecondary school did not differ significantly by high school-leaving status or length of time out of secondary school (table 6).

Table 7. Intensity of enrollment of young adults with disabilities ever enrolled in a postsecondary program, by parents' household income and young adults' race/ethnicity and gender

	$25,000 or less	$25,001 to $50,000	More than $50,000	White	African American	Hispanic	Male	Female
Mean number of months between having left high school and began going to a post-secondary school	8.6 (1.81)	9.0 (2.49)	6.1 (1.21)	7.2 (1.16)	7.7 (2.30)	7.5 (2.66)	8.2 (1.29)	6.1 (1.42)
Median number of months between having left high school and began going to a post-secondary school	3.0	3.0	3.0	3.0	2.0	3.0	3.0	3.0
Percentage enrolled continuously during the school year rather than "off and on"	69.1 (8.56)	62.1 (9.88)	86.5 (4.35)	75.0 (4.74)	85.3 (7.77)	74.0 (13.40)	78.5 (4.81)	74.7 (6.75)
Percentage enrolled full time (greater than or equal to 12credit hours)	70.7 (7.75)	62.4 (8.70)	73.1 (5.22)	67.1 (4.74)	77.0 (8.42)	80.8 (10.58)	68.8 (4.91)	70.6 (6.55)

Note: Standard errors are in parentheses. Findings are reported for young adults with disabilities out of high school up to 8 years. NLTS2 percentages are weighted population estimates based on samples that range from approximately 1,760 to 2,100 young adults with disabilities.

Source: U.S. Department of Education, Institute of Education Sciences, National Center for Special Education Research, National Longitudinal Transition Study-2 (NLTS2), Waves 2, 3, 4, and 5 parent interview and youth interview/survey, 2003, 2005, 2007, and 2009.

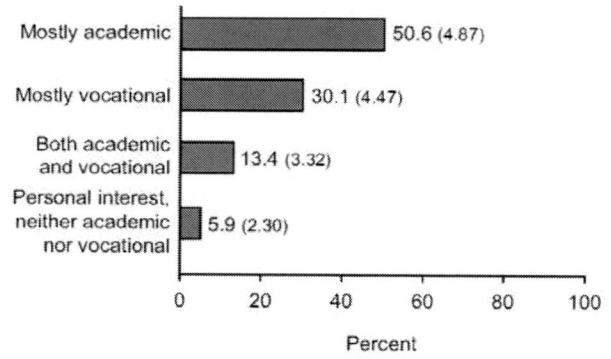

Note: Standard errors are in parentheses. Findings are reported for young adults with disabilities out of high school up to 8 years. NLTS2 percentages are weighted population estimates based on a sample of approximately 1,410 young adults with disabilities.

Source: U.S. Department of Education, Institute of Education Sciences, National Center for Special Education Research, National Longitudinal Transition Study-2 (NLTS2), Waves 2, 3, 4, and 5 parent interview and youth interview/survey, 2003, 2005, 2007, and 2009.

Figure 5. Primary focus of courses taken at a 2-year or community college by young adults with disabilities who were ever enrolled in postsecondary school.

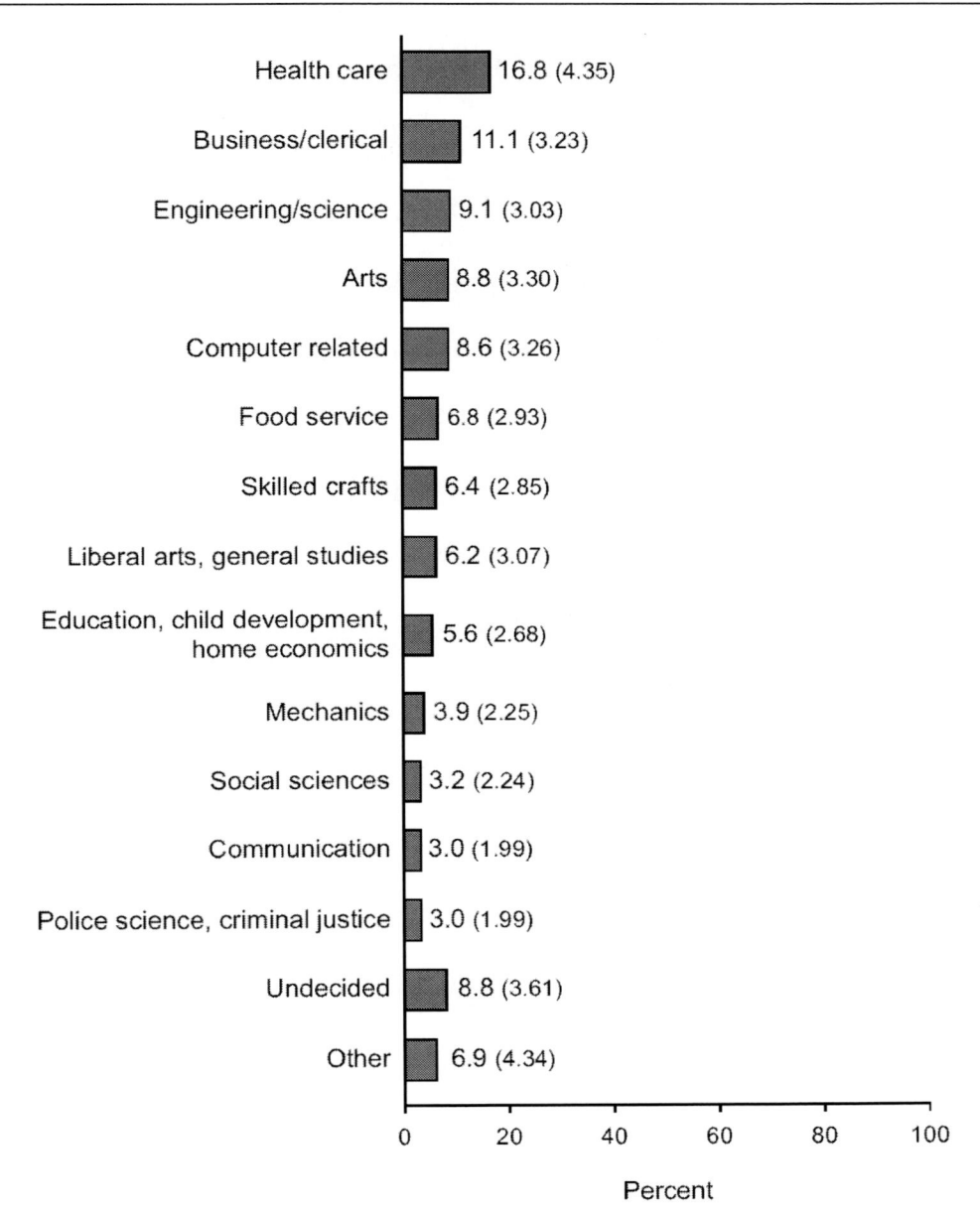

Percent

Note: Standard errors are in parentheses. Findings are reported for young adults with disabilities out of high school up to 8 years. NLTS2 percentages are weighted population estimates based on a sample of approximately 1,110 young adults with disabilities.

Source: U.S. Department of Education, Institute of Education Sciences, National Center for Special Education Research, National Longitudinal Transition Study-2 (NLTS2), Waves 2, 3, 4, and 5 parent interview and youth interview/survey, 2003, 2005, 2007, and 2009.

Figure 6. Major or primary course of study of young adults with disabilities ever enrolled at a 2-year or community college.

Demographic Differences in Timing and Intensity of Enrollment

The length of time between leaving high school and beginning postsecondary school and the intensity of enrollment in postsecondary programs did not differ significantly by demographic characteristics (table 7).

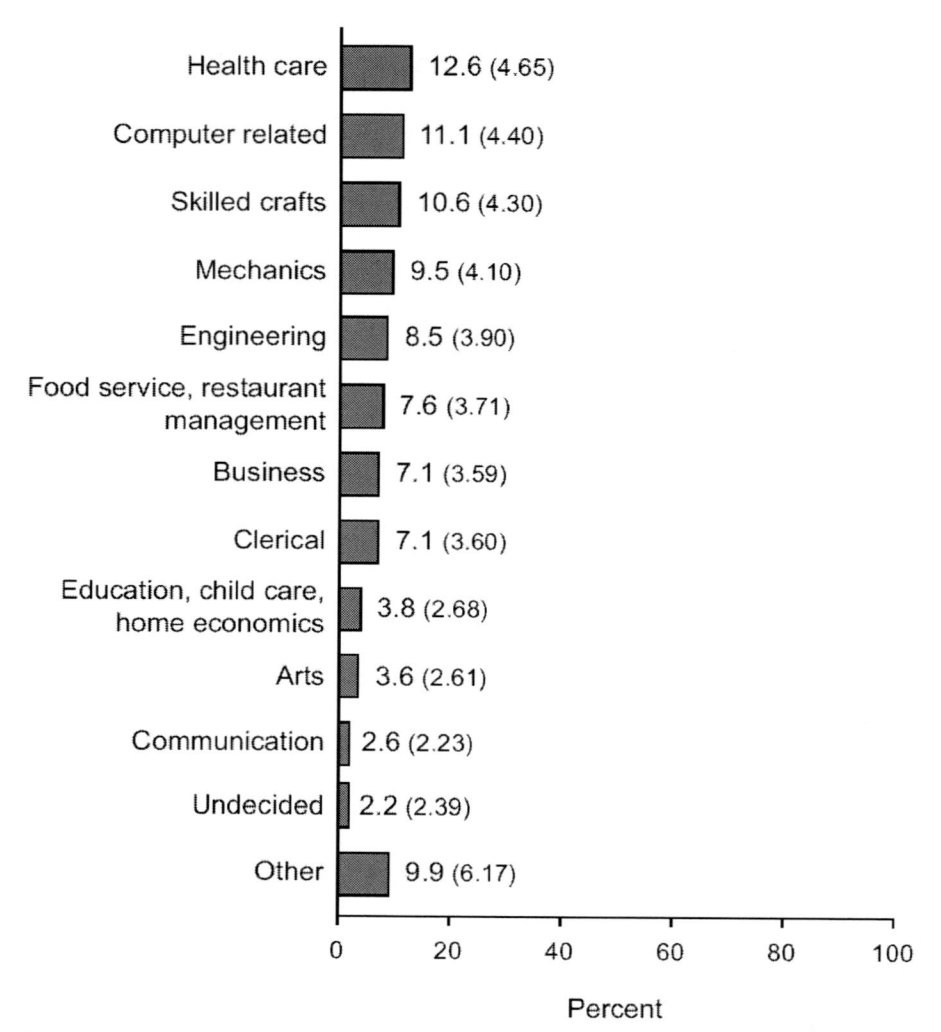

Note: Standard errors are in parentheses. Findings are reported for young adults with disabilities out of high school up to 8 years. NLTS2 percentages are weighted population estimates based on a sample of approximately 540 young adults with disabilities.

Source: U.S. Department of Education, Institute of Education Sciences, National Center for Special Education Research, National Longitudinal Transition Study-2 (NLTS2), Waves 2, 3, 4, and 5 parent interview and youth interview/survey, 2003, 2005, 2007, and 2009.

Figure 7. Major or primary course of study of young adults with disabilities ever enrolled in a vocational, business, or technical school.

Postsecondary Course of Study

Postsecondary schools frequently offer a wide range of instructional program options. For example, the National Center for Education Statistics' taxonomy describes more than 60 major postsecondary fields of study, not including hundreds of intermediate and specific instructional program subcategories (U.S. Department of Education National Center for Education Statistics 2002). With this range of options, students with disabilities varied in the types of courses they took while in postsecondary school.

Postsecondary students who attended 2-year colleges were more likely to be enrolled in an academic than a vocational course of study, with 51 percent majoring in academic areas and 30 percent in vocational areas ($p < .01$; figure 5).[37] Thirteen percent reported both an academic and vocational focus, and 6 percent attended classes primarily for recreation and personal interest.

Regardless of type of postsecondary school attended, young adults with disabilities had a range of majors. Among those who had ever been enrolled at 2-year colleges,[38] 17 percent majored in a field related to health care; 11 percent majored in business (including marketing, advertising, management, and finance); 9 percent each majored in engineering/science, arts, (visual and performing arts or design), computer-related fields (computer science, programming, information technologies, computer support), or engineering/science; 6 percent or 7 percent each majored in food service or restaurant management, skilled crafts (e.g., plumbing, electrical, carpentry), liberal arts, or general studies and education, (including childcare, early childhood, or home economics), 3 percent to 4 percent each majored in mechanics, social sciences, communications (journalism, television/radio, entertainment industry), and police science or criminal justice (figure 6). Nine percent were undecided about a major and 7 percent were in other majors.

Among young adults with disabilities who had attended vocational, business, or technical schools, the most common majors also were in the health care field (13 percent), followed by computer-related fields and skilled crafts (11 percent each); mechanics (10 percent); engineering (9 percent); food service or restaurant management (8 percent); business or clerical (7 percent each); education, child care, or home economics and arts (4 percent each); and communication (3 percent; figure 7). Approximately 2 percent were undecided, and 10 percent had majors in a range of other fields.

Business-related majors were most common among young adults with disabilities who had attended 4-year colleges (15 percent), followed by social sciences (12 percent); medical and health-related majors (11 percent); arts (10 percent); engineering or communication (9 percent each); education, child development, early childhood, or home economics (8 percent); sciences (biological or physical) or computer-related majors (6 percent each); and police science or criminal justice or foreign languages (3 percent each; figure 8). Nine percent were in other majors or had not yet chosen a major, and 3 percent were undecided in their area of focus.

Accommodations and Supports

Receiving appropriate supports and accommodations in postsecondary programs has been shown to be related to school success and retention for students with disabilities (Mull, Sitlington, and Alper 2001; Pierangelo and Crane 1997; Stodden and Dowrick 2000; Stodden, Jones, and Chang 2002). Although a college is required to provide "appropriate academic adjustments as necessary to ensure that it does not discriminate on the basis of disability"

(Office for Civil Rights U.S. Department of Education 2007, p. 2), accommodations that are a fundamental alteration of a program or that would impose an undue financial or administrative burden are not mandatory (Wolanin and Steele 2004). Schools interpret these guidelines differently, and the types and extent of supports and accommodations available to students with disabilities vary widely (National Center for Education Statistics 1999; Stodden, Jones, and Chang 2002).

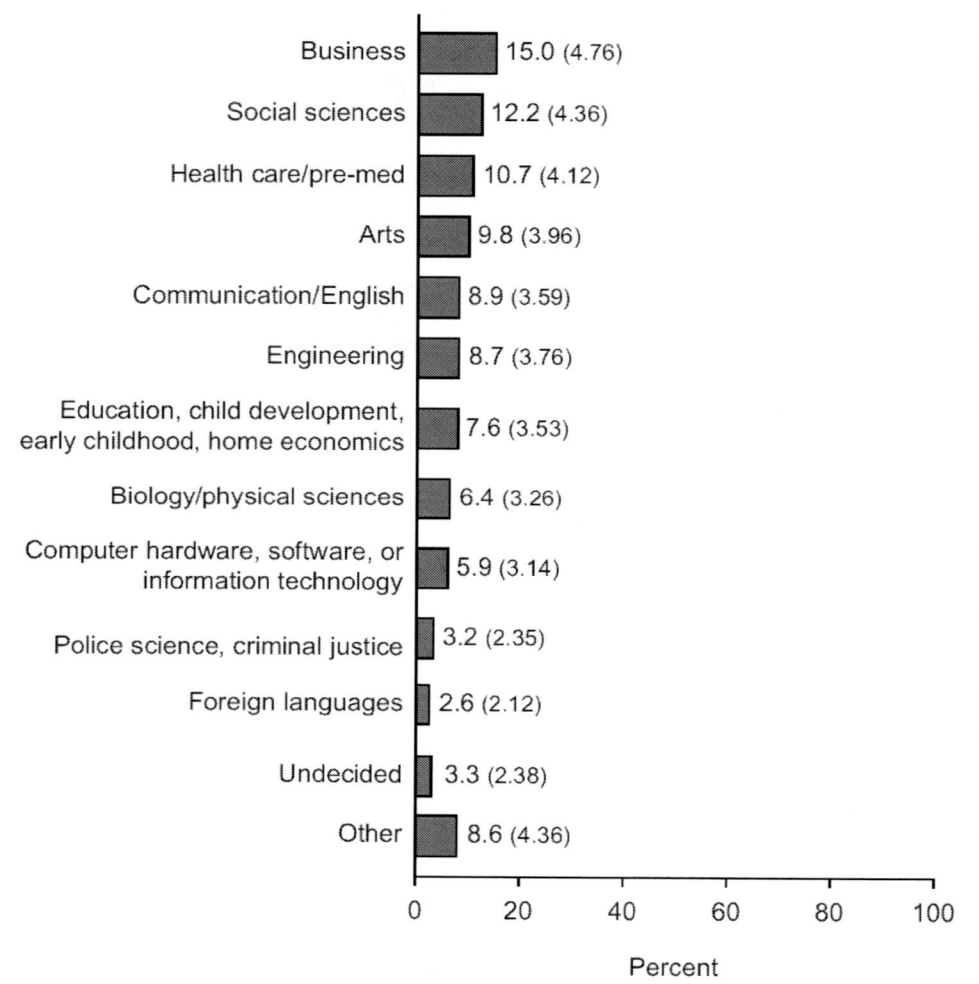

Percent

Note: Standard errors are in parentheses. Findings are reported for young adults with disabilities out of high school up to 8 years. NLTS2 percentages are weighted population estimates based on a sample of approximately 840 young adults with disabilities.

Source: U.S. Department of Education, Institute of Education Sciences, National Center for Special Education Research, National Longitudinal Transition Study-2 (NLTS2), Waves 2, 3, 4, and 5 parent interview and youth interview/survey, 2003, 2005, 2007, and 2009.

Figure 8. Major or primary course of study of young adults with disabilities ever enrolled in a 4-year college or university.

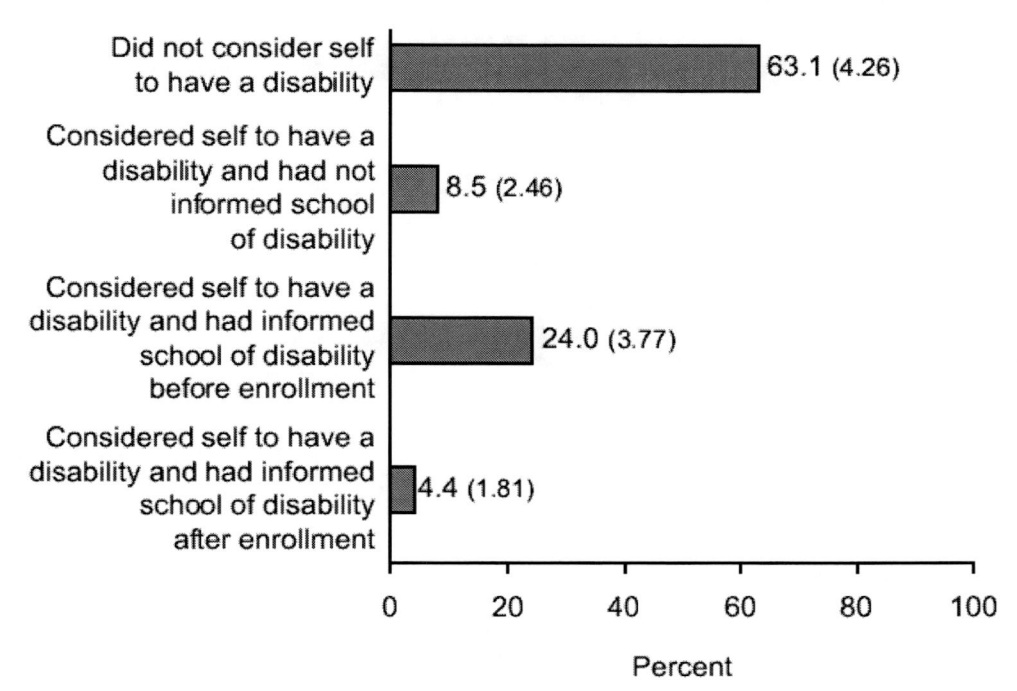

Note: Standard errors are in parentheses. Findings are reported for young adults with disabilities out of high school up to 8 years. NLTS2 percentages are weighted population estimates based on a sample of approximately 1,960 young adults with disabilities.

Source: U.S. Department of Education, Institute of Education Sciences, National Center for Special Education Research, National Longitudinal Transition Study-2 (NLTS2), Waves 2, 3, 4, and 5 parent interview and youth interview/survey, 2003, 2005, 2007, and 2009.

Figure 9. Extent to which young adults with disabilities ever enrolled in a postsecondary school considered themselves as having a disability and informed postsecondary schools of disability.

As noted earlier, when students leave secondary school and enter postsecondary institutions, the responsibility for arranging for accommodations and supports shifts from the school to the students. At the postsecondary level, students with disabilities are expected to advocate for themselves (Stodden, Jones, and Chang 2002). "To receive accommodations, students with disabilities must disclose their disabilities and take the initiative in requesting accommodations" (Wolanin and Steele 2004, p. ix). However, disclosure of a disability is voluntary. NLTS2 findings show that almost two-thirds (63 percent) of postsecondary students who were identified by their secondary school as having a disability did not consider themselves to have a disability by the time they had transitioned to postsecondary school (figure 9).[39] An additional 9 percent reported considering themselves to have a disability but chose not to disclose it to their postsecondary schools. Approximately one-quarter (24 percent) of postsecondary students with disabilities identified themselves as having a disability and had informed their postsecondary schools of their disability before enrollment, and 4 percent considered themselves to have a disability and had waited to inform the postsecondary schools of their disability until after enrollment.[40]

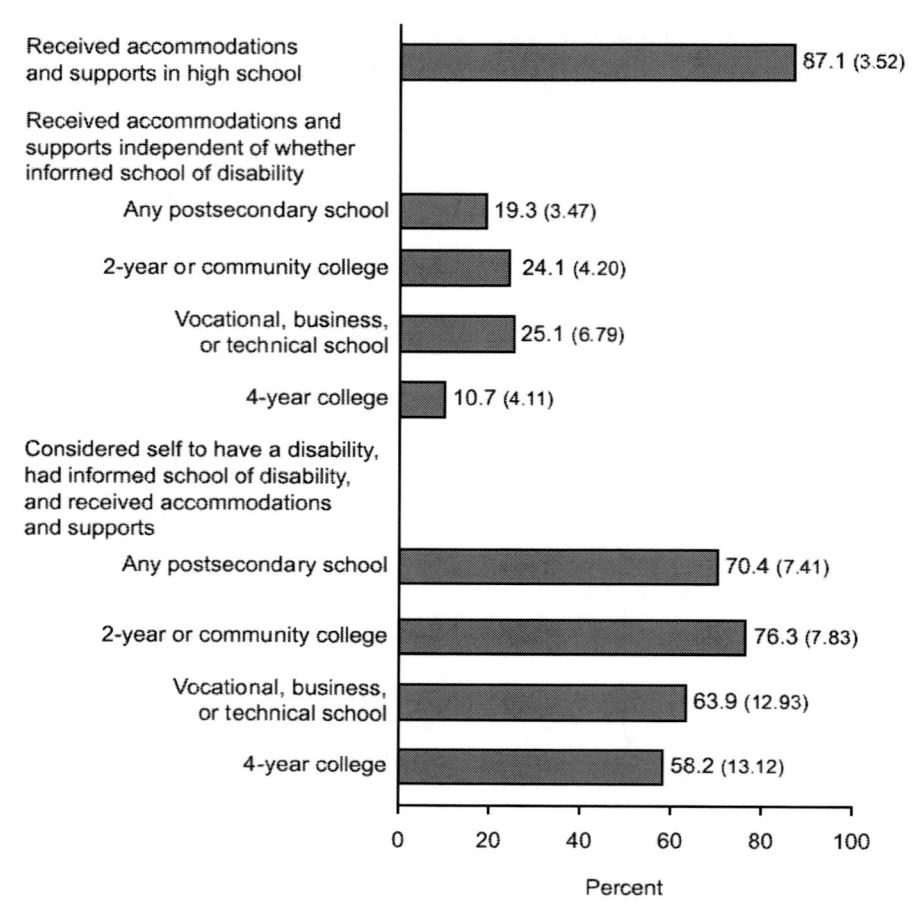

Note: Standard errors are in parentheses. Findings are reported for young adults with disabilities out of high school up to 8 years. NLTS2 percentages are weighted population estimates based on samples that range from approximately 300 to 2,010 young adults with disabilities.

Source: U.S. Department of Education, Institute of Education Sciences, National Center for Special Education Research, National Longitudinal Transition Study-2 (NLTS2), Wave 1 school program survey, 2002, and Waves 2, 3, 4, and 5 parent interview and youth interview/survey, 2003, 2005, 2007, and 2009.

Figure 10. Receipt of accommodations and supports from school because of disability by young adults with disabilities ever enrolled in postsecondary school.

To receive accommodations or supports from a postsecondary school because of a disability, students first must disclose a disability to their school. Approximately 28 percent of postsecondary students who were considered by their secondary schools as having a disability disclosed a disability to their postsecondary schools (sum of third and fourth bars in figure 9). Less than one in five (19 percent) of postsecondary students who were identified as having a disability by their secondary schools were reported to have received any accommodations or supports because of their disability from their postsecondary schools (figure 10).[41]

In contrast, when these postsecondary students were in high school, more than four times as many (87 percent) received some type of accommodation or support because of a disability ($p < .001$).[42] This pattern of less disability-related assistance at the postsecondary than the secondary level was consistent across the various types of postsecondary schools. Twenty-five percent of 2-year college students; 11 percent of postsecondary vocational, business, or technical school students; and 24 percent of 4-year college students received assistance from their schools because of their disability ($p < .001$ for all comparisons with rate in high school).

Restricting responses to the 28 percent of students who had disclosed a disability to their postsecondary programs, 70 percent were reported to have received accommodations and supports from their postsecondary programs. Although students with disabilities who had disclosed a disability were more likely than postsecondary students with disabilities as a whole to receive accommodations and supports ($p < .001$), they remained less likely to receive this type of help from their postsecondary schools than from their high schools (70 percent vs. 92 percent, $p < .01$).[43]

The rate of receiving accommodations and supports in postsecondary schools for those who had disclosed a disability ranged from 58 percent at 4-year colleges or universities to 64 percent at vocational, business, or technical schools and 76 percent at 2-year or community colleges. Of those who considered themselves to have a disability and had not received accommodations or supports related to their disability from their postsecondary schools, 17 percent had applied for this type of assistance.

Postsecondary students who were given assistance because of their disability were reported to have received a range of accommodations, supports, and services from their schools.[44] Additional time to complete tests was a frequent type of assistance—received by approximately two-thirds (79 percent) of those who got accommodations, supports, and services (figure 11). Tests were administered in a different-than-usual setting for 19 percent, and 9 percent were provided with other testing accommodations. Thirty-seven percent used technology aids, such as computer software designed for students with disabilities, or had tutors. Seventeen percent received help from note takers or received help from a reader, interpreter, or in-class aide. Approximately one-quarter (23 percent) received learning strategies, study skills, or behavior management support. Assignments were modified or deadlines were extended for 23 percent of postsecondary students who received some type of assistance. Eleven percent received written materials, and less than 10 percent received physical adaptations to their classrooms, large print or Braille materials and books on tape, social work services, case management, independent living supports, or early registration.

With the exception of early registration and independent living supports, the types of accommodations received by students in postsecondary schools paralleled those provided during high school. Consistent with experiences in high school general education courses, students with disabilities also frequently received testing modifications in postsecondary school. For example, 75 percent were given more time to complete tests in high school (Newman, Marder, and Wagner 2003), and two-thirds of postsecondary students who received accommodations got additional time for tests. In contrast, students were less likely in postsecondary school than in high school to receive additional time for or modifications to assignments (23 percent vs. 86 percent, $p < .001$).[45]

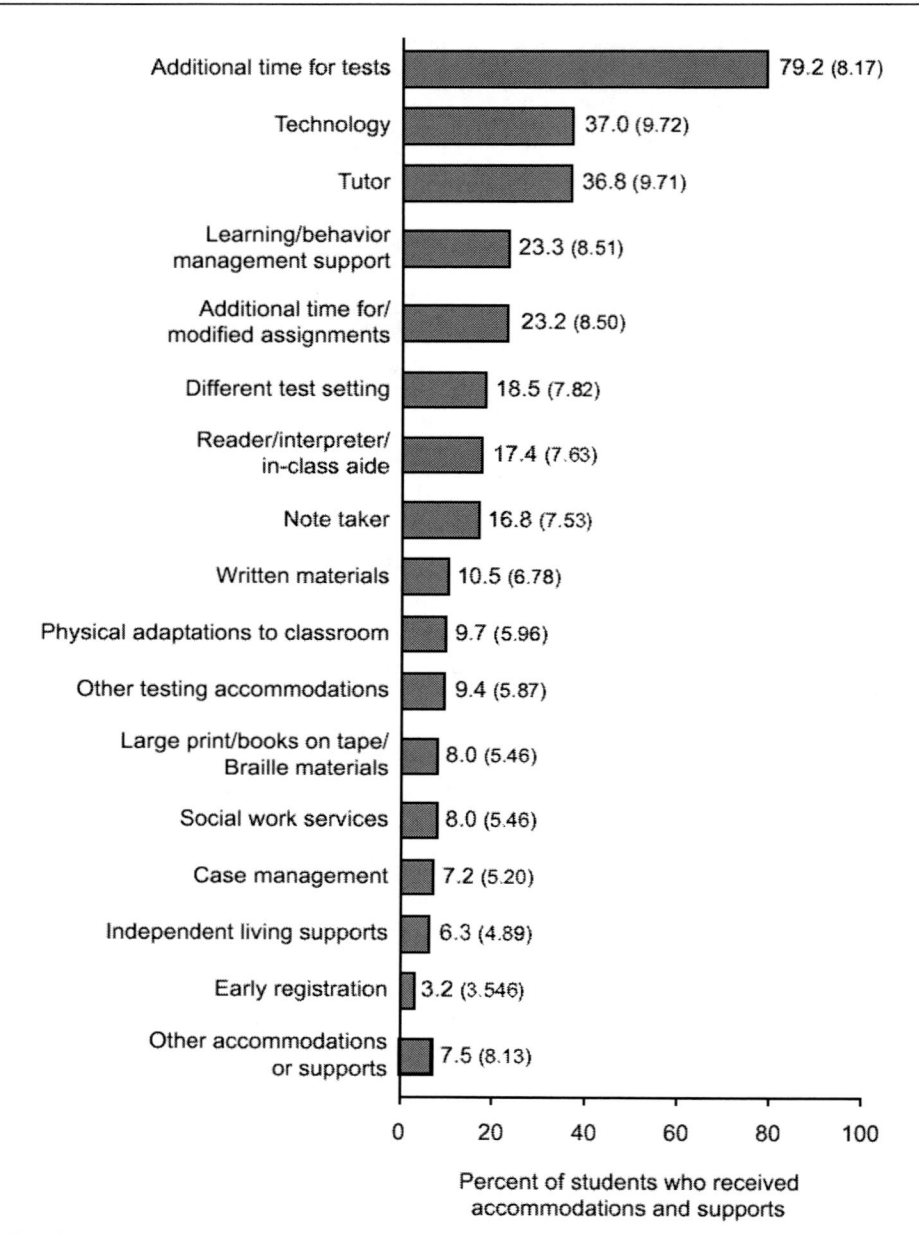

Note: Standard errors are in parentheses. Findings are reported for young adults with disabilities out of
      high school up to 8 years. NLTS2 percentages are weighted population estimates based on a
      sample of approximately 710 young adults with disabilities.
Source: U.S. Department of Education, Institute of Education Sciences, National Center for Special
      Education Research, National Longitudinal Transition Study-2 (NLTS2), Waves 2, 3, 4, and 5
      parent interview and youth interview/survey, 2003, 2005, 2007, and 2009.

Figure 11. Types of accommodations and supports received from postsecondary schools by young
adults with disabilities who had ever enrolled in a postsecondary school and had received these types of
assistance.

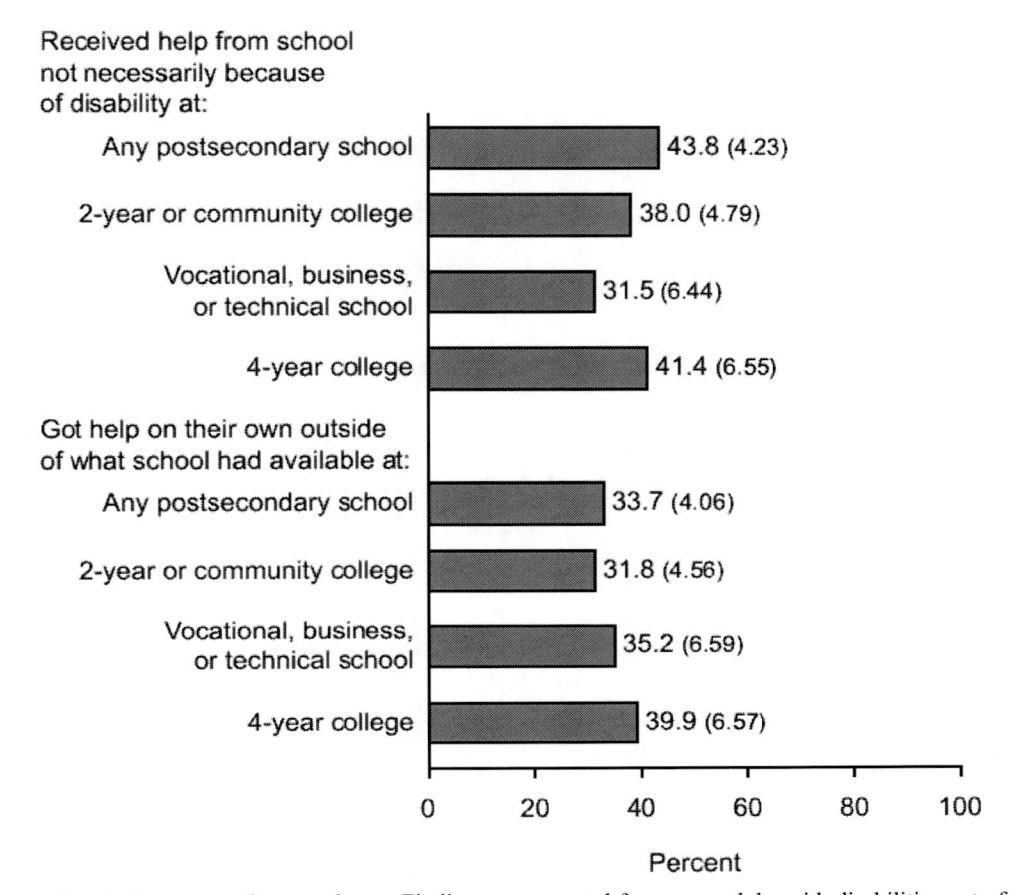

Received help from school not necessarily because of disability at:

- Any postsecondary school: 43.8 (4.23)
- 2-year or community college: 38.0 (4.79)
- Vocational, business, or technical school: 31.5 (6.44)
- 4-year college: 41.4 (6.55)

Got help on their own outside of what school had available at:

- Any postsecondary school: 33.7 (4.06)
- 2-year or community college: 31.8 (4.56)
- Vocational, business, or technical school: 35.2 (6.59)
- 4-year college: 39.9 (6.57)

Percent

Note: Standard errors are in parentheses. Findings are reported for young adults with disabilities out of high school up to 8 years. NLTS2 percentages are weighted population estimates based on samples that range from approximately 2,010 to 2,110 young adults with disabilities.

Source: U.S. Department of Education, Institute of Education Sciences, National Center for Special Education Research, National Longitudinal Transition Study-2 (NLTS2), Waves 2, 3, 4, and 5 parent interview and youth interview/survey, 2003, 2005, 2007, and 2009.

Figure 12. Receipt of help with schoolwork by young adults with disabilities who had ever enrolled in a postsecondary school.

Postsecondary students received help beyond the support provided by schools because of their disability. When students were asked whether they had received help with their schoolwork from their postsecondary schools—regardless of whether the assistance was related to their disability—44 percent had received some type of help (figure 12).[46] Of those students who had received help, 70 percent received tutoring assistance and approximately one-quarter sought help from a study or writing center (27 percent and 24 percent,respectively; not presented in figure). Rates of receiving assistance with schoolwork ranged from 32 percent for those at postsecondary vocational, business, or technical schools to 41 percent for those at 4-year colleges or universities.

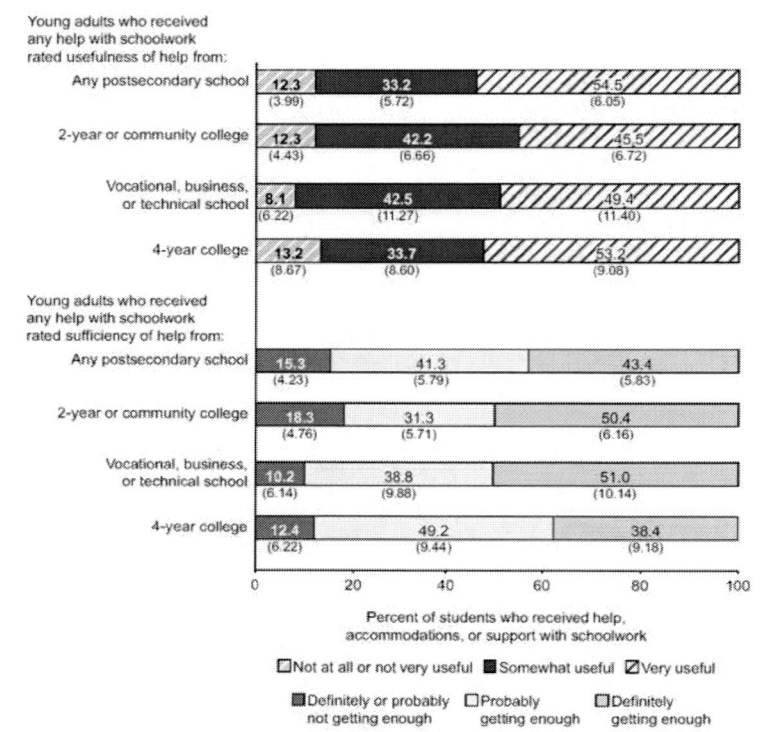

Note: Standard errors are in parentheses. Response categories "not at all useful"and "not very useful" and "probably not getting enough" and "definitely not getting enough" have been collapsed forreporting purposes. Findings are reported for young adults with disabilities out of high school up to 8 years. NLTS2 percentages are weighted population estimates based on samples that range from approximately 320 to 1,270 young adults with disabilities.

Source: U.S. Department of Education, Institute of Education Sciences, National Center for Special Education Research, National Longitudinal Transition Study-2 (NLTS2), Waves 2, 3, 4, and 5 youth interview/survey, 2003, 2005, 2007, and 2009.

Figure 13. Perceptions of assistance with schoolwork by young adults with disabilities who ever had enrolled in postsecondary school and had received assistance.

Some students also sought help on their own outside of what their postsecondary schools provided.[47] Approximately one-third (34 percent) had got help on their own. Forty percent of 4-year college students were reported to have received help with their schoolwork beyond that provided by their schools, as were 35 percent of postsecondary vocational, business, or technical school students and 32 percent of community college students.

When postsecondary students who had received any type of help with their schoolwork— accommodations or supports from the schools independent of a disability or because of a disability or help outside what the schools provided—were asked to rate how useful those supports were in helping them stay in school and do their best,[48] 33 percent reported that the supports were "somewhat useful," and 55 percent rated them as "very useful" (figure 13). Twelve percent felt they were "not very" or "not at all useful" ($p < .001$ for comparisons with "somewhat" and "very useful"). Students' of their schoolwork assistance as "very useful" ranged from 46 percent at 2-year or community colleges to 53 percent at 4-year colleges.

Young adults asserted it
would have been helpful
to have had some services,
accommodations, or help
with schoolwork from:

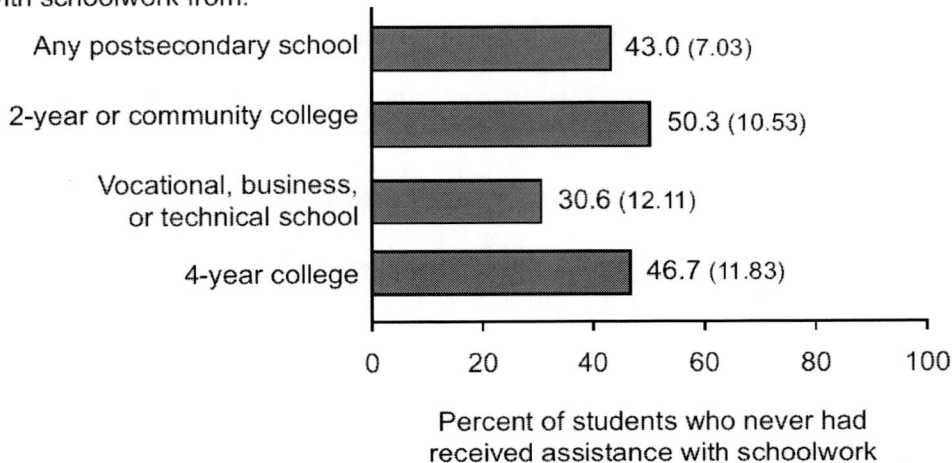

Note: Standard errors are in parentheses. Findings are reported for young adults with disabilities out of
   high school up to 8 years. NLTS2 percentages are weighted population estimates based on samples
   that range from approximately 160 to 580 young adults with disabilities.
Source: U.S. Department of Education, Institute of Education Sciences, National Center for Special
   Education Research, National Longitudinal Transition Study-2 (NLTS2), Waves 4 and 5 youth
   interview/surveys, 2007 and 2009.

Figure 14. Perceptions of need for assistance with schoolwork by young adults with disabilities who
ever had enrolled in postsecondary school and had not received assistance.

Students who had received assistance also were asked whether they thought they were
receiving enough help to do their best at school.[49] Of students who had ever enrolled in
postsecondary school, 41 percent reported they "probably" were, and 43 percent reported they
"definitely" were getting enough assistance, whereas 15 percent reported they "definitely" or
"probably" were not getting enough help ($p < .001$ for comparisons with "probably" and
"definitely" get enough assistance). Thirty-eight percent of students with disabilities at 4-year
colleges or universities, 50 percent of those at 2-year colleges, and 51 percent of those at
postsecondary vocational, business, or technical schools stated they were "definitely getting
enough" services, accommodations, or help with schoolwork.

The 38 percent of postsecondary students who had not received any type of help with
their schoolwork—neither accommodations nor supports from the schools independent of a
disability or because of a disability nor help outside what the schools provided—were asked
whether it would have been helpful to have had some assistance.[50] Forty-three percent
reported it would have been helpful to have had additional assistance (figure 14). Almost one-
third (31 percent) at vocational, business, or technical schools; 47 percent at 4-year colleges
or universities; and 50 percent at 2-year or community colleges reported the need for
additional help with schoolwork.

Disability Differences in Disclosure of Disability and Receipt of Accommodations

Students with different disabilities varied widely in the extent to which they identified themselves as an individual with a disability; the rate of not considering themselves to have a disability ranged from 19 percent to 74 percent (table 8). Students with speech/language impairments (74 percent), learning disabilities (69 percent), or other health impairments (65 percent) were more likely to have reported not considering themselves as having a disability than were those with orthopedic (19 percent), visual (21 percent), or hearing impairments (32 percent); autism (24 percent); multiple disabilities (26 percent); or deaf-blindness (32 percent) ($p < .001$ for all comparisons other than with deaf-blindness and $p < .01$ for all comparisons with deaf-blindness). Students with speech/language impairments or learning disabilities also were more likely to have reported not considering themselves as having a disability than were those with traumatic brain injuries (37 percent, $p < .01$ for both comparisons) or mental retardation (37 percent, $p < .01$ for comparison with speech/language impairment only). In addition, students with emotional disturbances (53 percent) were more likely than those with visual or orthopedic impairments ($p < .01$ for both comparisons) to view themselves as not having a disability.

A similar pattern of disability differences was apparent for those who had informed their postsecondary schools of a disability. Students with orthopedic or visual impairments (76 percent and 73 percent, respectively), multiple disabilities (71 percent), deaf-blindness (68 percent), autism (63 percent), or hearing impairments (59 percent) were more likely to consider themselves as having a disability and to have disclosed that disability to their postsecondary schools than were those with speech/language impairments (17 percent), learning disabilities (24 percent), other health impairments (25 percent), or emotional disturbances (27 percent, $p < .001$ for all comparisons). Students with mental retardation (58 percent) also were more likely to disclose a disability than were those with learning disabilities ($p < .01$) or speech/language or other health impairments ($p < .001$ for both comparisons). In addition, students with traumatic brain injuries (48 percent) were more likely to disclose their disability than those with speech/language impairments ($p < .01$).

Postsecondary students also differed in their rates of receipt of accommodations and supports from their schools. Rates of receiving accommodations or supports because of a disability ranged from 12 percent to 60 percent (table 9). Students with deaf-blindness (60 percent); visual (59 percent), hearing (53 percent), or orthopedic impairments (55 percent); or multiple disabilities (46 percent) were more likely to receive accommodations or supports because of a disability than were those with speech/language impairments (12 percent), other health impairments (15 percent), or learning disabilities (17 percent, $p < .001$ for all comparisons). Students with deaf-blindness or visual, hearing, or orthopedic impairments also were more likely to receive disability-related accommodations than were those with emotional disturbances (20 percent, $p < .001$ for all comparisons). In addition, students with visual or orthopedic impairments were more likely to receive accommodations than were students with mental retardation (24 percent, $p < .001$ for both comparisons).

The rate of receiving help with schoolwork overall—whether or not specifically due to a disability—did not differ across disability categories, with two exceptions. Students with traumatic brain injuries (70 percent) were more likely to receive help than were those with autism (36 percent) or emotional disturbances (37 percent, $p < .01$ for both comparisons).

Table 8. Extent to which young adults ever enrolled in a postsecondary school considered themselves as having a disability and informed postsecondary schools of disability, by disability category

	Learning disability	Speech/ language impairment	Mental retardation	Emotional disturbance	Hearing impairment	Visual impairment	Orthopedic impairment	Other health impairment	Autism	Traumatic brain injury	Multiple disabilities	Deaf-blindness
	Percent											
Young adult did not consider self to have a disability	68.9 (5.84)	74.0 (4.87)	37.1 (10.95)	52.5 (7.64)	31.6 (6.29)	20.8 (5.94)	18.5 (4.86)	64.9 (5.75)	23.9 (6.90)	37.4 (10.51)	25.9 (8.15)	32.4 (10.08)
Young adult considered self to have a disability and had informed school of disability	24.2 (5.40)	16.6 (4.13)	57.8 (11.20)	26.8 (6.78)	59.4 (6.64)	73.0 (6.50)	76.1 (5.34)	25.4 (5.24)	62.7 (7.83)	47.8 (10.85)	70.7 (8.47)	67.6 (10.08)
Young adult considered self to have a disability and had not informed school of disability	6.9 (3.20)	9.4 (3.24)	5.1 (4.99)	20.7 (6.20)	9.0 (3.87)	6.2 (3.53)	5.4 (2.83)	9.7 (3.57)	13.4 (5.51)	14.8 (7.71)	3.4 (3.37)	#

Rounds to zero.

Note: Standard errors are in parentheses. Findings are reported for young adults with disabilities out of high school up to 8 years. Response categories "student considers self to have a disability and has informed school of disability before enrollment" and "student considers self to have a disability and has informed school of disability after enrollment" have been collapsed for reporting purposes. NLTS2 percentages are weighted population estimates based on a sample of approximately 1,960 young adults with disabilities.

Source: U.S. Department of Education, Institute of Education Sciences, National Center for Special Education Research, National Longitudinal Transition Study-2 (NLTS2), Waves 2, 3, 4, and 5 parent interview and youth interview/survey, 2003, 2005, 2007, and 2009.

Table 9. Receipt of accommodations, supports, and help with schoolwork by young adults ever enrolled in a postsecondary school, by disability category

	Learning disability	Speech/language impairment	Mental retardation	Emotional disturbance	Hearing impairment	Visual impairment	Orthopedic impairment	Other health impairment	Autism	Traumatic brain injury	Multiple disabilities	Deaf-blindness
	Percent											
Accommodations and supports received from school because of disability, independent of informing school of disability	17.0 (4.67)	12.4 (3.62)	24.4 (9.62)	19.8 (6.07)	53.0 (6.48)	59.3 (7.17)	54.5 (6.19)	14.5 (4.21)	34.6 (7.35)	34.2 (10.05)	45.9 (9.31)	59.9 (10.41)
Received help with schoolwork from school overall	43.2 (5.94)	44.5 (5.25)	50.0 (10.73)	37.3 (6.95)	51.7 (7.19)	43.4 (7.17)	54.4 (6.12)	49.0 (5.86)	35.6 (7.25)	70.2 (9.62)	56.8 (9.19)	51.7 (10.33)
Student got help on own	33.4 (5.68)	34.5 (5.05)	42.3 (10.54)	28.0 (6.52)	40.0 (7.11)	52.0 (7.35)	37.4 (5.93)	29.2 (5.36)	33.8 (7.23)	30.7 (9.44)	53.8 (9.22)	47.6 (10.33)

Note: Standard errors are in parentheses. Findings are reported for young adults with disabilities out of high school up to 8 years. NLTS2 percentages are weighted population estimates based on samples that range from approximately 2,010 to 2,110 young adults with disabilities.

Source: U.S. Department of Education, Institute of Education Sciences, National Center for Special Education Research, National Longitudinal Transition Study-2 (NLTS2), Waves 2, 3, 4, and 5 parent interview and youth interview/survey, 2003, 2005, 2007, and 2009.

Table 10. Perceptions of assistance with schoolwork by young adults with disabilities who had ever enrolled in postsecondary school and had received assistance, by disability category

	Learning disability	Speech/ language impairment	Mental retardation	Emotional disturbance	Hearing impairment	Visual impairment	Orthopedic impairment	Other health impairment	Autism	Traumatic brain injury	Multiple disabilities	Deaf-blindness
	Percent											
Young adults who received any help with schoolwork rated the help as:												
Very useful	54.6 (8.59)	43.3 (7.24)	73.0 (12.66)	51.2 (10.92)	46.8 (9.76)	59.8 (8.14)	62.2 (6.56)	54.8 (7.78)	49.3 (10.78)	54.3 (12.36)	54.3 (11.38)	‡
Somewhat useful	36.9 (8.32)	40.4 (7.17)	8.3 (7.87)	23.6 (9.28)	14.3 (6.84)	25.6 (7.24)	28.8 (6.13)	27.1 (6.94)	27.6 (9.64)	36.2 (11.93)	15.2 (8.20)	‡
Not at all or not very useful	8.5 (4.81)	16.3 (5.39)	18.7 (11.1)	25.2 (9.49)	39.0 (9.54)	14.6 (5.86)	9.0 (3.87)	18.1 (6.02)	23.2 (9.10)	9.5 (7.28)	30.5 (10.51)	‡
Young adults who received any help with schoolwork thought they were:												
Definitely getting enough	42.8 (8.13)	51.8 (7.26)	39.0 (13.69)	36.5 (10.06)	51.5 (9.73)	62.5 (7.99)	53.1 (6.79)	45.4 (7.58)	36.7 (11.33)	45.8 (12.15)	53.6 (11.14)	‡
Probably getting enough	42.4 (8.12)	38.8 (7.08)	34.9 (13.38)	45.1 (10.40)	28.2 (8.76)	21.3 (6.76)	36.8 (6.56)	40.6 (7.47)	53.4 (11.73)	34.6 (11.60)	32.8 (10.49)	‡
Probably or definitely not getting enough	14.8 (5.84)	9.4 (4.24)	26.1 (12.33)	18.4 (8.09)	20.3 (7.83)	16.3 (6.10)	10.1 (4.10)	14.0 (5.28)	9.9 (7.02)	19.6 (9.68)	13.6 (7.66)	‡
Young adults who never received any help with schoolwork thought ssistance would have been helpful	43.6 (9.38)	42.2 (8.46)	‡	31.7 (10.50)	41.9 (13.00)	30.6 (12.47)	49.4 (10.30)	32.2 (9.21)	54.1 (12.58)	‡	‡	‡

‡ Responses for items with fewer than 30 respondents are not reported.

Note: Standard errors are in parentheses. Findings are reported for young adults with disabilities out of high school up to 8 years. Response categories "not at all useful" and "not very useful" and response categories "probably not getting enough" and "definitely not getting enough" have been collapsed for reporting purposes. NLTS2 percentages are weighted population estimates based on samples that range from approximately 1,230 to 1,270 young adults with disabilities.

Source: U.S. Department of Education, Institute of Education Sciences, National Center for Special Education Research, National Longitudinal Transition Study-2 (NLTS2), Waves 2, 3, 4, and 5 parent interview and youth interview/survey, 2003, 2005, 2007, and 2009.

Table 11. Disclosure of disability to postsecondary school and receipt of and perceptions of accommodations, supports, and help with schoolwork by young adults with disabilities who had ever enrolled in postsecondary school, by highest level of educational attainment

	Completers	Non-completers	Less than 3 years	3 up to 5 years	5 up to 8 years
	Percent				
Disclosure of disability					
Did not consider self to have a disability	63.5 (4.33)	42.1 (20.76)	47.7 (11.98)	62.0 (7.75)	66.6 (5.49)
Considered self to have a disability and had informed school of disability	28.1 (4.04)	40.3 (20.62)	42.7 (11.87)	31.1 (7.39)	24.0 (4.97)
Considered self to have a disability and had not informed school of disability	8.4 (2.49)	17.6 (16.01)	9.6 (7.07)	6.9 (4.05)	9.4 (3.40)
Receipt of accommodations and supports					
Received from school because of disability, independent of informing school of disability	19.4 (3.53)	12.4 (13.88)	36.9 (11.39)	22.1 (6.64)	14.3 (4.03)
Received help with school-work from school overall	13.5 (13.79)	44.4 (4.31)	41.8 (10.97)	44.5 (7.68)	43.8 (5.63)
Got help on own	33.9 (4.14)	27.5 (18.13)	29.3 (10.13)	34.0 (7.31)	34.4 (5.45)
Young adults who received any help with schoolwork rated the help as:					
Very useful	54.2 (6.11)	‡	56.5 (15.67)	54.4 (10.90)	54.2 (7.92)
Somewhat useful	33.5 (5.79)	‡	35.7 (15.15)	36.8 (10.56)	29.8 (7.27)
Not at all or not very useful	12.3 (4.03)		(8.48)	(6.20)	(5.83)
Young adults who received any help with schoolwork thought they were:					
Definitely getting enough	43.0 (5.92)	‡	49.1 (15.79)	36.4 (10.39)	47.1 (7.61)
Probably getting enough	41.7 (5.90)	‡	33.3 (14.89)	52.3 (10.79)	35.3 (7.29)
Probably or definitely not getting enough	15.4 (4.32)	‡	17.5 (12.00)	11.3 (6.84)	17.6 (5.81)
Young adults who never received any help with sch-ool work thought assistance would have been helpful	43.5 (7.13)		57.0 (20.28)	35.8 (11.18)	46.3 (9.84)

‡ Responses for items with fewer than 30 respondents are not reported.

Note: Standard errors are in parentheses. Findings are reported for young adults with disabilities out of high school up to 8 years.NLTS2 percentages are weighted population estimates based on samples that range from approximately 1,230 to 1,270 young adults with disabilities.

Source: U.S. Department of Education, Institute of Education Sciences, National Center for Special Education Research, National Longitudinal Transition Study-2 (NLTS2), Waves 2, 3, 4, and 5 parent interview and youth interview/survey, 2003, 2005, 2007, and 2009.

Students' rate of receiving help with schoolwork outside of what was provided by their postsecondary schools did not differ significantly across disability categories.

Students' perceptions of their accommodations, supports, and help with schoolwork did notperceptions of their differ significantly by disability category, except that young adults with hearing impairments were more likely than those with orthopedic impairments to describe the help they received as being "not at all or not very useful" (39 percent vs. 9 percent,$p < .01$; table 10).

Assertion of the need for help with schoolwork by those who had not received assistance did not differ significantly by disability category.

Differences in Disclosure of Disability and Receipt of Accommodations by High School-Leaving Characteristics

Self-identification as a student with disabilities, disclosure of a disability to postsecondary schools; receipt of accommodations, supports, and help with schoolwork from school and on their own; and perceptions of accommodations, supports, and help did not differ significantly by students' high school-leaving characteristics (table 11).

Demographic Differences in Disclosure of Disability and Receipt of Accommodations

Self-identification as a student with disabilities; disclosure of a disability to postsecondary schools; receipt of accommodations, supports, and help with schoolwork from school and on their own; and perceptions of accommodations, supports, and help did not differ significantly by students' demographic characteristics (table 12).

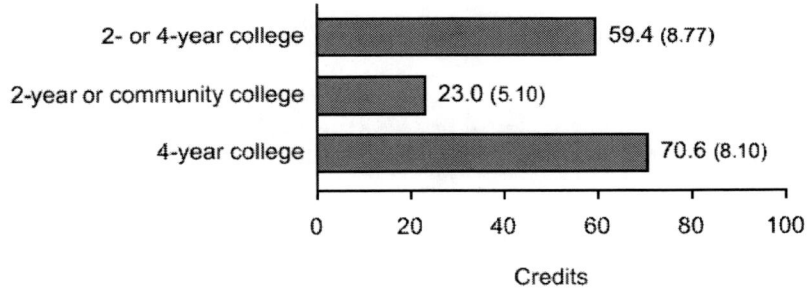

Note: Standard errors are in parentheses. Findings are reported for young adults with disabilities out of high school up to 8 years. NLTS2 percentages are weighted population estimates based on samples that range from approximately 610 to 1,330 young adults with disabilities.

Source: U.S. Department of Education, Institute of Education Sciences, National Center for Special Education Research, National Longitudinal Transition Study-2 (NLTS2), Waves 4 and 5 parent interview and youth interview/survey, 2007 and 2009.

Figure 15. Number of college credits earned by young adults with disabilities who ever had been enrolled in college.

Table 12. Disclosure of disability to postsecondary school and receipt of and perceptions of accommodations, supports, and help with schoolwork by young adults with disabilities who had ever enrolled in postsecondary school, by parents' household income and young adults' race/ethnicity and gender

	$25,000 or less	$25,001 to $50,000	More than $50,000	White	African American	Hispanic	Male	Female
	Percent							
Disclosure of disability								
Didnot consider self to have a disability	66.4 (8.04)	64.2 (8.92)	59.9 (5.94)	61.1 (5.05)	65.3 (9.80)	70.1 (12.77)	57.8 (5.47)	71.8 (6.57)
Considered self to have a disability and had informed sch-ool of disability	27.6 (7.61)	27.4 (8.30)	30.3 (5.57)	29.5 (4.72)	28.3 (9.27)	23.0 (11.74)	32.1 (5.17)	22.2 (6.07)
Considered self to have a disability and had not informed school of disability	6.1 (4.07)	8.4 (5.16)	9.8 (3.60)	9.4 (3.02)	6.4 (5.04)	6.9 (7.07)	10.1 (3.34)	6.0 (3.47)
Receipt of accommodations and supports								
Received from school because of disability, independent of informing school of disability	19.5 (6.89)	17.2 (6.95)	21.1 (4.91)	19.6 (4.06)	18.0 (8.05)	19.8 (11.11)	21.9 (4.52)	15.1 (5.27)
Received help with school-work from school overall	39.2 (8.32)	36.5 (8.58)	50.1 (5.90)	36.9 (4.84)	64.2 (9.58)	47.1 (13.35)	39.6 (5.18)	50.8 (7.18)
Got help on own	31.0 (7.96)	35.9 (8.57)	33.6 (5.60)	31.3 (4.67)	44.6 (10.07)	27.6 (12.13)	31.3 (4.96)	37.4 (6.94)
Young adults who received any help with schoolwork rated the help as:								
Very useful	59.0 (11.28)	67.7 (12.91)	46.4 (8.38)	49.0 (7.28)	59.4 (12.92)	70.6 (16.46)	50.3 (8.02)	59.5 (9.10)
Somewhat useful	28.5 (10.36)	21.1 (11.26)	40.8 (8.26)	35.1 (6.95)	35.1 (12.56)	19.6 (14.35)	38.8 (7.82)	26.5 (8.18)
Not at all or not very useful	12.6 (7.61)	11.3 (8.74)	12.8 (5.62)	15.9 (5.32)	5.4 (5.95)	9.8 (10.74)	10.9 (5.00)	14.0 (6.43)
Young adults who received any help with schoolwork thought they were:								
Definitely getting enough	51.0 (10.96)	33.2 (12.74)	45.8 (8.08)	43.2 (7.04)	37.4 (12.37)	54.8 (16.89)	37.2 (7.55)	51.0 (8.92)
Probably getting enough	39.0 (10.69)	39.8 (13.24)	41.2 (7.98)	41.3 (6.99)	49.6 (12.78)	26.4 (14.95)	43.7 (7.75)	38.3 (8.67)

	$25,000 or less	$25,001 to $50,000	More than $50,000	White	African American	Hispanic	Male	Female
	Percent							
Probably or definitely not getting enough	10.0 (6.58)	27.0 (12.01)	13.0 (5.45)	15.5 (5.14)	13.1 (8.63)	18.7 (13.23)	19.2 (6.15)	10.6 (5.49)
Young adults who never received any help with school work thought assistance would have been helpful	50.9 (15.28)	55.9 (13.06)	36.7 (9.27)	40.2 (7.85)	36.0 (17.42)	83.9 (21.23)	39.3 (7.73)	49.8 (13.94)

Note: Standard errors are in parentheses. Findings are reported for young adults out of high school up to 8 years. NLTS2 percentages are weighted population estimates based on samples that range from approximately 1,230 to 1,270 young adults.

Source: U.S. Department of Education, Institute of Education Sciences, National Center for Special Education Research, National Longitudinal Transition Study-2 (NLTS2), Waves 2,3,4,and 5 parent interview and youth interview/survey, 2003, 2005, 2007, and 2009.

Table 13. Number of collegecredits earned by young adults with disabilities who had ever been enrolled in college, by disability category

	Learning disability	Speech/ language impairment	Mental retardation	Emotional disturbance	Hearing impairment	Visual impairment	Orthopedic impairment	Other health impairment	Autism	Traumatic brain injury	Multiple disabilities	Deaf-blindness
	Average number of credits											
Young adults who ever had been enrolled in:												
2-year or community college	29.8 (5.47)	34.4 (4.17)	‡	19.8 (5.24)	41.7 (6.94)	43.1 (6.77)	32.4 (5.22)	21.9 (4.35)	38.4 (8.34)	38.3 (10.78)	27.46 (8.43)	‡
4-year college	72.8 (11.89)	82.7 (9.00)	‡	‡	93.9 (10.28)	93.5 (11.60)	70.8 (8.91)	61.4 (12.30)	76.5 (11.24)	‡	‡	‡

‡ 30 respondents are not reported.Responses for items with fewer than

Note: Standard errors are in parentheses. Findings are reported for young adults with disabilities out of high school up to 8 years. NLTS2 percentages are weighted population estimates based on samples of approximately 610 and 1,010 young adults with disabilities attending 2- and 4-year colleges.

Source: U.S. Department of Education, Institute of Education Sciences, National Center for Special Education Research, National Longitudinal Transition Study-2 (NLTS2), Waves 4 and 5 parent interview and youth interview/survey, 2007 and 2009.

Table 14. Number of college credits earned by young adults with disabilities who had ever been enrolled in college, by high school-leaving status and years since leaving high school

	Completers	Non-completers	Less than 3 years	3 up to 5 years	5 up to 8 years
	Average number of credits				
Young adults who ever had been enrolled in:					
2-year or community college	23.1 (5.14)	‡	18.9 (7.92)	29.3 (5. 43)	30.0 (6.17)
4-year college	70.7 (8.78)	‡	46.1 (12.82)	59.2 (13.30)	84.2 (11.86)

‡ Responses for items with fewer than 30 respondents are not reported.
Note: Standard errors are in parentheses. Findings are reported for young adults with disabilities out of high school up to 8 years. NLTS2 percentages are weighted population estimates based on samples that range from approximately 610 to 1,010 young adults with disabilities.
Source: U.S. Department of Education, Institute of Education Sciences, National Center for Special Education Research, National Longitudinal Transition Study-2 (NLTS2), Waves 4 and 5 parent interview and youth interview/survey, 2007 and 2009.

Postsecondary Credits Earned

To complete college and obtain a degree, students must earn a certain number of credits overall—typically approximately 60 credits for an associate's degree and 120 for a bachelor's degree. Chen and Carol (2005) reported that individuals in the general population who had been out of high school for 8 years and had been enrolled in postsecondary education had earned an average of 91 credits and that parents' education was positively associated with college credit accumulation. However, to date, little has been known about the credit accumulation of postsecondary school students with disabilities.

On average, young adults with disabilities who were out of high school up to 8 years and had attended a 2-year or 4-year college at some point in time had earned 59 semester credits (figure 15).[51] Those who had attended 2-year or community colleges had earned on average 23 semester credits, and those who ever had attended a 4-year college had earned 71 semester credits.

Disability Differences in Number of Credits Earned

The average numbers of credits earned in 2-year colleges ranged from approximately 20 credits for students with emotional disturbances to 43 credits for students with visual impairments (table 13). Students with hearing impairments and those with visual impairments earned significantly more postsecondary school credits (42 credits and 43 credits) than did students with emotional disturbances (20 credits; $p < .01$). At 4-year colleges, the average number of credits earned ranged from 61 for students with other health impairments to 94 for students with hearing impairments or visual impairments. No significant differences were found across disability categories for number of credits earned in 4-year colleges.

Table 15. Number of colleg ecredits earned by young adults with disabilities who had ever been enrolled in college, by parents' household income and young adults' race/ethnicity and gender

	$25,000 or less	$25,001 to $50,000	More than $50,000	White	African American	Hispanic	Male	Female
	Average number of credits							
Young adults who ever had been enrolled in:								
2-year or community college	24.2 (9.17)	24.7 (6.22)	29.8 (4.93)	29.6 (4.74)	27.8 (10.25)	26.0 (8.22)	28.5 (4.69)	28.7 (6.94)
4-year college	75.2 (17.58)	51.5 (19.26)	73.0 (10.53)	75.4 (9.77)	62.7 (17.19)	89.8 (25.22)	67.1 (10.97)	80.6 (13.28)

Note: Standard errors are in parentheses. Findings are reported for young adults with disabilities out of high school up to 8 years. NLTS2 percentages are weighted population estimates based on samples that range from approximately 610 to 1,010 young adults with disabilities.

Source: U.S. Department of Education, Institute of Education Sciences, National Center for Special Education Research, National Longitudinal Transition Study-2 (NLTS2), Waves 4 and 5 parent interview and youth interview/survey, 2007 and 2009.

Differences in Number of Credits Earned by High School-Leaving Characteristics

The average numbers of credits earned in 2- year and 4-year colleges did not differ significantly by secondary school-leaving characteristics (table 14).

Differences in Number of Credits Earned by Demographic Characteristics

Number of credits earned did not differ significantly by gender, race/ethnicity, or parents' household income (table 15).

Postsecondary School Completion

For many students in the general population, postsecondary school enrollment does not result in degree attainment or program completion. Fewer than two-thirds of students in the general population who began as full-time freshmen in 4-year universities in 1995 received a bachelor's degree within a 6-year period (Berkner, He, and Cataldi 2002). Many individuals who begin postsecondary education but fail to graduate do not realize the economic importance of college graduation. For example, whereas the earnings gap between individuals with a bachelor's degree and those with a high school diploma has continuously widened over the past 30 years, those who enroll in college but do not graduate "have made only slight gains" (Carey 2004).

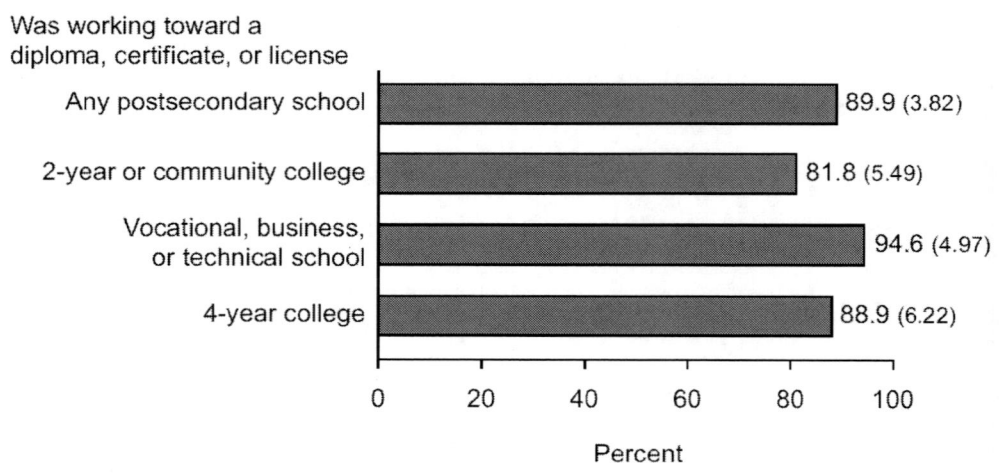

Note: Standard errors are in parentheses. Findings are reported for young adults with disabilities out of high school up to 8 years. NLTS2 percentages are weighted population estimates based on samples that range from approximately 280 to 960 young adults with disabilities.

Source: U.S. Department of Education, Institute of Education Sciences, National Center for Special Education Research, National Longitudinal Transition Study-2 (NLTS2), Waves 2, 3, 4, and 5 parent interview and youth interview/survey, 2003, 2005, 2007, and 2009.

Figure 16. School completion goal of young adults with disabilities enrolled in postsecondary school at the time of the interview.

Ninety percent of young adults with disabilities who were currently enrolled in postsecondary school at the time of the interview asserted that they were "working toward a diploma, certificate, or license" (figure 16).[52] The percentages so reporting did not differ significantly for students in different types of postsecondary institutions.

Examining completion rates[53] across types of postsecondary schools ("any" postsecondary program), approximately 41 percent of students had graduated from their most recent postsecondary program (figure 17), 31 percent had left their most recent postsecondary school prior to completing (not in figure), and the remaining students still were currently enrolled in their postsecondary program at the time of the interview. Completion rates of postsecondary students with disabilities were lower than those of similar-aged postsecondary students in the general population (41 percent vs. 52 percent, $p < .001$).

Completion rates varied by type of postsecondary institution. Students with disabilities who attended postsecondary vocational, business, or technical schools were more likely to complete their programs than were those who enrolled in 4-year colleges (57 percent vs. 34 percent, $p < .01$). Compared with their peers in the general population, completion rates at 4-year colleges were lower for students with disabilities than for their peers (34 percent vs. 51 percent, $p < .001$). In contrast, their completion rates at 2-year or community college were higher than those of students in the general population (41 percent vs. 22 percent, $p < .001$).

Reasons for leaving postsecondary school varied for the 31 percent of postsecondary school leavers who did not graduate or complete their programs.[54] The most common reason for leaving school concerned its cost: 17 percent of young adults with disabilities reportedly left for this reason (figure 18). Employment or the military, poor grades, and changing schools were the next most common reasons for leaving, with 14 percent, 13 percent, and 13 percent of young adults with disabilities, respectively, leaving for these reasons. Seven percent of young adults with disabilities cited finishing the classes they wanted as their reason for leaving, with similar percentages of young adults with disabilities asserting not liking school or having health or time demands as reasons. Six percent cited pregnancy, childbirth, or childcare; and 4 percent reported not getting the services they needed as reasons. Twenty percent indicated they had left for other reasons, with no single reason within the "other"category accounting for more than 3 percent of exits.

Disability Differences in Postsecondary School Completion

The majority of young adults in all disability categories who were enrolled in postsecondary school at the time of the interview reported that they were working toward a diploma, certificate, or license, with rates ranging from 73 percent of students with multiple disabilities to 97 percent of students with orthopedic or other health impairments ($p < .01$ for both comparisons with multiple disabilities; table 16).

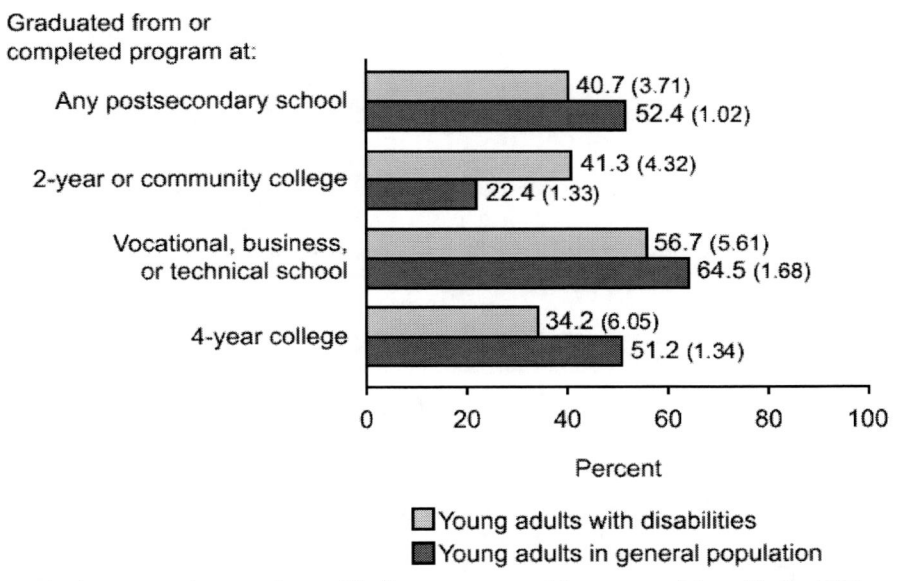

Note: Standard errors are in parentheses. Findings are reported for young adults with disabilities out of high school up to 8 years. NLTS2 percentages are weighted population estimates based on samples that range from approximately 670 to 2,170 young adults with disabilities.

Source: U.S. Department of Education, Institute of Education Sciences, National Center for Special Education Research, National Longitudinal Transition Study-2 (NLTS2), Waves 2, 3, 4, and 5 parent interview and youth interview/survey, 2003, 2005, 2007, and 2009; U.S. Department of Labor, Bureau of Labor Statistics, National Longitudinal Survey of Youth 1997 (NLSY97) 2005 youth survey, responses for 21- to 25-year-olds.

Figure 17. Completion rates ofstudentswith disabilities from current or most recently attended postsecondary school.

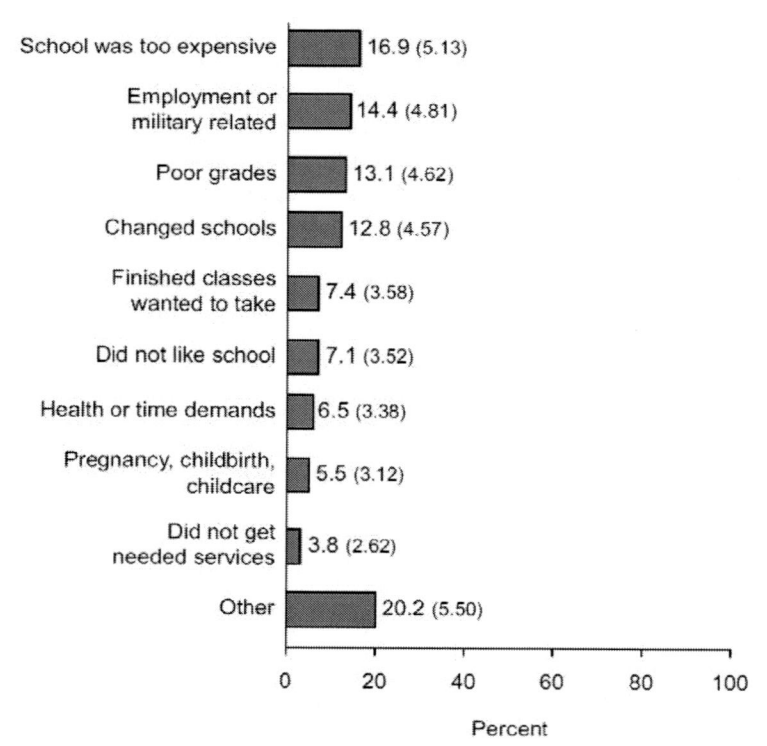

Note: Figure includes young adults with disabilities who left any given type of postsecondary school even if they were enrolled in another type of postsecondary school at the time of the interview. If a young adult with a disability left postsecondary schools more than once, the last reason for leaving is shown. Standard errors are in parentheses. Findings are reported for young adults with disabilities out of high school up to 8 years. NLTS2 percentages are weighted population estimates based on a sample of approximately 290 young adults with disabilities.

Source: U.S. Department of Education, Institute of Education Sciences, National Center for Special Education Research, National Longitudinal Transition Study-2 (NLTS2), Waves 3, 4, and 5 parent interview and youth interview/survey, 2005, 2007, and 2009.

Figure 18. Reasons why young adults with disabilities who had not completed postsecondary school and no longer were enrolled had left postsecondary school.

Within 8 years of leaving high school, completion rates from most recent postsecondary schools ranged from 28 percent for young adults with deaf/blindness to 53 percent of those with hearing impairments (no significant differences).

Differences in Postsecondary School Completion by High School-Leaving Characteristics

Among young adults with disabilities who attended postsecondary school, there were no significant differences in the percentages who expected to complete postsecondary school or actual rates of postsecondary school completion by high school-leaving characteristics or time since leaving secondary school (table 17).

Table 16. Completion rates ofstudents from current or most recently attended postsecondary school, by disability category

	Learning disability	Speech/ language impairment	Mental retardation	Emotional disturbance	Hearing impairment	Visual impairment	Orthopedic impairment	Other health impairment	Autism	Traumatic brain injury	Multiple disabilities	Deaf-blindness
	Percent											
Young adults enrolled at the time of the inter-view who were working toward a diploma, certificate, or license	89.1 (5.41)	91.6 (4.26)	‡	96.1 (4.84)	91.8 (4.88)	95.7 (4.63)	96.8 (3.33)	96.6 (3.64)	79.5 (8.56)	90.4 (8.66)	72.5 (11.24)	‡
Completion rate of students in current or most recently attended postsecondary school	40.9 (5.23)	43.8 (4.78)	44.2 (8.44)	35.1 (6.05)	52.9 (6.16)	42.8 (6.86)	34.7 (5.39)	40.4 (5.35)	38.8 (7.02)	49.9 (9.97)	42.1 (8.38)	27.7 (9.14)

‡ Responses for items with fewer than 30 respondents are not reported.

Note: Standard errors are in parentheses. Findings are reported for young adults with disabilities out of high school up to 8 years. NLTS2 percentages are weighted population estimates based on samples of approximately 960 young adults with disabilities for working toward a degree or diploma and 2,170 young adults with disabilities for graduation rate.

Source: U.S. Department of Education, Institute of Education Sciences, National Center for Special Education Research, National Longitudinal Transition Study-2 (NLTS2), Waves 2, 3, 4, and 5 parent interview and youth interview/survey, 2003, 2005, 2007, and 2009.

Table 17. Completion rates of students with disabilities from current or most recently attended postsecondary school, by high school-leaving status and years since leaving high school

	Completers	Non-completers	Less than 3 years	3 up to 5 years	5 years or more
	Percent				
Young adults enrolled at the time of the interview who were working toward a diploma, certificate, or license	90.0 (3.87)	‡	95.9 (6.03)	85.2 (7.31)	91.7 (5.19)
Completion rate of students in current or most recently attended postsecondary school	42.2 (4.00)	‡	35.7 (9.79)	32.6 (6.02)	47.5 (5.16)

‡ Responses for items with fewer than 30 respondents are not reported.

Note: Standard errors are in parentheses. Findings are reported for young adults with disabilities out of high school up to 8 years.NLTS2 percentages are weighted population estimates based on samples of approximately 960 young adults with disabilities for working toward a degree or diploma and 2,170 young adults with disabilities for graduation rate.

Source: U.S. Department of Education, Institute of Education Sciences, National Center for Special Education Research, National Longitudinal Transition Study-2 (NLTS2), Waves 2, 3, 4, and 5 parent interview and youth interview/survey, 2003, 2005, 2007, and 2009.

Table 18. Completion rates of students with disabilities from current or most recently attended postsecondary school, by parents' household income and young adults' race/ethnicity and gender

	$25,000 or less	$25,001 to $50,000	More than $50,000	White	African American	Hispanic	Male	Female
	Percent							
Young adults enrolled at the time of the interview who were working toward a diploma, certificate, or license	87.5 (8.84)	91.8 (7.90)	89.8 (4.91)	94.3 (3.50)	77.1 (11.53)	98.2 (5.29)	89.0 (5.21)	91.2 (5.53)
Completion rate of students in current or most recently attended postsecondary school	39.5 (7.67)	31.9 (7.14)	45.3 (5.15)	44.4 (4.50)	33.0 (8.19)	37.1 (11.11)	39.0 (4.67)	43.8 (6.10)

Note: Standard errors are in parentheses. Findings are reported for young adults with disabilities out of high school up to 8 years. NLTS2 percentages are weighted population estimates based on samples of approximately 960 young adults with disabilities for working toward a degree or diploma and 2,170 young adults with disabilities for graduation rate.

Source: U.S. Department of Education, Institute of Education Sciences, National Center for Special Education Research, National Longitudinal Transition Study-2 (NLTS2), Waves 2, 3, 4, and 5 parent interview and youth interview/survey, 2003, 2005, 2007, and 2009.

Demographic Differences in Postsecondary School Completion

Among young adults with disabilities who attended postsecondary school, there were no significant differences by demographic characteristics in the percentages who expected to complete postsecondary school or actual rates of postsecondary school completion (table 18).

This chapter has presented a national picture of the postsecondary experiences and outcomes of young adults with disabilities. Chapter 3 examines employment experiences and outcomes, and chapter 4 focuses on the overlap between postsecondary education and employment.

3. EMPLOYMENT

Many adults consider employment a central component of their lives, providing not only economic benefits, but also a social network and a sense of worth as a productive member of society (Levinson and Palmer 2005; Rogan, Grossi, and Gajewski 2002). Indeed, employment has been linked to a range of positive outcomes, including financial independence and enhanced self-esteem (Fabian 1992; Lehman et al. 2002; Polak and Warner 1996). Given the importance of post-high school employment, preparation for employment is a primary focus of many transition services for secondary-school-age youth with disabilities, and achieving employment is the primary transition goal of the majority of secondary students with disabilities served under IDEA (Cameto, Levine, and Wagner 2004).

Although some young adults go on to postsecondary education or training and do not work, and others both work and go to school, for some young adults with disabilities and young adults in the general population, the early years of adult life are a time to begin to engage in employment as a means of support. This chapter examines the employment status and experiences of young adults with disabilities who had been out of high school up to 8 years, including

- employment status;
- number and duration of jobs;
- types of jobs;
- hours worked per week;
- wages and benefits;
- job accommodations;
- perceptions of working conditions;
- job leaving; and
- job search activities.

Findings are reported for young adults with disabilities as a whole and for those who differed in their primary disability classification while in secondary school and by years since leaving high school, highest level of educational attainment, and selected demographic characteristics.

Employment Status

At the time of the 2009 Wave 5 interview, 60 percent of young adults with disabilities who had been out of high school for up to 8 years were employed for pay outside the home (figure 19),[55] compared with 66 percent of similarly aged young adults (21 to 25 years old) in the general population,[56] not a significant difference. About 91 percent of young adults with disabilities had been employed at some point since leaving high school,[57] and 31 percent had been employed after leaving high school but were unemployed at the time of the interview.

Disability Differences in Employment Status

The early post-high school employment experiences of young adults with disabilities varied with their primary disability classification. The percentages of young adults who were employed at the time of the interview ranged from 30 percent to 67 percent (table 19). Young adults with other health impairments, speech/language impairments, or learning disabilities were more likely to be employed at the time of the interview (64 percent to 67 percent) than young adults with deaf-blindness, orthopedic impairments, autism, multiple disabilities, mental retardation, or visual impairments (30 percent to 44 percent; $p < .001$ for all comparisons except $p < .01$ for young adults with speech/language or other health impairments compared with those with visual impairments). In addition, young adults with learning disabilities were more likely to be employed at the time of the interview than those with emotional disturbances (67 percent vs. 50 percent, $p < .01$), and young adults with hearing impairments were more likely to be employed at the time of the interview (57 percent) than young adults with deaf-blindness, orthopedic impairments, autism, or mental retardation (30 percent to 39 percent, $p < .01$ for all comparisons except $p < .001$ for comparison with young adults with orthopedic impairments).

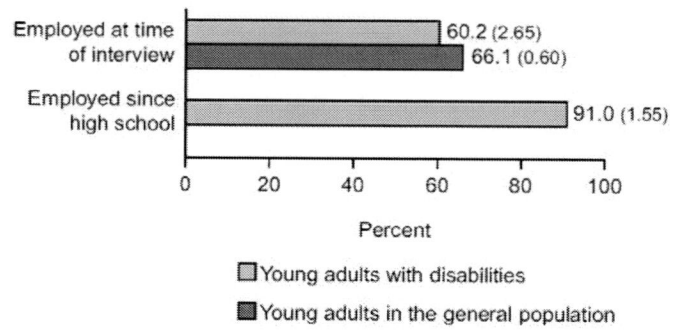

Note: Standard errors are in parentheses. Findings are reported for young adults with disabilities out of high school up to 8 years. NLTS2 percentages are weighted population estimates based on samples ranging from approximately 4,720 to 4,760 young adults with disabilities. General population comparison data not available for employed since high school.

Source: U.S. Department of Education, Institute of Education Sciences, National Center for Special Education Research, National Longitudinal Transition Study-2 (NLTS2), Waves 2, 3, 4, and 5 parent interview and youth interview/survey, 2003, 2005, 2007, and 2009; U.S. Census Bureau, Current Population Survey (CPS), May 2009. Data are for 21- to 25-year-olds.

Figure 19. Paid employment outside the home of young adults with disabilities and young adults in the general population.

Table 19. Paid employment outside the home of young adults, by disability category

	Learning disability	Speech/ language impairment	Mental retardation	Emotional disturbance	Hearing impairment	Visual impairment	Orthopedic impairment	Other health impairment	Autism	Traumatic brain injury	Multiple disabilities	Deaf-blindness
	Percent											
Percentage reported to have been:												
Employed at time of interview	67.3 (3.93)	63.9 (3.73)	38.8 (3.90)	49.6 (4.58)	57.2 (4.89)	43.8 (5.54)	35.0 (4.39)	64.4 (4.09)	37.2 (4.59)	51.6 (7.59)	39.2 (5.33)	30.1 (6.69)
Employed since high school	94.9 (1.83)	94.0 (1.84)	76.2 (3.40)	91.2 (2.58)	91.5 (2.74)	78.0 (4.59)	67.7 (4.29)	95.5 (1.77)	63.2 (4.57)	81.4 (5.93)	62.5 (5.24)	70.4 (6.58)

Note: Standard errors are in parentheses. Findings are reported for young adults with disabilities out of high school up to 8 years. NLTS2 percentages are weighted population estimates based on samples ranging from approximately 4,720 to 4,760 young adults with disabilities.

Source: U.S. Department of Education, Institute of Education Sciences, National Center for Special Education Research, National Longitudinal Transition Study-2 (NLTS2), Waves 2, 3, 4, and 5 parent interview and youth interview/survey, 2003, 2005, 2007, and 2009.

Table 20. Paid employment outside the home of young adults with disabilities, by years since leaving high school

	Less than 3 years	3 up to 5 years	5 up to 8 years
	Percent		
Percentage reported to have been:			
Employed at time of interview	49.5 (6.23)	65.3 (4.54)	59.1 (3.70)
Employed since high school	79.9 (4.99)	92.2 (2.55)	92.7 (1.95)

Note: Standard errors are in parentheses. Findings are reported for young adults with disabilities out of high school up to 8 years. NLTS2 percentages are weighted population estimates based on samples ranging from approximately 4,720 to 4,760 young adults with disabilities.

Source: U.S. Department of Education, Institute of Education Sciences, National Center for Special Education Research, National Longitudinal Transition Study-2 (NLTS2), Waves 2, 3, 4, and 5 parent interview and youth interview/survey, 2003, 2005, 2007, and 2009.

Table 21. Paid employment outside the home of young adults with disabilities, by highest level of educational attainment

	High school non-completer	High school completer	Some post-secondary school	Post-secondary school completion
	Percent			
Percentage reported to have been:				
Employed at time of interview	38.1 (7.41)	53.9 (4.16)	57.7 (5.04)	83.2 (4.68)
Employed since high school	78.2 (6.28)	88.7 (2.64)	92.4 (2.69)	98.7 (1.41)

Note: Standard errors are in parentheses. Findings are reported for young adults with disabilities out of high school up to 8 years. NLTS2 percentages are weighted population estimates based on samples ranging from approximately 4,720 to 4,760 young adults with disabilities.

Source: U.S. Department of Education, Institute of Education Sciences, National Center for Special Education Research, National Longitudinal Transition Study-2 (NLTS2), Waves 2, 3, 4, and 5 parent interview and youth interview/survey, 2003, 2005, 2007, and 2009.

The percentage of young adults who had been employed at some time since leaving high school ranged from 63 percent of those with autism or multiple disabilities to about 96 percent of young adults with other health impairments. Young adults with speech/language impairments, learning disabilities, or other health impairments (94 percent to 96 percent) were all more likely to have had a job at some time since high school than young adults with multiple disabilities, autism, orthopedic impairments, deaf-blindness, mental retardation, or visual impairments (63 percent to 78 percent, $p < .001$ for all comparisons except $p < .01$ comparing young adults with speech/language impairments and those with visual impairments). In addition, young adults with emotional disturbances or hearing impairments (91 and 92 percent, respectively) were more likely than those with multiple disabilities, autism, orthopedic impairments, deaf-blindness, or mental retardation (63 percent to 76 percent) to have been employed since high school ($p < .001$ for all comparisons except $p < .01$ for comparisons with young adults with deaf-blindness).

Differences in Employment Status by Years since Leaving High School

Young adults with disabilities who had been out of high school for different amounts of time did not have significantly different rates of employment at the time of the interview or since high school (table 20). Employment at the time of the interview ranged from 50 percent for young adults with disabilities who had been out of high school for less than 3 years to 65 percent for those who had been out of high school for between 3 and 5 years, and employment since high school ranged from 80 percent to 93 percent for young adults with disabilities who had been out of high school for different lengths of time.

Differences in Employment Status by Highest Level of Educational Attainment

For young adults with disabilities with different levels of educational attainment, employment at the time of the interview ranged from 38 percent to 83 percent, and employment since high school ranged from 78 percent to 99percent (table 21). At the time of the interview, young adults who had received a postsecondary education degree or certificate were more likely to be employed (83 percent) than young adults whose highest level of educational attainment was some postsecondary education (58 percent), high school completion (54 percent), or less than a high school education (38 percent, $p < .001$ for all comparisons). Young adults with disabilities who had completed a postsecondary program also were more likely to have been employed since high school (99 percent) than those who had not finished high school (78 percent) or those who had completed high school (89 percent, $p < .001$ for both comparisons).

Table 22. Paid employment outside the home of young adults with disabilities, by parents' household income and young adults' race/ethnicity and gender

	$25,000 or less	$25,001 to $50,000	More than $50,000	White	African American	Hispanic	Male	Female
	Percent							
Percentage reported to have been:								
Employed at time of interview	44.4 (4.67)	65.2 (5.30)	70.7 (3.76)	64.5 (3.10)	48.0 (6.03)	53.6 (8.46)	64.9 (3.19)	52.1 (4.62)
Employed since high school	85.2 (3.32)	93.6 (2.71)	94.5 (1.87)	93.6 (1.58)	86.4 (4.14)	85.1 (6.00)	91.6 (1.85)	90.1 (2.74)

Note: Standard errors are in parentheses. Findings are reported for young adults with disabilities out of high school up to 8 years. NLTS2 percentages are weighted population estimates based on samples ranging from approximately 4,720 to 4,760 young adults with disabilities.

Source: U.S. Department of Education, Institute of Education Sciences, National Center for Special Education Research, National Longitudinal Transition Study-2 (NLTS2), Waves 2, 3, 4, and 5 parent interview and youth interview/survey, 2003, 2005, 2007, and 2009.

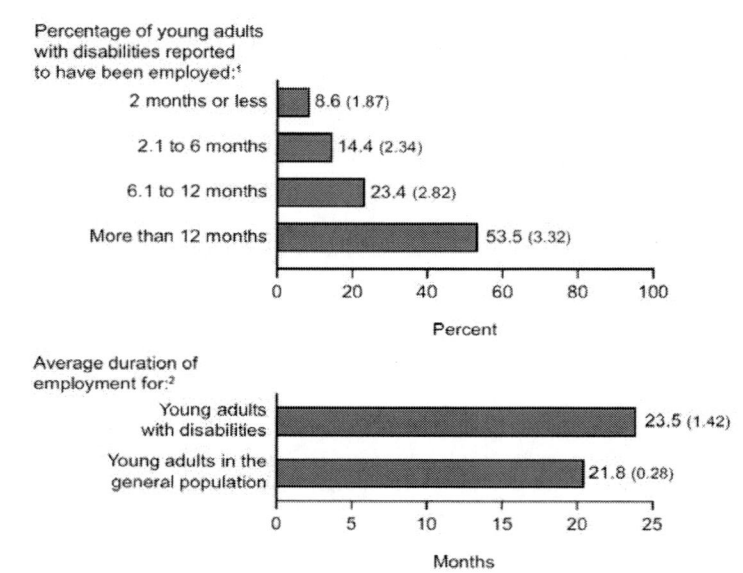

¹ For young adults with disabilities who had held at least one job since high school.
² For current or most recent job for young adults with disabilities.
Note: Standard errors are in parentheses. Findings are reported for young adults with disabilities out of high school up to 8 years. NLTS2 percentages are weighted population estimates based on a sample of approximately 2,740 young adults with disabilities.
Source: U.S. Department of Education, Institute of Education Sciences, National Center for Special Education Research, National Longitudinal Transition Study-2 (NLTS2), Wave 5 parent interview and youth interview/survey, 2009; U.S. Department of Labor, Bureau of Labor Statistics, National Longitudinal Survey of Youth 1997 (NLSY97), round 9 youth questionnaire, 2005. Data are for 21- to 25-year-olds.

Figure 20. Duration of jobs of young adults with disabilities and young adults in the general population who had been employed since high school.

Demographic Differences in Employment Status

Table 22 shows the percentages of young adults with disabilities employed at the time of the interview and since leaving high school by parents' race/ethnicity and gender. No significant differences in employment status at the time of the interview or employment since high school were noted for young adults with disabilities who differed in their racial/ethnic background (ranging from 48 percent to 65 percent) or gender (65 percent for males and 52 percent for females); however, differences related to parents' household income were significant. Young adults with disabilities from households earning more than $50,000 and those from households earning $25,001 to $50,000 were more likely than those from households earning $25,000 or less to have been employed at the time of the interview (71 percent and 65 percent vs. 44 percent, $p < .001$ for comparison between household earnings of more than $50,000 and less than $25,000 and $p < .01$ for comparison between household earnings of $25,001 to $50,000 and less than $25,000).

Job Characteristics

To gain a more complete understanding of the characteristics of young adults with disabilities' post-high school employment, analyses in this section focus on those who were post-high school employment, employed at the time of the interview or had been employed after leaving high school.[58]

Number and Duration of Jobs

On average, young adults with disabilities who had been employed had held about four jobs since leaving high school. The majority of young adults with disabilities (54 percent) had held their current or most recent job for 12 months or more. On average, their current or most recent job had lasted 24 months [59] (figure 20), which did not differ significantly from the average job duration of young adults in the general population (22 months).

Disability Differences in Number and Duration of Jobs

The average number of jobs young adults in different disability categories had held since high school (among those who had held at least one job) ranged from 2.2 to 4.6 jobs (table 23). Young adults with emotional disturbances, other health impairments, or learning disabilities had held more jobs on average (4.6, 4.5, and 4.2 jobs, respectively) than young adults with mental retardation, orthopedic impairments, or multiple disabilities (2.9, 2.8, and 2.2 jobs, $p < .001$ for all comparisons with young adults with multiple disabilities and comparisons between young adults with other health impairments and those with mental retardation or orthopedic impairments and $p < .01$ for all other comparisons). Young adults with other health impairments also had held more jobs (an average of 4.5 jobs) than young adults with hearing impairments (3.3 jobs, $p < .01$), and young adults with speech/language impairments had held more jobs than those with multiple disabilities on average (3.8 jobs vs. 2.2 jobs, $p < .001$). Average job duration ranged from 19 months to 30 months, with no significant differences by young adults in different disability categories.

Differences in Number and Duration of Jobs by Years since Leaving High School

The number and duration of jobs did not differ significantly between young adults who had been out of high school for different lengths of time (table 24). The average number of jobs held, among those who had held at least one job since high school, ranged from about 3 jobs for young adults who had been out of high school less than 3 years to about 5 jobs for those who had been out of high school for 5 or more years. The duration of their current or most recent job ranged from 20 months for those out of high school for less than 3 years to almost 27 months for those out of high school for 5 or more years.

Table 23. Number of jobs and duration of employment of young adults with disabilities, by disability category

	Learning disability	Speech/ language impairment	Mental retardation	Emotional disturbance	Hearing impairment	Visual impairment	Orthopedic impairment	Other health impairment	Autism	Traumatic brain injury	Multiple disabilities	Deaf-blindness
Average number of jobs held since high school[1]	4.2 (0.31)	3.8 (0.27)	2.9 (0.27)	4.6 (0.54)	3.3 (0.30)	4.1 (0.74)	2.8 (0.31)	4.5 (0.35)	3.1 (0.66)	3.5 (0.47)	2.2 (0.32)	3.9 (1.62)
Average duration of job (months)[2]	24.3 (2.09)	19.7 (1.77)	25.9 (2.37)	18.8 (2.08)	22.4 (2.59)	20.5 (2.86)	20.8 (2.86)	21.6 (2.29)	24.7 (3.08)	20.4 (4.06)	30.4 (4.70)	19.1 (3.74)

[1] For young adults who had held at least one job since high school.

[2] For current or most recent job for young adults with disabilities.

Note: Standard errors are in parentheses. Findings are reported for young adults with disabilities out of high school up to 8 years. NLTS2 percentages are weighted population estimates based on samples ranging from approximately 2,720 to 2,740 young adults with disabilities.

Source: U.S. Department of Education, Institute of Education Sciences, National Center for Special Education Research, National Longitudinal Transition Study-2 (NLTS2), Wave 5 parent interview and youth interview/survey, 2009.

Table 24. Number of jobs and duration of employment of young adults with disabilities, by years since leaving high school

	Less than 3 years	3 up to 5 years	5 up to 8 years
Average number of jobs held since high school[1]	3.1 (0.52)	3.9 (0.41)	4.5 (0.31)
Average duration of job (months)[2]	20.2 (3.30)	20.2 (2.08)	26.6 (2.14)

[1] For young adults with disabilities who had held at least one job since high school.
[2] For current or most recent job for young adults with disabilities.
Note: Standard errors are in parentheses. Findings are reported for young adults with disabilities out of high school up to 8 years. NLTS2 percentages are weighted population estimates based on samples ranging from approximately 2,720 to 2,740 young adults with disabilities.
Source: U.S. Department of Education, Institute of Education Sciences, National Center for Special Education Research, National Longitudinal Transition Study-2 (NLTS2), Wave 5 parent interview and youth interview/survey, 2009.

Table 25. Number of jobs and duration of employment of young adults with disabilities, by highest level of educational attainment

	High school non-completer	High school completer	Some post-secondary school	Post-secondary school completion
Average number of jobs held since high school[1]	5.7 (0.93)	3.3 (0.27)	4.2 (0.43)	4.7 (0.54)
Average duration of job (months)[2]	18.5 (4.15)	24.1 (2.21)	22.3 (2.80)	25.1 (2.85)

[1] For young adults who had held at least one job since high school.
[2] For current or most recent job for young adults with disabilities.
Note: Standard errors are in parentheses. Findings are reported for young adults with disabilities out of high school up to 8 years. NLTS2 percentages are weighted population estimates based on samples ranging from approximately 2,720 to 2,740 young adults with disabilities.
Source: U.S. Department of Education, Institute of Education Sciences, National Center for Special Education Research, National Longitudinal Transition Study-2 (NLTS2), Wave 5 parent interview and youth interview/survey, 2009.

Differences in Number and Duration of Jobs by Highest Level of Educational Attainment

The average number and duration of jobs of young adults with disabilities who had achieved different levels of educational attainment did not differ significantly (table 25). Among those who had held a job since high school, the average number of months they had held their current or most recent job ranged from 19 months for those whose highest level of education was less than a high school degree to 25 months for those who had completed a postsecondary education program. The average number of jobs they had held ranged from about 3 jobs for young adults whose highest level of education was high school completion to about 6 jobs for those who had not completed high school.

Demographic Differences in Number and Duration of Jobs

Table 26 shows the number and duration of jobs held since leaving high school by young adults with disabilities by parents' income and young household No significant differences in the number of jobs held or the duration of the current or most recent job were noted. The number of jobs held ranged from 3.7 to 4.4. The length of time young adults had held their jobs ranged from 21 months to 25 months by household income categories, 17 months to 26 months by race/ethnicity, and 21 months to 24 months by gender.

Types of Jobs

Young adults with disabilities held a variety of types of jobs[60] (figure 21). Thirteen percent worked in food preparation and serving-related occupations; 12 percent worked in sales and related occupations; 9 percent worked in office and administrative support occupations; and construction and extraction, personal care and service, and transportation and material moving occupational categories each included 8 percent of young adults with disabilities. Young adults with disabilities were significantly more likely to work in food preparation and serving-related occupations and sales and related occupations (13 percent and 12 percent, respectively) than in education, training, and library occupations (4 percent); computer, mathematical, architecture, engineering, and science occupations (3 percent); military-specific occupations (3 percent); or healthcare support occupations (3 percent, $p <$ .001 for all comparisons). In addition, more young adults with disabilities reported working in food preparation and serving-related occupations than installation, maintenance, and repair occupations (13 percent vs. 6 percent, $p < .01$). Young adults with disabilities were also more likely to work in office and administrative support occupations (9 percent), construction and extraction occupations (8 percent), or personal care and service occupations (8 percent) than healthcare support occupations (3 percent). About 10 percent of young adults with disabilities held jobs in the "other" category, which includes a large number of job categories held by small numbers of young adults with disabilities.

Disability Differences in Types of Jobs

The likelihood of young adults with disabilities holding a particular type of job did not differ significantly across disability categories for most types of jobs investigated. However, differences did exist for young adults with disabilities employed in food preparation and serving-related occupations, production occupations, and occupations included in the "other" category (table 27).

Table 26. Number of jobs and duration of employment of young adults with disabilities, by parents' household income and young adults' race/ethnicity and gender

	$25,000 or less	$25,001 to $50,000	More than $50,000	White	African America n	Hispanic	Male	Female
Average number of jobs held since high school[1]	4.1 (0.36)	3.9 (0.49)	4.1 (0.35)	4.1 (0.29)	3.7 (0.31)	4.4 (0.78)	4.3 (0.31)	3.7 (0.27)
Average duration of job (months)[2]	20.8 (2.79)	25.3 (2.92)	24.1 (1.95)	24.0 (1.66)	25.7 (3.97)	17.3 (3.57)	24.8 (1.78)	21.0 (2.30)

[1] For young adults who had held at least one job since high school.

[2] For current or most recent job for young adults with disabilities.

Note: Standard errors are in parentheses. Findings are reported for young adults with disabilities out of high school up to 8 years. NLTS2 percentages are weighted population estimates based on samples ranging from approximately 2,720 to 2,740 young adults with disabilities.

Source: U.S. Department of Education, Institute of Education Sciences, National Center for Special Education Research, National Longitudinal Transition Study-2 (NLTS2), Wave 5 parent interview and youth interview/survey, 2009.

The percentage of young adults with different disabilities who were employed in food preparation and serving-related jobs ranged from none to 25 percent, with young adults with mental retardation being more likely to be employed in these types of occupations than those with traumatic brain injuries (7 percent) or deaf-blindness (zero, $p < .01$ for comparison with young adults with traumatic brain injuries and $p < .001$ for comparison with young adults with deaf-blindness). Young adults with traumatic brain injury were more likely to hold production jobs than those with other health impairments (24 percent vs. 3 percent, $p < .01$). Young adults with visual or speech/language impairments were more likely than those with traumatic brain injuries to have a job in the "other" category (17 percent and 16 percent vs. 3 percent, $p < .01$ for both comparisons).

Differences in Types of Jobs by Years since Leaving High School

The types of jobs held by young adults with disabilities did not differ significantly by length of time out of high school (table 28). For example, the percentage of young adults employed in food preparation and serving occupations ranged from 11 percent to 22 percent for young adults out of high school for 3 to 5 years and less than 3 years, respectively, not a significant difference.

Differences in Types of Jobs by Highest Level of Educational Attainment

There were no significant differences in the types of jobs held by young adults with disabilities who differed in their highest level of educational attainment (table 29). For example, the percentage of young adults whose current or most recent job was in sales and related occupations ranged from 9 percent of those with a postsecondary diploma or certificate to 16 percent of those with some postsecondary education.

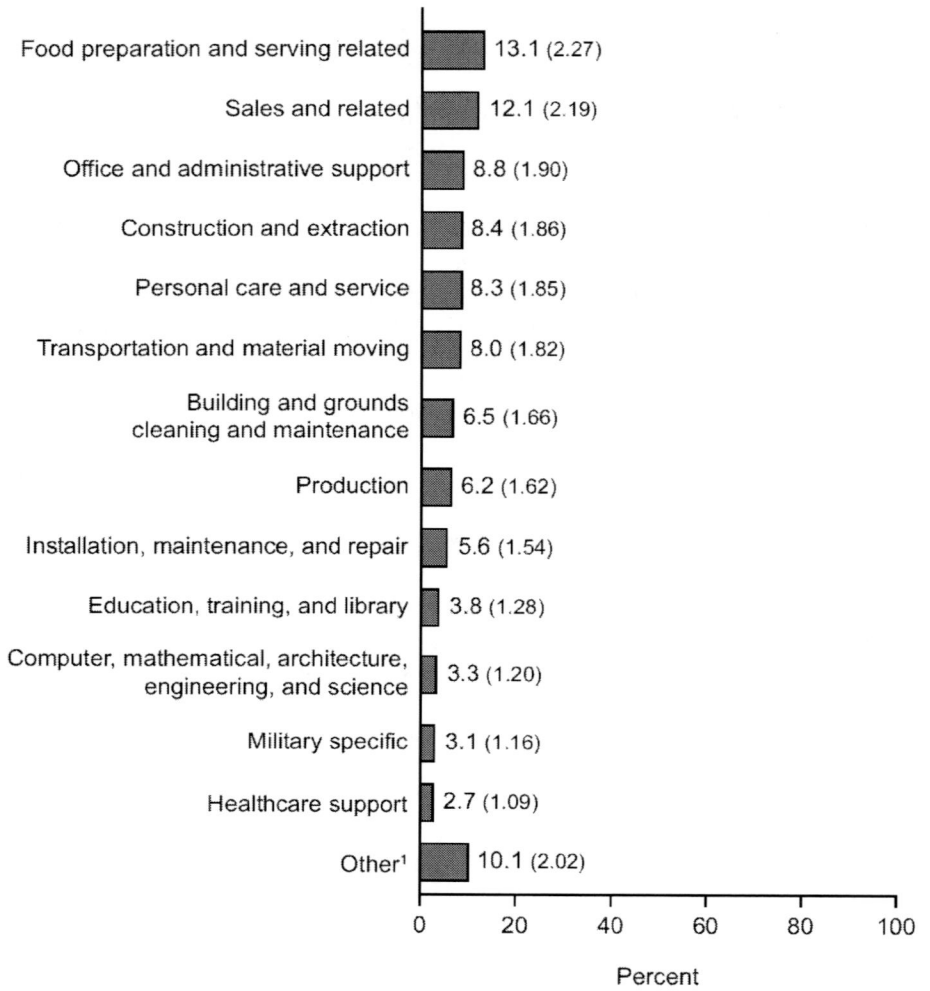

Food preparation and serving related   13.1 (2.27)
Sales and related   12.1 (2.19)
Office and administrative support   8.8 (1.90)
Construction and extraction   8.4 (1.86)
Personal care and service   8.3 (1.85)
Transportation and material moving   8.0 (1.82)
Building and grounds cleaning and maintenance   6.5 (1.66)
Production   6.2 (1.62)
Installation, maintenance, and repair   5.6 (1.54)
Education, training, and library   3.8 (1.28)
Computer, mathematical, architecture, engineering, and science   3.3 (1.20)
Military specific   3.1 (1.16)
Healthcare support   2.7 (1.09)
Other[1]   10.1 (2.02)

Percent

[1] Job categories held by fewer than 2.7 percent of youth with disabilities were combined into the "other" category. A large number of job categories had small numbers of respondents and were collapsed into this category.

Note: Standard errors are in parentheses. Job characteristics are reported for the current or most recent job of young adults with disabilities out of high school up to 8 years. NLTS2 percentages are weighted population estimates based on a sample of approximately 2,660 young adults with disabilities.

Source: U.S. Department of Education, Institute of Education Sciences, National Center for Special Education Research, National Longitudinal Transition Study-2 (NLTS2), Wave 5 parent interview and youth interview/survey, 2009.

Figure 21. Type of employment of young adults with disabilities.

Table 27. Type of employment of young adults, by disability category

	Learning disability	Speech/ language impairment	Mental retardation	Emotional disturbance	Hearing impairment	Visual impairment	Orthopedic impairment	Other health impairment	Autism	Traumatic brain injury	Multiple disabilities	Deaf-blindness
	Percent											
Percentage whose current or most recent job was:												
Food preparation and serving related	10.8 (3.06)	10.5 (2.86)	25.1 (4.95)	18.2 (4.32)	16.3 (4.90)	14.7 (5.11)	11.1 (4.38)	13.0 (3.45)	12.8 (4.85)	6.5 (4.95)	9.5 (5.11)	0.0 (0.00)
Sales and related occupations	13.6 (3.37)	12.3 (3.07)	5.3 (2.56)	9.0 (3.20)	16.0 (4.86)	8.9 (4.11)	19.7 (5.55)	10.8 (3.18)	7.5 (3.82)	12.6 (6.66)	5.5 (3.97)	7.3 (5.76)
Office and administrative Support	7.4 (2.58)	10.3 (2.84)	11.2 (3.60)	7.7 (2.98)	12.8 (4.43)	23.2 (6.09)	20.9 (5.67)	17.7 (3.91)	19.1 (5.70)	8.0 (5.45)	12.8 (5.82)	20.9 (9.00)
Construction and extraction	9.4 (2.87)	4.3 (1.89)	2.1 (1.64)	11.3 (3.54)	6.6 (3.29)	2.7 (2.34)	1.9 (1.90)	7.4 (2.68)	0.0 (0.00)	4.7 (4.25)	1.5 (2.12)	0.0 (0.00)
Personal care and service	9.6 (2.90)	8.2 (2.56)	2.8 (1.88)	7.9 (3.02)	4.9 (2.86)	6.5 (3.56)	7.3 (3.63)	4.8 (2.19)	2.4 (2.22)	1.4 (2.36)	6.4 (4.26)	9.7 (6.55)
Transportation and material moving	8.4 (2.73)	8.5 (2.60)	9.4 (3.33)	4.3 (2.27)	4.6 (2.78)	4.1 (2.86)	2.4 (2.13)	9.5 (3.01)	14.6 (5.08)	13.1 (6.73)	7.4 (4.56)	8.9 (5.31)
Building and grounds cleaning and maintenance	4.9 (2.12)	3.7 (1.76)	14.3 (3.99)	9.3 (3.25)	3.5 (2.43)	5.8 (3.37)	4.3 (2.83)	7.3 (2.67)	10.8 (4.50)	14.2 (7.01)	23.7 (7.40)	0.0 (0.00)
Production	4.3 (2.00)	4.7 (1.98)	19.0 (4.47)	7.1 (2.87)	6.1 (3.17)	6.2 (3.48)	7.8 (3.74)	3.4 (1.86)	11.5 (4.63)	5.4 (4.54)	23.8 (7.42)	25.8 (9.69)
Installation, maintenance, and repair	6.0 (2.34)	6.3 (2.27)	1.1 (1.19)	7.6 (2.97)	3.4 (2.40)	0.7 (1.20)	0.8 (1.24)	6.5 (2.53)	4.3 (2.94)	2.5 (3.14)	0.8 (1.55)	4.0 (4.34)
Education, training, and Library	4.2 (1.97)	5.5 (2.13)	2.5 (1.78)	3.2 (1.97)	5.0 (2.89)	5.3 (3.23)	4.2 (2.80)	1.5 (1.25)	1.9 (1.98)	8.5 (5.60)	1.4 (2.05)	6.4 (5.42)
Computer, mathematical, architecture, engineering, and science	4.5 (2.04)	2.3 (1.40)	#	0.5 (0.79)	5.8 (3.10)	3.0 (2.46)	3.0 (2.38)	1.0 (1.02)	3.8 (2.77)	1.8 (2.67)	#	2.4 (3.39)
Military specific	3.5 (1.81)	1.3 (1.06)	0.0 (0.00)	4.1 (2.22)	0.0 (0.00)	0.0 (0.00)	5.1 (3.07)	3.5 (1.88)	4.5 (3.01)	13.4 (6.84)	0.3 (0.95)	

Table 27. (Continued)

	Learning disability	Speech/ language impairment	Mental retardation	Emotional disturbance	Hearing impairment	Visual impairment	Orthopedic impairment	Other health impairment	Autism	Traumatic brain injury	Multiple disabilities	Deaf-blindness
	Percent											
Healthcare support	2.7 (1.60)	6.2 (2.25)	1.3 (1.29)	2.2 (1.64)	3.6 (2.47)	1.9 (1.97)	0.7 (1.16)	3.1 (1.78)	0.0 (0.00)	5.1 (4.42)	0.1 (0.55)	0.0 (0.00)
Other[1]	10.7 (3.04)	16.0 (3.42)	5.9 (2.69)	7.4 (2.93)	11.4 (4.21)	17.1 (5.43)	10.9 (4.35)	10.6 (3.16)	6.4 (3.55)	2.6 (3.20)	6.8 (4.38)	14.5 (7.80)

\# Rounds to zero.

‡ Fewer than three respondents in the cell.

[1] Job categories held by fewer than 2.7 percent of all youth with disabilities were combined into the "other" category. A large number of job categories had small numbers of respondents and were collapsed into this category.

Note: Standard errors are in parentheses. Job characteristics are reported for the current or most recent job of young adults with disabilities out of high school up to 8 years. NLTS2 percentages are weighted population estimates based on a sample of approximately 2,660 young adults with disabilities.

Source: U.S. Department of Education, Institute of Education Sciences, National Center for Special Education Research, National Longitudinal Transition Study-2 (NLTS2), Wave 5 parent interview and youth interview/survey, 2009.

**Table 28. Type of employment of young adults with disabilities,
by years since leaving high school**

	Less than 3 years	3 up to 5 years	5 up to 8 years
	Percent		
Percentage whose current or most recent job was:			
Food preparation and serving related	21.8 (6.92)	10.6 (3.57)	12.8 (3.11)
Sales and related occupations	13.9 (5.80)	11.4 (3.69)	12.2 (3.05)
Office and administrative support	12.5 (5.54)	11.0 (3.63)	6.3 (2.26)
Construction and extraction	8.3 (4.62)	6.1 (2.78)	10.1 (2.80)
Personal care and service	10.4 (5.11)	12.5 (3.84)	4.7 (1.97)
Transportation and material moving	4.1 (3.32)	9.3 (3.37)	7.9 (2.51)
Building and grounds cleaning and maintenance	5.2 (3.72)	7.7 (3.10)	5.9 (2.19)
Production	12.4 (5.52)	4.6 (2.43)	6.0 (2.21)
Installation, maintenance, and repair	3.1 (2.90)	4.2 (2.33)	7.3 (2.42)
Education, training, and library	0.6 (1.29)	2.7 (1.88)	5.4 (2.10)
Computer, mathematical, architecture, engineering, and science	0.5 (1.18)	2.5 (1.81)	4.6 (1.95)
Military specific	0.7 (1.40)	2.9 (1.95)	3.9 (1.80)
Healthcare support	1.9 (2.29)	2.7 (1.88)	2.9 (1.56)
Other[1]	4.7 (3.55)	11.8 (3.75)	10.1 (2.80)

[1] Job categories held by fewer than 2.7 percent of all youth with disabilities were combined into the "other" category. A large number of job categories had small numbers of respondents and consequently were collapsed into this category.

Note: Standard errors are in parentheses. Job characteristics are reported for the current or most recent job of young adults with disabilities out of high school up to 8 years. NLTS2 percentages are weighted population estimates based on a sample of approximately 2,660 young adults with disabilities.

Source: U.S. Department of Education, Institute of Education Sciences, National Center for Special Education Research, National Longitudinal Transition Study-2 (NLTS2), Wave 5 parent interview and youth interview/survey, 2009.

Demographic Differences in Types of Jobs

There were no significant differences among young adults with disabilities who differed in parents' adults'ty regarding the types of jobs heldhousehold income or young (table 30); however, some gender differences were apparent.Personal care and services occupations were more likely to be held by young women with disabilities than young men (20 percent vs. 2 percent, $p < .001$). Young men with disabilities were more likely to be employed in installation, maintenance and repair occupations (8 percent) than young women (less than 1 percent $p < .01$).

Table 29. Type of employment of young adults with disabilities, by highest level of educational attainment

Percentage whose current or most recent job was:	High school non-completer	High school completer	Some post-secondary school	Post-secondary school completion
	Percent			
Food preparation and serving related	10.4 (6.78)	13.5 (3.64)	12.4 4.09)	13.9 (4.80)
Sales and related occupations	13.6 (7.61)	10.5 (3.27)	15.7 (4.52)	9.4 (4.05)
Office and administrative support	7.8 (5.95)	8.8 (3.02)	8.7 (3.50)	9.1 (3.99)
Construction and extraction	10.9 (6.92)	11.4 (3.39)	9.7 (3.67)	2.3 (2.08)
Personal care and service	4.5 (4.60)	5.9 (2.51)	15.9 (4.54)	3.8 (2.66)
Transportation and material moving	13.7 (7.64)	10.3 (3.24)	7.6 (3.29)	4.0 (2.72)
Building and grounds cleaning and maintenance	23.2 (9.37)	6.5 (2.63)	7.1 (3.19)	2.1 (1.99)
Production	1.7 (2.87)	10.9 (3.32)	5.8 (2.90)	1.5 (1.69)
Installation, maintenance, and repair	7.6 (5.88)	7.5 (2.81)	2.2 (1.82)	6.7 (3.47)
Education, training, and library	1.5 (2.70)	0.6 (0.82)	1.4 (1.46)	11.4 (4.41)
Computer, mathematical, architecture, engineering, and science	#	0.1 (0.34)	3.0 (2.12)	8.7 (3.91)
Military specific	0.0 (0.00)	4.0 (2.09)	0.7 (1.03)	5.5 (3.17)

	High school non-completer	High school completer	Some post-secondary school	Post-secondary school completion
	Percent			
Healthcare support	0.6 (1.71)	2.0 (1.49)	0.8 (1.11)	6.2 (3.35)
Other[1]	4.7 (4.70)	8.0 (2.89)	8.9 (3.53)	15.5 (5.03)

\# Rounds to zero.

[1] Job categories held by fewer than 2.7 percent of all youth with disabilities were combined into the "other" category. A large number of job categories had small numbers of respondents and consequently were collapsed into this category.

Note: Standard errors are in parentheses. Job characteristics are reported for the current or most recent job of young adults with disabilities out of high school up to 8 years. NLTS2 percentages are weighted population estimates based on a sample of approximately 2,660 young adults with disabilities.

Source: U.S. Department of Education, Institute of Education Sciences, National Center for Special Education Research, National Longitudinal Transition Study-2 (NLTS2), Wave 5 parent interview and youth interview/survey, 2009.

Table 30. Type of employment of young adults with disabilities, by parents' household income and young adults' race/ethnicity and gender

	$25,000 or less	$25,001 to $50,000	More than $50,000	White	African American	Hispanic	Male	Female
	Percent							
Percentage whose current or most recent job was:								
Food preparation and serving related	13.5 (4.30)	11.5 (4.34)	13.1 (3.27)	12.7 (2.67)	10.5 (4.91)	15.0 (7.41)	13.1 (2.73)	13.0 (4.03)
Sales and related occupations	9.2 (3.64)	18.0 (5.22)	11.0 (3.03)	12.4 (2.64)	10.1 (4.82)	15.3 (7.47)	8.8 (2.29)	18.1 (4.61)
Office and admini-strative support	9.5 (3.69)	7.3 (3.54)	9.6 (2.85)	7.4 (2.10)	11.4 (5.09)	14.1 (7.22)	5.5 (1.84)	14.8 (4.25)
Construction and extraction	11.4 (4.00)	10.3 (4.13)	4.2 (1.94)	8.8 (2.27)	5.6 (3.68)	11.1 (6.52)	12.9 (2.71)	‡
Personal care and service	6.1 (3.01)	14.3 (4.76)	6.5 (2.39)	6.6 (1.99)	16.1 (5.88)	6.6 (5.15)	1.9 (1.10)	20.1 (4.80)
Transportation and material moving	9.4 (3.67)	8.9 (3.87)	6.9 (2.45)	9.1 (2.31)	5.3 (3.59)	5.8 (4.85)	10.7 (2.50)	2.9 (2.01)
Building and grounds cleaning and maintenance	9.0 (3.60)	3.8 (2.60)	6.8 (2.44)	4.1 (1.59)	11.5 (5.11)	8.8 (5.88)	8.3 (2.23)	3.2 (2.11)
Production	7.5 (3.31)	5.1 (2.99)	6.3 (2.35)	7.6 (2.13)	4.5 (3.32)	1.6 (2.60)	7.0 (2.06)	4.8 (2.56)

Table 30. (Continued)

	$25,000 or less	$25,001 to $50,000	More than $50,000	White	African American	Hispanic	Male	Female
	Percent							
Installation, maintenance, and repair	6.7 (3.15)	5.1 (2.99)	5.5 (2.21)	7.6 (2.13)	1.6 (2.01)	1.4 (2.44)	8.4 (2.24)	0.6 (0.92)
Education, training, and library	2.5 (1.96)	0.9 (1.28)	6.8 (2.44)	2.8 (1.32)	9.6 (4.71)	2.0 (2.91)	0.7 (0.67)	9.5 (3.51)
Computer, mathematical, architecture, engine-ering, and science	0.8 (1.12)	5.4 (3.07)	4.0 (1.90)	3.2 (1.41)	2.7 (2.59)	5.6 (4.77)	4.8 (1.73)	0.5 (0.84)
Military specific	3.6 (2.34)	1.6 (1.71)	3.9 (1.87)	2.9 (1.35)	2.3 (2.40)	4.0 (4.07)	4.8 (1.73)	‡
Healthcare support	2.3 (1.88)	1.9 (1.86)	1.4 (1.14)	2.8 (1.32)	2.3 (2.40)	2.9 (3.48)	0.5 (0.57)	6.7 (2.99)
Other[1]	8.6 (3.53)	5.9 (3.20)	14.1 (3.37)	12.0 (2.61)	6.6 (3.97)	5.7 (4.81)	12.5 (2.67)	5.6 (2.75)

‡ Fewer than three respondents in the cell.

[1] Job categories held by fewer than 2.7 percent of all youth with disabilities were combined into the "other" category. A large number of job categories had small numbers of respondents and consequently were collapsed into this category.

Note: Standard errors are in parentheses. Job characteristics are reported for the current or most recent job of young adults with disabilities out of high school up to 8 years. NLTS2 percentages are weighted population estimates based on a sample of approximately 2,660 young adults with disabilities.

Source: U.S. Department of Education, Institute of Education Sciences, National Center for Special Education Research, National Longitudinal Transition Study-2 (NLTS2), Wave 5 parent interview and youth interview/survey, 2009.

Hours Worked per Week

About two-thirds of young adults with disabilities (67 percent) worked full time (35 or more hours per week) at the job they held at the time of the interview or at their most recent job[61] (figure 22).

The percentage of young adults with disabilities who worked part time ranged from 16 percent who worked 21 to 34 hours per week to 3 percent who worked 5 or fewer hours per week. On average, young adults with disabilities worked 36 hours per week, which did not differ significantly from similarly aged young adults in the general population, who worked an average of 37 hours per week. Half of young adults with disabilities who worked part time reportedly wanted to do so, whereas the other half who worked part time reported that they would prefer to work full time.[62]

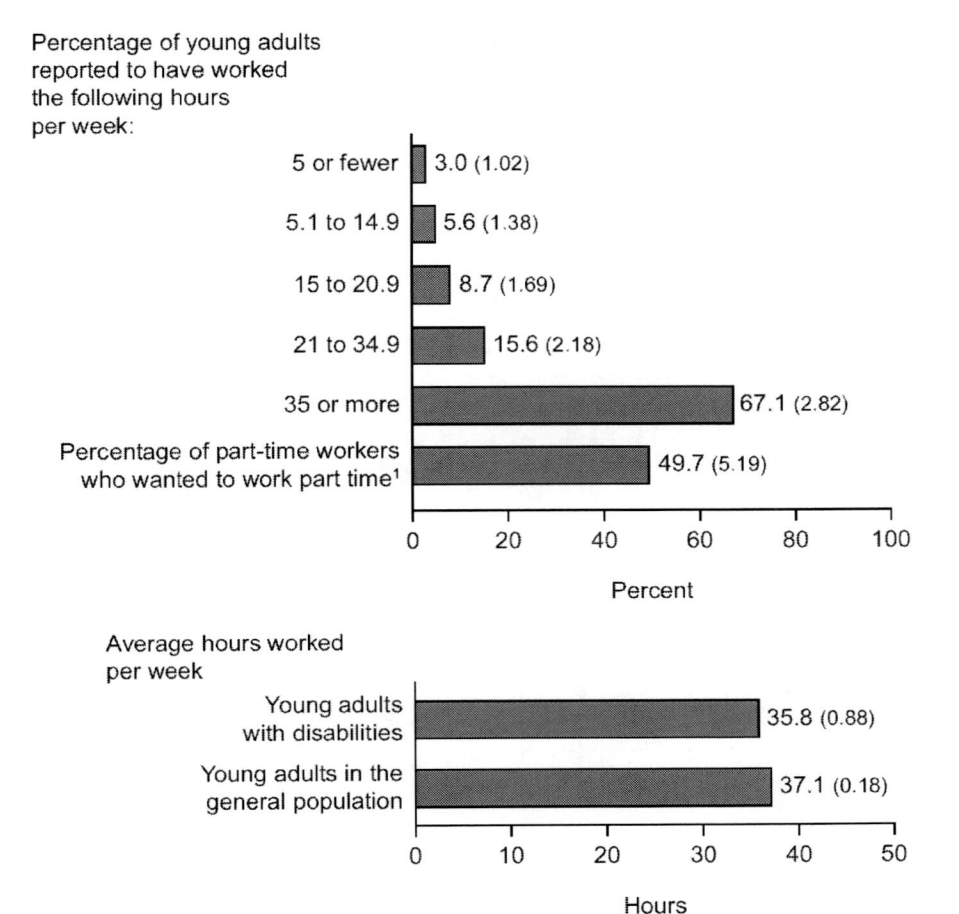

Percentage of young adults reported to have worked the following hours per week:

Hours	Percent
5 or fewer	3.0 (1.02)
5.1 to 14.9	5.6 (1.38)
15 to 20.9	8.7 (1.69)
21 to 34.9	15.6 (2.18)
35 or more	67.1 (2.82)
Percentage of part-time workers who wanted to work part time[1]	49.7 (5.19)

Average hours worked per week

Group	Hours
Young adults with disabilities	35.8 (0.88)
Young adults in the general population	37.1 (0.18)

[1] For young adults with disabilities working part time (less than 35 hours per week) at current or most recent job.

Note: Standard errors are in parentheses. Job characteristics are reported for the current or most recent job of young adults with disabilities out of high school up to 8 years. NLTS2 percentages are weighted population estimates based on samples of approximately 3,470 young adults with disabilities for hours worked per week and 1,300 young adults with disabilities for wanting to work part time.

Source: U.S. Department of Education, Institute of Education Sciences, National Center for Special Education Research, National Longitudinal Transition Study-2 (NLTS2), Wave 5 parent interview and youth interview/survey, 2009; U.S. Department of Labor, Bureau of Labor Statistics, National Longitudinal Survey of Youth 1997 (NLSY97), round 9 youth questionnaire, 2005. Data are for 21- to 25-year-olds.

Figure 22. Hours worked by young adults with disabilities and young adults in the general population.

Table 31. Hours worked by young adults, by disability category

	Learning disability	Speech/language impairment	Mental retardation	Emotional disturbance	Hearing impairment	Visual impairment	Orthopedic impairment	Other health impairment	Autism	Traumatic brain injury	Multiple disabilities	Deaf-blindness
Average hours worked per week	37.7 (1.23)	34.2 (1.12)	27.6 (1.34)	35.6 (1.58)	31.3 (1.47)	31.5 (2.06)	26.8 (1.76)	35.0 (1.26)	24.1 (2.07)	35.5 (3.18)	24.8 (2.02)	24.7 (2.77)
Percentage of part-time workers who wanted to work part time[1]	48.7 (8.92)	46.3 (7.64)	49.2 (7.24)	49.7 (10.32)	64.1 (7.81)	53.1 (9.52)	52.5 (8.13)	56.5 (8.07)	47.7 (8.27)	29.3 (13.03)	57.6 (8.67)	‡

‡ Responses for items with fewer than 30 respondents are not reported.

[1]For young adults with disabilities working part time (less than 35 hours per week) at current or most recent job.

Note: Standard errors are in parentheses. Job characteristics are reported for the current or most recent job of young adults with disabilities out of high school up to 8 years. NLTS2 percentages are weighted population estimates based on samples of approximately 3,470 young adults with disabilities for hours worked per week and 1,300 young adults with disabilities for wanting to work part time.

Source: U.S. Department of Education, Institute of Education Sciences, National Center for Special Education Research, National Longitudinal Transition Study-2 (NLTS2), Wave 5 parent interview and youth interview/survey, 2009.

**Table 32. Hours worked by young adults with disabilities,
by years since leaving high school**

	Less than 3 years	3 up to 5 years	5 up to 8 years
Average hours worked per week	30.7 (2.19)	37.6 (1.68)	35.6 (1.08)
Percentage of part-time workers who wanted to work part time[1]	46.7 (11.29)	48.1 (9.19)	51.9 (7.52)

[1] For young adults with disabilities working part time (less than 35 hours per week) at current or most recent job.

Note: Standard errors are in parentheses. Job characteristics are reported for the current or most recent job of young adults with disabilities out of high school up to 8 years. NLTS2 percentages are weighted population estimates based on samples of approximately 3,470 young adults with disabilities for hours worked per week and 1,300 young adults with disabilities for wanting to work part time.

Source: U.S. Department of Education, Institute of Education Sciences, National Center for Special Education Research, National Longitudinal Transition Study-2 (NLTS2), Wave 5 parent interview and youth interview/survey, 2009.

Disability Differences in Hours Worked

Young adults in several disability categories, including learning disabilities, emotional disturbances, speech/language or other health impairments, or traumatic brain injuries worked more hours per week on average (34 to 38 hours per week) than did those with autism, deaf-blindness, multiple disabilities, orthopedic impairments, or mental retardation (24 to 28 hours per week, all comparisons $p < .001$ except $p < .01$ comparing young adults with speech/language impairments and those with deaf-blindness; table 31). Young adults with learning disabilities also worked more hours (38 hours on average) than young adults with hearing impairments or visual impairments (31 hours, $p < .001$ compared with young adults with hearing impairments and $p < .01$ compared with those with visual impairments). In addition, young adults with hearing impairments worked more hours per week (31 hours) on average than those with autism (24 hours) or multiple disabilities (25 hours, $p < .01$ for both comparisons), and those with traumatic brain injury worked more hours (35 hours) than those with autism, deaf-blindness, or multiple disabilities (24 to 25 hours, $p < .01$ for all comparisons).

Differences in Hours Worked by Years since Leaving High School

There were no significant differences in hours worked by young adults with disabilities based on the number of years since leaving high school. The average number of hours worked per week ranged from 31 hours for those out of high school for less than 3 years to 38 hours for those out of high school 3 to 5 years (table 32). In addition, the percentage of young adults with disabilities working part time who wanted to work part time did not significantly differ by the number of years since leaving high school.

**Table 33. Hours worked by young adults with disabilities,
by highest level of educational attainment**

	High school non-completer	High school completer	Some post-secondary school	Post-secondary school completion
Average hours worked per week	33.6 (2.74)	36.8 (1.44)	34.2 (1.48)	37.0 (1.95)
Percentage of part-time workers who wanted to work part time[1]	60.4 (19.55)	42.6 (6.47)	49.0 (10.20)	57.2 (10.64)

[1]For young adults with disabilities working part time (less than 35 hours per week) at current or most recent job.

Note: Standard errors are in parentheses. Job characteristics are reported for the current or most recent job of young adults with disabilities out of high school up to 8 years. NLTS2 percentages are weighted population estimates based on samples of approximately 3,470 young adults with disabilities for hours worked per week and 1,300 young adults with disabilities for wanting to work part time.

Source: U.S. Department of Education, Institute of Education Sciences, National Center for Special Education Research, National Longitudinal Transition Study-2 (NLTS2), Wave 5 parent interview and youth interview/survey, 2009.

**Table 34. Hours worked by young adults with disabilities,
by parents' household income and young adults' race/ethnicity and gender**

	$25,000 or less	$25,001 to $50,000	More than $50,000	White	African American	Hispanic	Male	Female
Average hours worked per week	34.3 (1.70)	37.8 (1.81)	35.6 (1.22)	37.0 (1.01)	32.0 (1.84)	34.3 (3.38)	38.1 (1.04)	31.5 (1.51)
Percentage of part-time workers who wanted to work part time[1]	44.7 (8.61)	39.4 (11.59)	58.8 (7.34)	49.9 (6.31)	48.2 (11.51)	51.6 (15.57)	47.4 (6.82)	52.3 (7.90)

[1]For young adults with disabilities working part time (less than 35 hours per week) at current or most recent job.

Note: Standard errors are in parentheses. Job characteristics are reported for the current or most recent job of young adults with disabilities out of high school up to 8 years. NLTS2 percentages are weighted population estimates based on samples of approximately 3,470 young adults with disabilities for hours worked per week and 1,300 young adults with disabilities for wanting to work part time.

Source: U.S. Department of Education, Institute of Education Sciences, National Center for Special Education Research, National Longitudinal Transition Study-2 (NLTS2), Wave 5 parent interview and youth interview/survey, 2009.

Differences in Hours Worked by Highest Level of Educational Attainment

The number of hours worked by young adults with disabilities did not significantly differ by their highest level of educational attainment (table 33). The average number of hours worked per week ranged from 34 hours for those with less than a high school education to 37 hours for those who completed a postsecondary education program. In addition, the percentage of young adults with disabilities working part time who wanted to work part time did not significantly differ by the highest level of educational attainment.

Demographic Differences in Hours Worked

Although no significant differences related to parents' household income or young adults' race/ethnicity were noted for the hours worked by young adults with disabilities, there were significant gender differences (table 34). Young men with disabilities worked on average 38 hours per week, whereas young women worked 32 hours per week ($p < .001$).

Wages and Benefits

Employed young adults with disabilities who had been out of high school for up to 8 years earned an average of $10.40 per hour[63] at the time of the interview (figure 23), a significant difference from the average hourly wage of young adults in the general population ($11.40, $p < .01$). Although 13 percent of young adults with disabilities were paid less than the federal minimum wage ($6.55 in 2008), the majority (72 percent) earned more than $8.00 per hour, and 50 percent earned more than $9.00 per hour.

The average hourly wage of young adults with disabilities who were employed full time was significantly higher than that of those working part time ($11.10 vs. $9.00, $p < .01$; figure 24). Young adults with disabilities who worked full time were significantly more likely than young adults with disabilities who worked part time to earn wages ranging from $10.01 to $15.00 per hour (28 percent vs. 13 percent, $p < .01$). In addition, those who worked part time were significantly more likely than full-time workers to earn less than $6.55 per hour (21 percent vs. 8 percent, $p < .01$).

Paid vacation or sick leave, health insurance, and a retirement plan are benefits that may be provided by employers. Figure 25 presents the percentage of young adults with disabilities who received each of these types of benefits at their current or most recent job[64] and compares them with peers in the general population; no significant differences are noted.[65] For example, 55 percent of young adults with disabilities and 57 percent of young adults in the general population received paid vacation or sick leave. Forty-eight percent of young adults with disabilities received health insurance from their employer, and 56 percent of young adults in the general population did so. The same percentage of young adults in the two groups received retirement benefits (39 percent).

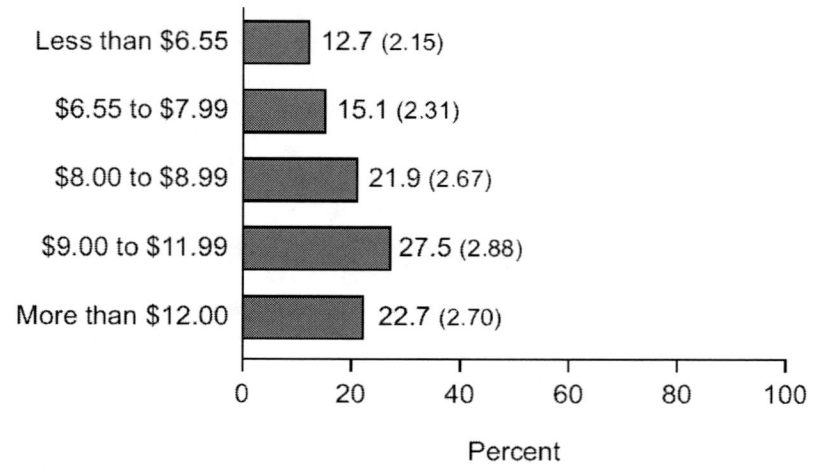

Percentage of young adults
with disabilities reported
to have earned an hourly
wage of:

Less than $6.55 — 12.7 (2.15)
$6.55 to $7.99 — 15.1 (2.31)
$8.00 to $8.99 — 21.9 (2.67)
$9.00 to $11.99 — 27.5 (2.88)
More than $12.00 — 22.7 (2.70)

Percent

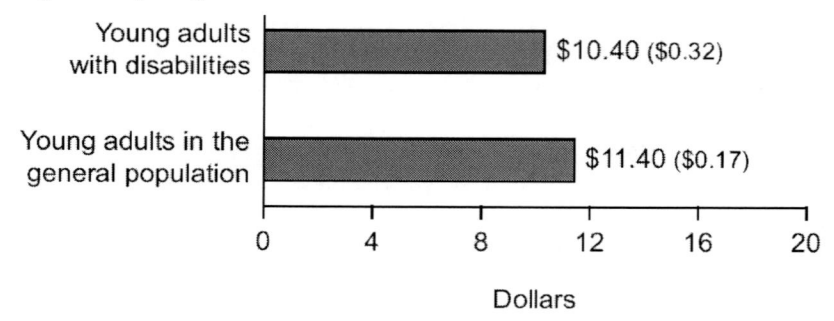

Average hourly wage:[1]

Young adults
with disabilities — $10.40 ($0.32)

Young adults in the
general population — $11.40 ($0.17)

Dollars

[1] Rounded to nearest $0.10.

Note: Standard errors are in parentheses. Job characteristics are reported for young adults with disabilities out of high school up to 8 years for young adult's rcentages are weighted population estimates based on a sample ofcurrent or most recent job. NLTS2 pe approximately 3,050 young adults with disabilities.

Source: U.S. Department of Education, Institute of Education Sciences, National Center for Special Education Research, National Longitudinal Transition Study-2 (NLTS2), Wave 5 parent interview and youth interview/survey, 2009. U.S. Census Bureau, Current Population Survey (CPS), May 2009. Data are for 21- to 25-year-olds.

Figure 23. Wages of young adults with disabilities and young adults in the general population.

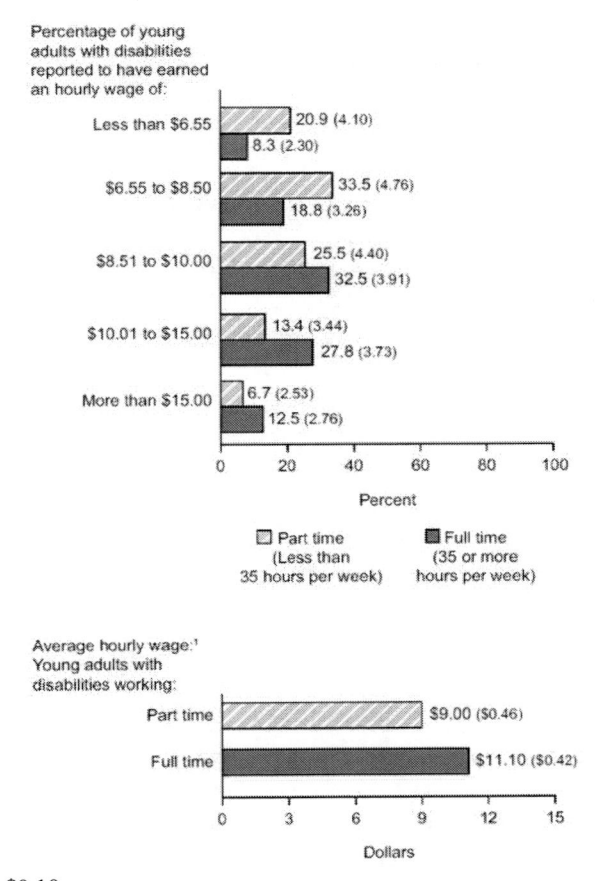

Percentage of young adults with disabilities reported to have earned an hourly wage of:

Wage	Part time	Full time
Less than $6.55	20.9 (4.10)	8.3 (2.30)
$6.55 to $8.50	33.5 (4.76)	18.8 (3.26)
$8.51 to $10.00	25.5 (4.40)	32.5 (3.91)
$10.01 to $15.00	13.4 (3.44)	27.8 (3.73)
More than $15.00	6.7 (2.53)	12.5 (2.76)

Percent

☐ Part time (Less than 35 hours per week)   ■ Full time (35 or more hours per week)

Average hourly wage:[1] Young adults with disabilities working:

Part time	$9.00 ($0.46)
Full time	$11.10 ($0.42)

Dollars

[1] Rounded to nearest $0.10.

Note: Standard errors are in parentheses. Job characteristics are reported for the current or most recent job of young adults with disabilities out of high school up to 8 years. NLTS2 percentages are weighted population estimates based on a sample of approximately 3,030 young adults with disabilities.

Source: U.S. Department of Education, Institute of Education Sciences, National Center for Special Education Research, National Longitudinal Transition Study-2 (NLTS2), Wave 5 parent interview and youth interview/survey, 2009.

Figure 24. Wages of young adults with disabilities, by part-time and full-time employment.

Young adults with disabilities who worked full time were significantly more likely than those who worked part time to receive any employment benefits (77 percent vs. 31 percent, $p < .001$; figure 26). More specifically, young adults with disabilities who worked full time were significantly more likely than part-time workers to receive paid vacation or sick leave (69 percent vs. 27 percent, $p < .001$), health insurance (63 percent vs. 17 percent, $p < .001$), or retirement benefits (50 percent vs. 17 percent, $p < .001$).

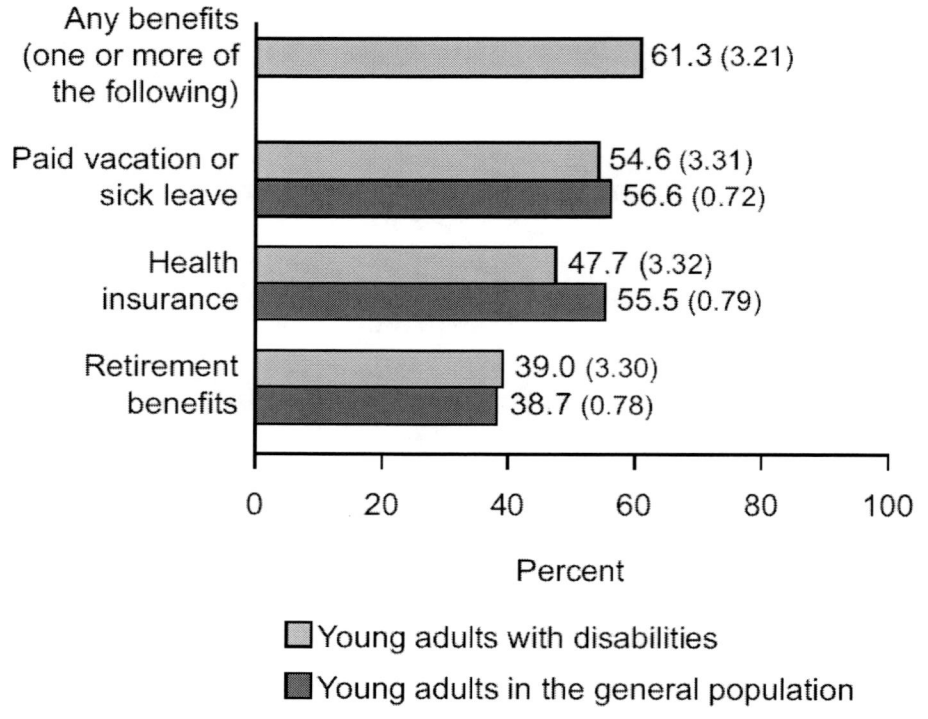

Note: Standard errors are in parentheses. Job characteristics are reported for the current or most recent job of young adults with disabilities out of high school up to 8 years. NLTS2 percentages are weighted population estimates based on a sample of approximately 2,670 young adults with disabilities. General population comparison data were not available for whether young adults received any benefits.

Source: U.S. Department of Education, Institute of Education Sciences, National Center for Special Education Research, National Longitudinal Transition Study-2 (NLTS2), Wave 5 parent interview and youth interview/survey, 2009. U.S. Department of Labor, Bureau of Labor Statistics, National Longitudinal Survey of Youth 1997 (NLSY97), round 9 youth questionnaire, 2005. Data are for 21- to 25-year-olds.

Figure 25. Benefits received by young adults with disabilities and young adults in the general population.

Disability Differences in Wages and Benefits

The hourly wage rate for young adults with disabilities ranged from $7.90 to $11.10 across disability categories (table 35). Young adults with learning disabilities; speech/language, hearing, visual, or other health impairments; or emotional disturbances ($10.50 to $11.10) earned more per hour than their peers with mental retardation ($7.90, $p <$ .001 for all comparisons except $p <$ .01 comparing young adults in the other health impairment vs. mental retardation categories). The only significant difference in the percentage of young adults receiving any benefits was between young adults with learning disabilities and those with orthopedic impairments (66 percent vs. 42 percent, $p <$ .01).

Table 35. Wages and benefits of young adults, by disability category

	Learning disability	Speech/ language impairment	Mental retardation	Emotional disturbance	Hearing impairment	Visual impairment	Orthopedic impairment	Other health impairment	Autism	Traumatic brain injury	Multiple disabilities	Deaf-blindness
Average hourly wage[1]	$10.60	$10.80	$7.90	$11.00	$10.50	$11.10	$9.10	$10.70	$9.20	$9.30	$8.80	$9.20
	(0.42)	(0.47)	(0.49)	(0.57)	(0.58)	(0.89)	(1.25)	(0.78)	(0.81)	(0.73)	(0.78)	(1.64)
Percentage reported having received:												
Any benefits (one or more of the following)	65.5	60.2	48.6	53.3	60.1	60.4	42.4	53.9	52.8	53.9	47.0	43.8
	(4.56)	(4.44)	(5.61)	(5.50)	(6.28)	(6.89)	(6.74)	(4.99)	(7.08)	(9.61)	(8.51)	(10.67)
Paid vacation or sick leave	59.3	50.9	42.6	44.9	49.6	52.1	38.9	45.3	47.4	46.8	42.4	43.8
	(4.72)	(4.59)	(5.64)	(5.58)	(6.46)	(7.14)	(6.84)	(5.02)	(7.20)	(9.88)	(8.52)	(10.67)
Health insurance	52.0	48.4	30.1	40.7	40.4	43.6	33.6	43.9	30.3	41.1	34.0	29.2
	(4.81)	(4.56)	(5.24)	(5.47)	(6.31)	(7.05)	(6.55)	(5.00)	(6.64)	(9.74)	(8.26)	(9.78)
Retirement benefits	42.1	43.5	27.5	29.4	41.5	34.7	32.0	36.9	26.6	38.8	35.0	31.5
	(4.85)	(4.59)	(5.19)	(5.18)	(6.43)	(6.75)	(6.59)	(4.89)	(6.02)	(10.01)	(8.22)	(9.99)

[1] Rounded to nearest $0.10.

Note: Standard errors are in parentheses. Job characteristics are reported for the current or most recent job of young adults with disabilities out of high school up to 8 years. NLTS2 percentages are weighted population estimates based on a sample of approximately 2,670 young adults with disabilities.

Source: U.S. Department of Education, Institute of Education Sciences, National Center for Special Education Research, National Longitudinal Transition Study-2 (NLTS2), Wave 5 parent interview and youth interview/survey, 2009.

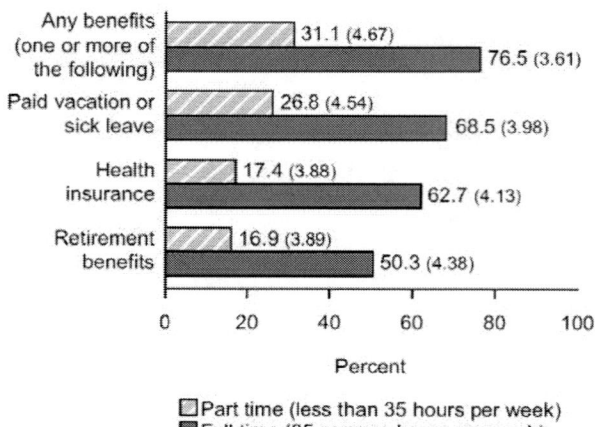

Note: Standard errors are in parentheses. Job characteristics are reported for the current or most recent job of young adults with disabilities out of high school up to 8 years. NLTS2 percentages are weighted population estimates based on a sample of approximately 2,670 young adults with disabilities.

Source: U.S. Department of Education, Institute of Education Sciences, National Center for Special Education Research, National Longitudinal Transition Study-2 (NLTS2), Wave 5 parent interview and youth interview/survey, 2009.

Figure 26. Benefits received by young adults with disabilities, by part-time and full-time employment.

Table 36. Wages and benefits of young adults with disabilities, by years since leaving high school

	Less than 3 years	3 up to 5 years	5 up to 8 years
Average hourly wage[1]	$9.40 (0.82)	$9.60 (0.50)	$11.10 (0.47)
Percentage reported having received:			
Any benefits (one or more of the following)	42.9 (8.15)	64.2 (5.49)	63.2 (4.37)
Paid vacation or sick leave	31.8 (7.76)	58.9 (5.69)	56.5 (4.54)
Health insurance	27.4 (7.41)	49.1 (5.78)	51.2 (4.56)
Retirement benefits	29.1 (7.65)	40.0 (5.74)	40.5 (4.60)

[1] Rounded to nearest $0.10.

Note: Standard errors are in parentheses. Job characteristics are reported for the current or most recent job of young adults with disabilities out of high school up to 8 years. NLTS2 percentages are weighted population estimates based on samples ranging from approximately 2,670 to 3,050 young adults with disabilities.

Source: U.S. Department of Education, Institute of Education Sciences, National Center for Special Education Research, National Longitudinal Transition Study-2 (NLTS2), Wave 5 parent interview and youth interview/survey, 2009.

Differences in Wages and Benefits by Years since Leaving High School

Young adults with disabilities who had been out of high school for different amounts of time had significantly different wages and benefits (table 36). Those who had been out of high school for more than 5 years were more likely to receive paid vacation or sick leave (57 percent vs. 32 percent, $p < .01$) and health insurance (51 percent vs. 27 percent, $p < .01$) than those who had been out of high school for less than 3 years.

Differences in Wages and Benefits by Highest Level of Educational Attainment

There were significant differences in the wages and benefits received by young adults with disabilities based on their highest level of education attained (table 37). Average hourly wages were significantly higher for young adults with disabilities who had completed postsecondary education than for those who had completed high school or who had some postsecondary education ($12.50 vs. $9.50 per hour, $12.50 per hour v. $9.80 per hour, $p <$ .01 for both comparisons). There were no significant differences in the percentage of young adults with disabilities of different educational levels in receiving any benefits, paid vacation or sick leave, retirement benefits, or health insurance.

Table 37. Wages and benefits of young adults with disabilities, by highest level of educational attainment

	High school non-completer	High school completer	Some post-secondary school	Post-secondary school completion
Average hourly wage[1]	$9.80 (1.05)	$9.50 (0.48)	$9.80 (0.49)	$12.50 (0.80)
Percentage reported having received:				
Any benefits (one or more of the following)	46.4 (10.54)	65.1 (4.98)	56.1 (6.06)	66.7 (6.47)
Paid vacation or sick leave	34.1 (10.23)	58.0 (5.23)	49.3 (6.18)	62.0 (6.67)
Health insurance	40.9 (10.52)	46.9 (5.27)	43.5 (6.11)	55.8 (6.83)
Retirement benefits	34.9 (10.15)	37.0 (5.18)	35.9 (6.10)	46.5 (6.93)

[1] Rounded to nearest $0.10.

Note: Standard errors are in parentheses. Job characteristics are reported for the current or most recent job of young adults with disabilities out of high school up to 8 years. NLTS2 percentages are weighted population estimates based on samples ranging from approximately 2,670 to 3,050 young adults with disabilities.

Source: U.S. Department of Education, Institute of Education Sciences, National Center for Special Education Research, National Longitudinal Transition Study-2 (NLTS2), Wave 5 parent interview and youth interview/survey, 2009.

Table 38. Wages and benefits of young adults with disabilities, by parents' household income and young adults' race/ethnicity and gender

	$25,000 or less	$25,001 to $50,000	More than $50,000	White	African American	Hispanic	Male	Female
Average hourly wage[1]	$9.00 (0.48)	$9.90 (0.61)	$11.60 (0.51)	$10.70 (0.40)	$10.10 (0.72)	$9.50 (0.72)	$10.90 (0.42)	$9.40 (0.48)
Percentage reported having received:								
Any bene-fits (one or more of the following)	54.6 (6.00)	62.6 (6.50)	64.8 (4.55)	61.8 (3.83)	55.8 (7.78)	61.1 (9.92)	64.2 (3.81)	56.0 (5.78)
Paid vacation or sick leave	50.7 (6.06)	57.0 (6.73)	56.5 (4.79)	55.7 (3.95)	51.1 (7.89)	52.3 (10.27)	55.5 (4.00)	53.1 (5.86)
Health insurance	39.8 (5.93)	51.6 (6.79)	51.1 (4.80)	49.3 (3.96)	36.8 (7.65)	48.9 (10.29)	52.0 (4.00)	39.9 (5.76)
Retirement benefits	30.9 (5.71)	40.1 (6.75)	42.6 (4.83)	38.6 (3.92)	34.4 (7.69)	42.5 (10.48)	43.4 (4.07)	30.9 (5.48)

[1] Rounded to nearest $0.10.

Note: Standard errors are in parentheses. Job characteristics are reported for the current or most recent job of young adults with disabilities out of high school up to 8 years. NLTS2 percentages are weighted population estimates based on samples ranging from approximately 2,670 to 3,050 young adults with disabilities.

Source: U.S. Department of Education, Institute of Education Sciences, National Center for Special Education Research, National Longitudinal Transition Study-2 (NLTS2), Wave 5 parent interview and youth interview/survey, 2009.

Demographic Differences in Wages and Benefits

No significant differences were noted in wages or benefits between young adults with disabilities who differed in their demographic characteristics (table 38). The lack of a significant difference in average hourly wage by gender also was apparent for general population peers, i.e., $12.10 vs. $10.70 for males and females in the general population[66] and $10.90 per hour and $9.40 per hour for male and female young adults with disabilities, respectively.

Job Accommodations

About 26 percent of young adults with disabilities reported that their employers were aware of their disabilities[67] (figure 27), and 7 percent reported that they received employment accommodations.[68] Job accommodations[69] included a range of individual adaptations involving materials or technology used on the job (e.g., large print or Braille, TTY or TTD, or modified work stations, 10 percent), scheduling accommodations (e.g., flexible work times, more or longer breaks, or more paid time off for medical needs; 39 percent), human aides (e.g., interpreters or job coaches, 41 percent), and adaptations to assignments and/or supervision (e.g., modifications to training or instructions or different expectations for productivity, 47 percent).

Disability Differences in Job Accommodations

There were variations in the percentage of young adults in different disability categories who reported that their employers were aware of their disability (table 39). Young adults with mental retardation; visual, hearing, or orthopedic impairments; autism; multiple disabilities; or deaf-blindness (60 percent to 75 percent) were significantly more likely to report that their employers were aware of their disability than young adults with learning disabilities, speech/language or other health impairments, emotional disturbances, or traumatic brain injuries (19 percent to 30 percent, $p < .001$ for all comparisons except $p < .01$ for hearing, impairments vs. traumatic brain injury).

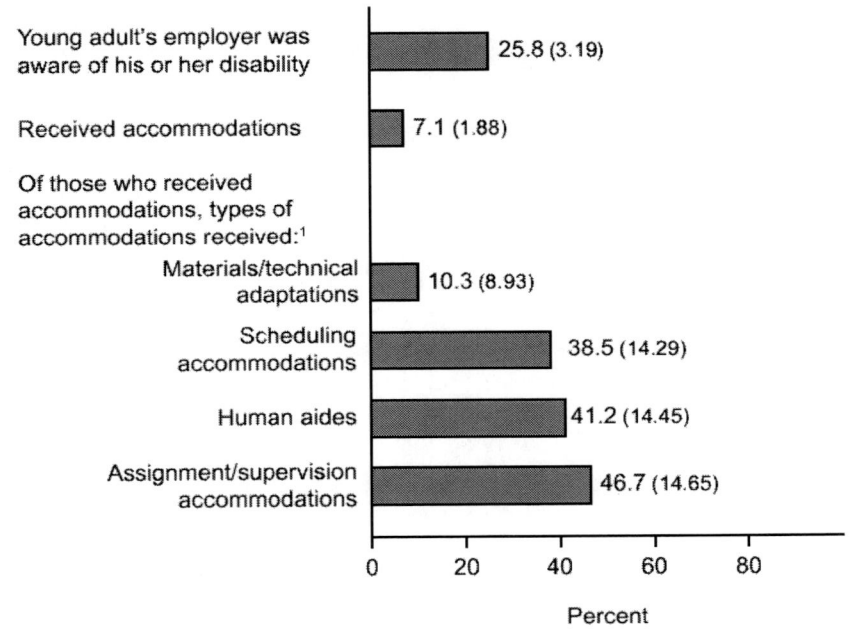

[1] Percentages do not sum to 100 because young adult with disabilities may have received more than one type of accommodation.

Note: Standard errors are in parentheses. Job characteristics are reported for the current or most recent job of young adults with disabilities out of high school up to 8 years. NLTS2 percentages are weighted population estimates based on samples of approximately 2,420 young adults with disabilities for employers' adult'sh awareness of disabilities for receiving accommodations, and 420 young adults with disabilities for type of accommodation received.

Source: U.S. Department of Education, Institute of Education Sciences, National Center for Special Education Research, National Longitudinal Transition Study-2 (NLTS2), Wave 5 parent interview and youth interview/survey, 2009.

Figure 27. Employers' awareness of young adults' disabilities and receipt of employment accommodations.

Table 39. Employers' awareness of young adults' disabilities and receipt of employment accommodations, by disability category

	Learning disability	Speech/language impairment	Mental retardation	Emotional disturbance	Hearing impairment	Visual impairment	Orthopedic impairment	Other health impairment	Autism	Traumatic brain injury	Multiple disabilities	Deaf-blindness
	Percent											
Percentage of employed young adults reported to have had:												
Their employers aware of their disability	18.6 (4.13)	22.5 (4.20)	59.8 (6.05)	24.3 (5.36)	63.9 (6.54)	74.9 (6.37)	67.9 (6.62)	29.9 (4.99)	73.1 (6.77)	30.0 (9.36)	72.1 (7.92)	75.2 (9.71)
Received accommodations	4.6 (2.22)	3.4 (1.84)	22.3 (5.24)	3.5 (2.30)	15.4 (4.99)	35.6 (7.10)	27.4 (6.39)	7.9 (2.93)	37.2 (7.53)	5.4 (4.62)	34.5 (8.46)	50.4 (11.24)

Note: Standard errors are in parentheses. Job characteristics are reported for the current or most recent job of young adults with disabilities out of high school up to 8 years. NLTS2 percentages are weighted population estimates based on samples ranging from approximately 2,390 to 2,400 young adults with disabilities.

Source: U.S. Department of Education, Institute of Education Sciences, National Center for Special Education Research, National Longitudinal Transition Study-2 (NLTS2), Wave 5 parent interview and youth interview/survey, 2009.

Table 40. Employers' awareness of young adults' disabilities and receipt of employment accommodations, by years since leaving high school

	Less than 3 years	3 up to 5 years	5 up to 8 years
	Percent		
Percentage of employed young adults reported to have had:			
Their employers aware of their disability	33.6 (8.69)	27.2 (5.60)	23.0 (4.22)
Received accommodations	15.2 (6.68)	4.7 (2.69)	7.0 (2.56)

Note: Standard errors are in parentheses. Job characteristics are reported for the current or most recent job of young adults with disabilities out of high school up to 8 years. NLTS2 percentages are weighted population estimates based on samples ranging from approximately 2,390 to 2,420 young adults with disabilities.

Source: U.S. Department of Education, Institute of Education Sciences, National Center for Special Education Research, National Longitudinal Transition Study-2 (NLTS2), Wave 5 parent interview and youth interview/survey, 2009.

Receipt of employment accommodations also significantly differed by disability category. Young adults with visual or orthopedic impairments, autism, multiple disabilities, or deaf-blindness (27 percent to 50 percent) were significantly more likely to receive accommodations than young adults with learning disabilities, speech/language or other health impairments, emotional disturbances, or traumatic brain injuries (3 percent to 8 percent, $p < .001$ for all comparisons except $p < .01$ for multiple disabilities vs. other health impairments and traumatic brain injuries). Young adults with deaf-blindness also were more likely to report receiving employment accommodations than those with hearing impairments (52 percent vs. 15 percent, $p < .01$). In addition, young adults with mental retardation (22 percent) were more likely to receive accommodations at work than young adults with learning disabilities, speech/language impairments, or emotional disturbances (22 percent vs. 3 percent to 5 percent, $p < .001$ for all comparisons except $p < .01$ for comparison with learning disabilities).

Differences in Job Accommodations by Years since Leaving High School

There were no significant differences in employers' awareness of young adults' disabilities based on years since leaving high school; percentages ranged from 23 percent to 34 percent (table 40). Similarly, differences in the receipt of accommodations, ranging from 5 percent to 15 percent, were not significant.

Differences in Job Accommodations by Highest Level of Educational Attainment

Employers' awareness of young adults having disabilities and their receipt of accommodations varied by level of educational attainment (table 41). Young adults with disabilities who had not completed high school were more likely to have employers who were aware of their disabilities than those who had completed a postsecondary education program (36 percent vs. 13 percent, p < .01). Young adults with disabilities whose highest education level was high school completion reported a significantly higher rate of being accommodated at work than their peers who had not completed high school or those who had completed a postsecondary education program (14 percent vs. 1 percent and 2 percent, respectively, p < .01 for both comparisons).

Table 41. Employers' awareness of young adults' disabilities and receipt of employment accommodations, by highest level of educational attainment

	High school non-completer	High school completer	Some post-secondary school	Post-secondary school completion
	Percent			
Percentage of employed young adults reported to have had:				
Their employers aware of their disability	22.5 (9.98)	36.2 (5.57)	26.0 (5.91)	13.3 (5.10)
Received accommodations	0.6 (1.85)	14.4 (4.10)	4.7 (2.88)	2.0 (2.11)

Note: Standard errors are in parentheses. Job characteristics are reported for the current or most recent job of young adults with disabilities out of high school up to 8 years. NLTS2 percentages are weighted population estimates based on samples ranging from approximately 2,390 to 2,420 young adults with disabilities.

Source: U.S. Department of Education, Institute of Education Sciences, National Center for Special Education Research, National Longitudinal Transition Study-2 (NLTS2), Wave 5 parent interview and youth interview/survey, 2009.

Table 42. Employers' awareness of young adults' disabilities and receipt of employment accommodations, by parents' household income and young adults' race/ethnicity and gender

	$25,000 or less	$25,001 to $50,000	More than $50,000	White	African American	Hispanic	Male	Female
	Percent							
Percentage of employed young adults reported to have had:								
Their employers aware of their disability	33.0 (6.43)	20.7 (6.07)	23.4 (4.39)	27.1 (3.80)	29.8 (8.21)	16.2 (8.87)	28.9 (3.92)	19.7 (5.33)
Received accommodations	9.2 (3.98)	5.2 (3.34)	5.5 (2.37)	7.5 (2.26)	3.4 (3.27)	10.6 (7.43)	7.9 (2.35)	5.4 (3.04)

Note: Standard errors are in parentheses. Job characteristics are reported for the current or most recent job of young adults with disabilities out of high school up to 8 years. NLTS2 percentages are weighted population estimates based on samples ranging from approximately 2,390 to 2,420 young adults.

Source: U.S. Department of Education, Institute of Education Sciences, National Center for Special Education Research, National Longitudinal Transition Study-2 (NLTS2), Wave 5 parent interview and youth interview/survey, 2009.

Demographic Differences in Job Accommodations

No significant differences in employers'areness of young adults'disabilities or their receipt of accommodations were found based on their demographic characteristics (table 42). Rates of employer awareness of disability ranged from 16 percent to 33 percent across categories, whereas rates of accommodation receipt ranged from 3 percent to 11 percent.

Perceptions of Working Conditions

The majority of young adults with disabilities had positive perceptions about their jobs.[70] In response to being asked whether they "usually like [their] job...very much, like it fairly well, not like it much, or not like it at all," 43percentresponded that they liked their job very much (figure 28), and an additional 45 percent responded that they liked their job fairly well, significantly more than the 8 percent who responded that they did not like their job much and the 4 percent who responded that they did not like their job at all ($p < .001$ for all comparisons). Most young adults (90 percent) also reported being "treated pretty well by others at [their] job."[71]

Seventy-three percent of young adults with disabilities reported that their education and training was being "put to good use," and 68 percent reported that they had "lots of chances to work [their] way up" (figure 29).[72] Sixty-two percent stated they were "pretty well paid" for their work. Indeed, for young adults who had been employed 6 months or more, 70 percent had "been promoted or taken on more responsibility" since they started the job, and 75 percent were "paid more than when [they] started the job."[73]

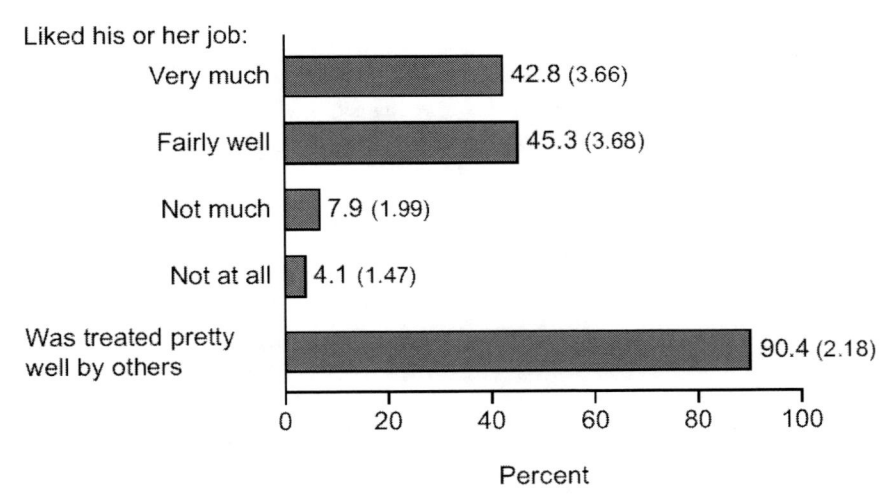

Note: Standard errors are in parentheses. Job characteristics are reported for the current or most recent job of young adults with disabilities out of high school up to 8 years. NLTS2 percentages are weighted population estimates based on samples ranging from approximately 2,170 to 2,190 young adults with disabilities.

Source: U.S. Department of Education, Institute of Education Sciences, National Center for Special Education Research, National Longitudinal Transition Study-2 (NLTS2), Wave 5 youth interview/survey, 2009.

Figure 28. Job satisfaction of young adults with disabilities.

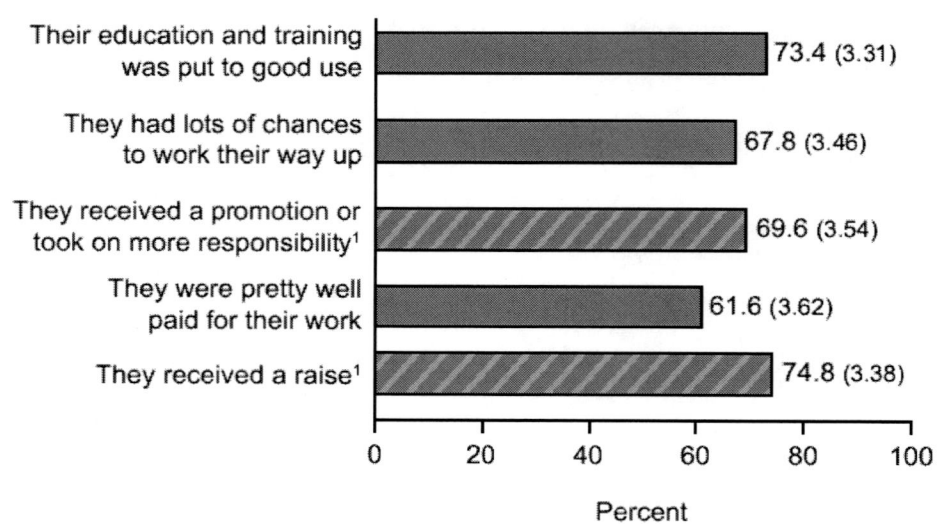

Percent

[1] For young adults with disabilities employed 6 months or more at the job they had at the time of the interview or their most recent job.

Note: Standard errors are in parentheses. Job characteristics are reported for the current or most recent job of young adults with disabilities out of high school up to 8 years. NLTS2 percentages are weighted population estimates based on samples of approximately 2,160 young adults with disabilities for education and training put to good use, 2,160 for chances for advancement, 2,170 for how well paid, and 2,060 for received promotion and/or raise.

Source: U.S. Department of Education, Institute of Education Sciences, National Center for Special Education Research, National Longitudinal Transition Study-2 (NLTS2), Wave 5 youth interview/survey, 2009.

Figure 29. Perceptions of their working conditions of young adults with disabilities.

Disability Differences in Perceptions of Working Conditions

A majority of young adults in all disability categories reported liking their jobs at least fairly well (84 percent to 94 percent, table 43) and feeling well treated by others at work (85 percent to 98 percent).

A majority of young adults in each disability category also reported positive perceptions of their working conditions. Between 63 percent and 86 percent reported that their education and training was being put to good use, and from 55 percent to 77 percent indicated they had opportunities for advancement. A majority of young adults in each disability category who had been employed for 6 months or more also reported taking on increased job responsibilities or receiving a promotion (51 percent to 74 percent) or a raise in pay (63 percent to 77 percent). Young adults with learning disabilities were more likely than those with speech/language or hearing impairments to have been promoted or taken on more job responsibilities (74 percent vs. 56 percent and 51 percent, respectively, $p < .01$ for both comparisons). Young adults with visual or orthopedic impairments were more likely to report being paid pretty well at work than young adults with learning disabilities (80 percent and 78 percent, respectively, vs. 57 percent, $p < .01$ for both comparisons).

**Table 43. Job satisfaction and perceptions of working conditions of young adults,
by disability category**

	Learning disability	Speech/ language impairment	Mental retardation	Emotional disturbance	Hearing impairment	Visual impairment	Orthopedic impairment	Other health impairment	Autism	Traumatic brain injury	Multiple disabilities	Deaf-blindness
	Percent											
Percentage who reported:												
Liking his/her job:												
Very much	40.7 (5.11)	41.8 (4.88)	53.8 (6.69)	44.2 (6.12)	39.4 (7.42)	57.5 (7.59)	52.3 (6.84)	49.0 (5.50)	42.4 (9.47)	43.0 (10.02)	68.1 (10.84)	‡
Fairly well	48.2 (5.20)	42.3 (4.89)	32.1 (6.27)	40.4 (6.05)	44.4 (7.55)	29.6 (7.01)	36.8 (6.61)	41.8 (5.42)	47.5 (9.57)	46.6 (10.10)	26.0 (10.20)	‡
Not much	7.2 (2.69)	14.0 (3.43)	5.8 (3.14)	10.6 (3.79)	14.0 (5.27)	10.2 (4.64)	9.1 (3.94)	7.1 (2.82)	9.3 (5.56)	9.3 (5.88)	1.1 (2.43)	‡
Not at all	3.9 (2.01)	1.9 (1.35)	8.4 (3.72)	4.8 (2.63)	2.1 (2.18)	2.7 (2.49)	1.8 (1.82)	2.1 (1.58)	0.8 (1.71)	1.1 (2.11)	4.8 (4.97)	‡
Being treated pretty well by others at work	90.9 (3.00)	90.8 (2.86)	89.3 (4.17)	87.5 (4.07)	84.8 (5.48)	98.4 (1.93)	91.5 (3.83)	90.8 (3.18)	88.4 (6.17)	87.7 (6.65)	95.7 (4.72)	‡
Their education and training was put to good use	72.2 (4.72)	74.6 (4.34)	86.0 (4.68)	73.5 (5.49)	73.3 (6.74)	80.2 (6.12)	79.7 (5.53)	69.0 (5.11)	72.6 (8.60)	62.6 (9.79)	79.3 (9.57)	‡
Having lots of chances to work their way up	68.7 (4.83)	62.7 (4.81)	76.8 (5.68)	59.8 (6.01)	54.6 (7.63)	70.3 (7.06)	68.8 (6.41)	67.7 (5.17)	58.8 (9.82)	63.0 (9.80)	68.8 (10.84)	‡
Receivinga promotion or took on more responsibility[1]	74.2 (4.72)	56.1 (5.02)	57.5 (6.53)	60.0 (6.55)	51.0 (7.45)	56.1 (8.11)	55.1 (8.21)	69.4 (5.47)	53.4 (8.59)	70.5 (11.19)	50.7 (9.97)	‡

Table 43. (Continued)

	Learning disability	Speech/ language impairment	Mental retardation	Emotional disturbance	Hearing impairment	Visual impairment	Orthopedic impairment	Other health impairment	Autism	Traumatic brain injury	Multiple disabilities	Deaf-blindness
	Percent											
Beingpaid pretty well	57.4 (5.17)	63.6 (4.78)	74.2 (5.91)	70.4 (5.59)	65.8 (7.20)	80.3 (6.10)	78.3 (5.72)	73.2 (4.88)	68.6 (8.98)	64.4 (9.72)	75.9 (9.95)	‡
Receivinga raise[1]	77.2 (4.57)	68.7 (4.71)	68.1 (6.28)	68.7 6.26)	64.7 (7.22)	69.8 (7.52)	63.8 (7.97)	75.3 (5.11)	68.5 (8.14)	63.3 (11.83)	70.1 (9.22)	‡

‡ Responses for items with fewer than 30 respondents are not reported.

[1] For young adults with disabilities employed 6 months or more at current or most recent job.

Note: Standard errors are in parentheses. Job characteristics are reported for the current or most recent job of young adults with disabilities out of high school up to 8 years. NLTS2 percentages are weighted population estimates based on samples ranging from approximately 2,060 to 2,160 young adults.

Source: U.S. Department of Education, Institute of Education Sciences, National Center for Special Education Research, National Longitudinal Transition Study-2 (NLTS2), Wave 5 youth interview/survey, 2009.

Table 44. Job satisfaction and perceptions of working conditions of young adults with disabilities, by highest level of educational attainment

	High school non-completer	High school completer	Some post-secondary school	Post-secondary school completion
	Percent			
Percentage who reported:				
Liking his/her job:				
Very much	38.0 (12.68)	39.0 (6.02)	44.9 (6.55)	44.7 (7.33)
Fairly well	51.9 (13.06)	45.5 (6.14)	41.8 (6.50)	48.5 (7.37)
Not much	8.9 (7.44)	8.1 (3.37)	9.7 (3.90)	5.4 (3.33)
Not at all	1.3 (2.96)	7.3 (3.21)	3.5 (2.42)	1.4 (1.73)
Being treated pretty well by others at work	86.4 (9.07)	89.7 (3.77)	86.1 (4.56)	96.7 (2.63)
Their education and training was put to good use	65.1 (12.84)	84.2 (4.54)	63.2 (6.46)	74.3 (6.45)
Having lots of chances to work their way up	57.6 (12.96)	68.9 (5.73)	65.7 (6.27)	72.2 (6.59)
Receivinga promotion or takingon more responsibility[1]	60.3 (13.30)	68.7 (5.70)	69.4 (6.68)	73.7 (6.70)
Being paid pretty well	56.8 (12.94)	60.7 (6.04)	60.8 (6.47)	63.6 (7.17)
Receiving a raise[1]	74.1 (12.24)	76.0 (5.36)	67.9 (6.80)	80.0 (6.08)

[1] For young adults with disabilities employed 6 months or more at current or most recent job.

Note: Standard errors are in parentheses. Job characteristics are reported for the current or most recent job of young adults with disabilities out of high school up to 8 years. NLTS2 percentages are weighted population estimates based on samples ranging from approximately 2,060 to 2,160 young adults with disabilities.

Source: U.S. Department of Education, Institute of Education Sciences, National Center for Special Education Research, National Longitudinal Transition Study-2 (NLTS2), Wave 5 youth interview/survey, 2009.

Differences in Perceptions of Working Conditions by Highest Level of Educational Attainment

There were no differences in the job satisfaction or perceptions of working conditions of young adults with disabilities who differed in their highest level of educational attainment (table 44) with one exception. Young adults whose highest education level was high school completion were more likely than those whose highest education level was some postsecondary education to report that their education was put to good use (84 percent vs. 63 percent, $p < .01$).

Table 45. Job satisfaction and perceptions of working conditions of young adults with disabilities, by years since leaving high school

	Less than 3 years	3 up to 5 years	5 up to 8 years
	Percent		
Percentage who reported:			
Liking his/her job:			
Very much	44.0 (9.11)	37.7 (6.26)	46.4 (5.06)
Fairly well	34.2 (8.70)	53.0 (6.45)	42.0 (5.01)
Not much	13.9 (6.35)	6.7 (3.23)	7.3 (2.64)
Not at all	8.0 (4.98)	2.5 (2.02)	4.3 (2.06)
Being treated pretty well by others at work	88.7 (5.76)	90.2 (3.86)	91.0 (2.91)
Their education and training was put to good use	68.5 (8.59)	76.0 (5.59)	72.5 (4.59)
Having lots of chances to work their way up	67.3 (8.61)	66.8 (6.12)	68.6 (4.71)
Receivinga promotion or took on more responsibility[1]	62.6 (9.07)	67.3 (6.48)	72.5 (4.63)
Beingpaid pretty well	69.0 (8.42)	63.5 (6.28)	58.4 (5.03)
Receiving a raise[1]	69.3 (8.79)	78.0 (5.78)	73.6 (4.63)

[1] For young adults with disabilities employed 6 months or more at current or most recent job.

Note: Standard errors are in parentheses. Job characteristics are reported for the current or most recent job of young adults with disabilities out of high school up to 8 years. NLTS2 percentages are weighted population estimates based on samples ranging from approximately 2,060 to 2,160 young adults with disabilities.

Source: U.S. Department of Education, Institute of Education Sciences, National Center for Special Education Research, National Longitudinal Transition Study-2 (NLTS2), Wave 5 youth interview/survey, 2009.

Differences in Perceptions of Working Conditions by Years since Leaving High School

Young adults with disabilities who differed in the length of time they had been out of high school were similar in their reports of job satisfaction and perceptions of their working conditions (table 45). For example, from 38 percent to 46 percent reported liking their job very much, and from 89 percent to 91 percent reported being treated pretty well by others at work. From 69 percent to 76 percent said their education was put to good use at work, and about two-thirds of young adults, regardless of years out of high school, reported having opportunities to advance at work. From 58 percent to 69 percent of young adults with disabilities reported being paid pretty well. Among those who had been in their job at least 6 months, from 63 percent to 73percent indicated receiving a promotion or an increase in responsibility, and from 69 percent to 78 percent indicated they had received a raise.

Table 46. Job satisfaction and perceptions of working conditions of young adults with disabilities, by parents' household income and young adults' race/ethnicity and gender

	$25,000 or less	$25,001 to $50,000	More than $50,000	White	African American	Hispanic	Male	Female
	Percent							
Percentage who reported:								
Liking his/her job:								
Very much	41.4 (6.60)	38.4 (7.47)	45.1 (5.31)	42.7 (4.38)	35.4 (8.38)	50.6 (11.35)	43.5 (4.54)	41.8 (6.16)
Fairly well	41.6 (6.60)	55.6 (7.63)	42.2 (5.27)	46.3 (4.41)	49.8 (8.76)	37.3 (10.98)	43.7 (4.54)	47.8 (6.24)
Not much	10.4 (4.09)	3.6 (2.86)	9.3 (3.10)	7.5 (2.33)	11.9 (5.67)	5.3 (5.09)	8.5 (2.55)	6.8 (3.14)
Not at all	6.6 (3.33)	2.5 (2.40)	3.3 (1.91)	3.6 (1.65)	3.0 (2.99)	6.8 (5.72)	4.4 (1.88)	3.5 (2.29)
Being treated pretty well by others at work	85.6 (4.73)	91.5 (4.30)	92.8 (2.77)	93.6 (2.17)	81.0 (6.93)	88.6 (7.15)	91.5 (2.55)	88.7 (3.97)
Their education and training was put to good use	71.5 (6.14)	76.1 (6.67)	71.7 (4.84)	73.9 (3.94)	66.1 (8.35)	81.6 (8.87)	73.9 (4.06)	72.5 (5.67)
Having lots of chances to work their way up	69.0 (6.22)	67.0 (7.24)	67.1 (5.02)	64.9 (4.23)	69.0 (8.11)	82.9 (8.59)	71.1 (4.15)	62.3 (6.08)
Receiving a promotion or took on more responsibility[1]	60.1 (7.24)	72.6 (6.98)	72.1 (4.86)	73.1 (4.08)	60.8 (8.89)	62.1 (11.63)	74.6 (4.05)	60.4 (6.64)
Being paid pretty well	54.1 (6.68)	51.3 (7.68)	71.8 (4.86)	64.1 (4.26)	53.4 (8.81)	64.3 (11.00)	62.6 (4.45)	59.9 (6.17)
Receiving a raise[1]	67.5 (6.96)	72.4 (7.08)	79.5 (4.44)	74.5 (4.06)	75.3 (7.97)	79.0 (9.72)	76.8 (3.98)	71.0 (6.20)

[1] For young adults employed 6 months or more at current or most recent job.

Note: Standard errors are in parentheses. Job characteristics are reported for the current or most recent job of young adults with disabilities out of high school up to 8 years. NLTS2 percentages are weighted population estimates based on samples ranging from approximately 2,060 to 2,160 young adults with disabilities.

Source: U.S. Department of Education, Institute of Education Sciences, National Center for Special Education Research, National Longitudinal Transition Study-2 (NLTS2), Wave 5 youth interview/survey, 2009.

Demographic Differences in Perceptions of Working Conditions

Young adults with disabilities had similar views of their jobs, regardless of their parents' household income, or their race/ethnicity or gender (table 46). For example, from 35 percent to 51 percent reported liking their job very much, and from 51 percent to 72 percent reported being paid pretty well.

Job Leaving and Job Search Activities

Despite the positive feelings many young adults with disabilities had about their jobs, 53 percent of those who had been employed and left a job reported that they had quit[74] (figure 30). Twenty-one percent said they left because they had a temporary job that ended, 14 percent had been laid off, and 11 percent had been fired. They were more likely to have quit than to have left their job for any of the other reasons (53 percent vs. 11 percent to 21 percent, $p < .001$ for all comparisons).

At the time of the interview, 40 percent of young adults with disabilities were not working, although 49 percent of these young adults with disabilities were actively looking for a paid job[75] (figure 31). The average length of the ongoing job search of unemployed young adults with disabilities was 7.6 months.[76] Forty-four percent of young adults with disabilities who were looking for work had been doing so for 2 months or less, 28 percent had been looking for work for between 2 and 6 months, and 38 percent had been looking for work longer than 6 months.

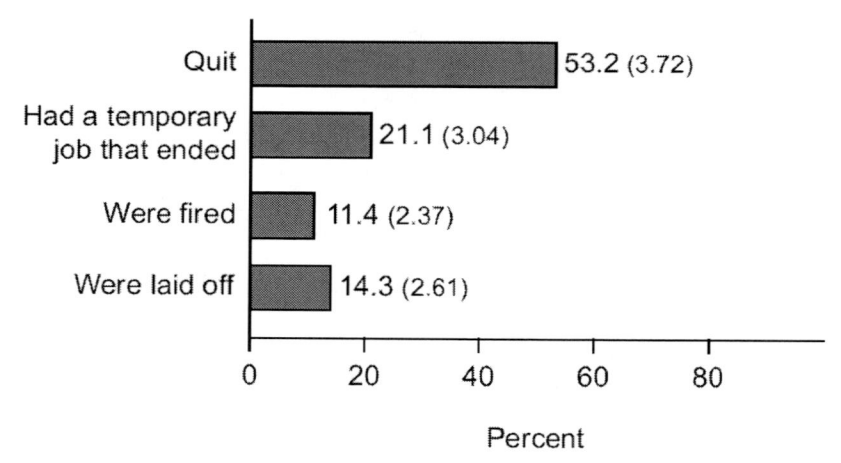

Percent

Note: Standard errors are in parentheses. Job characteristics are reported for the most recent job left by young adults with disabilities out of high school up to 8 years. NLTS2 percentages are weighted population estimates based on a sample of approximately 2,090 young adults with disabilities.

Source: U.S. Department of Education, Institute of Education Sciences, National Center for Special Education Research, National Longitudinal Transition Study-2 (NLTS2), Wave 5 parent interview and youth interview/survey, 2009.

Figure 30. Reasons young adults with disabilities had left their most recent job.

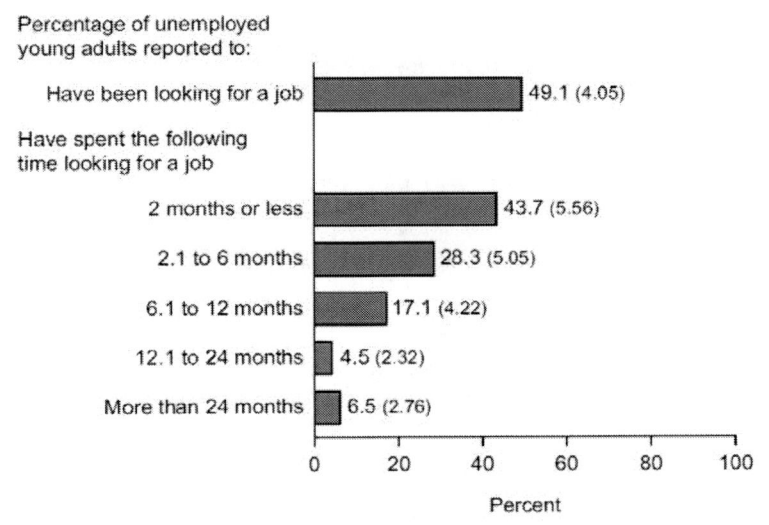

Note: Standard errors are in parentheses. Job search characteristics are reported for young adults with disabilities out of high school up to 8 years who were looking for paid employment at the time of the interview. NLTS2 percentages are weighted population estimates based on samples of approximately 2,200 young adults with disabilities for whether unemployed young adults were looking for work and 860 young adults with disabilities for length of job search for unemployed young adults.

Source: U.S. Department of Education, Institute of Education Sciences, National Center for Special Education Research, National Longitudinal Transition Study-2 (NLTS2), Wave 5 parent interview and youth interview/survey, 2009.

Figure 31. Length of job search of unemployed young adults with disabilities.

Among young adults with disabilities who were employed, 55 percent reported finding work on their own; the other 45 percent reported receiving help from a variety of sources.[77] Eighteen percent of employed young adults reported having help finding their job from a family member, and 17 percent had help from friends or acquaintances (figure 32). Eight percent received help from an employment agency, and 4 percent had help from a teacher or other school staff member. A successful job search was more likely to be attributed to the young adults' own efforts than to any other source of help (54 percent vs. 4 percent to 18 percent, $p < .001$ for all comparisons).

Disability Differences in Job Leaving and Job Search Activities

There were significant differences across disability categories in reported reasons for leaving a previously held job (table 47). Young adults with traumatic brain injuries; hearing, speech/language, or other health impairments; learning disabilities; multiple disabilities; or emotional disturbances were more likely to have quit their previous job (46 percent to 68 percent) than young adults with autism (23 percent, $p < .001$ for comparisons with traumatic brain injuries, hearing impairments, and learning disabilities and $p < .01$ for all other comparisons). In addition, young adults with autism were more likely to have a temporary job that ended than young adults with learning disabilities, mental retardation, emotional disturbances, or traumatic brain injuries (45 percent vs. 15 percent to 21 percent, $p < .01$).

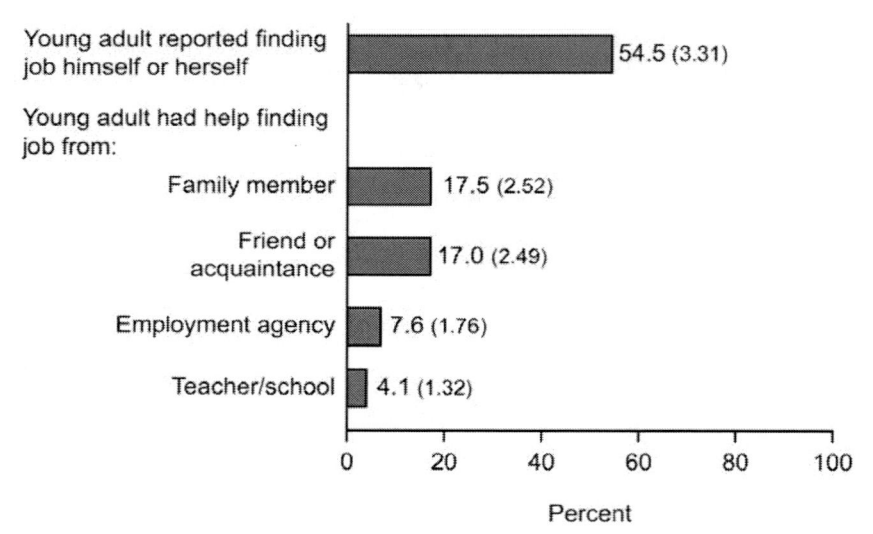

Note: Standard errors are in parentheses. Job characteristics are reported for the current or most recent job of young adults with disabilities out of high school up to 8 years. NLTS2 percentages are weighted population estimates based on a sample of approximately 2,740 young adults with disabilities.

Source: U.S. Department of Education, Institute of Education Sciences, National Center for Special Education Research, National Longitudinal Transition Study-2 (NLTS2), Wave 5 parent interview and youth interview/survey, 2009.

Figure 32. Job search activities of employed young adults with disabilities.

There also were significant differences in the percentages of young adults in different disability categories who were not working and were looking for a paid job at the time of the interview (table 48). Young adults with other health impairments were more likely to be looking for a paid job at the time of the interview than those with orthopedic impairments, mental retardation, autism, or multiple disabilities (67 percent vs. 29 percent to 36 percent, $p < .001$ for all comparisons). Young adults with emotional disturbances also were more likely to be looking for a paid job than young adults with orthopedic impairments, mental retardation, autism, or multiple disabilities (61 percent vs. 29 percent to 36 percent, $p < .01$ for those with orthopedic impairments or mental retardation and $p < .001$ for other comparisons). In addition, young adults with hearing impairments reported looking for a paid job at the time of the interview more often than young adults with multiple disabilities, autism, or mental retardation (60 percent vs. 29 percent to 35 percent, $p < .01$), as did young adults with speech/language impairments compared with those with mental retardation, orthopedic impairments, autism, or multiple disabilities (60 percent vs. 23 percent to 36 percent, $p < .001$ for all comparisons except $p < .01$ compared with those with multiple disabilities).

In contrast, there were no significant differences across disability categories in the average number of months unemployed young adults with disabilities had spent looking for a paid job before finding their current or most recent job. The average months of job search ranged from approximately 5 months for young adults with hearing impairments to 16 months for those with mental retardation.

Table 47. Reasons young adults with disabilities left previous or most recent job,by disability category

	Learning disability	Speech/ language impairment	Mental retardation	Emotional disturbance	Hearing impairment	Visual impairment	Orthopedic impairment	Other health impairment	Autism	Traumatic brain injury	Multiple disabilities	Deaf-blindness
	Percent											
Percentage reported to have:												
Quit	56.0	48.0	45.3	46.3	64.3	48.1	45.3	46.6	22.5	68.4	51.4	‡
	(5.26)	(5.02)	(6.85)	(5.90)	(7.19)	(8.09)	(8.21)	(5.57)	(6.79)	(10.33)	(9.03)	
Had a temporary job that ended	21.0	28.5	15.0	18.7	22.9	28.8	37.2	25.3	45.4	15.8	22.7	‡
	(4.32)	(4.53)	(4.91)	(4.62)	(6.31)	(7.34)	(7.97)	(4.86)	(8.10)	(8.10)	(7.57)	
Been fired	10.4	11.3	18.5	14.2	3.7	12.5	9.7	12.1	12.3	9.1	10.4	‡
	(3.23)	(3.18)	(5.34)	(4.13)	(2.83)	(5.36)	(4.88)	(3.64)	(5.34)	(6.39)	(5.52)	
Been laid off	12.7	12.2	21.1	20.7	9.2	10.6	7.8	15.9	19.8	6.7	15.4	‡
	(3.53)	(3.29)	(5.61)	(4.80)	(4.34)	(4.99)	(4.42)	(4.09)	(6.48)	(5.56)	(6.52)	

‡ Responses for items with fewer than 30 respondents are not reported.

Note: Standard errors are in parentheses. Job search characteristics are reported for young adults with disabilities out of high school up to 8 years who were looking for paid employment at the time of the interview. NLTS2 percentages are weighted population estimates based on a sample of approximately 2,100 young adults with disabilities.

Source: U.S. Department of Education, Institute of Education Sciences, National Center for Special Education Research, National Longitudinal Transition Study-2 (NLTS2), Wave 5 parent interview and youth interview/survey, 2009.

Table 48. Length of job search of unemployed young adults, by disability category

	Learning disability	Speech/ language impairment	Mental retardation	Emotional disturbance	Hearing impairment	Visual impairment	Orthopedic impairment	Other health impairment	Autism	Traumatic brain injury	Multiple disabilities	Deaf-blindness
Percentage of unemployed young adults with disabilities reported:												
Had been looking for a job	50.7 (7.62)	58.7 (6.32)	34.6 (5.24)	61.0 (6.91)	59.6 (7.33)	43.1 (7.50)	35.7 (5.76)	66.5 (7.11)	31.7 (5.06)	46.1 (10.54)	29.3 (6.03)	39.1 (8.80)
Average months spent looking for work	5.6 (2.12)	6.7 (1.55)	16.1 (4.52)	8.1 (1.79)	5.3 (1.36)	6.0 (2.11)	9.9 (2.47)	6.2 (2.10)	12.3 (3.92)	10.5 (4.13)	9.1 (2.55)	‡

‡ Responses for items with fewer than 30 respondents are not reported.

Note: Standard errors are in parentheses. Job search characteristics are reported for young adults with disabilities out of high school up to 8 years who were looking for paid employment at the time of the interview. NLTS2 percentages are weighted population estimates based on samples of approximately 2,200 young adults with disabilities for whether young adult is looking for work and 860 young adults with disabilities for length of job search.

Source: U.S. Department of Education, Institute of Education Sciences, National Center for Special Education Research, National Longitudinal Transition Study-2 (NLTS2), Wave 5 parent interview and youth interview/survey, 2009.

Table 49. Job search activities of employed young adults with disabilities, by disability category

	Learning disability	Speech/ language impairment	Mental retardation	Emotional disturbance	Hearing impairment	Visual impairment	Orthopedic impairment	Other health impairment	Autism	Traumatic brain injury	Multiple disabilities	Deaf-blindness
	Percent											
Percentage reported to have:												
Found their job himself or herself Had help finding job from:	57.9 (4.78)	57.3 (4.50)	30.4 (5.18)	57.3 (5.47)	49.1 (6.54)	51.7 (7.04)	40.9 (6.75)	56.3 (4.98)	23.6 (6.20)	51.2 (9.62)	23.5 (7.49)	31.4 (10.43)
Family member	18.2 (3.74)	15.0 (3.25)	21.4 (4.62)	12.7 (3.68)	16.1 (4.81)	13.7 (4.85)	17.1 (5.17)	17.4 (3.81)	15.2 (5.24)	7.7 (5.13)	16.0 (6.48)	19.8 (8.96)
Friend or acquaintance	15.3 (3.49)	19.7 (3.62)	20.2 (4.52)	23.4 (4.68)	18.2 (5.05)	17.9 (5.40)	18.4 (5.32)	17.3 (3.80)	17.5 (5.54)	30.1 (8.83)	4.6 (3.70)	29.8 (10.28)
Employment agency	5.8 (2.26)	5.7 (2.11)	18.1 (4.34)	5.5 (2.52)	12.3 (4.30)	14.1 (4.91)	21.0 (5.59)	9.0 (2.87)	25.5 (6.36)	7.1 (4.94)	32.3 (8.26)	9.1 (6.47)
Teacher/school	3.2 (1.70)	2.7 (1.48)	12.8 (3.76)	1.6 (1.39)	6.4 (3.20)	5.2 (3.13)	3.2 (2.42)	1.9 (1.37)	19.1 (5.74)	4.6 (4.03)	28.9 (8.01)	9.9 (6.71)

Note: Standard errors are in parentheses. Job characteristics are reported for the current or most recent job of young adults with disabilities out of high school up to 8 years. NLTS2 percentages are weighted population estimates based on a sample of approximately 2,740 young adults with disabilities.

Source: U.S. Department of Education, Institute of Education Sciences, National Center for Special Education Research, National Longitudinal Transition Study-2 (NLTS2), Wave 5 parent interview and youth interview/survey, 2009.

Table 50. Reasons young adults with disabilities left previous or most recent job, by years since leaving high school

	Less than 3 years	3 up to 5 years	5 up to 8 years
	Percent		
Percentage reported to have:			
Quit	47.4 (9.71)	46.3 (6.60)	58.9 (4.95)
Had temporary job that ended	24.4 (8.35)	23.5 (5.61)	18.9 (3.94)
Been fired	15.7 (7.07)	14.8 (4.70)	8.3 (2.77)
Been laid off	12.5 (6.43)	15.4 (4.78)	13.9 (3.48)

Note: Standard errors are in parentheses. Job characteristics are reported for the most recent job left by young adults with disabilities out of high school up to 8 years. NLTS2 percentages are weighted population estimates based on a sample of approximately 2,090 young adults with disabilities.

Source: U.S. Department of Education, Institute of Education Sciences, National Center for Special Education Research, National Longitudinal Transition Study-2 (NLTS2), Wave 5 parent interview and youth interview/survey, 2009.

Table 51. Length of job search of unemployed young adults with disabilities, by years since leaving high school

	Less than 3 years	3 up to 5 years	5 up to 8 years
Percentage of unemployed young adults with disabilities' reported:			
Had been looking for a job	51.0 (7.38)	48.7 (7.04)	48.8 (6.11)
Average months spent looking for work	8.1 (3.82)	5.8 (1.46)	8.6 (2.38)

Note: Standard errors are in parentheses. Job search characteristics are reported for young adults with disabilities out of high school up to 8 years who were looking for paid employment at the time of the interview. NLTS2 percentages are weighted population estimates based on samples of approximately 2,200 young adults with disabilities for whether young adult is looking for work and 860 young adults with disabilities for length of job search.

Source: U.S. Department of Education, Institute of Education Sciences, National Center for Special Education Research, National Longitudinal Transition Study-2 (NLTS2), Wave 5 parent interview and youth interview/survey, 2009.

Among young adults with disabilities who had successfully found employment, there were significant differences in job search activities across several disability categories (table 49). Young adults with learning disabilities, speech/language impairments, emotional disturbances, or other health impairments (56 to 58 percent) were more likely to have found their current or most recent job on their own than young adults with mental retardation (30 percent), autism (24 percent), or multiple disabilities (24 percent, $p < .001$ for all comparisons). In addition, young adults with visual impairments were more likely to have found their current or most recent job on their own than young adults with multiple disabilities or autism (51 percent vs. 24 percent for both categories, $p < .01$).

Young adults with disabilities received help from a variety of sources that also significantly differed across the disability categories. Young adults with traumatic brain injuries, emotional disturbances, speech/language impairments, or mental retardation were more likely to have had a friend or someone else help them find their current job (20 percent to 30 percent) than those with multiple disabilities (5 percent; p < .01 for all comparisons). However, young adults with multiple disabilities were more likely to have had a teacher or someone at school help find their current or most recent job than those with hearing, visual, speech/language, orthopedic, or other health impairments; traumatic brain injuries; learning disabilities; or emotional disturbances (29 percent vs. 2 percent to 6 percent, p < .01 for all comparisons except p < .001 compared with young adults with emotional disturbances or other health impairments). Those with multiple disabilities also were more likely to use an employment agency than young adults with speech/language or other health impairments, traumatic brain injuries, emotional disturbances, or learning disabilities (32 percent vs. 6 percent to 9 percent, p < .01 for all comparisons). Similarly, young adults with autism were more likely to have had a teacher or someone at school help find their current or most recent job than those with emotional disturbances, speech/language or other health impairments, or learning disabilities (19 percent vs. 2 percent and 3 percent, p < .01 for all comparisons) or to have used an employment agency than young adults with learning disabilities, speech/language impairments, or emotional disturbances (26 percent vs. 6 percent for all three categories, p < .01). Young adults with orthopedic impairments also were more likely to receive help from an employment agency than young adults with speech/language impairments (21 percent vs. 6 percent, p < .01).

Differences in Job Leaving and Job Search Activities by Years Since Leaving High School

There were no significant differences in the reason why young adults left their previous jobs based on years since leaving high school (table 50). For example, forty-seven percent of young adults out of high school less than 3 years reported to have quit their previous or most recent job, and 59 percent of young adults out of high school 5 to 8 years reported to have quit their previous or most recent job.

Unemployed young adults with disabilities did not vary significantly in their looking for work or in the length of their job search, based on the number of years since leaving high school (table 51). The average length of job searching was approximately 8 months for young adults with disabilities out of high school less than 3 years, 6 months for those out of high school 3 up to 5 years, and 9 months for young adults out of high school 5 up to 8 years.

Differences in how employed young adults found their jobs also were not apparent for young adults with disabilities based on years since leaving high school (table 52). Forty percent of employed young adults with disabilities out of high school less than 3 years reported to have found their job themselves. Employed young adults with disabilities out of high school 5 to 8 years reported to have found their job themselves at a rate of 53 percent.

Table 52. Job search activities of employed young adults with disabilities, by years since leaving high school

	Less than 3 years	3 up to 5 years	5 up to 8 years
	Percent		
Percentage reported to have:			
Found their job himself or herself	40.7 (8.13)	60.7 (5.64)	53.1 (4.55)
Had help finding job from:			
Family member	30.6 (7.63)	18.8 (4.51)	13.6 (3.13)
Friend or acquaintance	18.7 (6.45)	10.8 (3.59)	21.1 (3.72)
Employment agency	5.5 (3.77)	7.9 (3.12)	8.0 (2.48)
Teacher/school	5.6 (3.77)	2.6 (1.84)	5.1 (2.01)

Note: Standard errors are in parentheses. Job characteristics are reported for the current or most recent job of young adults with disabilities out of high school up to 8 years. NLTS2 percentages are weighted population estimates based on a sample of approximately 2,740 young adults with disabilities.

Source: U.S. Department of Education, Institute of Education Sciences, National Center for Special Education Research, National Longitudinal Transition Study-2 (NLTS2), Wave 5 parent interview and youth interview/survey, 2009.

Table 53. Reasons young adults with disabilities left previous or most recent job, by highest level of educational attainment

	High school non-completer	High school completer	Some post-Secondary school	Post-secondary School completion
	Percent			
Percentage who reported to have:				
Quit	39.2 (11.54)	58.3 (6.10)	47.2 (6.73)	56.6 (7.40)
Had a temporary job that ended	14.3 (8.28)	13.1 (4.17)	24.6 (5.81)	28.2 (6.71)
Been fired	28.1 (10.63)	12.2 (4.05)	12.6 (4.48)	5.6 (3.43)
Been laid off	18.4 (9.16)	16.4 (4.58)	15.7 (4.91)	9.6 (4.40)

Note: Standard errors are in parentheses. Job characteristics are reported for the current or most recent job of young adults with disabilities out of high school up to 8 years. NLTS2 percentages are weighted population estimates based on a sample of approximately 2,090 young adults with disabilities.

Source: U.S. Department of Education, Institute of Education Sciences, National Center for Special Education Research, National Longitudinal Transition Study-2 (NLTS2), Wave 5 parent interview and youth interview/survey, 2009.

Differences in Job Leaving and Job Search Activities by Highest Level of Educational Attainment

There were no significant differences in the reason why young adults left their previous jobs based on highest level of educational attainment (table 53). The percentage of young adults with disabilities who did not complete high school reported to have quit their job was 39 percent. Fifty-seven percent of young adults with disabilities with postsecondary school completion reported to have had quit their previous job.

Unemployed young adults with disabilities did not vary significantly in whether they were looking for work at the time of the interview or the length of their job search, by their highest level of educational attainment (table 54). The average amount of time spent looking for a job by a high school noncompleter as well as a young adult with postsecondary school completion was about 5 months.

Differences in how young adults found their current or most recent job also were not apparent for young adults with disabilities based on years since leaving high school (table 55). For example, the percentage of young adults with disabilities reported to have found their job themselves ranged from 42 percent for high school noncompleters to 67 percent of postsecondary school completers.

Demographic Differences in Job Leaving and Job Search Activities

No significant differences in the reason why young adults left their previous jobs were noted for young adults with disabilities who differed in gender or race/ethnicity (table 56); however, one household income difference was apparent. Young adults with disabilities from parents' households with incomes of $25,000 or less were more likely to be fired from their most recent job than those from household with incomes of more than $50,000 (20 percent vs. 4 percent, $p < .001$).

Table 54. Length of job search of unemployed young adults with disabilities, by highest level of educational attainment

	High school non-completer	High school completer	Some post-secondary school	Post-secondary school completion
Percentage of young adults with disabilities reported:				
Had been looking for a job	37.1 (9.71)	48.1 (5.88)	53.0 (8.07)	55.9 (10.19)
Average months spent looking for work	4.9 (1.83)	9.4 (2.47)	6.9 (2.82)	5.0 (1.66)

Note: Standard errors are in parentheses. Job search characteristics are reported for young adults with disabilities out of high school up to 8 years who were looking for paid employment at the time of the interview. NLTS2 percentages are weighted population estimates based on samples of approximately 2,200 young adults with disabilities for whether young adult is looking for work and 860 young adults with disabilities for length of job search.

Source: U.S. Department of Education, Institute of Education Sciences, National Center for Special Education Research, National Longitudinal Transition Study-2 (NLTS2), Wave 5 parent interview and youth interview/survey, 2009.

Table 55. Job search activities of employed young adults with disabilities, by highest level of educational attainment

	High school non-completer	High school completer	Some post-secondary school	Post-secondary school completion
	Percent			
Percentage reported to have:				
Found their job himself or herself	41.9 (10.91)	43.4 (5.22)	60.5 (6.00)	66.7 (6.48)
Had help finding job from:				
Family member	25.9 (9.69)	21.1 (4.30)	16.6 (4.57)	10.9 (4.29)
Friend or acquaintance	23.8 (9.42)	24.3 (4.51)	11.0 (3.84)	12.1 (4.49)
Employment agency	9.2 (6.39)	9.3 (3.06)	9.3 (3.56)	3.3 (2.46)
Teacher/school	0.3 (1.21)	3.7 (1.99)	2.8 (2.02)	7.1 (3.53)

Note: Standard errors are in parentheses. Job characteristics are reported for the current or most recent job of young adults with disabilities out of high school up to 8 years. NLTS2 percentages are weighted population estimates based on a sample of approximately 2,740 young adults with disabilities.

Source: U.S. Department of Education, Institute of Education Sciences, National Center for Special Education Research, National Longitudinal Transition Study-2 (NLTS2), Wave 5 parent interview and youth interview/survey, 2009.

In addition, unemployed young adults with disabilities did not vary significantly in whether they were looking for work at the time of the interview or the length of their job search, by household income, race/ethnicity, or gender (table 57). From 42 percent to 55 percent of unemployed young adults with disabilities across demographic categories indicated they had been looking for a job, spending from 5 to 12 months on average doing so.

Nor were differences apparent related to household income, race/ethnicity, or gender in how young adults with disabilities found their current or most recent job (table 58). For example, from 48 percent to 64 percent of young adults with disabilities across demographic categories reported finding their job themselves, and from 11 percent to 20 percent reported having help from a family member.

This chapter has presented a national picture of the employment experiences of young adults with disabilities. Chapter 2 examined postsecondary school experiences, and chapter 4 will focus on the overlap between these two outcomes, describing engagement in school, work, or preparation for work.

Table 56. Reasons young adults with disabilities left previous or most recent job, by parents' household income and young adults' race/ethnicity and gender

	$25,000 or less	$25,001 to $50,000	More than $50,000	White	African American	Hispanic	Male	Female
				Percent				
Percentage reported to have:								
Quit	47.9 (6.85)	52.8 (7.64)	54.5 (5.33)	52.3 (4.45)	56.9 (8.52)	49.0 (11.51)	49.7 (4.52)	59.2 (6.42)
Had a temporary job that ended	17.6 (5.22)	17.9 (5.87)	26.9 (4.75)	20.3 (3.58)	21.0 (7.01)	27.3 (10.26)	24.3 (3.87)	15.6 (4.74)
Beenfired	19.5 (5.43)	14.4 (5.37)	4.4 (2.20)	12.3 (2.93)	9.8 (5.12)	9.9 (6.87)	8.8 (2.56)	16.0 (4.79)
Been laid off	14.9 (4.88)	14.9 (5.45)	14.2 (3.74)	15.1 (3.19)	12.3 (5.65)	13.8 (7.94)	17.1 (3.40)	9.3 (3.80)

Note: Standard errors are in parentheses. Job characteristics are reported for the most recent job left by young adults with disabilities out of high school up to 8 years. NLTS2 percentages are weighted population estimates based on a sample of approximately 2,090 young adults with disabilities.

Source: U.S. Department of Education, Institute of Education Sciences, National Center for Special Education Research, National Longitudinal Transition Study-2 (NLTS2), Wave 5 parent interview and youth interview/survey, 2009.

Table 57. Length of job search of unemployed young adults with disabilities, by parents' household income and young adults' race/ethnicity and gender

	$25,000 or less	$25,001 to $50,000	More than $50,000	White	African American	Hispanic	Male	Female
Percentage of unemployed young adults with disabilities reported:								
Had been looking for a job	45.6 (6.29)	52.7 (8.38)	53.3 (6.63)	45.2 (5.24)	55.6 (7.70)	53.6 (11.37)	54.9 (5.27)	41.9 (6.19)
Average months spent looking for work	11.8 (2.85)	4.7 (1.66)	5.4 (1.60)	8.2 (2.01)	7.9 (3.09)	4.5 (1.43)	8.4 (1.83)	6.3 (2.23)

Note: Standard errors are in parentheses. Job search characteristics are reported for young adults with disabilities out of high school up to 8 years who were looking for paid employment at the time of the interview. NLTS2 percentages are weighted population estimates based on a sample of approximately 2,200 young adults with disabilities.

Source: U.S. Department of Education, Institute of Education Sciences, National Center for Special Education Research, National Longitudinal Transition Study-2 (NLTS2), Wave 5 parent interview and youth interview/survey, 2009.

Table 58. Job search activities of employed young adults with disabilities, by parents' household income and young adults' race/ethnicity and gender

	$25,000 or less	$25,001 to $50,000	More than $50,000	White	African American	Hispanic	Male	Female
				Percent				
Percentage reported to have:								
Found their job himself or herself	52.6 (6.07)	58.3 (6.66)	54.9 (4.80)	52.3 (3.96)	63.9 (7.55)	48.2 (10.40)	50.8 (4.01)	61.4 (5.71)
Had help finding job from:								
Family member	16.6 (4.52)	13.0 (4.54)	18.4 (3.73)	20.3 (3.19)	10.7 (4.86)	13.4 (7.09)	16.5 (2.98)	19.4 (4.64)
Friend or acquaintance	18.2 (4.69)	21.3 (5.53)	14.0 (3.34)	18.5 (3.08)	12.5 (5.20)	16.5 (7.72)	19.0 (3.15)	13.2 (3.97)
Employment agency	10.9 (3.79)	5.7 (3.13)	7.0 (2.43)	6.8 (1.99)	7.3 (4.09)	14.2 (7.26)	9.9 (2.40)	3.5 (2.16)
Teacher/school	2.0 (1.70)	2.9 (2.27)	6.8 (2.43)	3.2 (1.39)	5.7 (3.64)	8.1 (5.68)	4.8 (1.72)	2.9 (1.97)

Note: Standard errors are in parentheses. Job characteristics are reported for the current or most recent job of young adults with disabilities out of high school up to 8 years. NLTS2 percentages are weighted population estimates based on a sample of approximately 2,740 young adults with disabilities.

Source: U.S. Department of Education, Institute of Education Sciences, National Center for Special Education Research, National Longitudinal Transition Study-2 (NLTS2), Wave 5 parent interview and youth interview/survey, 2009.

4. PRODUCTIVE ENGAGEMENT IN THE COMMUNITY

According to the Individuals with Disabilities Education Improvement Act of 2004 (IDEA 2004), one of the primary purposes of special education is to prepare students "for further education, employment, and independent living" [20 U.S.C. § 1400(33)(c)(1)]. At the time they were in high school, the majority of young adults with disabilities included in this report had employment and postsecondary education as primary transition goals (Newman et al. 2009; Wagner et al. 2007). Research and policies related to transition from high school to early adulthood have primarily focused on employment and postsecondary school attendance (e.g., Johnson et al. 2002; Savage 2005; Wehman and Evans Getzel 2005); improving high school transition planning, services, and strategies (Carter et al. 2009; Guy et al. 2009); and promoting the career awareness of young adults with disabilities (Carter et al. 2010b). Other transition-related topics have included research into outcomes for young adults who differ in their primary disability category (Carter et al. 2010a; Neece, Kraemer, and Blacher 2009), gender (Powers et al. 2008), and cultural or linguistic background (Fabian 2007; Povenmire et al. 2010).

Chapters 2 and 3 of this report describe separately involvement in two important post-high school outcomes—employment and postsecondary education.However, some young adults engage in one of these activities but not in the other. For example, some might spend their early post-high school years attending postsecondary school but are not employed. To provide a broader understanding of the extent to which young adults are productively engaged in their communities, this chapter focuses on a broader measure of successful transition—the combination and the overlap of these two types of engagement—employment and postsecondary education.

Addressing this broader concept of engagement, rather than considering individual outcomes separately, was encouraged by the advisory panel during the design of the initial NLTS; as a result, NLTS was one of the first studies to present a broader perspective on how young adults with disabilities could be productively engaged in their communities. The advisory panel for the current study continued to endorse that view of engagement. The importance of this broader view of what constitutes a successful transition is now incorporated in the current federal policy that requires states to collect data on "Indicator 14"—i.e., "the percent of youth who had IEPs, are no longer in secondary school, and who have been competitively employed, enrolled in some type of postsecondary school, or both, within one year of leaving high school" [20 U.S.C. 1416(a)(3)(B)]. The NLTS2 operationalization of this concept, as endorsed by the NLTS2 design advisory panel, is somewhat broader than Indicator 14 in that NLTS2 includes all forms of employment, not just competitive employment, and includes job training as a productive form of preparation for work in addition to enrollment in postsecondary education.

In this chapter, young adults with disabilities are considered productively engaged in the community if they had participated in one or more of the following activities since leaving secondary school:

- Employment—worked for pay, other than work around the house, including supported or sheltered employment.[78]
- Education—attended a vocational, business, or technical school; a 2-year, junior, or community college; or a 4-year college or university.
- Job training—received training in specific job skills (e.g., car repair, web page design, food service) from someone other than an employer or a family member, such as an agency or a government training program.

Engagement in Employment and Postsecondary Education or Training for Employment at the Time of the Interview and since Leaving High School

At the time of the Wave 5 interview, 65 percent of young adults with disabilities reported having been productively engaged in postsecondary education, training for employment, and/or employment (figure 33). Forty-eight percent of young adults with disabilities reported having paid employment as their only mode of engagement at the time of the interview. Nine percent of post-high school young adults with disabilities reported being involved in both employment and education concurrently at the time of the interview—juggling the demands of going to school while working. Postsecondary education was the only mode of engagement at the time of the interview for 5 percent of young adults with disabilities. Two percent were involved in employment and job training concurrently, and 1 percent of young adults with disabilities reported "other" modes of engagement. Other modes included involvement in job training only, involvement in postsecondary education and job training, and involvement in employment, job training and postsecondary education.

A larger proportion of young adults with disabilities (94 percent) reported having been productively engaged in postsecondary education or training for employment and employment at some time since leaving high school (figure 34). Thirty percent of young adults with disabilities reported having paid employment as their only mode of engagement. Others had been employed since leaving high school and had concurrently been involved in other activities, including

- postsecondary education (42 percent);
- postsecondary education and job training (14 percent); or
- job training (5 percent).

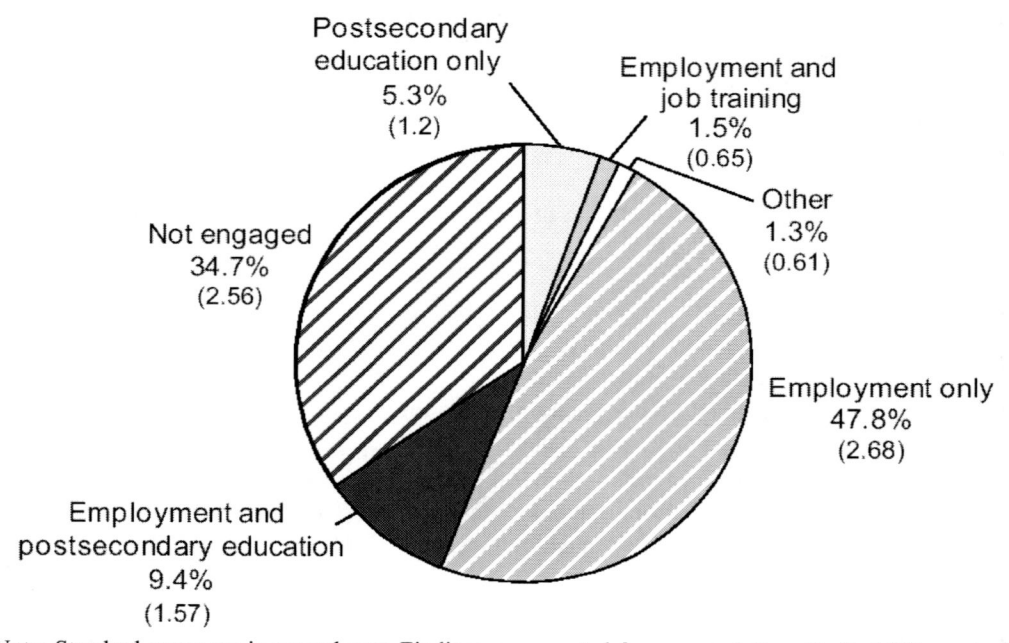

Note: Standard errors are in parentheses. Findings are reported for young adults with disabilities out of high school up to 8 years. NLTS2 percentages are weighted population estimates based on a sample of approximately 4,800 young adults with disabilities.

Source: U.S. Department of Education, Institute of Education Sciences, National Center for Special Education Research, National Longitudinal Transition Study-2 (NLTS2), Wave 5 parent interview and youth interview/survey, 2009.

Figure 33. Modes of engagement of young adults with disabilities at the time of the interview.

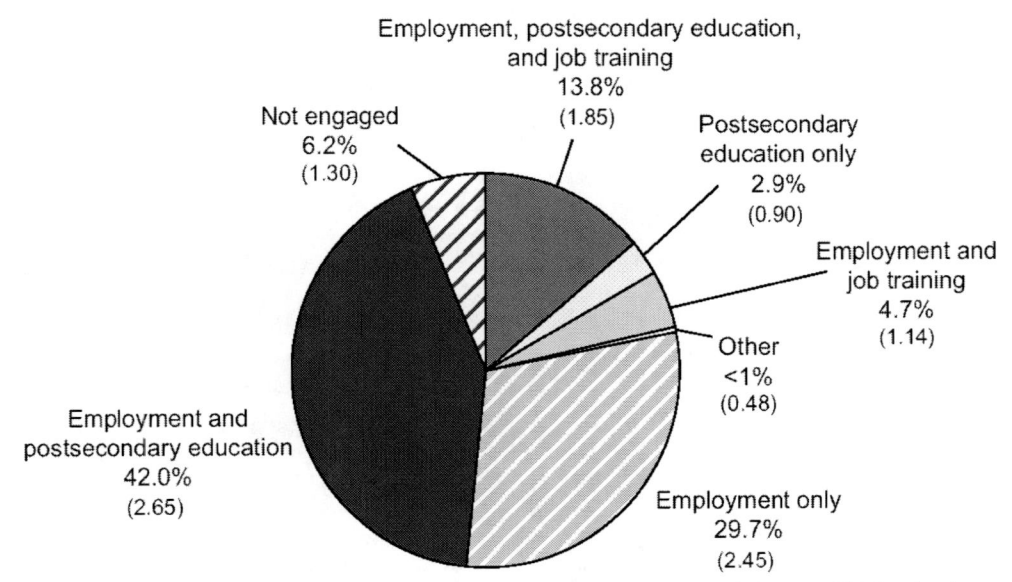

Note: Standard errors are in parentheses. Findings are reported for young adults out of high school up to 8 years. NLTS2 percentages are weighted population estimates based on a sample of approximately 4,800 young adults with disabilities.

Source: U.S. Department of Education, Institute of Education Sciences, National Center for Special Education Research, National Longitudinal Transition Study-2 (NLTS2), Wave 5 parent interview and youth interview/survey, 2009.

Figure 34. Modes of engagement of young adults with disabilities since leaving high school.

Postsecondary education was the only mode of engagement since high school for 3 percent of young adults with disabilities. Less than 1 percent of young adults with disabilities reported "other" modes of engagement. Other modes included job training only, and postsecondary education and job training.

Disability Differences in Engagement in Employment and Postsecondary Education or Training for Employment since Leaving High School

Engagement in employment and postsecondary education or training since leaving high school varied by disability category, ranging from 71 percent to 98 percent (figure 35). Young adults in several disability categories were more likely to report ever having been engaged than were those with autism. Ninety-eight percent of those with other health impairments, 97 percent of those with learning disabilities, 96 percent of those with speech and language impairments, 95 percent of those with hearing impairments, and 94 percent of those with emotional disabilities had ever been engaged, compared with 71 percent of young adults with autism ($p < .001$ for all comparisons) Young adults with other health impairments also were more likely ever to have been engaged in productive activities (98 percent) than were those with multiple disabilities (74 percent), mental retardation (79 percent), and orthopedic impairments (83 percent, $p < .001$ for all comparisons).

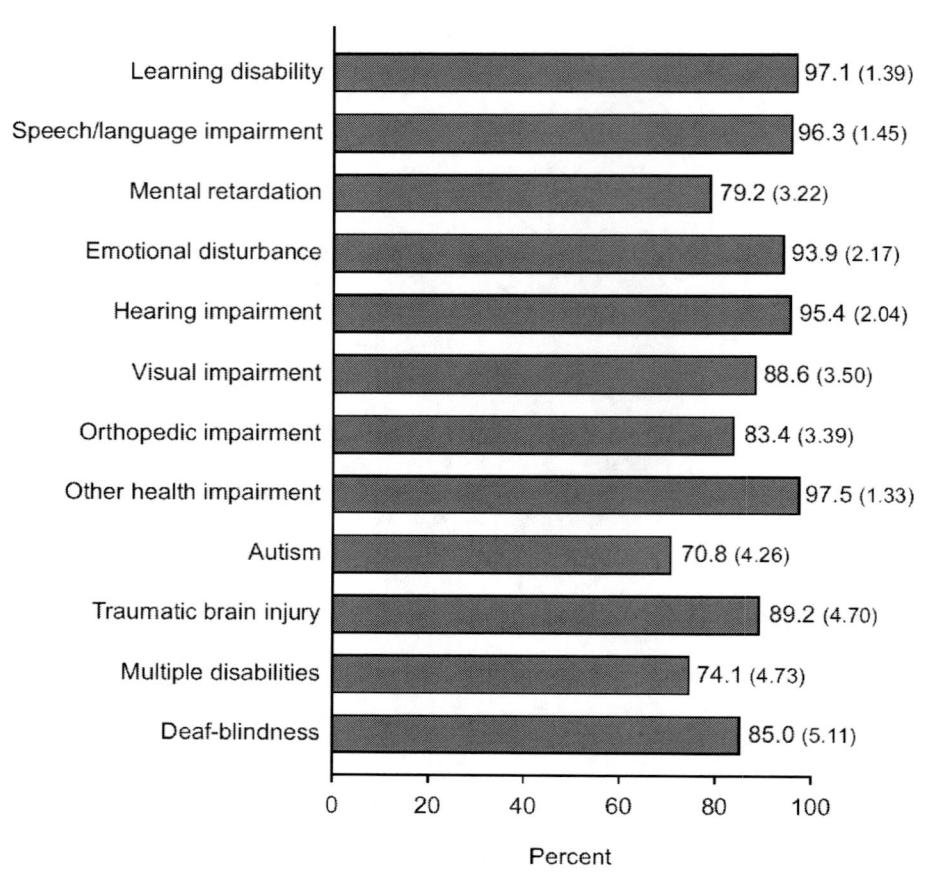

Note: Standard errors are in parentheses. Findings are reported for young adults out of high school up to
8 years. NLTS2 percentages are weighted population estimates based on a sample of
approximately 4,800 young adults with disabilities.

Source: U.S. Department of Education, Institute of Education Sciences, National Center for Special
Education Research, National Longitudinal Transition Study-2 (NLTS2), Wave 5 parent interview
and youth interview/survey, 2009.

Figure 35. Engagement in education, employment, or training for employment of young adults, by
disability category since leaving high school.

Young adults with other health impairments also were more likely ever to have been
engaged in productive activities (98 percent) than were those with multiple disabilities (74
percent), mental retardation (79 percent), and orthopedic impairments (83 percent, p < .001
for all comparisons).

Modes of engagement also varied by disability category (table 59). Thirty-nine percent of
young adults with mental retardation and 38 percent of those with emotional disturbances
were more likely than those in several other categories to have paid employment as their only
mode of engagement: 13 percent of those with orthopedic impairments (*p* < .001 for both
comparisons), 15 percent of those with visual impairments (*p* < .001 for both comparisons),
16 percent of young adults with autism (*p* < .001 for both comparisons), and 17 percent of
those with hearing impairments (*p* < .001 for both comparisons).

Table 59. Modes of engagement of young adults, by disability category since leaving high school

	Learning disability	Speech/ language impairment	Mental retardation	Emotional disturbance	Hearing impairment	Visual impairment	Orthopedic impairment	Other health impairment	Autism	Traumatic brain injury	Multiple disabilities	Deaf-blindness
	Percent											
Employment only	27.8 (3.70)	25.5 (3.36)	39.2 (3.88)	37.6 (4.40)	16.7 (3.64)	14.9 (4.02)	12.9 (3.06)	27.5 (3.80)	16.3 (3.46)	25.3 (6.58)	28.9 (4.89)	19.2 (5.64)
Postsecondary education only	2.9 (1.39)	2.7 (1.25)	1.9 (1.08)	2.4 (1.39)	3.3 (1.74)	8.5 (3.07)	12.8 (3.05)	1.9 (1.16)	2.8 (1.55)	7.1 (3.89)	6.0 (2.56)	8.0 (3.88)
Employment and postsecondary education	47.7 (4.13)	53.3 (3.84)	15.5 (2.87)	37.1 (4.38)	45.7 (4.86)	39.0 (5.37)	33.2 (4.29)	46.8 (4.25)	20.6 (3.79)	35.9 (7.26)	13.3 (3.67)	27.2 (6.37)
Employment, postsecondary education, and job training	14.3 (2.89)	11.0 (2.41)	11.8 (2.56)	12.4 (2.99)	24.4 (4.19)	20.5 (4.45)	13.0 (3.07)	16.3 (3.14)	16.7 (3.50)	16.2 (5.58)	9.8 (3.21)	14.3 (5.01)
Employment and job training	4.0 (1.62)	3.7 (1.45)	9.3 (2.31)	3.4 (1.64)	3.9 (1.89)	2.8 (1.82)	8.2 (2.50)	4.8 (1.82)	8.4 (2.66)	3.3 (2.70)	10.4 (3.30)	9.1 (4.12)
Other combination of activities	0.4 (0.52)	0.1 (0.24)	1.6 (1.00)	1.1 (0.95)	1.4 (1.15)	3.0 (1.88)	3.3 (1.63)	0.3 (0.47)	6.0 (2.23)	1.3 (1.71)	5.8 (2.52)	7.3 (3.73)
No engagement	2.9 (2.41)	3.7 (1.94)	20.8 (3.72)	6.1 (2.28)	4.6 (2.66)	11.4 (3.9)	16.6 (3.71)	2.5 (2.13)	29.2 (4.4)	10.8 (5.39)	25.9 (5.07)	15.0 (6.23)

Note: Standard errors are in parentheses. Findings are reported for young adults with disabilities out of high school up to 8 years. NLTS2 percentages are weighted population estimates based on a sample of approximately 4,800 young adults with disabilities.

Source: U.S. Department of Education, Institute of Education Sciences, National Center for Special Education Research, National Longitudinal Transition Study-2 (NLTS2), Wave 5 parent interview and young adult interview/survey, 2009.

Young adults with learning disabilities were more likely to have employment as their only mode of engagement (28 percent) than were those with orthopedic impairments (14 percent, $p < .01$).

Postsecondary school enrollment as the only form of engagement was more likely for young adults with orthopedic impairments (13 percent) than for those in five of the other disability categories: young adults with learning disabilities (3 percent, $p < .01$), speech/language impairments (3 percent, $p < .01$), hearing impairments (3 percent, $p < .01$), emotional disturbances (2 percent, $p < .01$), mental retardation (2 percent, $p < .001$), and other health impairments (2 percent, $p < .001$).

Young adults with speech/language impairments (53 percent) or learning disabilities (48 percent) were more likely to report having been employed and to have enrolled in postsecondary education at some point since high school than were those with autism (21 percent), mental retardation (16 percent), or multiple disabilities (13 percent), ($p < .001$ for all comparisons). Young adults with other health impairments (47 percent) or hearing impairments (46 percent) were more likely than those with autism (21 percent, $p < .001$) mental retardation (16 percent, $p < .001$ for both comparisons) or multiple disabilities (13 percent, $p < .001$ for both comparisons) to have been employed and to have attended postsecondary school since leaving high school.

Table 60. Modes of engagement in education, employment, or training for employment of young adults with disabilities, by years since leaving high school

	Less than 3 years	3 up to 5 years	5 up to 8 years
	Percent		
Engaged in at least one of the three modes of engagement	85.3 (4.41)	93.8 (2.28)	95.8 (1.49)
Employment only	27.7 (5.57)	30.2 (4.33)	29.7 (3.40)
Postsecondary education only	4.4 (2.55)	1.9 (1.29)	3.3 (1.33)
Employment and postsecondary education	38.5 (6.05)	42.2 (4.66)	42.4 (3.68)
Employment, postsecondary education, and job training	9.5 (3.65)	12.8 (3.15)	15.5 (2.69)
Employment and job training	4.1 (2.47)	6.2 (2.28)	3.9 (1.44)
Other combination of activities	1.0 (1.24)	0.3 (0.67)	1.0 (0.74)
No engagement	14.7 (4.41)	6.2 (2.28)	4.2 (1.49)

Note: Standard errors are in parentheses. Findings are reported for young adults with disabilities out of high school up to 8 years. NLTS2 percentages are weighted population estimates based on based on a sample of approximately 4,800 young adults with disabilities.

Source: U.S. Department of Education, Institute of Education Sciences, National Center for Special Education Research, National Longitudinal Transition Study-2 (NLTS2), Wave 5 parent interview and young adult interview/survey, 2009.

Engagement since high school in employment and postsecondary education and job training did not differ significantly by disability category, nor did engagement since high school in employment and training in job skills or other combinations of modes of engagement.

Differences in Engagement in Employment and Postsecondary Education or Training for Employment by Years since Leaving High School

Both the overall engagement rate in employment, postsecondary education, and/or training and engagement in the various combinations of modes of engagement did not vary significantly by years since leaving high school (table 60).

Differences in Engagement in Employment and Postsecondary Education or Training for Employment by Highest Level of Educational Attainment

As would be expected by the definition of the engagement variable, all young adults with disabilities who had completed postsecondary education or had attended some postsecondary school reported engagement in employment, postsecondary education, or training for employment (table 61). Young adults who had attended and/or completed postsecondary school were more likely to have been productively engaged than were those who had not completed high school (77 percent, $p < .001$ for both comparisons) or who had finished their high school programs (90 percent, $p < .001$ for both comparisons).

Demographic Differences in Engagement in Employment and Postsecondary Education or Training for Employment

Modes of engagement varied by income levels. Young adults with disabilities from families with incomes of more than $50,000 were more likely than those from families with incomes of $25,000 or less to have been employed and to have attended postsecondary school (50 percent vs. 32 percent, $p < .01$; table 62). The modes of engagement of young adults with disabilities did not vary significantly by parent's household income, race/ethnicity or gender.

The beginning chapters of this report have focused on the postsecondary education and employment experiences of young adults with disabilities. The following chapters shift the focus from these two post-high school outcomes to household circumstances and social and community involvement.

5. HOUSEHOLD CIRCUMSTANCES OF YOUNG ADULTS WITH DISABILITIES

Although postsecondary education and employment are important postschool outcomes for young adults, household circumstances (e.g., independent residence) also are important to transition success (Chambers, Rabren, and Dunn 2009). Markers on the path to adult responsibility typically have included financial and residential independence and self-sufficiency, marriage, and parenting (Arnett 2000; Rindfuss 1991; Settersten 2006). However, youth in the general population are taking longer to attain these traditional markers as they transition from high school to adulthood than in the past (Furstenberg et al. 2004; Mortimer and Larson 2002; Shanahan 2000). NLTS2 provides the opportunity to examine such trends among young adults with disabilities.

This chapter examines these key aspects of independence for young adults with disabilities who have been out of high school for up to 8 years. Specifically, it explores the experience of young adults with disabilities with regard to

- residential independence;
- dimensions of independent lifestyle activities and family formation, including parenting and marital status; and
- indicators of financial independence, such as the use of personal financial management tools, reliance on government benefit programs, and young adults' household income.

Table 61. Modes of engagement in education, employment, or training for employment of young adults with disabilities, byhighest level of educational attainment since leaving high school

	High school non-completer	High school completer	Some post-secondary school	Post-secondary school completion
	Percent			
Engaged in at least one of the three modes of engagement	76.5 (6.48)	89.7 (2.53)	100.0	100.0
Employment only	63.4 (7.36)	60.4 (4.06)	0.0	0.0
Postsecondary education only	2.2 (2.24)	0.7 (0.69)	6.5 (2.49)	2.4 (1.89)
Employment and postsecondary education	6.2 (3.69)	14.2 (2.9)	76.2 (4.30)	59.9 (6.06)
Employment, postsecondary education, and job training	0.5 (1.08)	2.9 (1.39)	15.6 (3.66)	37.2 (5.97)
Employment and job training	4.1 (1.86)	11.0 (1.51)	0.0 (1.64)	0.0 (2.33)
Other combination of activities	0.0	0.5 (0.59)	1.6 (0.95)	0.5 (0.87)
No engagement	23.5 (6.48)	10.3 (2.53)	0.0	0.0

Note: Standard errors are in parentheses. Findings are reported for young adults with disabilities out of high school up to 8 years. NLTS2 percentages are weighted population estimates based on a sample of approximately 4,800 young adults with disabilities.

Source: U.S. Department of Education, Institute of Education Sciences, National Center for Special Education Research, National Longitudinal Transition Study-2 (NLTS2), Wave 5 parent interview and young adult interview/survey, 2009.

Table 62. Modes of engagement of young adults with disabilities by parents' household income and young adults' race/ethnicity and gender

	$25,000 or less	$25,001 to $50,000	More than $50,000	White	African American	Hispanic	Male	Female
				Percent				
Engaged in at least one of the three modes of engagement	90.0 (2.8)	94.4 (2.53)	96.9 (1.42)	95.3 (1.36)	90.0 (3.62)	92.2 (4.48)	94.1 (1.57)	93.4 (2.26)
Employment only	34.2 (4.42)	30.8 (5.07)	24.8 (3.53)	31.2 (2.97)	26.2 (5.30)	24.5 (7.19)	32.2 (3.11)	25.3 (3.96)
Postsecondary education only	4.5 (1.93)	1.6 (1.38)	2.3 (1.23)	2.3 (0.96)	2.2 (1.77)	7.3 (4.35)	2.5 (1.07)	3.7 (1.72)
Employment and postsecondary education	32.2 (4.35)	44.6 (5.46)	49.7 (4.09)	45.3 (3.19)	37.4 (5.84)	33.2 (7.87)	41.2 (3.27)	43.0 (4.51)
Employment, postsecondary education, and job training	12.0 (3.03)	10.7 (3.40)	16.6 (3.04)	11.2 (2.02)	16.3 (4.45)	23.5 (7.09)	13.5 (2.27)	14.4 (3.2)
Employment and job training	6.4 (2.28)	5.6 (2.53)	2.8 (1.35)	4.8 (1.37)	6.2 (2.91)	3.0 (2.85)	4.2 (1.33)	5.7 (2.11)
Other combination of activities	0.7 (0.78)	1.1 (1.15)	0.7 (0.68)	0.6 (0.50)	1.6 (1.51)	0.8 (1.49)	0.5 (0.47)	1.3 (1.03)
No engagement	10.0 (2.8)	5.6 (2.53)	3.1 (1.42)	4.7 (1.36)	10.0 (3.62)	7.8 (4.48)	5.9 (1.57)	6.6 (2.26)

Note: Standard errors are in parentheses. Findings are reported for young adults with disabilities out of high school up to 8 years. NLTS2 percentages are weighted population estimates based on samples that range from approximately 4,720 to 4,800 young adults with disabilities.

Source: U.S. Department of Education, Institute of Education Sciences, National Center for Special Education Research, National Longitudinal Transition Study-2 (NLTS2), Wave 5 parent interview and young adult interview/survey, 2009.

Descriptive findings are reported for young adults with disabilities as a whole and for those who differed in their primary disability category, years since leaving high school, highest level of educational attainment, and selected demographic characteristics.

Residential Independence

When youth with disabilities were in high school, less than 1 percent had lived independently (i.e., on their own or with a spouse, partner, or roommate) (Wagner et al. 2003). Within 8 years of leaving high school, however, 59 percent had lived independently at some time since high school[79] ($p < .001$; figure 36). Fewer young adults had lived semi-independently since leaving high school (4 percent, $p < .001$)—a transitional living arrangement between "leaving the parental home and establishing an independent residence" (Goldscheider and Davanzo 1986, p. 187), including in a college dormitory, military housing, or a group home.[80]

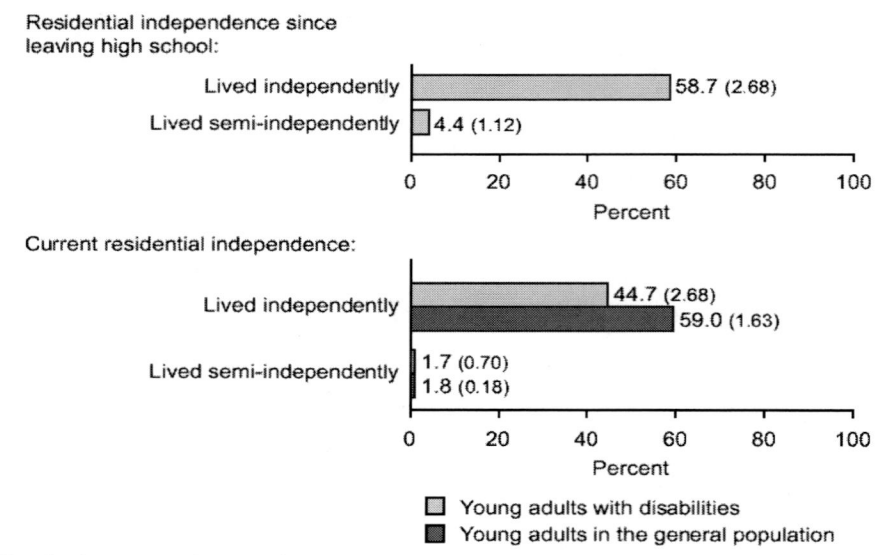

Note: Standard errors are in parentheses. Findings are reported for young adults with disabilities out of high school up to 8 years. NLTS2 percentages are weighted population estimates based on a sample of approximately 4,640 young adults with disabilities. Young adults with disabilities are considered to be living independently if they were living alone or with a spouse, partner, or roommate. Young adults with disabilities are considered to be living semi-independently if they were living in a college dormitory, military housing, or a group home.

Source: U.S. Department of Education, Institute of Education Sciences, National Center for Special Education Research, National Longitudinal Transition Study-2 (NLTS2), Waves 2, 3, 4, and 5 parent interview and youth interview/survey, 2003, 2005, 2007, and 2009; U.S. Department of Labor, Bureau of Labor Statistics, National Longitudinal Survey of Youth 1997 (NLSY97), 2005 youth survey; responses calculated for 21- to 25-year-olds.

Figure 36. Residential independence of young adults with disabilities and young adults in the general population.

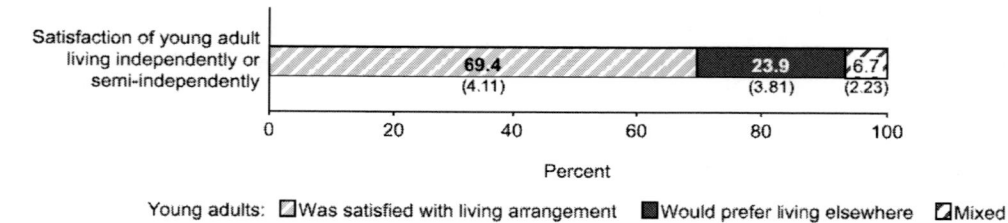

Note: Standard errors are in parentheses. Findings are reported for young adults with disabilities out of high school up to 8 years. NLTS2 percentages are weighted population estimates based on samples that range from approximately 1,470 to 3,100 young adults with disabilities across variables.

Source: U.S. Department of Education, Institute of Education Sciences, National Center for Special Education Research, National Longitudinal Transition Study-2 (NLTS2), Wave 5 parent interview and youth interview/survey, 2009.

Figure 37. Satisfaction with current living arrangement of young adults with disabilities.

At the time of the interview, 45 percent of young adults with disabilities were living independently[81] ($p < .001$). Young adults with disabilities were less likely to live independently than were their peers in the general population[82] (45 percent vs. 59 percent, $p < .001$).

Of the 59 percent of young adults with disabilities who had lived independently at some time since high school, 36 percent currently lived alone and 37 percent currently lived with a spouse, partner, or roommate.[83] Of those who had lived semi-independently, 4 percent currently lived in a college dormitory and 18 percent were in military housing.

When young adults with disabilities who were living independently or semi-independently were asked about their satisfaction with their living arrangement at the time of the interview, 69 percent reported being satisfied with their residential arrangement, 24 percent said they would prefer living elsewhere, and 7 percent were ambivalent[84] (figure 37).

Disability Differences in Residential Independence

Rates of living independently ranged from 16 percent to 65 percent of young adults across disability categories (table 63). Fifty percent or more of young adults in several disability categories who had been out of high school up to 8 years lived independently (65 percent of those with learning disabilities, 51 percent of those with speech/language and hearing impairments, 63 percent of those with emotional disturbances, 55 percent of those with visual impairments, and 58 percent of those with other health impairments). The rates of living independently were significantly higher for young adults in all six of these disability categories than the rates for young adults with orthopedic impairments (31 percent, $p < .01$ compared with young adults with hearing impairments and $p < .001$ for all other comparisons), autism (17 percent and $p < .001$ for all comparisons), multiple disabilities (16 percent, and $p < .001$ for all comparisons), or deaf-blindness (26 percent, $p < .01$ compared with young adults with speech/language and hearing impairments and $p < .001$ for all other comparisons).

Young adults in five of these six disability categories (excluding those with hearing impairments) also were more likely to live independently than young adults with mental retardation (36 percent, $p < .01$ compared with young adults with speech/language or visual impairments and $p < .001$ for all other comparisons). Young adults in the category of learning disability were more likely than those with traumatic brain injuries to live independently (43 percent, $p < .01$). In addition, young adults with mental retardation or traumatic brain injuries were more likely to live independently than young adults with autism or multiple disabilities ($p < .001$ compared with young adults with mental retardation and $p < .01$ compared with those with traumatic brain injuries).

Young adults with learning disabilities or speech/language impairments were more likely to have lived semi-independently at some time since high school than were those with mental retardation (5 percent vs. < 1 percent, $p < .01$ for both comparisons). In addition, young adults with visual (9 percent), orthopedic (7 percent), or other health impairments (6 percent) were more likely to live semi-independently than those with mental retardation ($p < .01$ for all comparisons). Reported satisfaction with living arrangements did not differ significantly by disability category.

Table 63. Residential independence and satisfaction of young adults since leaving high school, by disability category

	Learning disability	Speech/language impairment	Mental retardation	Emotional disturbance	Hearing impairment	Visual impairment	Orthopedic impairment	Other health impairment	Autism	Traumatic Brain injury	Multiple disabilities	Deaf-blindness
	Percent											
Lived independently	64.9 (4.01)	51.2 (3.91)	36.3 (3.90)	63.1 (4.42)	50.5 (5.01)	55.4 (5.56)	30.5 (4.24)	58.2 (4.24)	17.0 (3.66)	42.8 (7.55)	16.4 (4.08)	26.4 (6.56)
Lived semi-independently	5.2 (1.86)	5.0 (1.71)	0.2 (0.36)	2.8 (1.51)	6.0 (2.38)	9.0 (3.2)	6.5 (2.27)	5.8 (2.01)	3.4 (1.76)	6.2 (3.68)	1.5 (1.34)	8.2 (4.09)
Satisfaction of young adult living independently or semi-independently	68.2 (5.66)	70.9 (5.70)	76.7 (8.04)	72.5 (6.18)	72.3 (8.45)	65.2 (8.09)	80.9 (7.14)	68.1 (6.26)	45.8 (16.96)	79.7 (10.62)	68.0 (13.62)	76.2 (13.35)

Note: Standard errors are in parentheses. Findings are reported for young adults with disabilities out of high school up to 8 years. NLTS2 percentages are weighted population estimates based on a sample of approximately 4,640 young adults with disabilities for residential independence and approximately 1,470 young adults with disabilities for satisfaction of living arrangement.

Source: U.S. Department of Education, Institute of Education Sciences, National Center for Special Education Research, National Longitudinal Transition Study-2 (NLTS2), Waves 2, 3, 4, and 5 parent interview and youth interview/survey, 2003, 2005, 2007, and 2009.

**Table 64. Residential independence and satisfaction of
young adults with disabilities, by years since leaving high school**

	Less than 3 years	3 up to 5 years	5 up to 8 years
	Percent		
Lived independently	38.9(6.22)	47.8(4.79)	70.5(3.43)
Lived semi-independently	3.2(2.24)	7.7(2.56)	2.3(1.13)
Satisfaction of young adult living independently or semi-independently	79.0(9.97)	72.1(7.41)	66.8(5.40)

Note: Standard errors are in parentheses. Findings are reported for young adults with disabilities out of high school up to 8 years. NLTS2 percentages are weighted population estimates based on a sample of approximately 4,640 young adults with disabilities for residential independence and approximately 1,470 young adults with disabilities for satisfaction of living arrangement.

Source: U.S. Department of Education, Institute of Education Sciences, National Center for Special Education Research, National Longitudinal Transition Study-2 (NLTS2), Waves 2, 3, 4, and 5 parent interview and youth interview/survey, 2003, 2005, 2007, and 2009.

**Table 65. Residential independence and satisfactionof young
adults with disabilities, by highest level of educational attainment**

	High school non-completer	High school completer	Some post-secondary school	Post-secondary school completion
	Percent			
Lived independently	55.1(7.73)	50.2(4.27)	60.7(4.93)	73.8(5.46)
Lived semi-independently	0.8(1.39)	2.2(1.25)	5.7(2.34)	7.9(3.35)
Satisfaction of young adult living independently or semi-independently	63.9(15.37)	72.5(7.09)	68.2(7.12)	69.3(7.71)

Note: Standard errors are in parentheses. Findings are reported for young adults with disabilities out of high school up to 8 years. NLTS2 percentages are weighted population estimates based on a sample of approximately 4,640 young adults with disabilities for residential independence and approximately 1,470 young adult with disabilities for satisfaction of living arrangement.

Source: U.S. Department of Education, Institute of Education Sciences, National Center for Special Education Research, National Longitudinal Transition Study-2 (NLTS2), Waves 2, 3, 4, and 5 parent interview and youth interview/survey, 2003, 2005, 2007, and 2009.

Differences in Residential Arrangements by Years since Leaving High School

The percentages of young adults with disabilities who were reported to live independently ranged from 39 percent of those out of high school less than 3 years to 71 percent for those out of high school between 5 and 8 years (table 64). Young adults with disabilities out of high school the longest time (5 to 8 years) were more likely to report living independently (71 percent) than both those out of high school the shortest time (less than 3 years, 39 percent, $p < .001$) and those out of high school 3 to 5 years (48 percent, $p < .001$). Eight percent of young adults with disabilities out of school 3 to 5 years lived semi-independently, whereas 2 percent of those out of school between 5 and 8 years lived semi-independently ($p < .01$). Reported satisfaction with living arrangements did not differ significantly by years since leaving high school.

Table 66. Residential independence and satisfaction of young adults with disabilities since leaving high school, by parents' household income and young adults' race/ethnicity and gender

	$25,000 or less	$25,001 to $50,000	More than $50,000	White	African American	Hispanic	Male	Female
	Percent							
Lived independently	55.0 (4.72)	60.1 (5.47)	60.7 (4.02)	63.2 (3.13)	47.4 (6.15)	51.2 (8.45)	54.6 (3.35)	65.7 (4.40)
Lived semi-independently	1.3 (1.07)	4.1 (2.22)	7.6 (2.18)	4.7 (1.37)	5.0 (2.68)	0.5 (1.19)	5.9 (1.59)	1.7 (1.20)
Satisfaction of young adult living independently or semi-independently	72.3 (7.43)	66.1 (8.69)	68.0 (5.97)	74.1 (4.54)	57.8 (10.78)	50.1 (16.79)	70.0 (5.25)	68.5 (6.62)

Note: Standard errors are in parentheses. Findings are reported for young adults with disabilities out of high school up to 8 years. NLTS2 percentages are weighted population estimates based on a sample of approximately 4,640 young adults with disabilities for residential independence and approximately 1,470 young adults with disabilities for satisfaction of living arrangement.

Source: U.S. Department of Education, Institute of Education Sciences, National Center for Special Education Research, National Longitudinal Transition Study-2 (NLTS2), Waves 2, 3, 4, and 5 parent interview and youth interview/survey, 2003, 2005, 2007, and 2009.

Differences in Residential Arrangements by Highest Level of Educational Attainment

Young adults with disabilities who had completed postsecondary education were significantly more likely to have lived independently than were those whose highest level of education was a completed high school program (74 percent vs. 50 percent, $p < .001$; table 65). Level of satisfaction with residential arrangements and the rate of living semi-independently did not differ significantly by level of educational attainment.

Demographic Differences in Residential Independence

Rates of living independently or semi-independently and satisfaction with living situation did not differ significantly by gender, race/ethnicity, or parents' household income (table 66). For example, the rate of living independently ranged from 47 percent of African American young adults with disabilities to 63 percent of White young adults with disabilities.

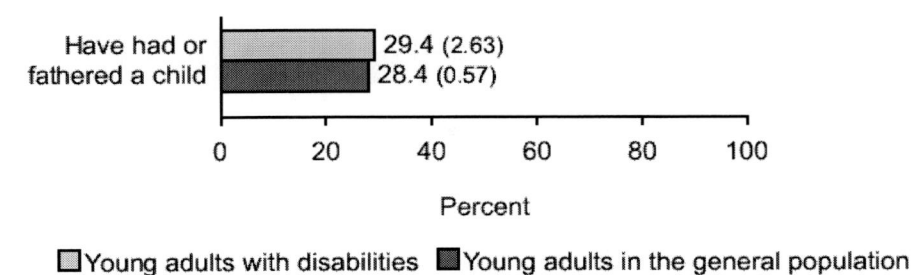

Percent

Note: Standard errors are in parentheses. Findings are reported for young adults with disabilities out of high school up to 8 years. NLTS2 percentages are weighted population estimates based on a sample of approximately 4,800 young adults with disabilities.

Source: U.S. Department of Education, Institute of Education Sciences, National Center for Special Education Research, National Longitudinal Transition Study-2 (NLTS2), Wave 5 parent interview and youth interview/survey, 2009; U.S. Department of Labor, Bureau of Labor Statistics, National Longitudinal Survey of Youth 1997 (NLSY97), 2005 youth survey, responses calculated for 21- to 25-year-olds.

Figure 38. Parenting status of young adults with disabilities and young adults in the general population.

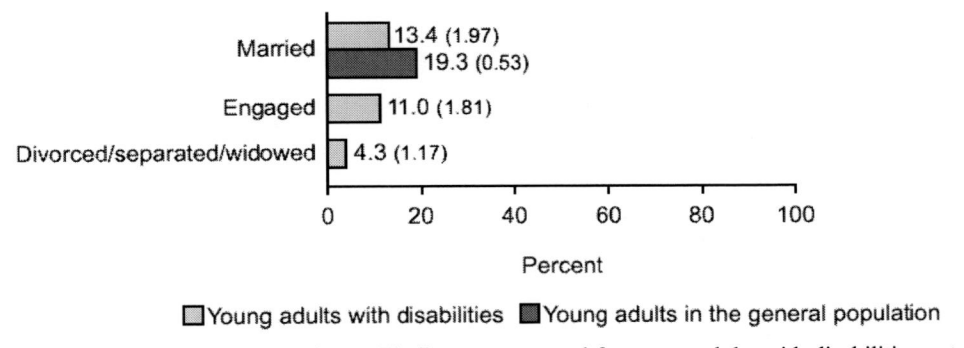

Percent

Note: Standard errors are in parentheses. Findings are reported for young adults with disabilities out of high school up to 8 years. NLTS2 percentages are weighted population estimates based on a sample of approximately 4,150 young adults with disabilities. General population comparison data not available for engagement or divorced, separated or widowed.

Source: U.S. Department of Education, Institute of Education Sciences, National Center for Special Education Research, National Longitudinal Transition Study-2 (NLTS2), Wave 5 parent interview and youth interview/survey, 2009; U.S. Department of Labor, Bureau of Labor Statistics, National Longitudinal Survey of Youth 1997 (NLSY97) 2005 youth survey, responses calculated for 21- to 25-year-olds.

Figure 39. Marital status of young adults with disabilities and young adults in the general population at the time of the interview.

Parenting and Marriage

This section focuses on several dimensions of independent lifestyle activities and family formation, including parenting and marital status.

Table 67. Parenting and marital status of young adults, by disability category

	Learning disability	Speech/ language impairment	Mental retardation	Emotional disturbance	Hearing impairment	Visual impairment	Orthopedic impairment	Other health impairment	Autism	Traumatic brain injury	Multiple disabilities	Deaf-blindness
						Percent						
Ever had or fathered a child	31.6 (4.21)	17.6 (3.11)	25.3 (3.72)	39.1 (4.85)	20.6 (4.48)	10.7 (3.57)	8.1 (2.64)	21.8 (3.81)	3.0 (1.61)	17.3 (5.94)	6.9 (2.93)	7.4 (3.95)
Were married	15.1 (3.25)	13.2 (2.77)	10.5 (2.62)	11.1 (3.14)	11.4 (3.50)	8.3 (3.20)	2.2 (1.42)	15.3 (3.34)	0.9 (0.90)	10.9 (4.89)	1.3 (1.32)	3.8 (2.86)

Note: Standard errors are in parentheses. Findings are reported for young adults with disabilities out of high school up to 8 years.NLTS2 percentages are weighted population estimates based on samples of approximately 4,800 young adults with disabilities for having or fathering a child to 4,150 young adults with disabilities for marriage status.

Source: U.S. Department of Education, Institute of Education Sciences, National Center for Special Education Research, National Longitudinal Transition Study-2 (NLTS2), Wave 5 parent interview and youth interview/survey, 2009.

Parenting Status

Twenty-nine percent of young adults with disabilities reported that they had had or had fathered a child[85] by the time they had been out of high school up to 8 years (figure 38). This proportion did not differ significantly from the 28 percent of similar-age young adults in the general population[86] who were parents. Of young adults with disabilities who had had or had fathered children, 49 percent had had one child, 27 percent had had two, and 25 percent had had three or more children.[87] Eighty-three percent of young adults with disabilities who had had or had fathered a child reported that their children currently lived with them.[88]

Marital Status

Within 8 years of leaving high school, 13 percent of young adults with disabilities reported being married[89] (figure 39). The marriage rate for young adults with disabilities was lower than that of their peers in the general population (19 percent, $p < .01$).[90] An additional 11 percent reported being engaged to be married, and 4 percent were divorced, separated, or widowed.

Disability Differences in Parenting and Marriage

Young adults' reports of ever having had or fathered a child ranged from 3 percent of young adults with autism to 39 percent of those with emotional disturbances (table 67). Young adults with emotional disturbances were more likely to have had or fathered a child than were those in 9 of the 11 other disability categories, including young adults with speech/language (18 percent), hearing (21 percent), visual (11 percent), orthopedic (8 percent), or other health impairments (22 percent); autism (3 percent); traumatic brain injuries (17 percent); multiple disabilities (7 percent); or deaf-blindness (7 percent), ($p < .01$ compared with young adults with hearing or other health impairments or traumatic brain injuries and $p < .001$ for all other comparisons).

Young adults with learning disabilities; mental retardation; or speech/language, hearing, or other health impairments were more likely than were those with autism to have had or fathered a child ($p < .001$ for all comparisons). Young adults with learning disabilities, mental retardation, or other health impairments also were more likely to have had or fathered children than were those with multiple disabilities ($p < .01$ compared with young adults with other health impairment and $p < .001$ for other comparisons), orthopedic impairments ($p < .01$ compared with young adults with other health impairments and $p < .001$ for other comparisons) or deaf-blindness ($p < .01$ compared with young adults with other health impairments and $p < .001$ for other comparisons).

In addition, young adults with learning disabilities or mental retardation were more likely to have had or fathered a child than were those with visual impairments ($p < .01$ compared with young adults with mental retardation and $p < .001$ compared with those with learning disabilities), and young adults with learning disabilities were more likely to have had or fathered a child than were those with speech/language impairments ($p < .01$).

Marriage rates ranged from 1 percent for young adults with autism to 15 percent for those with other health impairments. Young adults with other health impairments (15 percent), learning disabilities (15 percent), speech/language impairments (13 percent), mental retardation (11 percent), or emotional disturbances (11 percent) were more likely to be married at the time of the interview than were those with orthopedic impairments (2 percent,

$p < .01$ compared with those with mental retardation or emotional disturbances and $p < .001$ for all other comparisons), multiple disabilities (1 percent, $p < .01$ compared with those with mental retardation or emotional disturbances and $p < .001$ for all other comparisons), or autism (1 percent, $p < .01$ compared with those emotional disturbances and $p < .001$ for all other comparisons). Similarly, young adults with hearing impairments were more likely to be married (11 percent) than were those with multiple disabilities or autism ($p < .01$ for both comparisons). In addition, young adults with other health impairments or learning disabilities were more likely to be married than were young adults with deaf-blindness (4 percent, $p < .01$ for both comparisons).

Table 68. Parenting and marital status of young adults with disabilities, by years since leaving high school

	Less than 3 years	3 up to 5 years	5 up to 8 years
	Percent		
Ever had or fathered a child	17.8 (4.93)	23.7 (4.32)	36.3 (3.90)
Were married	3.4 (2.34)	12.6 (3.37)	16.6 (3.03)

Note: Standard errors are in parentheses. Findings are reported for young adults with disabilities out of high school up to 8 years. NLTS2 percentages are weighted population estimates based on samples that range from approximately 4,800 young adults with disabilities for having or fathering a child to 4,150 young adults with disabilities for marriage status.

Source: U.S. Department of Education, Institute of Education Sciences, National Center for Special Education Research, National Longitudinal Transition Study-2 (NLTS2), Wave 5 youth survey, 2009.

Table 69. Parenting and marital status of young adults with disabilities, by highest level of educational attainment

	High school non-completer	High school completer	Some post-secondary school	Post-secondary school completion
	Percent			
Ever had or fathered a child	47.7 (8.47)	31.4 (4.04)	28.7 (4.98)	21.7 (5.38)
Were married	7.3 (4.45)	13.9 (3.02)	10.1 (3.33)	19.2 (5.16)

Note: Standard errors are in parentheses. Findings are reported for young adults with disabilities out of high school up to 8 years. NLTS2 percentages are weighted population estimates based on samples that range from approximately 4,800 young adults with disabilities for having or fathering a child to 4,150 young adults with disabilities for marriage status.

Source: U.S. Department of Education, Institute of Education Sciences, National Center for Special Education Research, National Longitudinal Transition Study-2 (NLTS2), Wave 5 youth survey, 2009.

Table 70. Parenting and marital status of young adults with disabilities, by by parents' household income and young adults' race/ethnicity and gender

	$25,000 or less	$25,001 to $50,000	More than $50,000	White	African American	Hispanic	Male	Female
					Percent			
Ever had or fathered a child	38.0 (8.47)	37.3 (5.71)	15.4 (3.16)	25.7 (3.08)	44.7 (6.24)	26.0 (7.71)	22.0 (2.98)	41.6 (4.74)
Were married	13.5 (3.40)	16.8 (4.45)	11.6 (2.80)	16.7 (2.63)	4.4 (2.60)	10.0 (5.28)	11.4 (2.29)	16.8 (3.61)

Note: Standard errors are in parentheses. Findings are reported for young adults with disabilities out of high school up to 8 years. NLTS2 percentages are weighted population estimates based on samples that range from approximately 4,800 young adults with disabilities for having or fathering a child to 4,150 young adults with disabilities for marriage status.

Source: U.S. Department of Education, Institute of Education Sciences, National Center for Special Education Research, National Longitudinal Transition Study-2 (NLTS2), Wave 5 parent interview and youth interview/survey, 2009.

Differences in Parenting and Marriage by Years since Leaving High School

Young adults with disabilities out of high school between 5 and 8 years were more likely to report having had or fathered a child than those out of high school less than 3 years (36 percent vs. 18 percent, $p < .01$). Similarly, the marriage rate among those out of high school between 5 and 8 years was significantly higher than that for those less than 3 years out of high school (17 percent vs. 3 percent, $p < .001$; table 68).

Differences in Parenting and Marriage by Highest Level of Educational Attainment

Young adults with disabilities who had not completed high school were more than twice as likely to have had or fathered a child than young adults with disabilities who had earned a postsecondary degree or license/certificate (48 percent vs. 21 percent, $p < .01$; table 69). There were no statistically significant differences in marriage status by level of educational attainment for young adults with disabilities out of high school up to 8 years.

Demographic Differences in Parenting and Marriage

Forty-two percent of women with disabilities out of high school up to 8 years were reported to have had a child since high school, whereas 22 percent of young men with disabilities reportedly had fathered a child ($p < .001$; table 70). In addition, young adults with disabilities from families in the lowest and middle income brackets were more likely to have had or fathered a child than were those from households with incomes of more than $50,000 (38 percent and 37 percent, respectively vs. 15 percent, $p < .001$ for both comparisons). African American young adults with disabilities were more likely to have had or fathered a child than their White counterparts (45 percent vs. 26 percent, $p < .01$).

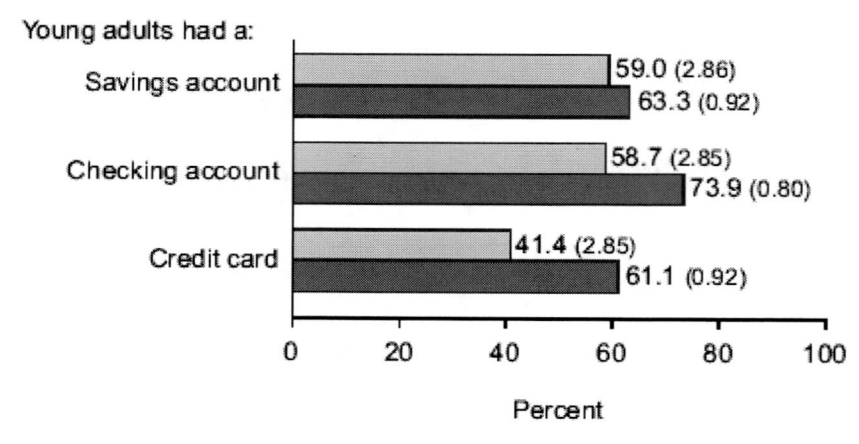

Note: Standard errors are in parentheses. Findings are reported for young adults with disabilities out of high school up to 8 years. NLTS2 percentages are weighted population estimates based on samples that range from approximately 4,100 to 4,120 young adults with disabilities.

Source: U.S. Department of Education, Institute of Education Sciences, National Center for Special Education Research, National Longitudinal Transition Study-2 (NLTS2), Wave 5 parent interview and youth interview/survey, 2009; National Institutes of Health, National Institute of Child Health and Human Development (NICHD), The National Longitudinal Study of Adolescent Health (Add Health), Wave 3, 2001–02, responses calculated for 21- to 25-year-olds.

Figure 40. Financial management tools used by young adults with disabilities and young adults in the general population at the time of the interview.

The percentage of young adults with disabilities who were reported to be married did not differ significantly by household income or gender. White young adults with disabilities were more likely to be reported to be married than were their African American peers (17 percent vs. 4 percent, $p < .001$).

Financial Independence

Being able to manage bank accounts and credit cards is a stepping-stone for young adults to achieve financial security and responsibility (Bell et al. 2006). This section focuses on whether young adults with disabilities have obtained bank accounts, credit cards, and government benefits.

By the time they had been out of high school up to 8 years, 59 percent of young adults with disabilities were reported to have a savings account[91] and a similar percentage had a checking[92] account (figure 40). A significantly smaller percentage had a credit card in their own name[93] (41 percent, $p < .001$ for both comparisons). The rate at which they had a savings account did not differ significantly between young adults with disabilities and those in the general population. In contrast, young adults in the general population[94] were more likely than those with disabilities to have a checking account (74 percent vs. 59 percent, $p < .001$) or a credit card (61 percent vs. 41 percent, $p < .001$).

Although young adults with disabilities were accessing these financial management tools, 74 percent of them were reported to have annual individual incomes (or for those living with a spouse, household incomes) of $25,000 or less.[95] More than one fifth of young adults with disabilities (22 percent) had an annual income of less than $5,000 in a year. Twenty percent had annual incomes between $25,001 and $50,000, and 6 percent had incomes of more than $50,000.

In addition to these indicators, NLTS2 tracked participation in the Temporary Assistance for Needy Families (TANF) and Food Stamps programs by young adults with disabilities. Twenty-three percent of those who were living independently or semi-independently had received Food Stamps at some time since leaving high school.[96] Similarly, 23 percent of young adults with disabilities who were living independently or semi-independently and had had or fathered a child reported that they had received money from TANF or the state welfare program at some time since high school.[97]

Disability Differences in Financial Independence

Rates of having a savings or checking account or credit card varied by disability category. Rates of having a savings account ranged from 42 percent of young adults with mental retardation to 67 percent of those with other health impairments, and rates of having a checking account ranged from 29 percent of those with mental retardation to 74 percent of those with hearing impairments. In addition, personal credit card possession ranged from 19 percent of young adults with mental retardation to 57 percent of those with visual impairments (table 71).

Young adults with mental retardation were less likely to have used these types of financial tools than were young adults in several other disability categories. Young adults with mental retardation were less likely to have a savings account (42 percent) than were those with learning disabilities (63 percent); speech/language (65 percent), hearing (65 percent), visual (66 percent), orthopedic (62 percent), or other health impairments (67 percent); or deaf-blindness (64 percent), ($p < .01$ for those with orthopedic impairments and deaf-blindness and $p < .001$ for all other comparisons). Those with mental retardation also were less likely to have a checking account (29 percent) than were those with learning disabilities (65 percent); emotional disturbances (52 percent); speech/language (66 percent), hearing (74 percent), visual (73 percent), orthopedic (63 percent), or other health impairments (64 percent); traumatic brain injuries (53 percent), or autism (45 percent), ($p < .01$ for comparisons with autism and traumatic brain injuries and $p < .001$ for all other comparisons). In addition, young adults with mental retardation were less likely to have a credit card (19 percent) than were those with learning disabilities (47percent); speech/language (52 percent), hearing (53 percent), visual (57percent), orthopedic (47percent), or other health impairments (48 percent) ($p < .001$ for all comparisons).

Young adults with autism were less likely to have a checking account (45 percent) or a credit card (27 percent) than were those with visual, hearing, speech/language, or other health impairments, or learning disabilities ($p < .01$ compared with young adults with learning disabilities and other health impairments, and $p < .001$ for all other comparisons for having had a checking account; $p < .01$ compared with young adults with learning disabilities, and $p < .001$ for all other comparisons for having had a credit card). Young adults with autism also were less likely to have a checking account or a credit card than young adults with orthopedic impairments ($p < .01$).

Table 71. Financial independence of young adults at the time of the interview, by disability category

	Learning disability	Speech/ language impairment	Mental retardation	Emotional disturbance	Hearing impairment	Visual impairment	Orthopedic impairment	Other health impairment	Autism	Traumatic brain injury	Multiple disabilities	Deaf-blindness
						Percent						
Young adult had a:												
Savings account	62.8	64.7	42.0	51.5	64.7	66.2	61.8	66.7	56.7	50.9	52.1	64.3
	(4.41)	(3.94)	(4.25)	(5.02)	(5.32)	(5.50)	(4.81)	(4.37)	(4.76)	(7.90)	(5.83)	(7.22)
Checking account	65.2	66.0	29.0	51.6	73.5	72.9	63.4	63.7	45.0	53.1	44.7	46.9
	(4.32)	(3.89)	(3.90)	(5.03)	(4.89)	(5.17)	(4.74)	(4.45)	(4.78)	(7.84)	(5.79)	(7.47)
Credit card	46.5	52.3	19.4	31.4	52.9	57.4	47.1	48.4	26.9	36.6	24.1	29.2
	(4.53)	(4.10)	(3.41)	(4.65)	(5.59)	(5.76)	(4.91)	(4.63)	(4.23)	(7.55)	(4.97)	(6.81)
Young adult's annual income:												
$25,000 or less	67.4	76.5	93.4	81.1	77.4	81.7	90.7	73.1	91.1	80.8	91.3	84.7
	(4.41)	(3.67)	(2.32)	(4.07)	(5.00)	(4.67)	(3.02)	(4.39)	(2.88)	(6.52)	(3.18)	(5.62)
$25,001 to $50,000	24.9	19.0	5.9	14.1	19.6	16.4	5.7	21.4	6.0	14.9	7.8	11.4
	(4.07)	(3.40)	(2.20)	(3.62)	(4.75)	(4.48)	(2.41)	(4.06)	(2.40)	(5.90)	(3.03)	(4.96)
More than $50,000	7.7	4.6	0.7	4.7	3.0	1.9	3.6	5.6	2.9	4.3	0.9	3.8
	(2.51)	(1.81)	(0.78)	(2.20)	(2.04)	(1.65)	(1.94)	(2.28)	(1.70)	(3.36)	(1.07)	(2.98)
Young adults living independently/semi-independently who received:												
Food Stamps	19.2	18.7	48.4	36.5	15.1	22.0	28.2	21.4	33.6	19.0	34.0	38.8
	(4.22)	(4.32)	(7.53)	(5.78)	(5.56)	(6.39)	(7.81)	(4.81)	(12.72)	(9.49)	(10.69)	(13.13)
TANF	22.8	29.1	26.5	21.8	16.4	15.9	‡	15.4	‡	‡	‡	‡
	(7.26)	(9.57)	(9.05)	(7.95)	(8.68)	(13.13)		(8.01)				

‡ Responses for items with fewer than 30 respondents are not reported.

Note: Standard errors are in parentheses. Findings are reported for young adults with disabilities out of high school up to 8 years. NLTS2 percentages are weighted population estimates based on samples of approximately 4,100 young adults with disabilities for financial management tools, 3,690 young adults with disabilities for annual income, 1,900 young adults with disabilities for Food Stamps, and 540 young adults with disabilities for TANF.

Source: U.S. Department of Education, Institute of Education Sciences, National Center for Special Education Research, National Longitudinal Transition Study-2 (NLTS2), Wave 5 parent interview and youth interview/survey, 2009.

Similarly, young adults with multiple disabilities were less likely to have a checking account (45 percent) or credit card (24 percent) than were those in several disability categories, including those with visual, hearing, speech/language, or other health impairments or learning disabilities ($p < .01$ compared with young adults with learning disabilities, speech/language impairments, and other health impairments and $p < .001$ for all other comparisons for having had a checking account; $p < .001$ for all comparisons for having had a credit card). In addition, multiple disabilities were less likely to have a credit card than were those with orthopedic impairments ($p < .001$).

Young adults with emotional disturbances or deaf-blindness were less likely to have a checking account (52 percent and 47 percent, respectively) or a credit card (31 percent and 29 percent, respectively) than were those with of hearing or visual impairments ($p < .01$ for all comparisons) and less likely to have a credit card than those with speech/language impairments ($p < .01$ for comparison with emotional disturbances and $p < .001$ for comparison with deaf-blindness). In addition, those with emotional disturbances were less likely to have a credit card than those with other health impairments ($p < .01$).

Income level also differed by disability category. Young adults with mental retardation, autism, orthopedic impairments, or multiple disabilities were more likely to be reported to have household incomes of $25,000 or less than were those with learning disabilities; speech/language or other health impairments (93 percent, 91 percent, 91 percent, 91 percent, respectively vs. 67 percent, 77 percent, 73 percent, $p < .001$ for all comparisons with the exception of $p < .01$ for comparison of youth with mental retardation with those with speech/language impairments). Young adults with mental retardation also were more likely to have household incomes of $25,000 or less than were those with emotional disturbances or hearing impairments (81 percent and 77 percent, respectively, $p < .01$ for both comparisons).

Young adults with mental retardation (48 percent) were more likely to receive Food Stamps than were young adults with learning disabilities or speech/language, hearing, visual, or other health impairments (19 percent, 19 percent, 15 percent, 22 percent, 21 percent, respectively $p < .001$ for all comparisons; with the exception of $p < .01$ for comparisons with those with hearing or other health impairments). In addition, young adults with emotional disturbances were more likely to receive Food Stamps than were those with hearing impairments (37 percent vs. 15 percent, $p < .01$).

Differences in Financial Independence by Years since Leaving High School

The annual incomes of young adults with disabilities did not differ significantly by school completion status, and none of the financial independence measures differed significantly by length of time out of high school. The percentages of out-of-high school young adults with disabilities who were reported to have a savings account ranged from 54 percent for young adults with disabilities out of high school up to 3 years to 62 percent for those out of high school from 3 to 5 years. The rate of having a checking account ranged from 53 percent for young adults out of high school up to 3 years to 60 percent for those out of high school from 5 up to 8 years, and the rate of having a credit card ranged from 39 percent for those out of high school up to 3 years to 45 percent for those out of school from 3 to 5 years (table 72).

Table 72. Financial independence of young adults with disabilities at the time of the interview, by years since leaving high school

Financial independence	Less than 3 years	3 up to 5 years	5 up to 8 years
	Percent		
Young adult had a:			
Savings account	53.5 (6.54)	62.3 (4.95)	58.1 (4.02)
Checking account	53.4 (6.52)	58.2 (5.05)	60.4 (3.97)
Credit card	38.8 (6.35)	45.1 (5.08)	39.4 (3.95)
Young adult's reported income:			
$25,000 or less	78.8 (5.72)	77.8 (4.39)	69.7 (3.95)
$25,001 to $50,000	16.8 (5.23)	16.4 (3.91)	23.7 (3.66)
More than $50,000	4.4 (2.87)	5.8 (2.47)	6.6 (2.14)
Young adults living independently/semi-independently who received:			
Food Stamps	30.3 (9.74)	15.6 (5.09)	26.7 (4.49)
TANF	9.2 (10.79)	12.0 (8.35)	28.1 (6.96)

Note: Standard errors are in parentheses. Findings are reported for young adults with disabilities out of high school up to 8 years. NLTS2 percentages are weighted population estimates based on samples of approximately 4,100 young adults with disabilities for financial management tools, 3,690 young adults with disabilities for annual income, 1,900 young adults with disabilities for Food Stamps, and 540 young adults with disabilities for TANF.

Source: U.S. Department of Education, Institute of Education Sciences, National Center for Special Education Research, National Longitudinal Transition Study-2 (NLTS2), Wave 5 parent interview and youth interview/survey, 2009.

Differences in Financial Independence by Highest Level of Educational Attainment

Young adults with disabilities who had completed postsecondary education were consistently more likely to have savings or checking accounts or credit cards than were young adults with lower levels of educational attainment (table 73). Young adults with disabilities who had completed postsecondary education were approximately three times as likely to have a savings or checking account or credit card than young adults who had not completed high school (78 percent vs. 25 percent, 86 percent vs. 25 percent, and 64 percent vs. 19 percent, respectively, $p < .001$ for all comparisons). In addition, young adults with disabilities who had completed postsecondary education were more likely than those whose highest level of education was completing high school to have a savings (49 percent, $p < .001$) or checking account (47 percent, $p < .001$) or credit card (32 percent, $p < .001$). Similarly, young adults with disabilities who had completed postsecondary education were more likely to have a checking account compared with young adults with disabilities who attended postsecondary school but had not completed their program (61 percent; $p < .001$).

Table 73. Financial independence of young adults with disabilities at the time of the interview, by highest level of educational attainment

Financial independence	High school non-completer	High school completer	Some post-Secondary school	Post-secondary school completion
	Percent			
Young adult had a:				
Savings account	24.9 (7.48)	49.4 (4.40)	65.2 (5.27)	77.9 (5.45)
Checking account	25.0 (7.40)	47.3 (4.38)	61.4 (5.36)	85.5 (4.64)
Credit card	19.3 (6.80)	31.5 (4.08)	43.0 (5.41)	63.8 (6.33)
Young adult's reported annual income:				
$25,000 or less	82.6 (6.83)	79.5 (3.77)	75.2 (5.00)	58.9 (6.64)
$25,001 to $50,000	17.1 (6.79)	16.0 (3.42)	20.4 (4.66)	28.7 (6.11)
More than $50,000	0.3 (0.99)	4.5 (1.94)	4.4 (2.37)	12.4 (4.45)
Young adults living independently/semi-independently who received:				
Food Stamps	38.7 (11.97)	23.6 (5.61)	34.8 (6.65)	8.1 (4.12)
TANF	23.3 (13.60)	16.8 (7.10)	36.0 (11.47)	10.4 (9.93)

Note: Standard errors are in parentheses. Findings are reported for young adults with disabilities out of high school up to 8 years. NLTS2 percentages are weighted population estimates based on samples of approximately 4,100 young adults with disabilities for financial management tools, 3,690 young adults with disabilities for annual income, 1,904 young adults with disabilities for Food Stamps, and 540 young adults with disabilities for TANF.

Source: U.S. Department of Education, Institute of Education Sciences, National Center for Special Education Research, National Longitudinal Transition Study-2 (NLTS2), Wave 5 parent interview and youth interview/survey, 2009.

Young adults with disabilities who attended postsecondary school were more likely to have a savings or checking account or credit card than young adults with disabilities who did not complete high school (65 percent vs. 25 percent, 61 percent vs. 25 percent, and 43 percent vs. 19 percent, respectively, $p < .01$ for credit card comparisons and $p < .001$ for savings or checking account comparisons). In addition, young adults who had completed high school were more likely than non-completers to have a savings or checking account (49 percent and 47 percent, respectively, $p < .01$ for both comparisons).

The annual incomes of young adults with disabilities also differed by level of educational attainment. Eighty percent of young adults with disabilities whose highest level of educational attainment was high school completion earned $25,000 or less annually, compared with 59 percent of young adults with disabilities who completed postsecondary education ($p < .01$). In addition, young adults who attended postsecondary education but had not completed their program were more likely to receive Food Stamps than were young adults with disabilities who completed postsecondary school (35 percent vs. 8 percent, $p < .001$).

Demographic Differences in Financial Independence

Young adults with disabilities from higher income parents' households were more likely than those from lower income households to have savings or checking accounts or credit cards (table 74). Compared with young adults with disabilities from parent households in the lowest income bracket ($25,000 or less), those in the highest income bracket (more than $50,000) were more likely to have a savings account (72 percent vs. 43 percent, $p < .001$), checking account (70 percent vs. 40 percent, $p < .001$), or credit card (50 percent vs. 26 percent, $p < .001$). In addition, young adults with disabilities from parent households in the middle income bracket ($25,001 to $50,000) were more likely than those from households in the lowest bracket ($25,000 or less) to have a savings account (63 percent vs. 43 percent, $p < .01$), checking account (66 percent vs. 40 percent, $p < .001$), or credit card (48 percent vs. 26 percent, $p < .01$). Young adults with disabilities with the lowest annual incomes ($25,000 or less) were more likely to come from parent households with incomes of $25,000 or less, than from households with incomes of $50,000 or more (87 percent vs. 68 percent, $p < .001$). In addition, young adults with disabilities from parent households with incomes of $25,000 or less were more likely to receive Food Stamps than were young adults with disabilities from households with higher incomes (more than $50,000; 41 percent vs. 11 percent, $p < .001$).

The rate of having a checking account or credit card also differed by racial/ethnic background. White young adults with disabilities were more likely to have a checking account or credit card than their African American peers (66 percent vs. 39 percent for checking account, $p < .001$; 44 percent vs. 26 percent for credit card, $p < .01$). The annual income of young adults with disabilities did not differ significantly by race/ethnicity.

Males and females did not differ significantly in their use of financial management tools or annual income. Young women with disabilities were more likely to have received Food Stamps since leaving high school than were their male counterparts (37 percent vs. 14 percent, $p < .001$).

This chapter has focused on the residential independence; parenting and marital status; and financial independence of young adults with disabilities. Chapter 6 will describe their social and community involvement.

Table 74. Financial independence of young adults with disabilities at the time of the interview, by parents' household income and young adults' race/ethnicity and gender

	$25,000 or less	$25,001 to $50,000	More than $50,000	White	African American	Hispanic	Male	Female
	Percent							
Young adult had a:								
Savings account	42.8 (4.96)	63.1 (5.81)	72.1 (3.92)	62.0 (3.45)	54.7 (6.32)	46.8 (8.91)	63.0 (3.51)	52.5 (4.82)
Checking account	39.6 (4.88)	66.4 (5.62)	70.4 (4.00)	66.0 (3.35)	39.3 (6.23)	50.3 (8.85)	59.6 (3.56)	57.3 (4.76)
Credit card	26.1 (4.36)	47.8 (5.96)	50.3 (4.38)	43.7 (3.51)	26.2 (5.63)	50.6 (8.64)	44.8 (3.59)	35.8 (4.62)
Young adult's annual income:								
$25,000 or less	86.6 (3.62)	69.2 (5.82)	68.1 (4.19)	71.2 (3.35)	82.1 (5.19)	73.9 (8.12)	72.2 (3.35)	76.4 (4.42)

	$25,000 or less	$25,001 to $50,000	More than $50,000	White	African American	Hispanic	Male	Female
	Percent							
$25,001 to $50,000	12.7 (3.54)	24.0 (5.38)	21.6 (3.70)	22.4 (3.09)	10.3 (4.12)	24.5 (7.95)	21.7 (3.08)	17.7 (3.97)
More than $50,000	0.7 (0.89)	6.8 (3.17)	10.2 (2.72)	6.4 (1.81)	7.7 (3.61)	1.6 (2.32)	6.1 (1.79)	5.9 (2.45)
Young adults living independently/semi-independently who received:								
Food Stamps	41.4 (7.15)	23.2 (6.70)	10.8 (3.44)	19.4 (3.56)	37.1 (9.23)	25.9 (12.64)	14.1 (3.39)	37.3 (6.19)
TANF	24.9 (8.63)	20.8 (9.70)	24.7 (8.28)	21.0 (6.46)	25.4 (11.30)	17.6 (15.11)	11.9 (5.64)	32.1 (8.50)

Note: Standard errors are in parentheses. Findings are reported for young adults with disabilities out of high school up to 8 years. NLTS2 percentages are weighted population estimates based on samples of approximately 4,100 young adults with disabilities for financial management tools, 3,690 young adults with disabilities for annual income, 1,904 young adults with disabilities for Food Stamps, and 540 young adults with disabilities for TANF.

Source: U.S. Department of Education, Institute of Education Sciences, National Center for Special Education Research, National Longitudinal Transition Study-2 (NLTS2), Wave 5 parent interview and youth interview/survey, 2009.

6. SOCIAL AND COMMUNITY INVOLVEMENT OF YOUNG ADULTS WITH DISABILITIES

Clearly, participating in postsecondary education and competitive employment are critical outcomes for young adults, whether or not they have identified disabilities. However, the broader notion of "social inclusion" isincreasingly being used to characterize transition success. Social inclusion "rests on the principle that democratic societies are enriched by the full inclusion of their citizens in the ebb and flow of community affairs" (Osgood et al. 2005, p. 12). Consistent with this notion, the domains encompassed in an understanding of a successful transition to young adulthood for individuals with disabilities have long included living successfully in one's community (Halpern 1985; National Center on Educational Outcomes 1993). An important aspect of whether a young adult is living successfully in the community is the "adequacy of his or her social and interpersonal network [which] is possibly the most important of all" aspects of adjustment for young adults with disabilities (Halpern 1985, p. 480). This chapter adds to an understanding of the social inclusion of young adults with disabilities who had been out of high school for up to 8 years by addressing three dimensions of their community integration:

- friendship interactions;
- participation in community/civic activities; and
- negative community involvement (i.e., involvement in violence-related activities and with the criminal justice system).

Findings for each of these dimensions of involvement are presented first for young adults with disabilities as a whole, followed by discussions of significant differences in these factors for those who differed in their primary disability category, in years since leaving high school, in highest level of educational attainment, and in selected demographic characteristics.

Friendship Interactions

Unlike adolescence, which is a time for discovering who one is and what one's role in the world is, the primary developmental task for young adults is forming intimate relationships (Erikson 1974). Considerable research has documented the importance of personal relationships as "protective factors" [98] against a variety of risk behaviors. For example, results regarding factors associated with emotional health, youth violence, substance use, and sexuality from the National Longitudinal Study on Adolescent Health (Add Health), the largest, most comprehensive survey of adolescents to date, provide "consistent evidence that perceived caring and connectedness to others is important in understanding the health of young people today" (Resnick et al. 1997, p. 830). Connectedness with friends has been found to be associated with a variety of behaviors in either a prosocial or antisocial direction, depending on the nature of the friendships (e.g., Bearman and Moody 2004; Crosnoe and Needham 2004; Fraser 1997; Rodgers and Rose 2002; Smith et al. 1995).

A majority of young adults with disabilities who had been out of high school from 1 to 8 years were reported to have active friendships[99] (figure 41); 78 percent saw friends outside of school or organized activities at least weekly, although 11 percent never saw friends informally ($p < .001$). The majority of young adults with disabilities were reported to use electronic means of communication[100] (i.e., e-mail, chat rooms, instant messaging) to some degree. Almost one-third (32 percent) reported using electronic communication at least daily, whereas 46 percent did so less than once a week.

Disability Differences in Friendship Interactions

Eighty percent or more of young adults with learning disabilities, speech/language impairments, or other health impairments who had been out of high school from 1 to 8 years were reported to see friends at least weekly (83 percent, 84 percent, and 80 percent, respectively; table 75). From 75 percent to 77 percent of young adults in the categories of emotional disturbance, hearing and visual impairment, and traumatic brain injury and 66 percent of those with orthopedic impairments also saw friends outside of school or work this often. The rates of seeing friends at least weekly were significantly higher for young adults in all eight of these disability categories than the rates for young adults with autism (48 percent; $p < .01$ compared with young adults with orthopedic impairments; $p < .001$ for all other comparisons). With the exception of young adults with orthopedic impairments, these groups also were more likely to see friends at least weekly than young adults with multiple disabilities (53 percent; $p < .01$ compared with young adults with emotional disturbances, hearing or visual impairments, or traumatic brain injuries; $p < .001$ for all other comparisons). Young adults in six of these disability categories (excluding young adults with orthopedic impairments or traumatic brain injuries), also were more likely to see friends at least weekly than those with mental retardation (58 percent; $p < .01$ compared with young adults with emotional disturbances or hearing or visual impairments; $p < .001$ for all other comparisons), and young adults with multiple disabilities ($p < .01$ compared with young adults with emotional disturbances, hearing or visual impairments; $p < .001$ for other comparisons).

Young adults with speech/language impairments also were more likely than those in the categories of orthopedic impairment and deaf/blindness to see friends at least weekly (66 percent and 62 percent, respectively; $p < .01$ for both comparisons), and young adults with learning disabilities were more likely to do so than young adults with orthopedic impairments ($p < .01$).

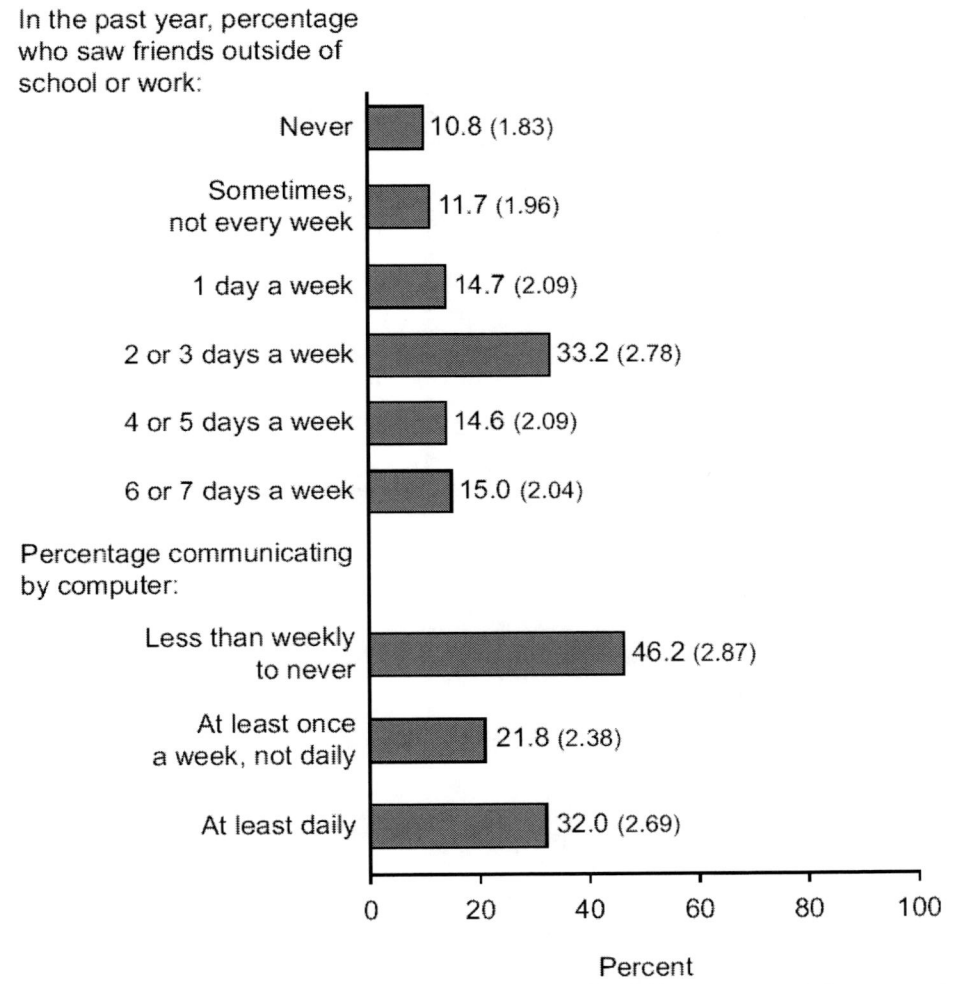

Percent

Note: Standard errors are in parentheses. Findings regarding friendships are reported for young adults with disabilities out of high school from 1 to 8 years so as not to include high school experiences; findings regarding electronic communication are for young adults with disabilities out of high school up to 8 years. NLTS2 percentages are weighted population estimates based on samples of approximately 4,000 young adults with disabilities for friendships and 4,120 for electronic communication.

Source: U.S. Department of Education, Institute of Education Sciences, National Center for Special Education Research, National Longitudinal Transition Study-2 (NLTS2), Wave 5 parent interview and youth interview/survey, 2009.

Figure 41. Friendship interactions of young adults with disabilities.

Table 75. Friendship interactions of young adults, by disability category

	Learning disability	Speech/language impairment	Mental retardation	Emotional disturbance	Hearing impairment	Visual impairment	Orthopedic impairment	Other health impairment	Autism	Traumatic brain injury	Multiple disabilities	Deaf-blindness
	Percent											
In the past year, percentage who saw friends out-side of school or work at least weekly	82.5 (3.51)	84.4 (3.03)	58.1 (4.28)	75.2 (4.42)	76.3 (4.79)	77.2 (4.96)	66.0 (4.68)	80.0 (3.75)	48.2 (4.94)	77.3 (6.69)	52.8 (5.97)	62.3 (7.31)
Percentage communicating by computer at least daily	33.8 (4.29)	43.0 (4.07)	17.0 (3.25)	31.5 (4.67)	51.4 (5.50)	49.0 (5.78)	41.5 (4.82)	34.2 (4.40)	24.5 (5.50)	32.3 (7.37)	20.9 (4.78)	41.2 (7.37)

Note: Standard errors are in parentheses. Findings regarding friendships are reported for young adults with disabilities out of high school from 1 to 8 years so as not to include high school experiences; findings regarding electronic communication are for young adults with disabilities out of high school up to 8 years. NLTS2 percentages are weighted population estimates based on samples of approximately 4,000 young adults with disabilities for friendships and 4,120 for electronic communication.

Source: U.S. Department of Education, Institute of Education Sciences, National Center for Special Education Research, National Longitudinal Transition Study-2 (NLTS2), Wave 5 parent interview and youth interview/survey, 2009.

**Table 76. Friendship interactions of young adults with disabilities,
by years since leaving high school**

	Less than 3 years	3 up to 5 years	5 up to 8 years
	Percent		
In the past year, percentage who saw friends outside of school or work at least weekly	67.4 (6.69)	74.7 (4.48)	81.7 (3.16)
Percentage communicating by computer at least daily	19.4 (5.15)	28.0 (4.55)	37.9 (3.92)

Note: Standard errors are in parentheses. Findings regarding friendships are reported for young adults with disabilities out of high school from 1 to 8 years so as not to include high school experiences; findings regarding electronic communication are for young adults with disabilities out of high school up to 8 years. NLTS2 percentages are weighted population estimates based on samples of approximately 4,000 young adults with disabilities for friendships and 4,120 for electronic communication.

Source: U.S. Department of Education, Institute of Education Sciences, National Center for Special Education Research, National Longitudinal Transition Study-2 (NLTS2), Wave 5 parent interview, and youth interview/survey, 2009.

**Table 77. Friendship interactions of young adults with disabilities,
by highest level of educational attainment**

	High school non-completer	High school completer	Some post-secondary school	Post-secondary school completion
	Percent			
In the past year, percentage who saw friends outside of school or work at least weekly	73.9 (7.65)	69.5 (4.11)	78.4 (4.61)	90.1 (4.01)
Percentage communicating by computer at least daily	19.4 (6.83)	20.7 (3.52)	32.9 (5.15)	54.8 (6.52)

Note: Standard errors are in parentheses.Findings regarding friendships are reported for young adults with disabilities out of high school from 1 to 8 years so as not to include high school experiences; findings regarding electronic communication are for young adults with disabilities out of high school up to 8 years. NLTS2 percentages are weighted population estimates based on samples of approximately 4,000 young adults with disabilities for friendships and 4,120 for electronic communication.

Source: U.S. Department of Education, Institute of Education Sciences, National Center for Special Education Research, National Longitudinal Transition Study-2 (NLTS2), Wave 5 parent interview and youth interview/survey, 2009.

The reported rate of communicating by computer at least daily was highest for young adults with hearing impairments (51 percent) and lowest for those with mental retardation (17 percent, $p < .001$). Young adults with learning disabilities; speech/language, visual, orthopedic, or other health impairments; or deaf-blindness also were more likely to have at least daily electronic communication (34 percent to 51 percent) than those with mental retardation (17 percent; $p < .001$ compared with young adults with speech/language, hearing, visual, or orthopedic impairments; $p < .01$ for other comparisons). Young adults with hearing impairments also were reported to be more likely than those with emotional disturbances, autism, or multiple disabilities to communicate by computer at least daily (51 percent vs. 32 percent, 25 percent, and 21 percent, respectively; $p < .01$ compared with young adults with emotional disturbances, $p < .001$ for other comparisons). Young adults with speech/language or visual impairments also were more likely to communicate by computer at least daily than those young adults with autism or multiple disabilities (43 percent and 49 percent vs. 25 percent and 21 percent, $p < .001$ for all comparisons), as were young adults with orthopedic impairments (42 percent vs. 24 percent and 21 percent, $p < .01$ for both comparisons).

Differences in Friendship Interactions by Years since Leaving High School

The percentages of out-of-high school young adults with disabilities who were reported to see friends at least weekly ranged from 67 percent for those out of high school from 1 up to 3 years to 82 percent for those out of high school from 5 up to 8 years (table 76). Young adults with disabilities out of high school the longest time were more likely to report communicating by computer at least daily than those out of high school the shortest time (38 percent vs. 19 percent, $p < .01$).

Table 78. Friendship interactions of young adults with disabilities, by parents' household income and young adults' race/ethnicity and gender

	$25,000 or less	$25,001 to $50,000	More than $50,000	White	African American	Hispanic	Male	Female
	Percent							
In the past year, percentage who saw friends outside of school or work at least weekly	74.5 (4.41)	75.8 (5.15)	81.7 (3.51)	79.2 (2.91)	77.9 (5.40)	69.2 (8.54)	78.2 (3.07)	76.4 (4.14)
Percentage communicating by computer at least daily	20.0 (3.93)	36.8 (5.76)	36.5 (4.21)	33.1 (3.31)	30.5 (5.93)	28.4 (7.77)	31.6 (3.36)	32.7 (4.48)

Note: Standard errors are in parentheses. Findings regarding friendships are reported for young adults with disabilities out of high school from 1 to 8 years so as not to include high school experiences; findings regarding electronic communication are for young adults with disabilities out of high school up to 8 years. NLTS2 percentages are weighted population estimates based on samples of approximately 4,000 young adults with disabilities for friendships and 4,120 for electronic communication.

Source: U.S. Department of Education, Institute of Education Sciences, National Center for Special Education Research, National Longitudinal Transition Study-2 (NLTS2), Wave 5 parent interview and youth interview/survey, 2009.

Differences in Friendship Interactions by Highest Level of Educational Attainment

The rate in which young adults with disabilities saw friends outside of organized activities at least weekly was higher among those who had completed postsecondary education than those whose highest level of education was completing high school (90 percent vs. 70 percent, $p < .001$, table 77). Young adults with disabilities who had completed postsecondary education also were more likely to communicate by computer at least daily (55 percent) than those in each of the other categories of educational attainment (19 percent to 33 percent, $p < .01$ compared with those with some postsecondary education; $p < .001$ for other comparisons).

Demographic Differences in Friendship Interactions

The percentage of out-of-high school young adults with disabilities who were reported to see friends at least weekly did not differ by parents' household income, or young adults' racial/ethnic background or gender (table 78). One difference was apparent, however, regarding the rate in which they communicated by computer. Young adults with disabilities from parent households with incomes of $50,000 or more were more likely to be reported to have electronic communication at least daily than those from households with incomes of $25,000 or less (37 percent vs. 20 percent, $p < .01$).

Community Participation

Engaging in activities in the community can provide opportunities for young adults to meet people with like interests, develop new skills, and experience the satisfaction of shared accomplishments and of making a contribution to the community. NLTS2 investigated three forms of community participation in the year preceding the Wave 5 interview/survey by young adults with disabilities:

- taking lessons or classes outside of formal school enrollment;[101]
- participating in a volunteer or community service activity;[102] and
- belonging to an organized community or extracurricular group.[103]

Because these items refer to activities in the preceding 12 months and because the focus of this report is activities of young adults with disabilities after high school, findings for these aspects of community participation are reported only for young adults who had been out of secondary school at least a year so as to avoid including secondary school experiences.[104] The full sample of young adults with disabilities is included in findings regarding whether they had driving privileges[105] and were registered to vote.[106]

Overall, young adults with disabilities who had been out of secondary school from 1 to 8 years were said to have engaged in some kind of extracurricular activity in the preceding year (figure 42), with the rates of participation in extracurricular lessons or classes, volunteer or community service activities, and community groups ranging from A driver's learner'sed by 78 percent of young adult slicense or with disabilities, and 71 percent were reported to be registered to vote. This voter registration of 72 percent rate is higher than the rate of 59 percent ($p < .001$) for young adults in the general population ages 18 through 24 (File and Crissey 2010).

Disability Differences in Community Participation

The proportions of young adults with disabilities who were reported to have taken part in at least one of the social activities investigated in NLTS2 ranged from 46 percent of those with mental retardation to 67 percent of those in the categories of visual impairment and deaf-blindness (table 79, $p < .001$ compared with young adults with license visual impairments and $p < .01$ compared with those with deaf-blindness). Young adults with visual or orthopedic impairments, deaf-blindness, or multiple disabilities were more likely than those with mental retardation to have taken lessons, volunteered in community service activities, and/or participated in community groups (67 percent, 62 percent, 67 percent, and 63 percent, respectively, vs. 46 percent, $p < .01$ for all comparisons). Young adults with visual impairments also were more likely to have participated in these types of activities than were young adults with emotional disturbances (47 percent, $p < .01$).

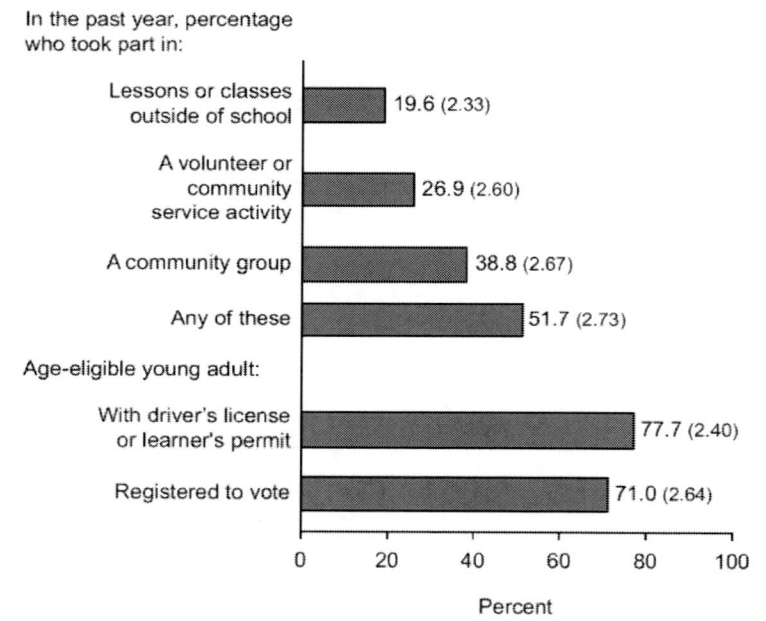

Note: Standard errors are in parentheses. Findings regarding participation in the past year are reported for young adults with disabilities out of high school from 1 to 8 years so as not to include high school experiences; other findings are for young adults with disabilities out of high school up to 8 years. NLTS2 percentages are weighted population estimates based on samples that range from approximately 4,000 to 4,790 young adults with disabilities across variables.

Source: U.S. Department of Education, Institute of Education Sciences, National Center for Special Education Research, National Longitudinal Transition Study-2 (NLTS2), Wave 5 parent interview and youth interview/survey, 2009.

Figure 42. Community participation of young adults with disabilities.

Table 79. Community participation of young adults, by disability category

	Learning disability	Speech/ language impairment	Mental retardation	Emotional disturbance	Hearing impairment	Visual impairment	Orthopedic impairment	Other health impairment	Autism	Traumatic brain injury	Multiple disabilities	Deaf- blindness
	Percent											
In the past year, percentage who took part in:												
Lessons or classes outside of school	19.7 (3.64)	24.2 (3.51)	13.2 (2.91)	20.6 (4.10)	25.3 (4.84)	37.9 (5.70)	29.3 (4.44)	20.5 (3.74)	32.2 (4.52)	12.0 (5.15)	24.2 (5.08)	38.1 (7.32)
A volunteer or community service activity	27.4 (4.08)	26.3 (3.64)	18.9 (3.38)	28.8 (4.57)	34.4 (5.29)	44.0 (5.87)	30.6 (4.52)	28.4 (4.21)	34.0 (4.61)	32.2 (7.39)	32.3 (5.57)	36.6 (7.26)
A community group (e.g., sports team, hobby club, religious group)	40.1 (4.12)	38.4 (3.82)	36.6 (3.88)	31.6 (4.31)	45.9 (4.95)	50.9 (5.64)	45.8 (4.58)	39.0 (4.19)	46.1 (4.77)	30.4 (7.08)	40.4 (5.46)	51.0 (7.20)
Any of these	52.7 (4.20)	53.4 (3.92)	46.7 (4.00)	45.9 (4.60)	59.3 (4.86)	66.9 (5.28)	62.2 (4.46)	53.1 (4.28)	61.1 (4.66)	49.0 (7.65)	63.0 (5.35)	66.9 (6.78)
Percentage who had a driver's license or learner's permit	88.2 (2.92)	81.4 (3.17)	39.2 (4.17)	73.9 (4.36)	83.5 (4.07)	23.3 (4.88)	52.8 (4.83)	83.3 (3.43)	33.4 (4.47)	74.1 (6.85)	31.2 (5.34)	26.9 (6.64)
Percentage registered to vote	70.9 (4.15)	79.3 (3.32)	62.1 (4.23)	77.0 (4.27)	71.0 (5.04)	81.2 (4.60)	77.6 (4.09)	78.2 (3.85)	55.4 (4.76)	72.5 (7.07)	55.0 (5.78)	56.9 (7.42)

Note: Standard errors are in parentheses. Findings regarding participation in the past year are reported for young adults with disabilities out of high school from 1 to 8 years so as not to include high school experiences; other findings are for young adults with disabilities out of high school up to 8 years. NLTS2 percentages are weighted population estimates based on samples that range from approximately 4,000 to 4,790 young adults with disabilities across variables.

Source: U.S. Department of Education, Institute of Education Sciences, National Center for Special Education Research, National Longitudinal Transition Study-2 (NLTS2), Wave 5 parent interview and youth interview/survey, 2009.

**Table 80. Community participation of young adults with disabilities,
by years since leaving high school**

	Less than 3 years	3 up to 5 years	5 up to 8 years
	Percent		
In the past year, percentage who took part in:			
Lessons or classes outside of school	23.6 (6.06)	20.7 (4.13)	18.1 (3.13)
A volunteer or community service activity	24.2 (6.15)	23.5 (4.30)	29.8 (3.72)
A community group (e.g., sports team, hobby club, religious group)	30.2 (6.30)	36.4 (4.58)	42.2 (3.70)
Any of these	47.8 (6.85)	50.6 (4.75)	53.3 (3.73)
Percentage who had a driver's Permit	60.1 (6.32)	76.4 (4.30)	82.9 (3.07)
Percentage registered to vote	62.1 (6.31)	69.7 (4.74)	74.2 (3.56)

Note: Standard errors are in parentheses. Findings regarding participation in the past year are reported for young adults with disabilities out of high school from 1 to 8 years so as not to include high school experiences; other findings are for young adults with disabilities out of high school up to 8 years. NLTS2 percentages are weighted population estimates based on samples that range from approximately 4,000 to 4,790 young adults with disabilities across variables.

Source: U.S. Department of Education, Institute of Education Sciences, National Center for Special Education Research, National Longitudinal Transition Study-2 (NLTS2), Wave 5 parent interview and youth interview/survey, 2009.

Young adults with visual impairments or deaf-blindness were more likely to take lessons or classes outside of formal school (38 percent for both groups) than those in several other disability categories. Young adults with visual impairments were significantly more likely than those with learning disabilities, mental retardation, other health impairments, or traumatic brain injuries to participate in lessons or classes outside school (38 percent vs. 20 percent, 13 percent, 21 percent, and 12 percent, respectively; $p < .001$ compared with young adults with mental retardation or traumatic brain injuries; $p < .01$ for other comparisons), and young adults in the deaf-blindness and autism categories were more likely than those with traumatic brain injuries to do so (38 percent and 32 percent vs. 12 percent, $p < .01$). Rates of participation in lessons or classes also were higher for young adults in the categories of orthopedic impairments and autism (29 percent and 32 percent) than for those with mental retardation (13 percent, $p < .01$ and $p < .001$, respectively).

The rate of participation in volunteer or community service activities was highest for young adults with visual impairments and lowest for those with mental retardation (44 percent and 19 percent, respectively; $p < .001$); young adults with visual impairments also exceeded those with speech/language impairments in the extent to which they volunteered or took part in community service activities (44 percent vs. 26 percent, $p < .01$). Rates of participation in community groups was highest for young adults with visual impairments (51 percent) and lowest for those with emotional disturbances (32 percent), a statistically significant difference ($p < .01$).

Approximately 80 percent or more of young adults with learning disabilities (88 percent) or speech/language, hearing, or other health impairments (81 percent, 84 percent, and 83 percent) were reported to have driving privileges, as were 74 percent of young adults with emotional disturbances or traumatic brain injuries. In contrast, between 23 percent and 53 percent of young adults with mental retardation, visual or orthopedic impairments, autism, multiple disabilities, or deaf-blindness had a driver'slicense or learner's $p < .001$ for all comparisons except $p < .01$ comparing those with emotional disturbances and those with orthopedic impairments, and the difference in rates between those with traumatic brain injuries and with orthopedic impairments was not statistically significant). Although the rate of having a driver's license or learner's permit among young adults with orthopedic impairments was much lower than that among young adults in several other categories, those with orthopedic impairments were more likely than young adults with multiple disabilities or deaf-blindness to have driving privileges (53 percent vs. 31 percent and 27 percent, $p < .001$).

Voter registration rates for young adults with disabilities ranged from 77 percent or more for young adults with speech/language, visual, orthopedic, or other health impairments or emotional disturbances to 55 percent to 62 percent for young adults with mental retardation, autism, multiple disabilities or deaf-blindness. Young adults with speech/language, visual, or orthopedic impairments were more likely to be registered to vote than were those with autism or multiple disabilities ($p < .001$ for all comparisons) or mental retardation ($p < .01$ for all comparisons). Those with other health impairments also were more likely to be registered to vote than were young adults with mental retardation ($p < .01$). In addition, young adults with emotional disturbances or orthopedic impairments had higher voter registration rates thanthose with multiple disabilities ($p < .01$) and those with visual impairments have higher rates than those with deaf-blindness ($p < .01$).

Differences in Community Participation by Years since Leaving High School

The rates of reported participation in extracurricular lessons or classes in the past year by young adults with disabilities who had been out of high school 1 to 8 years ranged from 18 percent to 24 percent (table 80). Rates of participation in volunteer or community service activities ranged from 24 percent for those out of high school less than 3 years to 30 percent for those who had left high school between 5 and 8 years earlier. Rates of participation in organized community groups ranged from 30 percent to 42 percent. From 62 percent of those who were out of school between 1 and 3 years to 74 percent of young adults with disabilities out between 5 and 8 years were reported to be registered to vote. Only rates of having a driver's license differed significantly by the number of years young adults with disabilities had been out of high school; 83 percent of those who had been out of high school between 5 and 8 years were reported to have driving privileges, compared with 60 percent who had been out of high school from 1 up to 3 years ($p < .001$).

Differences in Community Participation by Highest Level of Educational Attainment

Young adults with disabilities who had some postsecondary education and those who had earned a postsecondary degree or license/certificate were significantly more likely to have taken part in extracurricular lessons or classes (26 percent and 34 percent, respectively; table 81) than the two groups of young adults with disabilities who had completed high school and license orthose who had not (8 percent for each learner's group; $p < .01$ comparing those with some postsecondary education and high school noncompleters; $p < .001$ for other comparisons). Those who had completed a postsecondary education program also were more likely than high school completers to have participated in a volunteer or community service activity (39 percent vs. 18 percent, $p < .01$) and were more likely than high school noncompleters to have been a member of a community group (48 percent vs. 25 percent, $p < .01$). Both young adults with disabilities who had some postsecondary education and those who had completed a postsecondary program were more likely to have taken part in at least one of the modes of community participation investigated in NLTS2 than those who had not completed high school (54 percent and 66 percent vs. 29 percent, $p < .01$ and $p < .001$, respectively).

Having driving privileges was more common among young adults with disabilities who had completed a postsecondary education program than among either high school noncompleters or completers (95 percent vs. 62 percent and 66 percent, respectively; $p < .001$ for both comparisons). Young adults with disabilities who had some postsecondary education also were more likely than high school completers to have a driver's vs. 66 percent, $p < .01$). Being registered to vote also was more likely among postsecondary education attenders and completers (78 percent and 89 percent, respectively) than among high school completers and noncompleters (48 percent and 60 percent; $p < .01$ compared with postsecondary education attenders, $p < .001$ compared with postsecondary education completers).

Table 81. Community participation of young adults with disabilities, by highest level of educational attainment

	High school non-completer	High school completer	Some post-secondary school	Post-secondary school completion
	Percent			
In the past year, percentage who took part in:				
Lessons or classes outside of school	7.5 (4.45)	8.2 (2.43)	26.1 (4.90)	33.6 (6.34)
A volunteer or community service activity	18.9 (6.69)	17.9 (3.39)	30.3 (5.11)	39.1 (6.51)
A community group (e.g., sports team, hobby club, religious group)	24.0 (6.61)	35.7 (4.06)	39.4 (5.03)	48.4 (6.23)
Any of these	29.2 (6.90)	46.2 (4.21)	54.3 (5.13)	66.3 (5.89)
Percentage who had a driver's license or learner's permit	62.2 (8.16)	66.1 (4.12)	84.4 (3.96)	95.1 (2.86)
Percentage registered to vote	47.9 (8.59)	60.0 (4.33)	78.2 (4.54)	88.5 (4.24)

Note: Standard errors are in parentheses. Findings regarding participation in the past year are reported for young adults with disabilities out of high school from 1 to 8 years so as not to include high school experiences; other findings are for young adults with disabilities out of high school up to 8 years. NLTS2 percentages are weighted population estimates based on samples that range from approximately 4,000 to 4,790 young adults with disabilities across variables.

Source: U.S. Department of Education, Institute of Education Sciences, National Center for Special Education Research, National Longitudinal Transition Study-2 (NLTS2), Wave 5 parent interview and youth interview/survey, 2009.

Table 82. Community participation of young adults with disabilities, by parents' household income and young adults' race/ethnicity and gender

	$25,000 or less	$25,001 to $50,000	More than $50,000	White	African American	Hispanic	Male	Female
	Percent							
In the past year, percentage who took part in:								
Lessons or classes outside of school	13.5 (3.45)	15.2 (4.29)	26.7 (3.99)	19.5 (2.82)	19.2 (5.07)	20.0 (7.39)	20.8 (3.00)	17.8 (3.70)
A volunteer or community service activity	19.6 (3.96)	29.5 (5.45)	32.6 (4.23)	27.9 (3.19)	26.3 (5.68)	24.4 (7.89)	28.6 (3.33)	24.0 (4.14)
A community group (e.g., sports team, hobby club, religious group)	39.5 (4.64)	36.5 (5.40)	38.6 (4.05)	37.1 (3.14)	48.9 (6.17)	34.5 (8.15)	39.2 (3.31)	38.1 (4.50)
Any of these	48.5 (4.73)	49.8 (5.60)	54.3 (4.13)	51.8 (3.24)	58.5 (6.07)	43.0 (8.49)	53.9 (3.37)	47.9 (4.62)
Percentage who had a driver's license or learner's permit	67.4 (4.63)	77.3 (4.94)	86.5 (3.03)	83.9 (2.58)	62.6 (6.11)	67.3 (8.39)	79.8 (2.91)	74.1 (4.19)
Percentage registered to vote	66.7 (4.70)	61.0 (5.81)	80.9 (3.48)	69.5 (3.29)	83.9 (4.67)	61.9 (8.43)	71.5 (3.28)	70.2 (4.42)

Note: Standard errors are in parentheses. Findings regarding participation in the past year are reported for young adults with disabilities out of high school from 1 to 8 years so as not to include high school experiences; other findings are for young adults with disabilities out of high school up to 8 years. NLTS2 percentages are weighted population estimates based on samples that range from approximately 4,000 to 4,790 young adults with disabilities across variables.

Source: U.S. Department of Education, Institute of Education Sciences, National Center for Special Education Research, National Longitudinal Transition Study-2 (NLTS2), Wave 5 parent interview and youth interview/survey, 2009.

Demographic Differences in Community Participation

Only with regard to having driving privileges was there a significant difference associated with parents' household income or the racial/ethnic background of young adults with disabilitieshousehold income or the (table 82). Young adults with disabilities from families in the upper income group (more than $50,000) were significantly more likely to have driving privileges than those from households with incomes of $25,000 or less (87 percent vs. 67 percent, $p < .001$). Additionally, White young adults with disabilities were more likely than African American peers to have a driver's license or learner's permit (84 percent vs. 63 percent, $p < .01$).

There were no statistically significant differences in any form of community participation between male and female young adults with disabilities who had been out of high school from 1 to 8 years. Approximately one-fifth of both groups were reported to have taken lessons or classes outside of school; 29 percent of males and 24 percent of females had taken part in a volunteer or community service activity; 39 percent and 38 percent of young men and women with disabilities, respectively, were reported to have belonged to an organized community group; and 54 percent of males and 48 percent of females were reported to have taken part in at least one of these forms of community involvement. A driver's A driver's license or learner's permit reportedly had been earned by 80 percent of young adult males with disabilities and 74 percent of their female counterparts. Rates of voter registration were reported to be 72 percent and 70 percent for the two groups.

Negative Community Involvement

The preceding section described generally positive modes of community participation by young adults with disabilities. However, the community participation of some of them had negative repercussions, both for them and for their communities. NLTS2 has investigated two forms of negative community involvement: participation in violence-related activities and involvement with the criminal justice system.

Involvement in Violence-Related Activities

NLTS2 has investigated the reported involvement of young adults with disabilities in three forms of violence-related activities: physical fights,[107] carrying a weapon,[108] and belonging to a gang.[109] Less than one-half of 1 percent of young adults with disabilities reported belonging to a gang, so no further analysis of that form of violence-related activity is presented.

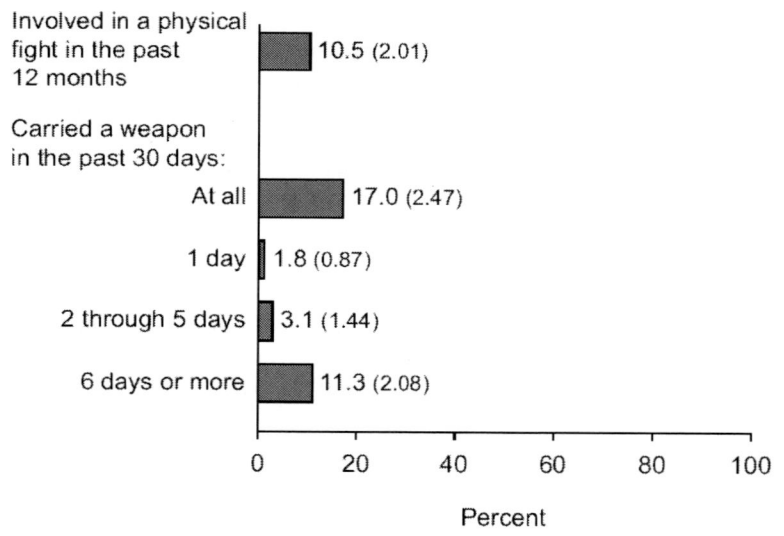

Note: Standard errors are in parentheses. Findings regarding participation in the past year are reported for young adults with disabilities out of high school from 1 to 8 years so as not to include high school experiences; other findings are for young adults with disabilities out of high school up to 8 years. NLTS2 percentages are weighted population estimates based on samples that range from approximately 3,010 and 3,090 young adults with disabilities across variables.

Source: U.S. Department of Education, Institute of Education Sciences, National Center for Special Education Research, National Longitudinal Transition Study-2 (NLTS2), Wave 5 youth interview/survey, 2009.

Figure 43. Involvementin violence-related activities of young adults with disabilities.

Table 83. Involvement in violence-related activities by young adults, by disability category

	Learning disability	Speech/language impairment	Mental retardation	Emotional disturbance	Hearing impairment	Visual impairment	Orthopedic impairment	Other health impairment	Autism	Traumatic brain injury	Multiple disabilities	Deaf-blindness
	Percent											
Reported involvement in a physical fight in the past 12 months	11.1 (3.12)	6.8 (2.28)	6.2 (2.57)	14.0 (3.86)	7.8 (3.51)	3.4 (2.31)	2.3 (1.58)	8.9 (2.91)	5.1 (3.09)	11.6 (5.59)	6.3 (4.50)	12.2 (6.22)
Reported carrying a weapon in the past 30 days	18.2 (3.81)	9.2 (2.58)	12.2 (3.44)	23.7 (4.69)	11.0 (4.07)	12.6 (4.16)	3.8 (1.99)	11.9 (3.30)	13.5 (4.69)	15.1 (6.20)	6.3 (4.32)	7.3 (4.95)

Note. Standard errors are in parentheses. Findings regarding participation in the past year are reported for young adults with disabilities out of high school from 1 to 8 years so as not to include high school experiences; other findings are for young adults with disabilities out of high school up to 8 years. NLTS2 percentages are weighted population estimates based on samples of approximately 3,010 and 3,090 young adults with disabilities for the two variables.

Source: U.S. Department of Education, Institute of Education Sciences, National Center for Special Education Research, National Longitudinal Transition Study-2 (NLTS2), Wave 5 youth interview/survey, 2009.

Because the question about fighting referred to involvement in the past 12 months and because the focus of this report is on experiences of young adults with disabilities after high school, those findings are reported only for those who had been out of high school at least 1 year so as to avoid including secondary school experiences. Findings for weapons carrying address activities in the preceding 30 days; thus, they include the full sample of young adults with disabilities who had been out of high school up to 8 years.

Eleven percent of young adults with disabilities who had been out of high school 1 to 8 years reported being in a physical fight in the 12 months preceding the Wave 5 interview/survey (figure 43); 17 percent reported carrying a weapon in the past 30 days, and 11 percent had carried a weapon for 6 or more days in that time period.

Disability Differences in Involvement in Violence Related Activities

Fourteen percent of young adults with emotional disturbances who had been out of high school 1 to 8 years reported being involved in a physical fight in the preceding year compared with 2 percent of young adults with orthopedic impairments ($p < .01$, table 83). Rates at which young adults with disabilities reported carrying a weapon in the preceding 30 days were 24 percent for those with emotional disturbances and 4 percent for those with orthopedic impairments ($p < .001$). Young adults with learning disabilities also were more likely to carry a weapon than those with orthopedic impairments (18 percent vs. 4 percent, $p < .001$). Young adults with emotional disturbances also had a significantly higher rate of carrying weapons than did those with speech/language impairments or multiple disabilities (9 percent and 6 percent, respectively; $p < .01$).

Differences in Involvement in Violence-Related Activities by Years since Leaving High School

There were no significant differences in involvement in either of the two forms of violence-related activities reported here between young adults with disabilities who differed in the years since they had left high school (table 84). From 7 percent to 12 percent across groups reported having been in a physical fight in the preceding year, and from 14 percent to 21 percent reported carrying a weapon in the preceding 30 days.

Differences in Violence Related Activities by Highest Level of Educational Attainment

There were no significant differences in involvement in either of the two forms of violence-related activities reported here between young adults with disabilities who differed in the years since they had left high school (table 85). From 8 percent to 17 percent across groups reported having been in a physical fight in the preceding year, and from 8 percent to 21 percent reported carrying a weapon in the preceding 30 days.

Table 84. Involvement in violence-related activities of young adults with disabilities, by years since leaving high school

	Less than 3 years	3 up to 5 years	5 up to 8 years
	Percent		
Reported involvement in a physical fight in the past 12 months	7.0 (4.04)	9.7 (3.43)	11.5 (2.91)
Reported carrying a weapon in the past 30 days	13.5 (5.22)	21.2 (4.73)	14.9 (3.24)

Note: Standard errors are in parentheses. Findings regarding participation in the past year are reported for young adults with disabilities out of high school from 1 to 8 years so as not to include high school experiences; other findings are for young adults with disabilities out of high school up to 8 years. NLTS2 percentages are weighted population estimates based on samples of approximately 3,010 and 3,090 young adults with disabilities for the two variables.

Source: U.S. Department of Education, Institute of Education Sciences, National Center for Special Education Research, National Longitudinal Transition Study-2 (NLTS2), Wave 5 parent interview and youth interview/survey, 2009.

Table 85. Investment in violence-related activities of young adults with disabilities, by highest level of educational attainment

	High school non-completer	High school completer	Some post-secondary school	Post-secondary school completion
	Percent			
Percentage reporting involvement in a physical fight in the past 12 months	17.0 (8.21)	12.0 (3.38)	8.4 (3.29)	9.3 (4.11)
Percentage reporting carrying a weapon in the past 30 days	7.9 (5.90)	21.1 (4.24)	16.0 (4.35)	15.0 (5.05)

Note: Standard errors are in parentheses. Findings regarding participation in the past year are reported for young adults with disabilities out of high school from 1 to 8 years so as not to include high school experiences; other findings are for young adults with disabilities out of high school up to 8 years. NLTS2 percentages are weighted population estimates based on samples of approximately 3,010 and 3,090 young adults with disabilities for the two variables.

Source: U.S. Department of Education, Institute of Education Sciences, National Center for Special Education Research, National Longitudinal Transition Study-2 (NLTS2), Wave 5 parent interview and youth interview/survey, 2009.

Demographic Differences in Involvement in Violence-Related Activities

There were no significant differences in reported involvement in violence-related activities between young adults of different racial/ethnic backgrounds or those who came from parent households with different income levels (table 86). Young men and women with disabilities also did not differ significantly in their reported participation in physical fights. However, they did differ in the proportion who reported carrying a weapon. Among young adults with disabilities who had been out of high school up to 8 years, 24 percent of males reported carrying a weapon in the past 30 days, compared with 7 percent of females ($p <$ .001).

Been stopped by police for an offense other than traffic violation: 50.2 (2.69) / 21.4 (2.62)

Been arrested: 32.3 (2.51) / 12.3 (1.98)

Spent a night in jail: 16.7 (2.01) / 8.2 (1.66)

Been on probation or parole: 17.8 (2.06) / 2.9 (2.97)

Had any of these experiences: 53.1 (2.68) / 18.7 (2.34)

Percent

☐ Involved ever   ■ Involved in past 2 years

Note: Standard errors are in parentheses. Findings regarding involvement in the past 2 years are reported for young adults with disabilities out of high school from 2 to 8 years so as not to include high school experiences; other findings are for young adults with disabilities out of high school up to 8 years NLTS2 percentages are weighted population estimates based on samples that range from approximately 2,750 to 3,820 young adults with disabilities across variables.

Source: U.S. Department of Education, Institute of Education Sciences, National Center for Special Education Research, National Longitudinal Transition Study-2 (NLTS2), Wave 5 youth interview/survey, 2009.

Figure 44. Criminal justice system involvement by young adults with disabilities.

Criminal Justice System Involvement

The actions of some young adults with disabilities violate the laws or norms of their communities to such a degree that they become involved with the criminal justice system. NLTS2 provides information on the percentages of young adults with disabilities out of high school up to 8 years who were reported ever and in the preceding 2 years to have

- been stopped by police for an offense other than a traffic violation;[110]
- been arrested;[111]
- spent a night in jail;[112]
- been on probation or parole;[113] or
- been involved with the criminal justice system in any of these ways.

At some time in their lives, 50 percent of young adults with disabilities out of high school up to 8 years were reported to have been stopped by police for an offense other than a traffic violation (figure 44), and 22 percent were reported to have been stopped by police in the preceding 2 years. Thirty-two percent of young adults with disabilities reportedly had been arrested at some time. The rate of arrest in the preceding 2 years for young adults with disabilities was 12 percent. Overall, 17 percent of young adults with disabilities had spent a night in jail, and 18 percent had been on probation or parole; 8 percent and 6 percent, respectively, had had those experiences in the preceding 2 years. Overall, 53 percent of young adults with disabilities had been involved with the criminal justice system in one or more of these ways; 19 percent had been involved in some way in the preceding 2 years.

Table 86. Involvement in violence-related activities by young adults with disabilities, by parents' household income and young adults' race/ethnicity and gender

	$25,000 or less	$25,001 to $50,000	More than $50,000	White	African American	Hispanic	Male	Female
	Percent							
Percentage reporting involvement in a physical fight in the past 12 months	13.6 (3.83)	4.0 (2.66)	12.6 (3.32)	9.3 (2.31)	10.8 (4.58)	18.8 (8.01)	13.9 (2.92)	5.4 (2.37)
Percentage reporting carrying a weapon in the past 30 days	19.5 (4.43)	17.7 (5.19)	15.4 (3.61)	21.1 (3.24)	9.9 (4.41)	6.1 (4.98)	23.9 (3.61)	6.7 (2.60)

Note. Standard errors are in parentheses. Findings regarding participation in the past year are reported for young adults with disabilities out of high school from 1 to 8 years so as not to include high school experiences; other findings are for young adults with disabilities out of high school up to 8 years. NLTS2 percentages are weighted population estimates based on samples of approximately 3,010 and 3,090 young adults with disabilities for the two variables.
Source: U.S. Department of Education, Institute of Education Sciences, National Center for Special Education Research, National Longitudinal Transition Study-2 (NLTS2), Wave 5 youth interview/survey, 2009.

Disability Differences in Criminal Justice System Involvement

There were many significant differences across disability categories in the various aspects of involvement with the criminal justice system, particularly involving young adults with emotional disturbances (table 87). Overall, 75 percent of young adults with emotional disturbances had been involved with the criminal justice system at some point in their lives, 33 percent in the preceding 2 years; 72 percent had been stopped by police for an offense other than a traffic violation, 43 percent in the past 2 years. Rates of ever being involved and being involved in the past 2 years are 61 percent and 27 percent, respectively, for arrests; 37 percent and 19 percent for overnight incarceration; and 44 percent and 15 percent for probation or parole.

Table 87. Criminal justice system involvement of young adults, by disability category

	Learning disability	Speech/ language impairment	Mental retardation	Emotional disturbance	Hearing impairment	Visual impairment	Orthopedic impairment	Other health impairment	Autism	Traumatic brain injury	Multiple disabilities	Deaf-blindness
	Percent											
Stopped by police for an offense other than a traffic violation												
Ever	51.8 (4.15)	39.7 (3.78)	33.4 (3.75)	71.8 (4.09)	36.7 (4.71)	28.6 (4.98)	21.6 (3.76)	52.7 (4.25)	23.0 (3.95)	49.2 (7.62)	25.8 (4.74)	27.2 (6.37)
In past 2 years	20.2 (4.00)	16.3 (3.24)	15.0 (3.36)	43.2 (5.64)	19.0 (4.63)	10.7 (3.85)	7.6 (2.70)	20.5 (4.03)	4.1 (2.15)	21.5 (7.37)	11.7 (4.20)	12.7 (5.32)
Arrested												
Ever	32.3 (3.87)	20.9 (3.13)	19.6 (3.15)	60.5 (4.44)	14.1 (3.40)	7.4 (2.88)	10.1 (2.75)	29.8 (3.89)	10.3 (2.85)	35.0 (7.27)	10.2 (3.27)	10.4 (4.37)
In past 2 years	11.9 (3.03)	7.3 (2.10)	6.6 (2.26)	27.1 (4.64)	3.6 (2.13)	2.1 (1.74)	4.3 (2.04)	12.5 (3.14)	0.6 (0.81)	12.2 (5.34)	3.9 (2.50)	3.7 (2.96)
Spent a night in jail												
Ever	15.6 (3.00)	8.5 (2.15)	11.0 (2.49)	37.3 (4.39)	5.4 (2.21)	5.2 (2.44)	3.8 (1.75)	17.0 (3.20)	2.1 (1.35)	16.5 (5.66)	3.8 (2.06)	3.8 (2.74)
In past 2 years	7.9 (2.53)	4.5 (1.74)	4.3 (1. 87)	18.7 (4.15)	2.3 (1.70)	1.6 (1.52)	2.3 (1.50)	7.1 (2.47)	0.2 (0.47)	8.5 (4.60)	2.7 (2.10)	2.5 (2.43)
Been on probation or parole												
Ever	15.9 (3.02)	10.0 (2.32)	9.8 (2.36)	44.2 (4.51)	6.5 (2.41)	3.7 (2.08)	6.3 (2.22)	17.9 (3.26)	3.4 (1.70)	23.3 (6.44)	6.0 (2.56)	2.8 (2.36)
In past 2 years	5.5 (2.13)	3.6 (1.56)	4.2 (1.81)	15.2 (3.74)	1.2 (1.21)	1.7 (1.56)	2.9 (1.68)	7.6 (2.52)	0.3 (0.54)	7.2 (4.22)	1.8 (1.73)	1.2 (1.73)

	Learning disability	Speech/ language impairment	Mental retardation	Emotional disturbance	Hearing impairment	Visual impairment	Orthopedic impairment	Other health impairment	Autism	Traumatic brain injury	Multiple disabilities	Deaf-blindness
	Percent											
Had any of these experiences												
Ever	54.7 (4.12)	43.0 (3.81)	37.0 (3.84)	74.7 (3.95)	39.1 (4.77)	29.2 (5.01)	22.8 (3.83)	53.5 (4.24)	26.7 (4.15)		52.4 (7.61)	27.3 (4.81)	27.2 (6.37)
In past 2 years	17.8 (3.57)	15.0 (2.98)	13.9 (3.14)	33.4 (4.80)	17.5 (4. 31)	10.3 (3.69)	7.4 (2.62)	18.4 (3.66)	3.9 (2.02)		18.3 (6.32)	11.5 (4.10)	12.0 (5.08)

Note: Standard errors are in parentheses. Findings regarding involvement in the past 2 years are reported for young adults with disabilities out of high school from 2 to 8 years so as not to include high school experiences; other findings are for young adults with disabilities out of high school up to 8 years. NLTS2 percentages are weighted population estimates based on samples that are approximately 4,800 young adults with disabilities for variables related to involvement "ever" and range from 2,750 to 3,820 young adults with disabilities for involvement in the past 2 years.

Source: U.S. Department of Education, Institute of Education Sciences, National Center for Special Education Research, National Longitudinal Transition Study-2 (NLTS2), Wave 5 youth interview/survey, 2009.

For all these forms of involvement, young adults with emotional disturbances were significantly more likely than those in most other categories to have been involved with the criminal justice system. The rate of ever having been involved in the criminal justice system at all and in each form of involvement all were significantly higher for young adults with emotional disturbances than the rates for those in all other disability categories ($p < .001$ for all comparisons except $p < .01$ for all comparisons with young adults with traumatic brain injuries). With the exception of those with traumatic brain injuries, young adults with emotional disturbances also had significantly higher rates of being stopped by police for other than a traffic violation in the past 2 years and arrested in the past 2 years than young adults in all other categories ($p < .01$ for both comparisons with young adults with other health impairments and for arrests with those with learning disabilities; $p < .001$ for all other comparisons. Young adults with emotional disturbances also exceeded those in all other categories except learning disability, other health impairment, and traumatic brain injuries in their rates of having been incarcerated over night in the past 2 years and having been on probation or parole in the past 2 years ($p < .001$ for all comparisons). Finally, with the exceptions of young adults with hearing impairments, other health impairments, or traumatic brain injuries, the rate of ever having been involved at all with the criminal justice system exceeded the rates of those in all other disability categories ($p < .01$ compared with youth with learning disabilities, speech/language impairments, or deaf-blindness; $p < .001$ for all other comparisons.

Young adults with learning disabilities, other health impairments, or traumatic brain injuries were significantly more likely than those in several disability categories to ever have been involved with the criminal justice system. Young adults in these three disability categories, learning disability, other health impairment, or traumatic brain injury, were reported to have higher rates of ever being stopped by police for other than a traffic violation (52 percent, 53 percent, and 49 percent respectively) than young adults with orthopedic impairments, autism, or multiple disabilities (22 percent, 23 percent, and 26 percent, respectively, $p < .01$ for all comparisons with those with traumatic brain injuries, $p < .001$ for all other comparisons). Young adults with learning disabilities, other health impairments, or traumatic brain injuries also were more likely ever to have been arrested (32 percent, 30 percent, 35 percent) than were those with hearing, visual, or orthopedic impairments; autism; multiple disabilities, or deaf-blindness (14 percent, 7 percent, 10 percent, 10 percent, 10 percent, and 10 percent, respectively, $p < .001$ for all comparisons with those with learning disabilities; $p < .001$ for all comparisons for those with other health impairments except $p < .01$ for their comparison with young adults with hearing impairments; $p < .01$ for all comparisons with those with traumatic brain injuries except $p < .001$ for their comparison with young adults with visual impairments).

Young adults with learning disabilities, other health impairments, or traumatic brain injuries also were more likely ever to have been on probation or parole (16 percent, 18 percent, 23 percent) than those in the categories of orthopedic impairment, autism, or multiple disabilities (6 percent, 3 percent, and 6 percent, respectively, $p < .001$ for all comparisons with those with learning disabilities or other health impairments, $p < .01$ for all comparisons with those with traumatic brain injuries). Finally, young adults with learning disabilities, other health impairments, and traumatic brain injuries also had higher rates of ever having any criminal justice system involvement (55 percent, 54 percent, and 52 percent, respectively) than those with orthopedic impairments, autism, or multiple disabilities (23 percent, 27 percent, and 27 percent, respectively, $p < .001$ for all comparisons with young adults with learning disabilities or other health impairments, $p < .001$ comparing those with traumatic brain injuries and orthopedic impairments, $p < .01$ comparing those with traumatic brain injuries and those with both autism and multiple disabilities).

Young adults with learning disabilities or other health impairments (although not those with traumatic brain injuries) were more likely than those with visual impairments or deaf-blindness ever to have been involved with the criminal justice system (29 percent and 27 percent, respectively, $p < .001$ for all comparisons). Those with other health impairments also were more likely than young adults with mental retardation to have any criminal justice system involvement (37 percent $p < .01$).

In the 2 years preceding the Wave 5 interview, young adults in the categories of learning disability (20 percent) and other health impairment (21 percent) were more likely than those with orthopedic impairments or autism to have been stopped by police for an offense other than a traffic violation (8 percent and 4 percent, respectively, $p < .01$ for comparisons with those with orthopedic impairments, $p < .001$ for comparisons with young adults with autism). Young adults with learning disabilities (12 percent) or other health impairments (13 percent) also were more likely than those with visual impairments or autism to have been arrested in the preceding 2 years (2 percent and 1 percent, $p < .01$ for comparisons with those with visual impairment, $p < .001$ for comparisons with young adults with autism). Those with learning disabilities (8 percent) or other health impairments (7 percent) also were more likely than young adults with autism to have been incarcerated over night or involved at all in the criminal justice system in the preceding 2 years (less than <1 percent, $p < .01$ for comparisons regarding overnight incarceration, $p < .001$ regarding comparisons of any involvement in the criminal justice system). Young adults with other health impairments (18 percent) were more likely than those with hearing or orthopedic impairments or multiple disabilities ever to have been on probation or parole (4 percent, 6 percent, and 6 percent, respectively, $p < .01$ for all comparisons). Those with other health impairments (8 percent) also were more likely than young adults with autism to have been on probation or parole in the preceding 2 years (less than <1 percent, $p < .01$).

Disability differences also were apparent for young adults in other disability categories. For example, young adults with learning disabilities were more likely than those with orthopedic impairments to to have been stopped by police for an offense other than a traffic violation in the past 2 years (20 percent vs. 8 percent, $p < .01$). Further, those with speech/language impairments were more likely than young adults with autism to have been stopped by the police for an offense other than a traffic violation in the past 2 years (16 percent vs. 4 percent, $p < .01$) and to have been involved with the criminal justice system ever and in the past 2 years (15 percent vs. 4 percent, $p < .01$). In addition, young adults with speech/language impairments were more likely than those with orthopedic impairments ever to have been stopped by police for an offense other than a traffic violation (40 percent vs. 22 percent, $p < .001$), and ever to have been arrested (21 percent vs. 10 percent, $p < .01$). Those with speech/language impairments also were more likely ever to have been arrested than were young adults with visual impairments (8 percent $p < .01$).

Young adults with hearing impairments (39 percent) were more likely than those with orthopedic impairments (23 percent) ever to have been involved with the criminal justice system and than those with autism to have had criminal justice system involvement in the past 2 years (18 percent vs. 4 percent, $p < .01$ for both comparisons). Those with mental retardation were more likely ever to have been incarcerated overnight or have had any criminal justice system involvement, compared with those with autism (11 percent vs. 2 percent and 37 percent vs. 27 percent $p < .01$ for both comparisons).

Differences in Criminal Justice System Involvement by Years Since Leaving High School

There were no differences in the indicators of criminal justice system involvement by years since leaving high school (table 88). The rates of ever having been involved with the criminal justice system in various ways ranged from 41 percent to 52 percent for police stops for an offense other than a traffic violation, 27 percent to 36 percent for arrest, 14 percent to 19 percent for overnight incarceration, 10 percent to 23 percent for being on probation or parole, and 48 percent to 55 percent for involvement in any one or more of these ways. Rates of involvement in the 2 years preceding the Wave 5 interview/survey ranged from were 18 percent to 22 percent for police stops and from 11 percent to 13 percent for arrest, 3 percent to 10 percent for overnight incarceration, 4 percent to 8 percent for having been on probation or parole, and 17 percent to 19 percent for any form of involvement in the past 2 years.

Differences in Criminal Justice System Involvement by Highest Level of Educational Attainment

Young adults with disabilities who had not completed high school were significantly more likely to have had involvement in the criminal justice system than those with higher levels of educational attainment (table 89). Three-fourths of young adults with disabilities who had not completed high school had at some time been stopped by police for an offense other than a traffic violation compared with 48 percent of high school completers and 42 percent of postsecondary school completers ($p < .001$). The rate of ever having been arrested was 59 percent for high school noncompleters compared with 32 percent of high school completers, 34 percent of those who had some postsecondary education, and 22 percent of those who had completed a postsecondary education program ($p < .001$ compared with postsecondary completers and $p < .01$ for other comparisons). Overnight incarceration at some time had been experienced by 40 percent of young adults with disabilities who had not completed high school, compared with 17 percent of high school completers, 16 percent of those who had some postsecondary education, and 10 percent of those who had completed a postsecondary education program ($p < .001$ compared with postsecondary completers and $p < .01$ for other comparisons). Thirty-nine percent of high school noncompleters with disabilities had at some time been on probation or parole, significantly more than the 17 percent of those with some postsecondary education and 10 percent of postsecondary completers with disabilities ($p < .001$ compared with postsecondary completers and $p < .01$ compared with those with some postsecondary education). Finally, 76 percent of young adults with disabilities who had not completed high school had had one or more of these forms of criminal justice system involvement at some time, compared with 51 percent of high school completers and 45 percent of postsecondary education program completers ($p < .01$ and $p < .001$, respectively).

**Table 88. Criminal justice system involvement of young adults with disabilities,
by years since leaving high school**

	Less than 3 years	3 up to 5 years	5 up to 8 years
	Percent		
Stopped by police for an offense other than a traffic violation			
Ever	41.1 (6.13)	50.7 (4.72)	51.9 (3.74)
In past 2 years	17.5 (6.87)	20.8 (4.34)	22.1 (3.67)
Arrested			
Ever	34.5 (5.91)	26.6 (4.17)	35.9 (3.57)
In past 2 years	10.7 (5.39)	11.4 (3.25)	13.2 (2.76)
Spent a night in jail			
Ever	16.4 (4.61)	14.0 (3.28)	18.7 (2.91)
In past 2 years	2.9 (2.97)	6.9 (2.63)	9.8 (2.44)
Been on probation or parole			
Ever	16.3 (4.60)	10.3 (2.87)	23.3 (3.15)
In past 2 years	3.5 (3.19)	3.9 (1.99)	8.4 (2.25)
Had any of these experiences			
Ever	48.3 (6.22)	51.8 (4.72)	55.0 (3.71)
In past 2 years	16.5 (6.46)	19.0 (4.01)	18.8 (3.17)

Note: Standard errors are in parentheses. Findings regarding involvement in the past 2 years are reported for young adults with disabilities out of high school from 2 to 8 years so as not to include high school experiences; other findings are for young adults with disabilities out of high school up to 8 years. NLTS2 percentages are weighted population estimates based on samples that are approximately 4,800 young adults with disabilities for variables related to involvement "ever" and range from 2,750 to 3,820 young adults with disabilities for involvement in the past 2 years.

Source: U.S. Department of Education, Institute of Education Sciences, National Center for Special Education Research, National Longitudinal Transition Study-2 (NLTS2), Wave 5 youth interview/survey, 2009.

Table 89. Criminal justice system involvement of young adults with disabilities, by highest level of educational attainment

	High school non-completer	High school completer	Some post-secondary school	Post-secondary school completion
	Percent			
Stopped by police for an offense other than a traffic violation				
Ever	74.7 (6.70)	47.7 (4.16)	53.2 (5.04)	42.4 (6.14)
In past 2 years	33.9 (9.33)	23.5 (4.19)	19.7 (4.81)	16.1 (5.18)
Arrested				
Ever	58.5 (7.59)	32.4 (3.89)	33.8 (4.77)	21.7 (5.10)
In past 2 years	23.8 (7.61)	15.4 (3.33)	9.3 (3.32)	8.0 (3.64)
Spent a night in jail				
Ever	40.0 (7.55)	17.1 (3.13)	15.6 (3.66)	10.2 (3.74)
In past 2 years	14.5 (6.51)	10.9 (2.89)	5.5 (2.62)	5.6 (3.10)
Been on probation or parole				
Ever	38.7 (7.51)	18.6 (3.23)	16.9 (3.78)	10.4 (3.78)
In past 2 years	14.4 (6.22)	8.0 (2.50)	5.4 (2.61)	2.1 (1.92)
Had any of these experiences				
Ever	76.1 (6.57)	51.0 (4.15)	56.4 (5.01)	44.6 (6.15)
In past 2 years	29.3 (8.05)	20.8 (3.74)	16.9 (4.27)	14.7 (4.73)

Note: Standard errors are in parentheses. Findings regarding involvement in the past 2 years are reported for young adults with disabilities out of high school from 2 to 8 years so as not to include high school experiences; other findings are for young adults with disabilities out of high school up to 8 years NLTS2 percentages are weighted population estimates based on samples that are approximately 4,800 young adults with disabilities for variables related to involvement "ever" and range from 2,750 to 3,820 young adults with disabilities for involvement in the past 2 years.

Source: U.S. Department of Education, Institute of Education Sciences, National Center for Special Education Research, National Longitudinal Transition Study-2 (NLTS2), Wave 5 youth interview/survey, 2009.

Table 90. Criminal justice system involvement of young adults with disabilities, by parents' household income and young adults' race/ethnicity and gender

	$25,000 or less	$25,001 to $50,000	More than $50,000	White	African American	Hispanic	Male	Female
				Percent				
Stopped by police for other than a traffic violation								
Ever	56.4 (4.63)	43.4 (5.47)	51.2 (4.10)	49.2 (3.21)	53.5 (6.07)	49.0 (8.35)	57.8 (3.30)	36.9 (4.40)
In the past 2 years	26.3 (4.83)	15.2 (4.72)	21.0 (3.98)	19.3 (3.07)	25.6 (6.24)	26.2 (8.93)	28.0 (3.69)	10.8 (3.19)
Arrested								
Ever	39.9 (4.58)	24.4 (4.72)	30.4 (3.76)	30.1 (2.94)	36.4 (5.83)	34.4 (7.94)	38.7 (3.24)	21.1 (3.72)
In the past 2 years	16.3 (3.85)	7.5 (3.24)	12.2 (3.00)	12.1 (2.39)	13.2 (4.52)	11.9 (6.17)	15.2 (2.71)	7.7 (2.67)
Spent a night in jail								
Ever	24.4 (4.02)	10.2 (3.32)	14.9 (2.91)	15.4 (2.31)	21.8 (5.00)	15.0 (5.97)	21.2 (2.72)	8.9 (2.59)
In the past 2 years	12.1 (3.45)	5.7 (2.85)	6.5 (2. 26)	8.1 (2.01)	9.3 (3.94)	6.7 (4.77)	11.6 (2.44)	2.6 (1.60)
On probation or parole								
Ever	20.1 (3.74)	17.5 (4.18)	16.5 (3.04)	18.6 (2.50)	20.3 (4.87)	7.3 (4.35)	21.4 (2.73)	11.4 (2.90)
In the past 2 years	10.0 (3.12)	3.6 (2.29)	4.9 (1.97)	6.4 (1.79)	9.4 (3.88)	1.0 (1.87)	8.2 (2.07)	3.1 (1.73)
Had any of these experiences								
Ever	61.2 (4.55)	44.5 (5.46)	51.8 (4.09)	50.5 (3.21)	60.5 (5.92)	53.5 (8.34)	61.5 (3.24)	38.3 (4.43)
In the past 2 years	23.4 (4.40)	13.2 (4.13)	18.7 (3.55)	17.4 (2.76)	21.0 (5.41)	23.5 (8.07)	24.0 (3.21)	10.0 (2.99)

Note. Standard errors are in parentheses. Findings regarding involvement in the past 2 years are reported for young adults with disabilities out of high school from 2 to 8 years so as not to include high school experiences; other findings are for young adults with disabilities out of high school up to 8 years NLTS2 percentages are weighted population estimates based on samples that range from approximately 2,750 to 3,820 young adults with disabilities.

Source: U.S. Department of Education, Institute of Education Sciences, National Center for Special Education Research, National Longitudinal Transition Study-2 (NLTS2), Wave 5 youth interview/survey, 2009.

None of the forms of criminal justice system involvement in the preceding 2 years were significantly different for young adults with disabilities who differed in their levels of educational attainment.

Demographic Differences in Criminal Justice System Involvement

There were no statistically significant differences in reported criminal justice system involvement between young adults with disabilities from parent households with different income levels or those who differed in their racial/ethnic backgrounds (table 90). However, significant gender differences were apparent. Males were more likely than females ever to have been stopped by police for an offense other than a traffic violation (58 percent vs. 37 percent, $p < .001$) and in the preceding 2 years (28 percent vs. 11 percent, $p < .001$). Males also were more likely than females ever to have been arrested (39 percent vs. 21 percent, $p < .001$). Reported rates also were more than twice for males compared with females regarding ever having spent a night in jail (21 percent vs. 9 percent, $p < .01$) and were more than four times higher for doing so in the preceding 2 years (12 percent vs. 3 percent, $p < .01$). With their higher rates of experiencing these various forms of criminal justice system involvement, males also were much more likely ever to have had any criminal justice involvement (62 percent vs. 38 percent, $p < .001$) and to have been involved in the preceding 2 years (24 percent vs. 10 percent, $p < .001$).

This chapter has focused on the social and community involvement of young adults with disabilities, and it is the final chapter in this report presenting a national picture of the post-high school experiences and outcomes of young adults with disabilities who had been out of high school for up to 8 years.

APPENDIX A. NLTS2 SAMPLING, DATA COLLECTION, AND ANALYSIS PROCEDURES

This appendix describes several aspects of the NLTS2 methodology relevant to the data reported here, including

- sampling local education agencies (LEAs) and students;
- data sources and response rates;
- weighting the data;
- estimation and use of standard errors;
- unweighted and weighted sample sizes;
- calculating statistical significance; and
- measurement and reporting issues.

NLTS2 Sample Overview

The NLTS2 sample was constructed in two stages. A stratified random sample of 3,634 LEAs was selected from the universe of approximately 12,000 LEAs that serve students receiving special education in at least one grade from 7th through 12th grades. These LEAs and 77 state-supported special schools that served primarily students with hearing and vision impairments and multiple disabilities were invited to participate in the study, with the intention of recruiting 497 LEAs and as many special schools as possible from which to select the target sample of about 12,000 students. The target LEA sample was reached; 501 LEAs and 38 special schools agreed to participate and provided rosters of students receiving special education in the designated age range, from which the student sample was selected.

The roster of all students in the NLTS2 age range who were receiving special education from each LEA[114] and special school was stratified by disability category. Students then were selected randomly from each disability category. Sampling fractions were calculated that would produce enough students in each category so that, in the final study year, findings will generalize to most categories individually with an acceptable level of precision, accounting for attrition and for response rates to the parent/youth interview. A total of 11,270 students were selected and eligible to participate in NLTS2.

Details of the LEA and student samples are provided below.

The NLTS2 LEA Sample

Defining the Universe of LEAs

The NLTS2 sample includes only LEAs that have teachers, students, administrators, and operating schools—that is, "operating LEAs." It excludes such units as supervisory unions; Bureau of Indian Affairs schools; public and private agencies (e.g., correctional facilities); LEAs from U.S. territories; and LEAs with 10 or fewer students in the NLTS2 age range, which would be unlikely to have students with disabilities.

The public school universe data file maintained by Quality Education Data (Quality Education Data 1999) was used to construct the sampling frame because it had more recent information than the alternative list maintained by the National Center for Education Statistics. Correcting for errors and duplications resulted in a master list of 12,435 LEAs that met the selection criteria. These comprised the NLTS2 LEA sampling frame.

Stratification

The NLTS2 LEA sample was stratified to increase the precision of estimates, to ensure that low-frequency types of LEAs (e.g., large urban districts) were adequately represented in the sample, to improve comparisons with the findings of other research, and to make NLTS2 responsive to concerns voiced in policy debate (e.g., differential effects of federal policies in particular regions, LEAs of different sizes). Three stratifying variables were used: region, size (student enrollment), and community wealth. The three variables generate a 64-cell grid into which the universe of LEAs was arrayed.

Region

This variable captures essential political differences, as well as subtle differences in the organization of schools, the economic conditions under which they operate, and the character of public concerns. The regional classification variable selected has been used by the Department of Commerce, the Bureau of Economic Analysis, and the National Assessment of Educational Progress (categories are Northeast, Southeast, Midwest, and West).

Size (Student Enrollment)

LEAs vary considerably in size, the most useful available measure of which is student enrollment. A host of organizational and contextual variables are associated with size that exert considerable potential influence over the operations and effects of special education and related programs. In addition, total enrollment serves as an initial proxy for the number of students receiving special education served by an LEA. The QED database provides enrollment data from which LEAs were sorted into four categories serving approximately equal numbers of students:

- very large (estimated[115] enrollment greater than 14,931 in grades 7 through 12);
- large (estimated enrollment from 4,661 to 14,930 in grades 7 through 12);
- medium (estimated enrollment from 1,622 to 4,660 in grades 7 through 12); and
- small (estimated enrollment from 11 to 1,621 in grades 7 through 12).

Community Wealth

As a measure of district wealth, the Orshansky index (the proportion of the student population living below the federal definition of poverty, Employment Policies Institute 2002) is a well-accepted measure. The distribution of Orshansky index scores was organized into four categories of LEA/community wealth, each containing approximately 25 percent of the student population in grades 7 through 12:

- high (0 percent to 13 percent Orshansky);
- medium (14 percent to 24 percent Orshansky);
- low (25 percent to 43 percent Orshansky); and
- very low (more than 43 percent Orshansky).

LEA Sample Size

On the basis of an analysis of LEAs' estimated enrollment across LEA size and estimated sampling fractions for each disability category, 497 LEAs (and as many state-sponsored special into account the rate at which LEAs were expected to refuse to participate, a sample of 3,635 LEAs was invited to participate, from which 497 participating LEAs might be recruited. A total of 501 LEAs actually provided students for the sample, 101 percent of the target number needed and 14 percent of those invited. Analyses of the region, size, and wealth of the LEA sample, both weighted and unweighted, confirmed that the weighted LEA sample closely resembled the LEA universe with respect to those variables.

In addition to matching the LEA sample to the universe of LEAs on variables used in sampling, it was important to ascertain whether the stratified random sampling approach resulted in skewed distributions on relevant variables not included in the stratification scheme. Several analyses were conducted.

First, three variables from the QED database were chosen to compare the "fit" between the first-stage sample and the population: the LEA's racial/ethnic distribution of students, the proportion who attended college, and the urban/rural status of the LEA. This analysis revealed that the sample of LEAs somewhat underrepresented African American students and college-bound students and overrepresented Hispanic students and LEAs in rural areas. Thus, in addition to accounting for stratification variables, LEA weights were calculated to achieve a distribution on the urbanicity and racial/ethnic distributions of students that matched the universe.

To determine whether the resulting weights, when applied to the participating NLTS2 LEAs, accurately represented the universe of LEAs serving the specified grade levels, data collected from the universe of LEAs by the U.S. Department of Education's Office of Civil Rights (OCR) and additional items from QED were compared for the weighted NLTS2 LEA sample and the universe. Finally, the NLTS2 participating LEAs and a sample of 1,000 LEAs that represented the universe of LEAs were surveyed to assess a variety of policies and practices known to vary among LEAs and to be relevant to secondary-school-age young adults with disabilities. Analyses of both the extant databases and the LEA survey data confirm that the weighted NLTS2 LEA sample accurately represents the universe of LEAs (Javitz and Wagner 2003).

The NLTS2 Student Sample

Determining the size of the NLTS2 student sample took into account the duration of the study, desired levels of precision, and assumptions regarding attrition and response rates. Analyses determined that approximately three students would need to be sampled for each student who would have a parent/youth interview in Wave 5 of NLTS2 data collection.

The NLTS2 sample design called for findings to be generalizable to students receiving special education as a whole and for the 12 special education disability categories currently in use and reported in this document. Standard errors were to be no more than 3.6 percent, except for the low-incidence categories of traumatic brain injury and deaf-blindness. Thus, by sampling 1,250 students per disability category (with the two exceptions noted), 402 students per category were expected to have a parent or youth interview in year 9 (Wave 5). Assuming a 50 percent sampling efficiency[116] (which is likely to be exceeded for most disability categories), 402 students would achieve a standard error of estimate of slightly less than 3.6 percent. All students with traumatic brain injury or with deaf-blindness in participating LEAs and special schools were selected. Students were disproportionately sampled by age to assure that there would be an adequate number of students who are age 24 or older at the conclusion of the study. Among the eligible students, 40.2 percent are 24 or older as of the final interview.

LEAs and special schools were contacted to obtain their agreement to participate in the study and request rosters of students receiving special education who were 13 to 16 years old on December 1, 2000, and in at least seventh grade.[117] Requests for rosters specified that they contain the names and addresses of students receiving special education under the jurisdiction of the LEA, the disability category of each student, and the students' birthdates or ages. Some LEAs would provide only identification numbers for students, along with the corresponding birthdates and disability categories. When students were sampled in these LEAs, identification numbers of selected students were provided to the LEA, along with materials to mail to their parents/guardians (without revealing their identity).

After estimating the number of students receiving special education in the NLTS2 age range, the appropriate fraction of students in each category was selected randomly from each LEA and special school. In cases in which more than one child in a family was included on a roster, only one was eligible to be selected. LEAs and special schools were notified of the students selected, and contact information for their parents/guardians was requested.[118]

Data Sources

Data are reported here for the subset of NLTS2 sample members (approximately 4,810) who were out of high school at the time of Wave 5 data collection and who have data from the Wave 5 youth telephone interview or mail survey or the Wave 5 parent telephone interview (2009). In addition to Wave 5 data, several variables that were created for this report indicate whether a young adult had had a particular experience "since high school," (e.g. postsecondary enrollment, employment status, wages, and living arrangements). Eight percent of out-of-high school respondents (approximately 390 young adults with disabilities) had left high school since the Wave 4 data collection; thus, Wave 5 data are all that are required to generate values for these variables for them. However, the remainder of the out-of-high school respondents were already out of school in Wave 2, 3, or 4. Thus, data from prior waves needed to be taken into account to generate values for variables measuring experiences "since high school."

Wave 2 through Wave 4 data collection mirrored procedures followed for Wave 5. The Wave 4 parent/youth interview/survey produced data for approximately 3,980 young adults included in the Wave 5 report. Wave 3 provided information for approximately, 2,080 report sample members and Wave 2 for approximately 850 report sample members who had been out of high school since Wave 2.

Because of the relatively small percentage of young adults enrolled in postsecondary schools at the time of the Wave 5 interview (15 percent), Wave 2 through Wave 4 data also were used to augment data for variables related to the postsecondary education experiences of young adults in the Wave 5 report who had been enrolled in these types of schools in prior waves but not in Wave 5. Including earlier wave data increased the sample size, enabling broader analyses of these variables, particularly analyses by disability category. Postsecondary experience variables included, timing and intensity of enrollment, course of study, receipt of and accommodations and supports. For young adults in the Wave 5 report who were not in postsecondary school in Wave 5, but who had been enrolled in postsecondary school in an earlier wave, data from the most recent wave in which they had been enrolled in postsecondary education were combined with the responses of postsecondary attendees in Wave 5.

Wave 1 parent telephone interview or mail survey data are the source for data about gender, race/ethnicity, and household income. High school transcripts provided data on high school completion status and completion date. Information about the primary disability category of NLTS2 sample members came from rosters of students in the NLTS2 age range receiving special education services in the 2000–01 school year under the auspices of participating school districts and state-supported special schools. Each source is described below. Although Wave 5 data have generated the majority of findings reported in this document, parent/youth telephone interviews/mail surveys are described in chronological order because procedures applied in earlier waves of data collection shape the respondent groups for Wave 5.

Wave 1 Parent Interview/Survey[119]

The NLTS2 conceptual framework suggests that a youth's nonschool experiences, such as extracurricular activities and friendships; historical information, such as age when disability was first identified; household characteristics, such as socioeconomic status; and a family's level and type of involvement in school-related areas are crucial to student outcomes. Parents/guardians are the most knowledgeable about these aspects of students' lives. They also are important sources of information on outcomes across domains. Thus, parents/guardians of NLTS2 sample members were interviewed by telephone or surveyed by mail in 2001, as part of Wave 1 data collection.

Matches of names, addresses, and telephone numbers of NLTS2 parents with existing national locator databases were conducted to maximize the completeness and accuracy of contact information and subsequent response rates. A student was required to have a working telephone number and an accurate address to be eligible for the parent interview sample.

Letters were sent to parents to notify them that their child had been selected for NLTS2 and that an interviewer would be attempting to contact them by telephone. The letter included a toll-free telephone number for parents to call to be interviewed if they did not have a telephone number where they could be reached reliably or if they wanted to make an appointment for the interview at a specific time.

Computer-assisted telephone interviewing (CATI) was used for parent interviews, which were conducted between mid-May and late September 2001. Ninety-five percent of interviews were conducted in English and 5 percent in Spanish.

All parents who could not be reached by telephone were mailed a self-administered questionnaire in a survey period that extended from September through December 2001. The questionnaire contained a subset of key items from the telephone interview. Overall, 91 percent of respondents reported that they were parents of sample members (biological, adoptive, or step), and 1 percent were foster parents. Six percent were relatives other than parents, 2 percent were nonrelative legal guardians, and less than 1 percent reported other relationships to sample members.

Wave 2 Parent/Youth Interviews

NLTS2 sample members for whom working telephone numbers and addresses were contacted for the Wave 2 parent/youth telephone interview or youth mail survey in 2003, independent of response status in Wave 1. Database matching procedures were used to maximize the eligible sample, as in Wave 1. Contact procedures alerting parents of the interviews also were similar for the two waves. The major distinction between the data collection methods in Waves 1 and 2 is that interviews in Wave 2 were sought both with parents of NLTS2 sample members and with the youth themselves if they were able to respond to questions.

The first interview contact was made with parents of eligible sample members. Those who agreed to participate were interviewed with CATI. Items in this portion of the interview, referred to as Parent Part 1, focused on topics for which the parent was considered the most appropriate respondent (e.g., services received, family expectations, and support). At the end of Parent Part 1, the respondent was asked the following:

> My next questions are about jobs (YOUTH'S NAME) may have had, schools (he/she) may have gone to, and about (his/her) feelings about (him/herself) and (his/her)

life.The questions are similar to those I've been asking you, where (he/she) will be asked toanswer using scales, like "very well," "pretty well," "not very well," or "not at all well." The interview would probably last about 20 to 30 minutes. Do you think that (YOUTH'S NAME) would be able to accurately answer these kinds of questions over the telephone?

If youth could answer questions by phone, they also were told:

> *I also have some questions about (his/her) involvement in risk behaviors, like smoking, drinking, and sexual activity. Is it all right for me to ask (YOUTH"S NAME) questions like that?*

If parents consented, interviewers asked to speak with the youth or asked for contact information to reach the youth in order to complete the youth portion of the interview, referred to as Youth Part 2.

Parents who reported that youth could not answer questions by telephone were asked:

> *Would (he/she) be able to accurately answer these kinds of questions using a written questionnaire?*

If parents indicated that youth could complete a written questionnaire, they were asked for the best address to which to send a questionnaire, and a questionnaire was sent. The questionnaire contained a subset of items from the telephone interview that were considered most important for understanding the experiences and perspectives of youth. Multiple follow-up phone or mail contacts were made to maximize the response rate for the mail survey. Data from the mail survey and Youth Part 2 of the telephone interview were merged for analysis purposes.

If parents reported that youth could not answer questions either by telephone or written questionnaire or declined to have youth asked questions related to risk behaviors, interviewers asked them to continue the interview, referred to as Parent Part 2. If youth were reported to be able to complete a telephone interview or a written questionnaire but did not do so after repeated attempts, parents were contacted again and asked to complete Parent Part 2 in lieu of Youth Part 2.

Waves 3 through 5 Parent/Youth Interviews/Surveys

As in early waves of data collection, NLTS2 sample members for whom working telephone numbers and addresses were available were contacted for the Wave 3 (2005), Wave 4 (2007) and Wave 5 (2009) parent/youth telephone interviews/surveys, independent of response status in prior waves. Database matching procedures were used to maximize the eligible sample, as previously. Contact procedures alerting respondents of the interviews also were similar across waves. Wave 3 through Wave 5 data collection was similar to Wave 2 in that both parents and youth were sought as respondents, and youth respondents who were reported to be able to respond for themselves but not by telephone were surveyed by mail. The major distinction between the data collection methods in Waves 2 and in later waves is that for youth for whom Wave 2 data had been collected, interviews were sought with parents and with youth themselves simultaneously, rather than interviewing parents first, relying on parents' reports in Wave 2 regarding youth's ability to respond for themselves by telephone or mail. For sample members who were eligible for Wave 3 through Wave 5 data collection but who could not be reached for data collection in an earlier wave, a telephone interview was sought first with parents, and the screening process for the youth interview survey that was described for Wave 2 was repeated when a parent was reached. Table A-1 reports the response rates for Wave 1 Parent telephone/mail survey and from Waves 2, 3, 4, and 5 Parent Part 1 and Parent Part 2 telephone interviews and Youth Part 2 telephone/mail surveys.

High School Transcripts

High school completion status and high school leave date were based on data from high school transcripts. High school transcripts were requested for all NLTS2 sample members. Transcript data were collected for approximately 3,990 young adults included in this report. For those for whom transcript data were not available, school completion status and leave dates were based on information from parent/youth interviews.

Table A-1. Response rates for NLTS2 Waves 1 through 5 parent/youth data collection

Respondents	Number	Percent
Wave 1		
Total sample	11,240	
Respondents		
Completed telephone interview	8,670	76.9
Completed partial telephone interview	300	2.7
Completed mail questionnaire	260	2.3
Total respondents	9,220	81.9
Total nonrespondents	2,0450	18.1
Wave 2		
Total sample	11,230	
Respondents		
Completed Parent Part 1 telephone interview	6,860	61.1
Completed Parent Part 2 telephone interview	2,960	26.4
Completed Youth Part 2 telephone interview or mail questionnaire	3,360	30.0
Total respondents with Part 1 and either Parent or Youth Part 2	6,320	56.3
Total nonrespondents (no parent or youth data)	1,350	12.0
Wave 3		
Total sample	11,220	
Respondents		
Completed Parent Part 1 telephone interview	5,190	46.2
Completed Parent Part 2 telephone interview	1,580	14.1
Completed Youth Part 2 telephone interview or mail questionnaire	3,290	29.3
Total respondents with Part 1 and either Parent or Youth Part 2	4,660	41.5
Total respondents with Parent Part 1 or Parent Part 2, or Youth Part 2	5,370	47.8
Total nonrespondents (no parent or youth data)	2,620	23.3
Wave 4		
Total sample	11,130	

Table A-1. (Continued)

Respondents	Number	Percent
Respondents		
Completed Parent Part 1 telephone interview	4,610	41.4
Completed Parent Part 2 telephone interview	1,590	14.3
Completed Youth Part 2 telephone interview or mail questionnaire	2,500	22.5
Total respondents with Part 1 and either Parent or Youth Part 2	3,790	34.1
Total respondents with Parent Part 1 or Parent Part 2, or Youth Part 2	4,900	44.0
Total nonrespondents (no parent or youth data)	3,230	29.0
Wave 5		
Total sample	11,080	
Respondents		
Completed Parent Part 1 telephone interview	4,450	41.0
Completed Parent Part 2 telephone interview	1,440	13.0
Completed Youth Part 2 telephone interview or mail questionnaire	3,190	29.0
Total respondents with Part 1 and either Parent or Youth Part 2	4,070	37
Total respondents with Parent Part 1 or Parent Part 2, or Youth Part 2	4,970	44.9
Total nonrespondents (no parent or youth data)	3,110	28.1
High School Transcripts		
Total transcript data	9,070	80.5

Note: Deceased youth were eliminated from the pool of sample members.

Combining Parent and Youth Data

As noted above, for youth who had a parent interview through which they were determined to be eligible for a youth interview/survey, interviews with both parents and youth were pursued simultaneously. Anticipating that for some young adults, only one of the two interviews would be completed, items related to key post-high school outcomes were included in both interviews. If a youth interview/survey was completed, youth's responses these items were used. If a youth interview/survey could not be completed for an eligible youth or if a youth was reported by parents not to be able to participate in an interview/survey, parents' responses were used. For the subsample of out-of-high school youth included in this report, the youth interview/survey was the source of data for post-high school outcomes for 65 percent of youth, and the parent interview was the source for 35 percent of youth.

Combining data across respondents raises the question of whether parent and youth responses would concur—i.e., would the same findings result if parents' responses were reported instead of youth's responses. Table A-2 shows the level of congruence in parents' and youth's responses to four items related to key outcomes of interest.

When both parents and youth were asked whether the youth had attended community college, belonged to an organized community group, currently worked for pay, and worked for pay in the past 2 years, their responses agreed from 73 percent to 88 percent of the time. The greatest congruence (88 percent, $K = .76$, $p < .001$) is noted regarding youth's current employment status. There was 86 percent congruence ($K = .63$, $p < .001$) evident regarding employment in the preceding 2 years; an 85 percent congruence ($K = .70$, $p < .001$) related to community college enrollment, and 73 percent agreement ($K = .44$, $p <. 001$) regarding whether youth belonged to an organized group in the community.

Table A-2. Congruence of parent and youth responses to key items

	Percentage with:			
	Congruent responses	Parent answering yes (higher), youth no (lower)	Parent answering no (lower), youth yes (higher)	Kappa (K) score[1]
Youth currently working for pay	88.1	5.4	6.5	.76
Youth worked for pay in past 2 years	86.0	5.3	8.7	.63
Youth belongs to an organized group in the community	72.9	13.9	13.2	.44
Youth ever enrolled in a community college since high school	85.0	5.5	9.5	.70

[1] Adjusted agreement score for amount of agreement that would have been expected by chance.

It is impossible to determine the cause of discrepant responses. Complete congruence would not be expected, even with both respondents answering accurately, because the parent interview and youth interview/survey could have been completed several months apart during the 7-month interview period; the status of youth could have changed in the intervening period. In such cases, both responses would be accurate at the time given. However, discrepancies also could result from one response being inaccurate, either because a respondent gave a socially desirable response (e.g., reported a youth was employed when he or she was not) or because the respondent (usually the parent) had inaccurate information (e.g., a youth no longer living with a parent had not informed the parent regarding a community group he or she had joined, leading to a negative parent response regarding group membership when a positive response was accurate). Although it is not possible to tell which of two discrepant responses is correct, it is noteworthy that with the exception of current employment, discrepant cases are more likely to result from a positive response from youth when parents responded negatively (e.g., youth reported higher wages or a higher rate of group membership than parents). Thus, for some items, youth for whom data were collected through the youth interview/survey may appear to have more positive experiences than those for whom data were collected through a parent interview because of the source of the data, in addition to or instead of actual differences in their experiences. Again, this difference does not necessarily imply inaccuracies in the data, but it does affirm the difference in the knowledge and perspectives of parents and youth.

Weighting the Wave 5 Young Adult/Parent Data

The percentages and means reported in the data tables throughout this report are estimates of the true values for the population of young adults with disabilities in the NLTS2 age range. The response for each sample member is weighted to represent the number of young adults in his or her disability category in the kind of LEA (i.e., region, size, and wealth) or special school from which he or she was selected. Responses also are weighted to represent the best estimate of the number of young adults with disabilities by racial/ethnic category (non-Hispanic White, non-Hispanic Black, non-Hispanic other, and Hispanic).

Table A-3 illustrates the concept of sample weighting and its effect on percentages or means that are calculated for young adults with disabilities as a group. In this example, 10 young adults are included in a sample, 1 from each of 10 disability groups, and each has a hypothetical value regarding whether that youth participated in organized group activities in the community (1 for yes, 0 for no). Six young adults participated in such activities. Summing the hypothetical values for the 10 youth results in an average of 60 percent for the full group. However, this would not accurately represent the national population of young adults with disabilities because many more young adults are classified as having a learning disability than as having orthopedic or other health impairments, for example. Therefore, in calculating a population estimate, weights in the example are applied that correspond to the proportion of young adults in the population who are from each disability category (actual NLTS2 weights account for disability category and several aspects of the districts from which young adults were chosen). The sample weights for this example appear in column C. Using these weights, the weighted population estimate is 88 percent. The percentages in all NLTS2 tables are similarly weighted population estimates, whereas the sample sizes are the actual numbers of cases on which the weighted estimates are based (similar to the 10 cases in column A in table A-3).

The students in LEAs and state schools with data for each survey were weighted to represent the universe of students in LEAs and state schools by using the following methodology:

- Let i=1, 2, 3, …, 64 index the NLTS2 LEA strata and i = 65 denote the state school stratum. Let $N(i)$ denote the number of LEAs or state schools in the i-th strata. Let $M(i)$ denote the prespecified sample size of LEAs or state schools in the i-th strata. Within each stratum, all $N(i)$ LEAs and state schools were assigned a uniformly distributed random number and were sorted on the basis of that random number in increasing order. The first $M(i)$ of those LEAs or state schools were selected for the sample in the i-th stratum; consequently the LEA/state school sample in each stratum was drawn with equal probabilities and without replacement. Let $P(i, j)$ denote the probability of selection of the j-th LEA or state school within the i-th stratum. Then $P(i, j) = M(i) / N(i)$. The j-th selected LEA or state school in the i-th stratum was assigned an initial weight of $W(i, j) = 1/P(i, j) = N(i) / M(i)$.

- Let $Q(i)$ denote the number of respondent LEAs or state schools in the i-th stratum. Let $R(i)$ denote the response rate in the i-th stratum. Then $R(i) = Q(i)/M(i)$. The adjusted weight for the j-th selected LEA or state school in the i-th stratum, denoted $W*(i, j)$, was set to 0 if the j-th selected LEA or state school in the i-th stratum was a nonrespondent and to $W*(i, j) = W(i, j)/R(i) = N(i)/Q(i)$ if the j-th selected LEA or state school was a respondent. Note that all LEAs in the i-th stratum have the same adjusted weight.

- When rosters were obtained from each respondent LEA or state school, they were separated by disability category and student age groups (13 to 15.99, and 16 to

17.99). Samples were independently selected and weighted for each disability and age category, using the same methodology (with the exception of deaf-blind as discussed later). Without loss of generality, therefore, discussion is restricted to the selection and weighting of students with learning disabilities in the older age category.

- Let (i, j, k) denote the k-th older students with learning disabilities in the j-th LEA/state school in the i-th stratum. Let $Ns(i, j)$ denote the number of older students with learning disabilities in the (i, j)-th LEA/state school. Let $V(i)$ denote the predetermined sampling fraction for older students with learning disabilities in the i-th stratum. A uniformly generated random number, denoted $U(i, j, k)$ was generated for each older student with learning disabilities in the (i, j)-th LEA/state school roster. The (i, j, k)-th older student with learning disabilities was selected for the study without replacement if $U(i, j, k) < V(i)$. Let $Ws(i, j, k)$ denote the initial weight for the (i, j, k)-th older student with learning disabilities. Then $Ws(i, j, k) = W^*(i, j) / V(i)$. Since $W^*(i, j)$ is a constant for all LEA/state schools in the i-th stratum, note that $Ws(i, j, k)$ is constant for all older students with learning disabilities in the i-th stratum.

- Let $Ms(i, j)$ be the number of sampled older students with learning disabilities in the (i, j)-th LEA/state school and let $Ms(i)$ be the total number of selected older students with learning disabilities in the i-th stratum. Let $Qs(i, j)$ be the number of responding older students with learning disabilities in the (i, j)-th LEA/state school and let $Qs(i)$ be the total number of responding older LD students in the i-th stratum. Let $Rs(i)$ denote the older students with learning disabilities response rate in the i-th stratum among selected students. Then $Rs(i) = Qs(i) / Ms(i)$. The adjusted weight for the (i, j, k)-th older student with learning disabilities, denoted $Ws^*(i, j, k)$ is defined to be 0 if the student is a non-respondent and $Ws^*(i, j, k) = Ws(i, j, k) / R(i)$ otherwise. Note that $Ws^*(i, j, k)$ is a constant for all responding older students with learning disabilities in the i-th stratum.

- Data from Department of Education reports, the Common Core, the rosters of the respondent LEAs and state schools, and the student weights were combined to estimate the following: (1) total number of students in each disability category by age category (for example, the total number of older students with learning disabilities in the universe), (2) the total number of students by disability and race/ethnicity (coded non-hispanic white, non-Hispanic Black, Hispanic, Asian/Pacific Islander, and American Indian/Alaska native), and (3) the total number of students by disability and LEA/state school strata. Deming's raking algorithm was used to adjust the $Ws^*(i, j, k)$ weights so that the sum of the adjusted weights in these subgroups (for example, older students with learning disabilities in the universe) approximated their known or estimated national totals.

- Analysis of NLTS2 data after the first wave revealed that respondents to the later waves differed from the Wave 1 respondents with respect to the distribution of their household incomes, whether the parents had volunteered at the school, and whether the student had been held back one or more grade levels. The Wave 1 weights and parental survey responses were used to estimate, by disability and age category, the national number of students in each household income category, each parental volunteering category, and each student advancement category (i.e., whether the student had ever been held back). To reduce nonresponse bias in these later waves, the Deming raking algorithm was extended to modify weights so that their totals also approximate these estimated national totals.

- Recruitment was attempted with all students with deaf-blindness who appeared on the rosters of the responding LEAs and state schools and these students were subject to the same weighting approach as described above (excluding the Deming raking). A few students in the hearing impairment disability category and in the visually impaired disability category with sufficiently severe hearing and vision problems to be classified as deaf-blind were identified. These students were retained in their original disability/age categories for purposes of developing weights for students in those categories, but were classified as deaf-blind for purposes of analysis. The sum of the weights for all students with deaf-blindness (i.e., those originally found in the deaf-blind category and those who were later reclassified as deaf-blind) was equal to 3,196. Due to the small number of students who qualified for the deaf-blind category, SRI and the Department of Education agreed that the weights for all of these students would be set to a constant, such that the sum of those weights was equal to 3,196.

Estimating Standard Errors

Each estimate reported in the data tables is accompanied by a standard error. A standard error acknowledges that any population estimate that is calculated from a sample will only approximate the true value for the population. The true population value will fall within the range demarcated by the estimate, plus or minus 1.96 times the standard error, 95 percent of the time. For example, if the estimate for young adult's 23.5 percent, with a standard error of 2.67, one can be 95 percent confident that the true current postsecondary enrollment rate for the population is between 18.3 percent and 28.7 percent.

Because the NLTS2 sample is both stratified and clustered, calculating standard errors by formula is not straightforward. Standard errors for means and proportions can, however, be estimated by using pseudoreplication, a procedure that is widely used by the U.S. Census Bureau and other federal agencies involved in fielding complex surveys. To that end, a set of weights was developed for each of 32 balanced half-replicate subsamples. Each half-replicate involved selecting half of the total set of LEAs that provided contact information, using a partial factorial balanced design (resulting in about half of the LEAs being selected within each stratum) and then weighting that half to represent the entire universe. The half-replicates could be used to estimate the variance of a sample mean by (1) calculating the mean of the variable of interest on the full sample and each half-sample, using the appropriate weights; (2) calculating the squares of the deviations of the half-sample estimate from the full-sample estimate; and (3) adding the squared deviations and dividing by (n-1), where n is the number of half-replicates. Since there were 32 replicates, the variance estimates would have 31 degrees of freedom.

Because the method of using replicate weights is computationally intensive and was not easily implemented in the Statistical Analysis System (SAS) during the first years of NLTS2, we sought a simpler formula-based procedure. We selected a variety of categorical and continuous Wave 1 variables and calculated their standard errors using replicate weights. We compared those standard error estimates with those obtained using a formula appropriate for an independent and identically distributed sample with unequal weights. (Under the latter assumptions, the effective sample size can be approximated as

$$N_{eff} = N\left(\frac{E^2[W]}{E^2[W] + V[W]}\right)$$

where N_{eff} is the effective sample size, $E^2[W]$ is the square of the arithmetic average of the weights, and $V[W]$ is the variance of the weights. For a variable X, the standard error of estimate can typically be approximated by $\sqrt{V[X]/N_{eff}}$, where $V[X]$ is the weighted variance of X.) As expected, due to the complex sampling design in NLTS2, the use of the formula given above was not fully adequate. However, we found that if we multiplied these formula-based standard errors by 1.25, this yielded estimates that slightly exceeded the variance estimates via pseudo-replication for approximately 90 percent of the categorical and 90 percent of the continuous variables that were examined. Therefore we modified our formula by including a design factor of 1.25, which accounts for the stratified and clustered nature of the sample.

Table A-3. Example of weighted percentage calculation

Disability category	A Number in sample	B Participated in group activities	C Example weight for category	D Weighted value for category
Total	10	6	10.0	8.8
Learning disability	1	1	5.0	5.0
Speech/language impairment	1	1	1.9	1.9
Mental retardation	1	1	1.0	1.0
Emotional disturbance	1	0	.8	0
Hearing impairment	1	1	.2	.2
Visual impairment	1	1	.1	.1
Orthopedic impairment	1	0	.1	0
Other health impairment	1	1	.6	.6
Autism	1	0	.2	0
Multiple disabilities	1	0	.1	0
	Unweighted sample percentage = 60 percent (Column B total divided by Column A total)		Weighted population estimate = 88 percent (Column D total divided by Column C total)	

All standard errors in this report were calculated using formula-based estimates rather than estimates based on the replicate weights. Since our formula based estimates tend to be slightly larger than the variances using pseudo-replicates, and the cutoff values for t-statistics based on infinite degrees of freedom rather than 31 degrees of freedom are similar, we calculated our p values based on infinite degrees of freedom. As a 10-year longitudinal study, NLTS2 has continued to use this formula-based procedure to calculate standard errors rather than use currently available procedures. This decision to maintain consistency in analytical approaches was based on the need to support comparisons of findings across NLTS2 reports. For example, key post-high school outcomes, such as employment rates, postsecondary enrollment rates, and wages, have been reported for NLTS2 data collection waves 2, 3, 4, and 5. Changing the analytic approach would call into question the longitudinal look at such variables. To examine possible differences between the approaches, replicate weights were created for-chapter 5 of this report. Findings using the replicate weights were then compared with the findings using formula-based estimates. Of the 904 possible comparisons in the chapter, 29 differences (3 percent) were noted: 14 differences that were reported at the $p < .01$ level dropped to $p < .05$; 2 differences dropped from $p < .01$ to less than 05; 9 decreased from $p < .001$ to $p < .01$; and 4 increased from $p < .01$ to $p < .001$.

Determining Statistical Significance

The following formula was used to determine the statistical significance of the differences between independent groups.

$$F = \frac{\left(P_1 - P_2\right)^2}{SE_1{}^2 + SE_2{}^2}$$

For example, this formula could be used to determine whether the difference in the percentages of students who report a particular view among students with learning disabilities and among those with hearing impairments is greater than would be expected to occur by chance. In this formula, P_1 and SE_1 are the first percentage and its standard error and P_2 and SE_2 are the second percentage and its standard error. The squared difference between the two percentages of interest is divided by the sum of the two squared standard errors.

If the product of a calculation is larger than 3.84 (i.e., 1.96^2), the difference is significant at the .05 level—that is, it would occur by chance fewer than 5 times in 100. If the result of the calculation is at least 6.63, the significance level is .01; products of 10.8 or greater are significant at the .001 level (Owen 1962, pp. 12, 51).

Testing for the significance of differences in responses to two survey items for the same individuals involves identifying for each young adult the pattern of response to the two items. Responses to items (e.g., the young adult reported receiving vacation or sick leave—yes or no—and reported receiving health insurance—yes or no) are scored as 0 or 1, producing difference values for individual students of +1 (responded affirmatively to the first item but not the second), 0 (responded affirmatively to both items or neither item), or -1 (responded affirmatively to the second item but not the first). The test statistic is the square of a ratio, where the numerator of the ratio is the weighted mean change score and the denominator is an estimate of the standard error of that mean. Since the ratio approaches a normal distribution by the Central Limit Theorem, for samples of the sizes included in the analyses, this test statistic approximately follows a chi-square distribution with one degree of freedom—i.e., an F (1, infinity) distribution.

Table A-4. Definitions of disabilities

Autism. A developmental disability significantly affecting verbal and nonverbal communication and social interaction, generally evident before age 3, that adversely affects a child's educational performance. Other characteristics often associated with autism are engagement in repetitive activities and stereotyped movements, resistance to environmental change or change in daily routines, and unusual responses to sensory experiences. The term does not apply if a child's educational performance is adversely affected primarily because the child has a serious emotional disturbance as defined below.

Deafness. A hearing impairment so severe that the child cannot understand what is being said even with a hearing aid.

Deaf-blindness. A combination of hearing and visual impairments causing such severe communication, developmental, and educational problems that the child cannot be accommodated in either a program specifically for the deaf or a program specifically for the blind.

Emotional disturbance.[1] A condition exhibiting one or more of the following characteristics, displayed over a long period of time and to a marked degree that adversely affects a child's educational performance:
   An inability to learn that cannot be explained by intellectual, sensory, or health factors
   An inability to build or maintain satisfactory interpersonal relationships with peers or teachers
   Inappropriate types of behavior or feelings under normal circumstances
   A general pervasive mood of unhappiness or depression
   A tendency to develop physical symptoms or fears associated with personal or school problems.
This term includes schizophrenia, but does not include students who are socially maladjusted, unless they have a serious emotional disturbance.

Hearing impairment. An impairment in hearing, whether permanent or fluctuating, that adversely affects a child's educational performance but that is not included under the definition of deafness as listed above.

Mental retardation. Significantly subaverage general intellectual functioning existing concurrently with deficits in adaptive behavior and manifested during the developmental period that adversely affects a child's educational performance.

Multiple disabilities. A combination of impairments (such as mental retardation-blindness, or mental retardation-physical disabilities) that causes such severe educational problems that the child cannot be accommodated in a special education program solely for one of the impairments. The term does not include deaf-blindness.

Orthopedic impairment. A severe orthopedic impairment that adversely affects educational performance. The term includes impairments such as amputation, absence of a limb, cerebral palsy, poliomyelitis, and bone tuberculosis.

Other health impairment. Having limited strength, vitality, or alertness due to chronic or acute health problems such as a heart condition, rheumatic fever, asthma, hemophilia, and leukemia, which adversely affect educational performance.[2]

Specific learning disability. A disorder in one or more of the basic psychological processes involved in understanding or in using language, spoken or written, that may manifest itself in an imperfect ability to listen, think, speak, read, write, spell, or do mathematical calculations. This term includes such conditions as perceptual disabilities, brain injury, minimal brain dysfunction, dyslexia, and developmental aphasia. This term does not include children who have learning problems that are primarily the result of visual, hearing, or motor disabilities; mental retardation; or environmental, cultural or economic disadvantage.

Table A-4. (Continued)

Speech or language impairment. A communication disorder such as stuttering, impaired articulation, language impairment, or a voice impairment that adversely affects a child's educational performance.
Traumatic brain injury. An acquired injury to the brain caused by an external physical force, resulting in total or partial functional disability or psychosocial impairment, or both, that adversely affects a child's educational performance. The term applies to open or closed head injuries resulting in impairments in one or more areas, such as cognition; language; memory; attention; reasoning; abstract thinking; judgment; problem solving; sensory, perceptual and motor abilities; psychosocial behavior; physical functions; information processing; and speech. The term does not apply to brain injuries that are congenital or degenerative, or brain injuries induced by birth trauma.
Visual impairment, including blindness. An impairment in vision that, even with correction, adversely affects a child's educational performance. The term includes both partial sight and blindness.

[1] P.L. 105-17, the Individuals with Disabilities Education Act Amendments of 1997, changed "serious emotional disturbance" to "emotional disturbance." The change has no substantive or legal significance. It is intended strictly to eliminate any negative connotation of the term "serious."

[2] OSEP guidelines indicate that "children with ADD, where ADD is a chronic or acute health problem resulting in limited alertness, may be considered disabled under Part B solely on the basis of this disorder under the 'other health impaired' category in situations where special education and related services are needed because of the ADD" (Davila, Williams, and MacDonald 1991).

Source: Definitions taken from Knoblauch and Sorenson (1998).

Regardless of whether comparisons are for independent or dependent samples, a large number of statistical analyses were conducted and are presented in this report. Since no explicit adjustments were made for multiple comparisons, the likelihood of finding at least one statistically significant difference when no difference exists in the population is substantially larger than the type I error for each individual analysis. This may be particularly true when many of the variables on which the groups are being compared are measures of the same or similar constructs, as is the case in this report. To partially compensate for the number of analyses that were conducted, we used a relatively conservative p value of .01. The text mentions only differences that reach a level of significance of at least $p < .01$. If no level of significance is reported, the group differences described do not attain the $p < .01$ level. Readers also are cautioned that the meaningfulness of differences reported here cannot be inferred from their statistical significance.

Measurement and Reporting Issues

The chapters in this report provide information on specific variables included in analyses. However, several general points about NLTS2 measures that are used repeatedly in analyses should be clear to readers as they consider the findings reported here.

Categorizing Students by Primary Disability

Information about the nature of students' disabilities came from rosters of all students in the NLTS2 age range receiving special education services in the 2000–01 school year under the auspices of participating LEAs and state-supported special schools. In analyses in this report, each student is assigned to a disability category on the basis of the primary disability designated by the student's school or district. Although there are federal guidelines in making category assignments (table A-4), criteria and methods for assigning students to categories vary from state to state and even between districts within states, with the potential for substantial variation in the nature and severity of disabilities included in the categories (see, for example, MacMillan and Siperstein 2002). Therefore, NLTS2 data should not be interpreted as describing students who truly had a particular disability, but rather as describing students who were categorized as having that primary disability.

The exception to reliance on school or district category assignment involves students with deaf-blindness. Because of district variation in assigning students with both hearing and visual impairments to the category of deaf-blindness many students with those dual disabilities are assigned to other primary disability categories, most often hearing impairment, visual impairment, and multiple disabilities. As a result of these classification differences, national estimates suggest that there were 3,196 students with deaf-blindness who were 12 to 17 years old in 1999 (National Technical Assistance Center 1999), whereas the federal child count indicates that 681 were classified with deaf-blindness as their primary disability (Office of Special Education Programs 2001).

To describe the characteristics and experiences of the larger body of young adults with deaf-blindness more precisely, students who were reported by parents or by schools or school districts[120] as having both a hearing and a visual impairment were assigned to the deaf-blindness category for purposes of NLTS2 reporting, regardless of the primary disability category assigned by the school or school district.

Comparisons with the General Population of Students

In cases in which databases for the general population of young adults are publicly available (e.g., the National Longitudinal Survey of Youth), comparisons have been calculated from those databases for young adults with disabilities who match in age to those included in NLTS2. However, some comparisons have been made by using published data. For some of these comparisons, differences in samples (e.g., ages of young adults) or measurement (e.g., question wording on surveys) reduce the direct comparability of NLTS2 and general population data. Where these limitations affect the comparisons, they are pointed out in the text and the implications for the comparisons are noted.

Reporting Statistics

Statistics are not reported for groups with fewer than 30 members. Statistics with a decimal of .5 or higher in the tables and figures are rounded to the next whole number when reported in the text.

A number of interview items related to post-high school experiences were presented to respondents as open-ended questions, with no predefined response categories. For example:

- "What kind of work do you do for this job?" (asked of employed young adult).
- "What services, accommodations, or other help have you received?" (asked of postsecondary school students who reported seeking help at school).

- "What was the main reason you quit?" (asked of young adult who quit their previous or most recent job).

For each such question, interviewers had a set of response categories into which they coded responses when the match of the response to the categories was straightforward. For example, a response from a young adult who reported he quit his most recent job because "it was September and I was going back to school" could readily be assigned to the precoded category of "went back to school." When responses did not readily match precoded categories, interviewers were trained to record the verbatim response and leave the item uncoded. Approximately the first 100 verbatim responses for each question were then reviewed by the survey data team to identify responses that were frequent enough to develop additional precoded categories and responses that could be included in existing precoded categories by expanding the response category description (e.g., "went back to school" could be expanded to include "started school" without changing the intent of the category to identify young adult who left employment to pursue their education). New categories or expanded category definitions were then incorporated.

APPENDIX A. REFERENCES

[1]   Davila, R. R., Williams, M. L. & MacDonald, J. T. (1991). *Clarification of Policy to Address the Needs of Children with Attention-Deficit Disorders within General and/or Special Education.* Memorandum to Chief State School Officers. Washington, DC: U.S. Department of Education, Office of Special Education and Rehabilitative Services.

[2]   Employment Policies Institute. (2002). *Measuring Poverty in America: Science or Politics?* Available at http://www.epionline.org/studies/epi_poverty_04-2002.pdf.

[3]   Javitz, H. & Wagner, M. (2003). *Analysis of Potential Bias in the Sample of Local Education Agencies (Leas) in the National Longitudinal Transition Study-2 (NLTS2).* Menlo Park, CA: SRI International.

[4]   Knoblauch, B. & Sorenson, B. (1998). IDEA's Definition of Disabilities (ERIC Ec Digest No. E560). In. Reston, VA: ERIC Clearinghouse on Disabilities and Gifted Education.

[5]   MacMillan, D. L. & Siperstein, G. N. (2002). Learning Disabilities as Operationally Defined by Schools. In L. Bradley, L. Danielson, and D.P. Hallahan (Eds.), *Identification of Learning Disabilities: Research to Practice.* Mahwah, NJ: Lawrence Erlbaum Associates Publishers.

[6]   National Technical Assistance Center. (1999). *National Deaf-Blind Child Count Summary.* Monmouth, OR: Teaching Research Division, Western Oregon University.

[7]   Office of Special Education Programs. (2001). *Table AD1. Number of Students Age 14 and Older Exiting Special Education, During the 1999-2000 School Year.* Available at http://www.ideadata.org/tables24th/ar_ad1.htm.

[8]   Owen, D. B. (1962). *Handbook of Statistical Tables.* Palo Alto, CA: Addison-Wesley Publishing.

[9]   Quality Education Data. (1999). *State School Guides.* Retrieved August 2, 2004, from http://www.qeddata.com/MarketKno/SchoolGuides/SchoolGuides.aspx.

APPENDIX B. ADDITIONAL ANALYSES

Characteristics of Out-of-High School Young Adults with Disabilities

NLTS2 represents youth with disabilities nationally who were ages 13 through 16, in secondary school, and receiving special education services in grade 7 or above in the 2000–01 school year. This report focuses on the subset of young adults no longer in secondary school in 2009. Understanding the characteristics of young adults with disabilities is important for interpreting their after-high school experiences. Tables B-1 through B-3 describe this subsample—young adults with disabilities who were out of high school and for whom data were reported, either by young adult themselves or by their parents, as part of the NLTS2 Wave 5 parent and youth telephone interviews and youth mail survey. They report data for young adults as a group and for those for whom parents and young adults themselves, respectively, were respondents.

The out-of-high school young adult's subsample, like the universe of secondary-school-age young adults with disabilities, is heavily dominated by young adults with learning disabilities; 63 percent of young adults represented by the out-of-high school subsample were classified for special education services in the learning disability category when they were in high school (table B-1). At 12 percent each, the categories of emotional disturbance and mental retardation are the next largest categories. All other categories comprise 13 percent of the weighted sample. The disability category distributions of the groups of young adults for whom parents were respondents and those who responded for themselves do not differ significantly.

Table B-1. Primary disability category of out-of-high school young adults, overall and by respondent

Primary disability category	All out-of-high school youth	Parent Respondents	Youth respondents
	Percent		
Learning disability	62.5 (2.60)	58.3 (4.67)	64.2 (3.16)
Speech/language impairment	4.1 (1.07)	3.0 (1.63)	4.6 (1.39)
Mental retardation	11.7 (1.73)	14.9 (3.37)	10.4 (2.01)
Emotional disturbance	11.5 (1.71)	12.9 (3.18)	10.8 (2.05)
Hearing impairment	1.4 (0.62)	1.5 (1.15)	1.3 (0.74)
Visual impairment	0.5 (0.37)	0.4 (0.57)	0.5 (0.48)
Orthopedic impairment	1.1 (0.57)	1.2 (1.03)	1.1 (0.69)
Other health impairment	4.6 (1.13)	3.8 (1.81)	5.0 (1.44)
Autism	0.6 (0.42)	1.0 (0.92)	0.4 (0.44)

Table B-1. (Continued)

Primary disability category	All out-of-high school youth	Parent Respondents	Youth respondents
	Percent		
Traumatic brain injury	0.3 (0.29)	0.3 (0.49)	0.3 (0.37)
Multiple disabilities	1.6 (0.67)	2.6 (1.50)	1.1 (0.69)
Deaf-blindness	0.1 (0.20)	0.2 (0.40)	0.1 (0.22)

Note: Standard errors are in parentheses.

Source: U.S. Department of Education, Institute of Education Sciences, National Center for Special Education Research, National Longitudinal Transition Study-2 (NLTS2), Wave 5 parent and youth telephone interview/mail survey, 2009.

Table B-2. Functional characteristics of out-of-high school young adult respondents and those for whom parents responded

Functional characteristics	All out-of-high school youth	Parent respondents	Young adult respondents
	Percent		
Functional cognitive skills scale score:			
High (13-16)	68.9 (2.96)	55.7 (5.78)	74.3 (3.35)
Medium (8-12)	27.8 (2.86)	36.6 (5.60)	24.2 (3.29)
Low (4-7)	3.3 (1.14)	7.7 (3.11)	1.5 (0.92)
Youth had at least "some trouble":			
Seeing	16.8 (2.10)	19.1 (3.94)	15.6 (2.49)
Speaking	27.3 (2.51)	31.7 (4.70)	25.2 (2.98)
Understanding speech	30.8 (2.60)	36.8 (4.84)	28.0 (3.08)
Conversing with others	31.8 (2.63)	39.2 (4.93)	28.5 (3.10)
Functional characteristics	**All out-of-high school youth**	**Parent respondents**	**Young adult respondents**
	Percent		
Using one or more appendages	11.1 (1.76)	13.9 (3.46)	9.6 (2.02)
Youth's general health was excellent	24.0 (2.38)	30.8 (4.90)	21.5 (2.71)

Note: Standard errors are in parentheses.

Source: U.S. Department of Education, Institute of Education Sciences, National Center for Special Education Research, National Longitudinal Transition Study-2 (NLTS2), Wave 5 parent and youth telephone interview/mail survey, 2009.

**Table B-3. Age at identification of and first services for disabilities
of out-of-high school young adults respondents and
those for whom parents responded**

Youth's age	All out-of-high school youth	Parent respondents	Youth respondents
	Percent		
Disability first identified at age:			
Birth-1	14.2 (2.11)	18.4 (4.24)	12.6 (2.42)
2-4	16.0 (2.22)	18.2 (4.22)	15.2 (2.62)
5-7	46.7 (3.01)	42.1 (5.40)	48.8 (3.64)
8-10	15.6 (2.19)	15.5 (3.96)	15.3 (2.62)
11 or older	7.5 (1.59)	5.8 (2.56)	8.2 (2.00)
Special education services in school first received at age:			
5-7	50.7 (3.01)	50.3 (3.62)	52.5 (5.48)
8-10	29.5 (2.75)	27.4 (3.23)	34.1 (5.20)
11-13	16.3 (2.22)	17.9 (2.77)	12.3 (3.60)
14 or older	3.5 (1.11)	4.5 (1.49)	1.2 (1.17)

Note: Standard errors are in parentheses.
Source: U.S. Department of Education, Institute of Education Sciences, National Center for Special Education Research, National Longitudinal Transition Study-2 (NLTS2), Wave 5 parent and youth telephone interview/mail survey, 2009.

The majority of out-of-high school young adults (69 percent) were reported to have high functional cognitive skills,[121] from 11 percent to 32 percent had at least some limitation in the functional domains reported in table B-2, and almost one-fourth (24 percent) had excellent health. More young adults were reported to have high functional cognitive skills (74 percent) than those for whom parents responded (56 percent, $p < .01$). The majority of out-of-high school young adults were identified as having a disability at school entry or in their early years in school (table B-3); 47 percent were reported to have had their health disability first identified at ages of 5 to 7, although almost a one-third (30 percent) had had their disabilities first identified in their infant, toddler, or preschool years. The majority of out-of-high school young adults first began receiving special education services in elementary school, with 51 percent receiving services in their first few years in school and 30 percent receiving services for the first time between ages 8 and 10. No significant differences in age disability was first identified or services were first received were apparent between the two respondent groups.

Table B-4a. Demographic characteristics of out-of-high school young adults with disabilities, by disability category

Characteristics	All disabilities	Learning disability	Speech/ language impairment	Mental retardation	Emotional disturbance	Hearing impairment	Visual impairment	Orthopedic impairment	Other health impairment	Autism	Traumatic brain injury	Multiple disabilities	Deaf-blindness
						Percent							
Age													
21	9.5	10.1	15.2	6.1	9.4	7.8	6.9	6.1	7.8	6.3	4.3	8.0	8.4
	(1.57)	(2.49)	(2.77)	(1.89)	(2.65)	(2.62)	(2.80)	(2.17)	(2.29)	(2.27)	(3.07)	(2.92)	(3.97)
22	24.9	26.9	29.9	19.6	22.3	20.6	18.5	17.4	22.3	23.1	18.7	14.4	25.8
	(2.32)	(3.66)	(3.53)	(3.15)	(3.78)	(3.94)	(4.28)	(3.45)	(3.54)	(3.95)	(5.90)	(3.79)	(6.27)
23	21.8	20.6	24.4	23.4	24.4	20.8	25.1	27.7	25.7	21.1	23.3	19.5	19.9
	(2.22)	(3.34)	(3.31)	(3.36)	(3.90)	(3.96)	(4.78)	(4.07)	(3.72)	(3.83)	(6.39)	(4.28)	(5.72)
24	24.0	21.9	20.6	31.3	23.7	31.6	27.0	30.6	29.5	27.4	39.0	35.3	25.1
	(2.30)	(3.41)	(3.12)	(3.68)	(3.86)	(4.53)	(4.89)	(4.20)	(3.88)	(4.18)	(7.38)	(5.16)	(6.21)
25	19.7	20.6	9.9	19.7	20.3	19.2	22.4	18.2	14.7	22.0	14.7	23.0	20.9
	(2.14)	3.34	(2.31)	(3.16)	(3.65)	(3.84)	(4.59)	(3.52)	(3.01)	(3.89)	(5.36)	(4.54)	(5.82)
Since leaving high school													
Less than 3 years	11.5	9.7	13.4	17.7	11.5	8.9	15.7	12.3	9.8	29.1	10.0	27.9	18.8
	(1.71)	(1.95)	(2.14)	(2.42)	(3.30)	(1.40)	(1.62)	(1.94)	(2.49)	(1.56)	(3.54)	(2.61)	(2.50)
3 up to 5 years	36.5	37.8	42.8	33.3	30.5	36.7	31.9	38.8	35.5	39.7	33.4	35.5	49.1
	(2.59)	(4.01)	(3.81)	(3.74)	(4.18)	(4.70)	(5.13)	(4.44)	(4.07)	(4.59)	(7.14)	(5.17)	(7.16)
5 up to 8 years	52.0	52.5	43.8	49.0	58.1	54.5	52.4	48.8	54.7	31.2	56.6	36.5	32.0
	(2.68)	(4.13)	(3.82)	(3.97)	(4.48)	(4.86)	(5.50)	(4.55)	(4.24)	(4.34)	(7.50)	(5.20)	(6.68)
High school-leaving status													
Completed high school	90.6	92.2	90.7	88.9	82.5	97.6	96.8	94.6	88.3	96.7	92.3	93.8	96.9
	(1.58)	(2.24)	(2.24)	(2.50)	(3.47)	(1.49)	(1.94)	(2.07)	(2.75)	(1.68)	(4.05)	(2.63)	(2.50)
Did not complete high school	9.4	7.9	9.3	11.1	17.5	2.4	3.2	5.4	11.7	3.3	7.7	6.2	3.1
	(1.58)	(2.24)	(2.24)	(2.50)	(3.47)	(1.49)	(1.94)	(2.07)	(2.75)	(1.68)	(4.05)	(2.63)	(2.50)
Highest level of educational attainment													

Characteristics	All disabilities	Learning disability	Speech/ language impairment	Mental retardation	Emotional disturbance	Hearing impairment	Visual impairment	Orthopedic impairment	Other health impairment	Autism	Traumatic brain injury	Multiple disabilities	Deaf-blindness
	Percent												
High school non-completer	7.6 (1.43)	5.8 (1.95)	8.4 (2.14)	10.3 (2.42)	15.6 (3.30)	2.1 (1.40)	2.2 (1.62)	4.7 (1.94)	9.4 (2.49)	2.8 (1.56)	5.8 (3.54)	6.1 (2.61)	3.1 (2.50)
High school completer	40.5 (2.65)	36.5 (4.01)	31.0 (3.57)	67.6 (3.73)	40.3 (4.46)	27.9 (4.38)	27.9 (4.94)	37.9 (4.44)	30.3 (3.92)	54.7 (4.69)	36.5 (7.29)	63.9 (5.21)	41.1 (7.05)
Some post-secondary school	30.3 (2.48)	32.1 (3.88)	34.5 (3.67)	15.6 (2.89)	29.0 (4.13)	40.1 (4.79)	37.6 (5.34)	36.6 (4.41)	40.9 (4.19)	25.0 (4.08)	32.3 (7.09)	20.2 (4.36)	37.6 (6.94)
Post-secondary school completion	21.6 (2.22)	25.6 (3.63)	26.1 (3.39)	6.5 (1.96)	15.2 (3.27)	30.0 (4.48)	32.3 (5.15)	20.8 (3.71)	19.3 (3.36)	17.5 (3.58)	25.4 (6.60)	9.7 (3.21)	18.1 (5.52)

Note: Standard errors are in parentheses.

Source: U.S. Department of Education, Institute of Education Sciences, National Center for Special Education Research, National Longitudinal Transition Study-2 (NLTS2), Wave 5 parent and youth telephone interview/mail survey, 2009.

Table B-4b. Demographic characteristics of out-of-high school young adults with disabilities, by disability category, concluded

Characteristics	All disabilities	Learning disability	Speech/ language impairment	Mental retardation	Emotional disturbance	Hearing impairment	Visual impairment	Ortho pedic impairment	Other health impairment	Autism	Traumatic brain injury	Multiple disabilities	Deaf-blindness
	Percent												
Gender													
Male	63.6 (2.59)	63.2 (3.98)	62.2 (3.74)	56.5 (3.94)	72.1 (4.07)	49.2 (4.88)	55.2 (5.48)	54.8 (4.53)	72.8 (3.79)	86.5 (3.20)	69.5 (6.97)	60.4 (5.28)	62.7 (6.92)

Characteristics	All disabilities	Learning disability	Speech/language impairment	Mental retardation	Emotional disturbance	Hearing impairment	Visual impairment	Ortho pedic impairment	Other health impairment	Autism	Traumatic brain injury	Multiple disabilities	Deaf-blindness
	Percent												
Female	36.4	36.8	37.8	43.5	27.9	50.8	44.8	45.2	27.2	13.5	30.5	39.6	37.3
	(2.59)	(3.98)	(3.74)	(3.94)	(4.07)	(4.88)	(5.48)	(4.53)	(3.79)	(3.20)	(6.97)	(5.28)	(6.92)
Race/ethnicity													
White	65.6	65.6	70.8	57.8	65.7	64.3	68.3	70.2	77.2	74.1	72.8	70.6	65.2
	(2.57)	(3.97)	(3.50)	(3.93)	(4.34)	(4.74)	(5.16)	(4.17)	(3.61)	(4.16)	(6.83)	(5.02)	(6.82)
African American	20.2	17.8	16.6	33.4	24.3	17.0	19.3	15.6	15.1	17.8	17.1	18.2	10.1
	(2.17)	(3.19)	(2.87)	(3.75)	(3.92)	(3.71)	(4.38)	(3.31)	(3.08)	(3.62)	(5.77)	(4.25)	(4.32)
Hispanic	14.2	16.6	12.6	8.8	10.1	18.8	12.4	14.2	7.7	8.2	10.2	11.3	24.7
	(1.89)	(3.11)	(2.55)	(2.26)	(2.75)	(3.86)	(3.66)	(3.18)	(2.30)	(2.60)	(4.63)	(3.48)	(6.18)
Household income													
$25,000 or less	35.2	34.8	23.4	50.5	37.6	25.0	26.6	26.4	16.8	17.7	30.4	28.3	30.1
	(2.57)	(3.95)	(3.28)	(4.02)	(4.41)	(4.26)	(4.92)	(4.04)	(3.21)	(3.60)	(6.95)	(5.00)	(6.61)
$25,001 - $50,000	26.5	26.9	27.0	25.1	26.4	24.4	27.5	29.1	26.3	28.8	17.8	27.1	18.1
	(2.38)	(3.68)	(3.43)	(3.49)	(4.01)	(4.23)	(4.97)	(4.16)	(3.78)	(4.27)	(5.78)	(4.93)	(5.55)
More than $50,000	38.3	38.4	49.6	24.4	36.1	50.7	45.9	44.5	56.9	53.5	51.8	44.6	51.8
	(2.62)	(4.03)	(3.87)	(3.46)	(4.37)	(4.92)	(5.55)	(4.56)	(4.26)	(4.70)	(7.55)	(5.51)	(7.20)

Note: Standard errors are in parentheses.

Source: U.S. Department of Education, Institute of Education Sciences, National Center for Special Education Research, National Longitudinal Transition Study-2 (NLTS2), Wave 5 parent and youth telephone interview/mail survey, 2009.

Distribution of Demographic Characteristics across Disability Categories

Findings in this report are presented for young adults with disabilities as a group and then are reported separately for young adults in each federal special education disability category. Findings also are reported for young adults who differ in secondary school-leaving status, highest level of education attainment, length of time since leaving high school, gender, race/ethnicity, and household income. These bivariate analyses should not be interpreted as implying that a factor on which subgroups are differentiated (e.g., disability category) has a causal relationship with the differences reported. Further, readers should be aware that demographic factors (e.g., race/ethnicity and household income) are correlated among young adults with disabilities, as well as being distributed differently across disability categories.

Table B-4a and B-4b presents demographic characteristics of out-of-high school young adults with disabilities overall and within each disability category.[122]

This report represents young adults who were in the 21- to 25-year-old age range. Fewer young adults were at the younger end of the age range. Ten percent of young adults were 21-year-olds compared with 25 percent who were 22-year-olds ($p < .001$), 22 percent who were 23-year-olds ($p < .001$), 24 percent who were 24-year-olds ($p < .001$), and 20 percent who were 25-year-olds ($p < .001$). Fewer young adults with speech/language impairments (10 percent) than young adults with disabilities as a group (20 percent) were in the oldest age category (25 years old, $p < .01$).

Twelve percent young adults with disabilities had left high school within 3 years. More young adults with autism (29 percent) than those with disabilities overall (12 percent) had left high school within 3 years ($p < .001$).

Nine percent of out-of-high school young adults with disabilities left high school without a diploma or a certificate of completion.[123] More young adults with emotional disturbances (18 percent) than those with disabilities overall (9 percent) did not complete high school ($p < .05$).

Forty-one percent of young adults with disabilities completed high school as the highest level of education compared with those who did not complete high school (8 percent, $p < .001$), received some post-secondary school (30 percent, $p < .01$), or completed postsecondary education or training (22 percent, $p < .001$). More young adults with mental retardation (68 percent) than those with disabilities overall (42 percent) completed high school as the highest level of education ($p < .001$).

Whereas about half of young adults in the general population (52 percent) were male,[124] almost two-thirds of out-of-high school young adults with disabilities (64 percent) were male ($p < .001$). Young adults with hearing impairments and autism differed significantly in their gender balance when compared with young adults with disabilities overall. (72 percent and 87 percent vs. 64 percent, $p < .01$ for hearing impairment and $p < .001$ for autism).

Young adults with disabilities differed from those in the general population in their racial/ethnic backgrounds. They were disproportionately likely to be African American, relative to the general population; African Americans comprised 14 percent of young adults in the general population[125] but 20 percent of young adults with disabilities ($p < .01$). Young adults with other health impairments were more likely to be White than were young adults with disabilities as a group (77 percent vs. 66 percent, $p < .01$). In addition, young adults with mental retardation were more likely to be African American than were young adults with disabilities as a group (33 percent vs. 20 percent, $p < .01$).

Young adults with disabilities who were out of high school were more likely than those in the general population to have parents' households with lower income levels. Approximately one-third of those with disabilities (35 percent) included in this report had families with incomes of $25,000 or less; in comparison, 29 percent[126] of their peers in the general population lived in low-income-level households ($p < .01$). There were few significant differences by disability category in comparison with household incomes of young adults with disabilities overall, with the exception that young adults with mental retardation (51 percent) were more likely to come from families with incomes of $25,000 or less than were young adults with disabilities as a group (35 percent, $p < .01$).

APPENDIX B. REFERENCE

[1]   Wagner, M., Marder, C., Levine, P., Cameto, R., Cadwallader, T. W., Blackorby, J., Cardoso, D. & Newman, L. (2003). *The Individual and Household Characteristics of Youth With Disabilities. A Report From the National Longitudinal Transition Study-2 (NLTS2)*. Menlo Park, CA: SRI International.

REFERENCES

[1]   Arnett, J. J. (2000). Emerging Adulthood: A Theory of Development From the Late Teens Through the Twenties. *American Psychologist, 55(5)*, 469-480.

[2]   Arnett, J. J. (2001). *Adolescence and Emerging Adulthood: A Cultural Approach.* Upper Saddle River, NJ: Prentice Hall.

[3]   Arnett, J. J. (2002). *Readings on Adolescence and Emerging Adulthood.* Upper Saddle River, NJ: Prentice Hall.

[4]   Bearman, P. S. & Moody, J. (2004). Suicide and Friendships Among American Adolescents. *American Journal of Public Health, 94*, 89-95.

[5]   Bell, L., Burtless, G., Gornick, J. & Smeeding, T. M. (2006). *A Cross-National Survey of Trends in the Transition to Economic Independence* (Working Paper). New York, NY: The Network on Transitions to Adulthood.

[6]   Berkner, L., He, S. & Cataldi, E. F. (2002). *Descriptive Summary of 1995-1996 Beginning Postsecondary Students: Six Years Later*. Washington, DC: U.S. Department of Education, National Center for Education Statistics.

[7]   Cameto, R., Levine, P. & Wagner, M. (2004). *Transition Planning for Students With Disabilities. A Special Topic Report From the National Longitudinal Transition Study-2 (NLTS2)*. Menlo Park, CA: SRI International.

[8]   Carey, K. (2004). *A Matter of Degrees: Improving Graduation Rates in Four-Year Colleges and Universities*. Washington, DC: The Education Trust.

[9]   Carnevale, A. P. & Desrochers, D. M. (2003). *Standards for What? The Economic Roots of K-16 Reform*. Princeton, NJ: Educational Testing Service.

[10]   Carnevale, A. P. & Fry, R. A. (2000). *Crossing the Great Divide: Can We Achieve Equity When Generation Y Goes to College?* Princeton, NJ: Educational Testing Service.

[11] Carter, E. W., Ditchman, N., Sun, Y., Trainor, A. A., Swedeen, B. & Owens, L. (2010). Summer Employment and Community Experiences of Transition-Age Youth With Severe Disabilities. *Exceptional Children, 76(2)*, 194-212. Carter, E. W., Trainor, A. A., Cakiroglu, O., Swedeen, B. & Owens, L. A. (2010). Availability of and Access to Career Development Activities for Transition-Age Youth With Disabilities. *Career Development for Exceptional Individuals, 33*, 13-24.

[12] Carter, E. W., Trainor, A. A., Sun, Y. & Owens, L. (2009). Assessing the Transition-Related Strengths and Needs of Adolescents With High-Incidence Disabilities: Youth, Teacher, and Parent Perspectives. *Exceptional Children, 76*, 74-94.

[13] Chambers, D., Rabren, K. & Dunn, C. (2009). A Comparison of Transition From High School to Adult Life of Students With and Without Disabilities. *Career Development for Exceptional Individuals, 32(1)*, 42-52.

[14] Chen, X. & Carol, C. D. (2005). *First Generation Students in Postsecondary Education: A Look at Their College Transcripts.* Retrieved June 8, 2010, from http://nces.ed.gov/pubs2005/2005171.pdf. Conover, W.J. (1999). *Practical Nonparametric Statistics* (3rd ed.). New York, NY: John Wiley and Sons. Corak, M., Lipps, G., and Zhao, J. (2005). Family Income and Participation in Post-Secondary Education. In C. Beach, R. Boadway, and M. McInnis (Eds.), *Higher Education in Canada*. Montreal: McGill-Queen's University Press.

[15] Crosnoe, R. & Needham, B. (2004). Holism, Contextual Variability, and the Study of Friendships in Adolescent Development. *Child Development, 75(1)*, 264-279.

[16] Erikson, E. H. (1974). *Dimensions of a New Identity*. New York, NY: Norton.

[17] Ewell, P. & Wellman, J. (2007). *Enhancing Student Success in Education: Summary Report of the NPEC Initiative and National Symposium on Postsecondary Student Success.* Washington, DC: National Postsecondary Education Cooperative.

[18] Fabian, E. (1992). Longitudinal Outcomes in Supported Employment: A Survival Analysis. *Rehabilitation Psychology, 37*, 23-35.

[19] Fabian, E. S. (2007). Urban Youth With Disabilities: Factors Affecting Transition Outcomes. *Rehabilitation Counseling Bulletin, 50*, 130-138.

[20] File, T. & Crissey, S. (2010). *Voting and Registration in the Election of November 2008*. Washington DC: U.S. Census Bureau.

[21] Fraser, M. W. (1997). *Risk and Resilience in Childhood: An Ecological Perspective*. Washington, DC: National Association of Social Workers Press.

[22] Furstenberg, F. F., Kennedy, S., McLoyd, V. C., Rumbaut, R. G. & Settersten, R. A., Jr. (2004). Growing up Is Harder to Do. *Contexts, 3(3)*, 33-41.

[23] Furstenberg, F. F., Rumbaut, R. G.& Settersten, R. A. (2005). On the Frontier of Adulthood: Emerging Themes and New Directions. In R.A. Settersten, F.F. Furstenberg, and R.G. Rumbaut (Eds.), *On the Frontier of Adulthood. Theory, Research, and Public Policy*. Chicago, IL: University of Chicago Press.

[24] Fussell, E. & Furstenberg, F. F. (2005). The Transition to Adulthood During the Twentieth Century: Race, Nativity, and Gender. In R.A. Settersten, F.F. Furstenberg, and R.G. Rumbaut (Eds.), *On the Frontier of Adulthood. Theory, Research, and Public Policy*. Chicago, IL: University of Chicago Press.

[25] Goldscheider, F. K. & Davanzo, J. (1986). Semiautonomy and Leaving Home in Early Adulthood. *Social Forces, 65*, 187-201.

[26] Guy, B. A., Sitlington, P. L., Larson, M. D. & Frank, A. R. (2009). What Are High Schools Offering as Preparation for Employment? *Career Development for Exceptional Individuals, 32*, 40-41.

[27] Hall, G. S. (1904). *Adolescence: Its Psychology and Its Relations to Physiology, Anthropology, Sociology, Sex, Crime, Religion, and Education* (Vol. I & II). New York, NY: Appleton & Co.

[28] Halpern, A. S. (1985). Transition: A Look at the Foundation. *Exceptional Children, 51*, 479-486.

[29] Heeringa, S. G., West, B. T. & Berglund, P. A. (2010). *Applied Survey Data Analysis.* Boca Raton, FL: Chapman & Hall/CRC Press.

[30] Inside Higher Ed. (2006). *The Full-Time Advantage.* Retrieved November 27, 2006, from http://insidehighered.com/news2006/11/27/ccsse.

[31] Johnson, D. R., Stodden, R., Emanuel, E., Luecking, R. & Mack, M. (2002). Current Challenges Facing Secondary Education and Transition Services: What Research Tells Us. *Exceptional Children, 68(4)*, 519-531.

[32] Johnson, N. & Kotz, S. (1995). *Distributions in Statistics: Continuous Distributions* (Vol. 2). New York, NY: John Wiley and Sons.

[33] Lehman, A. F., Goldberg, R., Dixon, L. B., McNary, S., Postrado, L., Hackman, A. & McDonell, K. (2002). Improving Employment Outcomes for Persons With Severe Mental Illnesses. *Archives of General Psychiatry, 59(2)*, 165-172.

[34] Levinson, E. M. & Palmer, E. J. (2005). Preparing Students With Disabilities for School-to-Work Transition and Postschool Life. *Principal Leadership, 5(8)*, 11-15.

[35] Marcotte, D. E., Bailey, T., Borkoski, C. & Kienzel, G. S. (2005). The Returns of a Community College Education: Evidence From the National Education Longitudinal Survey. *Educational Evaluation and Policy Analysis, 27(2)*, 157-175.

[36] Mortimer, J. T. & Larson, R. W. (2002). Macrostructural Trends and the Reshaping of Adolescence. In J.T. Mortimer, and R.W. Larson (Eds.), *The Changing Adolescent Experience: Societal Trends and the Transition to Adulthood* (pp. 1-17). Cambridge, UK: Cambridge University Press.

[37] Mull, C., Sitlington, P. & Alper, S. (2001). Postsecondary Education for Students With Learning Disabilities: A Synthesis of the Literature. *Exceptional Children, 68(1)*, 97-118.

[38] National Center for Education Statistics. (1999). *An Institutional Perspective on Students With Disabilities in Postsecondary Education.* Washington, DC: Office of Educational Research and Improvement, U.S. Department of Education.

[39] National Center on Educational Outcomes. (1993). *Educational Outcomes and Indicators for Individuals at the Post-School Level.* Minneapolis, MN: The College of Education, University of Minnesota. National Center on Secondary Education and Transition. (2003). *A National Leadership Summit on Improving Results for Youth: State Priorities and Needs for Assistance.* Retrieved July 19, 2004, from http://www.ncset.org/summit03/NCSETSummit03findings.pdf.

[40] Neece, C. L., Kraemer, B. R. & Blacher, J. (2009). Transition Satisfaction and Family Well Being Among Parents of Young Adults With Severe Intellectual Disability. *Intellectual and Developmental Disabilities, 47*, 31-43.

[41] Newman, L., Marder, C. & Wagner, M. (2003). Instruction of Secondary School Students With Disabilities in General Education Academic Classes. In M. Wagner, L.

Newman, R. Cameto, P. Levine, and C. Marder (Eds.), *Going to School: Instructional Contexts, Programs, and Participation of Secondary School Students With Disabilities.* Menlo Park, CA: SRI International.

[42] Newman, L., Wagner, M., Cameto, R. & Knokey, A. M. (2009). *The Post-High School Outcomes of Youth With Disabilities up to 4 Years After High School. A Report from the National Longitudinal Transition Study-2 (NLTS2)* (NCSER 2009-3017). Menlo Park, CA: SRI International.

[43] Newman, L., Wagner, M., Cameto, R. & Knokey, A. M. (2009). *The Post-High School Outcomes of Youth With Disabilities up to 4 Years After High School. A Report From the National Longitudinal Transition Study-2 (NLTS2)* (NCSER 2009-3017). Menlo Park, CA: SRI International.

[44] Office for Civil Rights, U.S. Department of Education. (2007). *Students With Disabilities Preparing for Postsecondary Education: Know Your Rights and Responsibilities.* Retrieved August 3, 2007, from http://www.ed.gov/about/offices/list/ocr /transition.html.

[45] Osgood, W., Foster, E. M., Flanagan, C. & Ruth, G. R. (2005). Introduction: Why Focus on the Transition to Adulthood for Vulnerable Populations? In W. Osgood, E.M. Foster, C. Flanagan, and G.R. Ruth (Eds.), *On Your Own Without a Net: The Transition to Adulthood for Vulnerable Populations.* Chicago, IL: University of Chicago Press.

[46] Peter, K. & Horn, L. (2005). *Gender Differences in Participation and Completion of Undergraduate Education and How They Have Changed Over Time* (NCES 2005-169). U.S. Department of Education, National Center for Education Statistics, Washington, DC: U.S. Government Printing Office.

[47] Pierangelo, R. & Crane, R. (1997). *Complete Guide to Special Education Transition Services.* West Nyack, NY: Center for Applied Research in Education.

[48] Polak, P. & Warner, R. (1996). The Economic Life of Seriously Mentally Ill People in the Community. *Psychiatric Services 47*, 270-274.

[49] Povenmire, K., Tiana, C., Lindstrom, L. & Bullis, M. (2010). De Escuela a La Vida Adulta/From School to Adult Life: Transition Needs for Latino Youth With Disabilities and Their Families. *Career Development for Exceptional Individuals, 33*, 41-51.

[50] Powers, K., Hogansen, J., Geenen, S., Powers, L. E. & Gil-Kashiwbara, E. (2008). Gender Matters in Transition to Adulthood: A Survey Study of Adolscent With Disabilities and Their Families. *Psychology in the Schools, 45*, 349-364.

[51] Resnick, M. D., Bearman, P. S., Blum, R. W., Bauman, K. E., Harris, K. M., Jones, J., Tabor, J., Beuhring, T., Sieving, R. E., Shew, M., Ireland, M., Bearinger, L. H. & Udry, J. R. (1997). Protecting Adolescents From Harm: Findings From the National Longitudinal Study on Adolescent Health. *Journal of the American Medical Association, 278(10)*, 823-832.

[52] Rindfuss, R. R. (1991). The Young Adult Years: Diversity, Structural Change and Fertility. Population Association of America Presidential Address. *Demography, 28*, 493-512.

[53] Rodgers, K. B. & Rose, H. A. (2002). Risk and Resiliency Factors Among Adolescents Who Experience Marital Transitions. *Journal of Marriage and the Family, 64(4)*, 1024-1037.

[54] Rogan, P., Grossi, T. A. & Gajewski, R. (2002). Vocational and Career Assessment. In C.L. Sax, and C.A. Thoma (Eds.), *Transition Assessment: Wise Practices for Quality Lives* (pp. 103–117). Baltimore, MD: Paul Brookes Publishing.

[55] Sanford, C., Newman, L., Wagner, M., Cameto, R. & Knokey, A. M. (2011). *The Post-High School Outcomes of Young Adults With Disabilities up to 6 Years After High School. A Report From the National Longitudinal Transition Study-2 (NLTS2)* (NCSER 2011-3004). Menlo Park, CA: SRI International.

[56] Savage, R. C. (2005). The Great Leap Forward: Transitioning into the Adult World. *Preventing School Failure, 49(4)*, 43-52.

[57] Settersten, R. A., Furstenberg, F. F. & Rumbaut, R. G. (Eds.). (2005). *On the Frontier of Adulthood. Theory, Research, and Public Policy.* Chicago, IL: University of Chicago Press.

[58] Settersten, R. A., Jr. (2006). *Becoming Adult: Meanings and Markers for Young Americans* (Working Paper). New York, NY: The Network on Transitions to Adulthood.

[59] Shanahan, M. J. (2000). Pathways to Adulthood in Changing Societies: Variability and Mechanisms in Life Course Perspective. *Annual Review of Sociology, 26*, 667-692.

[60] Smith, C., Lizotte, A. J., Thornberry, T. P. & Krohn, M. D. (1995). Resilient Youth: Identifying Factors That Prevent High-Risk Youth From Engaging in Delinquency and Drug Use. In J. Hagan (Ed.), *Delinquency and Disrepute in the Life Course* (pp. 217-247). Greenwich, CT: JAI Press.

[61] Stodden, R. A. & Dowrick, P. (2000). The Present and Future of Postsecondary Education for Adults With Disabilities. *IMPACT, 13*(1), 4-5.

[62] Stodden, R. A., Jones, M. A. & Chang, K. B. T. (2002). *Services, Supports and Accommodations for Individuals With Disabilities: An Analysis Across Secondary Education, Postsecondary Education and Employment.* Retrieved July 19, 2004, from http://www.ncset.hawaii.edu/publications/pdf/services_supports.pdf.

[63] U.S. Department of Commerce, U.S. Census Bureau. (2002). *The Big Payoff: Educational Attainment and Synthetic Estimates of Work-Life Earnings.* Washington, DC: Government Printing Office.

[64] U.S. Department of Education, National Center for Education Statistics. (2002). *Classification of Instructional Programs: 2000 Edition.* Washington, DC: U.S. Government Printing Office.

[65] U.S. Department of Health and Human Services. (2001). *Youth Violence: A Report of the Surgeon General.* Retrieved July 27, 2006, from http://www.surgeongeneral.gov/library/youthviolence/chapter4/sec4.html.

[66] Wagner, M., Marder, C., Levine, P., Cameto, R., Cadwallader, T. W., Blackorby, J., Cardoso, D. & Newman, L. (2003). *The Individual and Household Characteristics of Youth With Disabilities. A Report From the National Longitudinal Transition Study-2 (NLTS2).* Menlo Park, CA: SRI International.

[67] Wagner, M., Newman, L. & Cameto, R. (2004). *Changes Over Time in the Secondary School Experiences of Students With Disabilities. A Report of Findings From the National Longitudinal Transition Study (NLTS) and the National Longitudinal Transition Study-2 (NLTS2).* Menlo Park, CA: SRI International.

[68] Wagner, M., Newman, L., Cameto, R., Levine, P. & Marder, C. (2007). Perceptions and Expectations of Youth With Disabilities: A Special Topic Report on Findings From the

National Longitudinal Transition Study-2 (NLTS2). Executive Summary. *The Journal for Vocational Special Needs Education, 30(1)*, 13-17.

[69] Wehman, P. & Evans Getzel, E. (Eds.). (2005). *Going to College: Expanding Opportunities for People WithDisabilities*. Baltimore, MD: Paul H. Brookes.

[70] Wolanin, T. R. & Steele, P. E. (2004). *Higher Education Opportunities for Students With Disabilities: A Primer for Policymakers*. Washington, DC: The Institute for Higher Education Policy.

End Notes

[1] Only a subset of items was included in the mail survey because the full set of items was considered too lengthy to be feasible for a mail questionnaire format.

[2] The time period for Add Health Wave 4, collected in 2007-08 would have been a more appropriate comparison for the 2009 Wave 5 NLTS2 data; however, the items related to financial independence were not collected in Add Health Wave 4.

[3] Youth with disabilities are included in the general population comparison sample because excluding them would require using self-reported disability data, which frequently are not an accurate indicator of disability, resulting in both over- and underestimations of disability.

[4] Parent/guardian household income was analyzed using three categories: $25,000 or less, $25,001 to $50,000, and more than $50,000.

[5] NLTS2 analyses included three racial/ethnic categories: White, African American, and Hispanic.

[6] Demographic characteristics include gender, parents' household income, and race/ethnicity. Findings are reported hou for White, African American, and Hispanic young adults with disabilities; other racial/ethnic categories of young adults were too small (less than 3 percent of the population of youth with disabilities) to report findings for them separately. Household income was categorized based on the three categories used in the data collection instrument, (i.e., $25,000 or less, $25,001 to $50,000, and more than $50,000). NLTS2 household income item categories were based on a review of general population statistics to ensure that the household income response categories fairly evenly divided the population. In NLTS2 Wave 1 the income breakdown was 35 percent for the category of $25,000 or less, 31 percent for $25,001 to $50,000, and 34 percent for more than $50,000 For consistency across the report, all comparisons are presented for all variables unless otherwise noted in a section (i.e., by length of time out of high school, high school completion status, disability category, age, gender, household income, and race/ethnicity.)

[7] The age of young adults with disabilities in 2009 was based on birthdates provided by parents during interviews and the date of the Wave 5 interview.

[8] This report is an update of a report on analyses conducted of data from the third wave of NLTS2 data collection, when youth had been out of high school up to 4 years and were ages 17 through 21. The organization and content of this report intentionally mirror the Wave 3 report very closely, including the figures and table shells used and some context-setting text. The report focusing on the fourth wave of NLTS2 data collection, when youth had been out of high school up to 6 years is an abbreviated look at key post-high school outcomes (e.g. postsecondary enrollment and employment status) and does not include the post-high school experiences, such as focus of postsecondary coursework or type of job, that are included in this report.

[9] The definitions of the 12 primary disability categories used here are specified by law and presented in table A-4, appendix A.

[10] Additional information about NLTS2 is available at www.nlts2.org.

[11] Wave 1 included parent interviews (2001), surveys of school staff (2002), and assessments of the academic abilities of students who were 16 to 18 years old in 2002. Wave 2 involved interviews with both parents and youth(2003), a mail survey of youth whose parents reported they were able to respond to questions but not by phone(2003), school staff surveys for youth still in high school (2004), and assessments of the academic abilities of youth who were 16 to 18 years old in 2004. Wave 3 (2005) repeated the telephone interviews and mail survey of youth, as in Waves 4 and 5 (2007 and 2009). High school transcripts were collected annually for youth leaving high school each year.

[12] All unweighted sample sizes included in the text, figures, and tables of this report are rounded to the nearest 10, per IES Disclosure Review Board requirements.

[13] NLTS2 instruments are available at www.nlts2.org.

[14] Because the data reported here come primarily from telephone interviews or mailed surveys that were requested by respondents during a telephone contact, no prior consent was required; respondents were free to indicate

their consent by continuing with the interview or to decline and hang up. Interviewers provided respondents with the following information:

"This interview is voluntary. Everything you say will be kept completely confidential and you may choose not to answer any question that I ask you. Nothing you say will ever be reported individually about you, [YOUTH if parent was respondent], or your family, and no information you give will be shared with [YOUTH/YOUR] school. If you have any questions or concerns about the study, I can give you a toll-free number to call."

[15] All unweighted sample sizes included in the text, figures, and tables of this report are rounded to the nearest 10, per IES requirements.

[16] Only a subset of items was included in the mail survey because the full set of items was considered too lengthy to be feasible for a mail questionnaire format.

[17] See appendix A for more information on sample eligibility and a discussion of response rates for each wave of data collection.

[18] Parents were told that interview questions would pertain to "school or work and social activities, as well as a few questions about things like...." For youth younger than 18, the sentence was completed with "[his/her] attitudes and experiences, like ever having been arrested." For youth age 18 or older, the sentence was completed with "[his/her] attitudes and experiences, including smoking, drinking, and ever having been arrested"; items related to these kinds of risk behaviors were asked only of youth age 18 or older. A total of 164 parents reported that their children could respond to the telephone interview but did not give permission for their children to be interviewed (4percent of those reportedly able to respond); the interview then continued with the parents and obtained additional information on such subjects as employment and postsecondary education. Analyses of the disability category distribution and demographic factors of youth who were able to respond and given permission to do so and those who were not permitted to be interviewed revealed no significant or sizable differences between the two groups.

[19] If a young adult could not be reached by phone or did not return a mailed questionnaire, an attempt was made to recontact the parent and complete the second part of the telephone interview with the parent, if the young adult had not indicated that the parent should not be contacted. Material included in the lead letters mailed to young adults prior to the interviews and introductory language in the phone interview informed young adults that they could refuse to have their parents contacted. The second part of the parent interview included only items readily answerable by many parents about their young adult children with disabilities; 18 percent of parent part 2 interviews were completed by parents after the young adult could not be reached.

[20] Readers should be aware of the potential for differences in reports across modes of data collection (i.e., mail questionnaire vs. telephone interview). Differences between mail and telephone samples (e.g., the mail sample included more youth with hearing impairments) did not support examining these potential differences in data collection mode.

[21] Young adults with disabilities are included in the general population comparison sample because excluding them would require using self-reported disability data, which frequently are not an accurate indicator of disability, resulting in both over- and underestimations of disability. For example, a large proportion of self-identified disabilities in postsecondary school are visual impairments because of confusion by students who wear glasses. In addition, NLTS2 findings indicate that less than one-third (32 percent) of youth who were identified by their secondary school as having a disability consider themselves to have a disability by the time they are age 17 orolder.

[22] CPS variables were combined to make them equivalent to NLTS2 items. For this reason, the CPS survey questions will not be presented in the report chapters.

[23] Given that interview/survey respondents were weighted to represent the universe and individuals who failed to respond to the survey as a whole were assigned a weight of zero, imputing missing values for nonrespondents would not affect analysis results. In addition, for those who responded to the interview/survey, item nonresponse was relatively low—item nonresponse ranged from less than 1 percent to less than 3 percent for the key outcome variables.

[24] All standard errors in this report were calculated using formula-based estimates rather than estimates based on replicate weights. See appendix A for description of estimating standard errors. As a 10-year longitudinal study, NLTS2 has used this formula-based procedure to calculate standard errors throughout the duration of the study, rather than use currently available procedures. This decision to maintain consistency in analytical approaches was based on the need to support comparisons of findings across NLTS2 reports. To examine possible differences between approaches, replicate weights were created for chapter 5 of this report. Findings using the replicate weights were then compared with the findings using formula-based estimates. Of the 904 possible comparisons in the chapter, 29 differences (3 percent) were noted, supporting the decision to maintain the use of formula-based estimates.

[25] In the case of unweighted data, two percentages are usually compared by using nonparametric statistics, such as the Fisher exact test. In the case of NLTS2, the data were weighted, and the usual nonparametric tests would yield significance levels that are too small (Heeringa, West, and Berglund 2010) because the NLTS2 effective sample size is less than the nominal sample size. Instead, to test for the equality between the mean values of the responses to a single survey item in two disjoint subpopulations, we began by computing a ratio where the

numerator was the difference of the sample means for those subpopulations. (In the case of Bernoulli variables, each mean was a weighted percentage.) The denominator for the ratio was the estimated standard error of the numerator, where the standard errors were adjusted to take into account clustering, stratification, and unequal weights. The adjustment to the variances was determined in a design effect study that compared traditionally calculated variances with those calculated using 32 balanced repeated replicate weights. Sample sizes (and consequently degrees of freedom) for Student t types of ratios were typically reasonably large (i.e., never fewer than 30 in each group), so the ratio follows, by the Central Limit Theorem, an approximately normal distribution. For a two-tailed test, the test statistic is the square of the ratio, which then follows an approximate chi-square distribution with one degree of freedom. Because a chi-square distribution with one degree of freedom is the same as an F distribution with one degree of freedom in the numerator and an infinite number of degrees in the denominator, the test statistic approximately follows an F (1, infinity) distribution. Since the application of adjustments from the design effect study tended to slightly overestimate the standard errors from balanced repeated replicates, the use of infinite degrees of freedom, rather than 31 degrees of freedom, nevertheless resulted in actual p values that were slightly lower than nominal p values.

[26] Testing for the significance of differences in responses to two survey items for the same individuals involves identifying for each young adult the pattern of response to the two items. The response to each item (e.g., the young adult reported receiving vacation benefits—yes or no—and reported receiving health benefits—yes or no) is scored as 0 or 1, producing difference values for individual young adults of +1 (responded affirmatively to the first item but not the second), 0 (responded affirmatively to both or neither item), or -1 (responded affirmatively to the second item but not the first). The test statistic is the square of a ratio, where the numerator of the ratio is the weighted mean change score and the denominator is an estimate of the standard error of that mean. Because the ratio approaches a normal distribution by the Central Limit Theorem, this test statistic approximately follows a chi-square distribution with one degree of freedom, that is, an F (1, infinity) distribution.

[27] See Wagner et al. (2003) for relationships of demographic factors and disability categories for the full NLTS2 sample.

[28] See Newman et al. (2009) and Sanford et al. (in review).

[29] Respondents were asked, "Since leaving high school have you [has YOUTH] taken any classes from a [postsecondary school]?"

[30] U.S. Department of Labor, Bureau of Labor Statistics, National Longitudinal Survey of Youth 1997 (NLSY97) 2005 youth survey, responses for 21- to 25-year-olds.

[31] Respondents were asked, "Are you [is YOUTH] going to a [postsecondary school] now?" Those who had been enrolled in a postsecondary school but were not currently enrolled were asked, "Are you [is YOUTH] not going to a [postsecondary school] now because you are [YOUTH is]: on school vacation, graduated or completed the program, or some other reason?" Respondents who were on school vacation were recoded as being currently enrolled in postsecondary school.

[32] Because a relatively small proportion of young adults in the NLTS2 sample (15 percent) were enrolled in postsecondary schools at the time of the Wave 5 interview, data from Waves 2 through 4 were used to augment Wave5 data for most analyses in this chapter, as follows: If a young adult with disabilities did not attend a postsecondary school in the 2 years preceding the Wave 5 interview, but was reported in a prior waveto have been out of high school and to have attended a postsecondary school, data were taken from the most recent wave in which that young adult was reported to have attended postsecondary school. Augmenting the data in this way increased the sample size sufficiently to allow disaggregated analyses (e.g., by disability category) of variables concerning timing and intensity of enrollment, course of study, receipt of accommodations and supports, and postsecondary school completion.

[33] Respondents were asked, "About how long after leaving high school was it before you [YOUTH] started going to a [postsecondary school]?"

[34] For each type of postsecondary school, respondents were asked, "Have you [has YOUTH] been enrolled continuously since you first began at a [type of postsecondary school], not counting time off for vacations, or have you [has YOUTH] been enrolled off and on, taking classes some semesters or quarters but not others?"

[35] Bars in the figure reflect only youth who met the category's criterion (i.e., were enrolled continuously or on a full-time basis); the complements (i.e., were enrolled some semesters or quarters but not others, or enrolled on a part-time basis) are not presented in the figure.

[36] Respondents were asked, "Are you [is YOUTH] going to a[postsecondary school] full time or part time?" If they asked, respondents were told that "full time" means taking a full course load of 12 credits or more at a time.

[37] Respondents at 2-year colleges were asked, "Have you [has YOUTH] taken mostly vocational courses to train for a job, like computer or business courses, or have you [has YOUTH] taken mostly academic courses, like English or science?"

[38] Respondents who had attended 2-year colleges were asked, "What is [was] your [YOUTH's] major or primary course of study in a 2-year or community college?"

[39] Young adult respondents were asked, "Some people have a disability or special need that makes it hard for them to do some things. Do you consider yourself to have any kind of disability or special need?"

[40] Young adult respondents who asserted they had a disability were asked, "Was this school aware that you have a disability or special need before you enrolled there, after you enrolled, or is the school not aware of your disability or special need?"

[41] Respondents were asked, "Have you [YOUTH] received any services, accommodations, or other help from the school to help you do your best there, like a note taker or more time to take tests because of a learning problem, disability, or other special need?"

[42] Source for accommodations and supports received by postsecondary students when they were in high school: U.S. Department of Education, Institute of Education Sciences, National Center for Special Education Research, National Longitudinal Transition Study-2 (NLTS2), Wave1 school program survey, 2002; responses restricted to those high school students who had eventually enrolled in postsecondary school.

[43] Source for accommodations and supports received in high school by postsecondary students who disclosed a disability to their postsecondary school: U.S. Department of Education, Institute of Education Sciences, National Center for Special Education Research, National Longitudinal Transition Study-2 (NLTS2), Wave1 school program survey, 2002; responses restricted to those who eventually enrolled in postsecondary schools and had disclosed a disability to their postsecondary school.

[44] Respondents who indicated that they received help from their school because of a disability were asked, "What services, accommodations, or other help have you [YOUTH] received?"

[45] Source for high school accommodations: U.S. Department of Education, Institute of Education Sciences, National Center for Special Education Research, National Longitudinal Transition Study-2 (NLTS2), Wave1 general education teacher survey (2002). See Newman, Marder, and Wagner (2003) for discussion of accommodations received in general education classes in high school.

[46] Respondents were asked, "Did you [YOUTH] ever get help with school work from this school, like going to a tutor or a study center or writing center?"

[47] Respondents were asked, "Besides what the school had available, have you [YOUTH] gotten any services or help on your own to help you do your best at school?"

[48] Young adult respondents were asked, "How useful have the services, accommodations, and help with schoolwork been in helping you stay in school and do your best there?" Response categories were "very useful," "somewhat useful," "not very useful," or "not at all useful."

[49] Youngadults were asked, "Do you think you are getting enough services, accommodations, or help with schoolwork to do your best there?" Response categories were "definitely getting enough," "probably getting enough," "probably not getting enough," or "definitely not getting enough."

[50] Young adult respondents were asked, "Would it havebeen helpful to you to have had some services, accommodations, or help with schoolwork?"

[51] Respondents who had attended 2-yearcolleges were asked, "About how many total credits have you earned [did you earn] at the 2-yearor community college or colleges you've credits?" and respondents who had attended 4-yearcolleges were asked, "About how many total credits have you earned [did you earn] at the 4-year college or colleges you'vemester credits or quarter credits?" Quarter credits were multiplied by .67 to convert to semester credits for analysis and reporting. Respondents who attended vocational, business, or technical schools were not asked to report the number of earned credits.

[52] Respondents were asked, "Are you [is YOUTH]working toward a diploma, certificate, or license from this work?"

[53] Completion rate in this report is calculated as a percentage of students who enrolled in postsecondary programs; it includes in its base students currently attending postsecondary school. This approach is used more widely than that previously used to calculate NLTS2 completion rates. Completion rates in previous NLTS2 reports were calculated as a percentage of students who had left postsecondary school. For wave 5 the completion rate would have been based on the 72percentof students who had attended postsecondary school, but were not currently enrolled at the time of the Wave 5 interview. Based on the previous method of calculating completion rates, 47.6 percent of postsecondary students with disabilities and 55 percent of similar-aged peers in the general population had completed their postsecondary programs (not a significant difference).

[54] Respondents who had been in a postsecondary program earlier but were not currently enrolled and had not graduated were asked, "Why did you [YOUTH]stop going to college?"

[55] Respondents were asked, "Do you (does YOUTH) have a paid job now, other than work around the house?"

[56] Source for general population data: U.S. Census Bureau, Current Population Survey (CPS), May 2009. Data are for 21- to 25-year-olds.

[57] Respondents were asked, "Did you (YOUTH) do any workfor pay, other than work around the house, at any time since high school?" Respondents who in any wave had reported working for pay other than work around the house since high school were considered to have been employed since high school.

[58] For respondents who were employed at the time of the interview, questions were asked about the current job; for those who were not currently employed, questions were asked about the respondent'srecent job. For reporting purposes, employment items were combined to reflect either the young adult's current (at the time of the interview) or most recent job.

[59] Respondents were asked, "How long have you (has YOUTH) had this job?"

[60] Respondents were asked, "What is your (YOUTH's) job title? Briefly tell me about your (YOUTH's) main job duties at that job."

[61] Respondents were asked, "About how many hoursa week do you (YOUTH) usually work at this job?"

[62] Respondents who worked less than 35 hours per week were asked, "Are you working part time because you want to, or would you rather work full time?"

[63] Respondents were asked, "About how much are you (isYOUTH) paid at this job? Is that per hour?" Weekly, yearly, and monthly wages were converted to hourly wages by dividing the wage by the number of hours worked per week, and then multiplying by 4.3 for monthly-reported wages or by 52 for yearly-reported wages.

[64] Respondents were asked about each benefit type separately, "As part of thisjob, do you (does YOUTH) get paid vacation or sick leave; health insurance; retirement benefits, like a 401K?"

[65] Note that benefits information for NLTS2 and the general population were collected at two time points.

[66] Wages by gender for the general population were extracted from U.S. Census Bureau, Current Population Survey (CPS), May 2009. Data are for 21- to 25-year-olds.

[67] Respondents were asked, "Do you think your (YOUTH's) employer is aware that you have (YOUTH has) a disability or special need?"

[68] Respondents were asked, "Have you (Has YOUTH) received any accommodations or other help from your (his/her) employer because you have (he/she has) any kind of learning problem, disability, or other special need?"

[69] Respondents were asked, "What accommodations or other help have you (has YOUTH) received?"

[70] Young adults were asked, "Do you usually like your job?"

[71] Young adults were asked, "Do you think you are treated pretty well by others at your job?"

[72] Young adults were asked, "Do you think your education and training is put to good use?" and "Do you think in your job, you have lots of chances to work your way up?"

[73] Young adults were asked, "Have you been promoted ortaken on more responsibility since you started the job?" "Do you think you are pretty well paid for your work?" and "Are you paid more than when you started the job?"

[74] Respondents were asked, "When you (YOUTH) left that job did you (he/she) quit, were you (was he/she) fired, were you (was he/she) laid off, or was it a temporary job that ended?"

[75] Respondents were asked, "Are you (is YOUTH) looking for a paid job now?"

[76] Respondents were asked, "About how long have you (has YOUTH) been looking for work?"

[77] Respondents were asked, "Did you (YOUTH) find this job yourself, or did you have help – like from a temporary agency or someone you know?" "Who helped you? Was it someone in an employment agency or other program, a teacher or someone at school, a family member, a friend or someone else you know?"

[78] The focus of this chapter is on involvement in any type of paid employment (other than work around the house), mirroring much of what is presented in this report's employment chapter. Current federal policy requires states to measure transition from high school to post-high school years in terms of competitive employment. The State Performance Plan (SPP) and Annual Performance Report (APR) to the Office of Special Education Programs (OSEP) for the reporting of Indicator 14 require the "Percent of youth who had IEPs, are no longer in secondary school and who have been competitively employed, enrolled in some type of postsecondary school, or both, within one year of leaving high school"[20 U.S.C. 1416(a)(3)(B)]. In NLTS2, *when restricting the definition of employment to competitive employment,* 88percent of young adults with disabilities reported having been competitively employed and/or enrolled in postsecondary school within up to 8 years after leaving high school and 85 percent reported having been competitively employed and/or enrolled in postsecondary education within the 1 year post-high school period specified in the regulations.

[79] Respondents were asked where young adults had lived in the past 2 years and where they lived "now." A variable measuring the degree of residential independence since high school was derived from three items: if the young adult had lived independently or semi-independently in the past 2 years, was currently living independently or semi-independently, and when he or she had left school.

[80] This section focuses on young adults who lived independently or semi-independently. Young adults not included in this figure are those who lived with a parent or family member or guardian (52 percent at the time of the interview), in an institution (1 percent at the time of the interview), or in a group home (1 percent at the time of the interview).

[81] Respondents were asked where young adult lived currently.

[82] Calculated from the National Longitudinal Survey of Youth (NLSY), 2005, for out-of-high school young adults who were between 21 to 25 years old. This calculation was created based on two items in NLSY; current residence and relationship to others in the household. Response categories for the first item were, "home, condo, apartment, dormitory, hotel/boarding house, shelter, in jail, mobile home, hospital, group home, and farm." The second item focused on the respondent's relationship to others in the household. Respondents were coded as currently living independently if they lived in a house, condo, apartment, farm, mobile home, hotel/boarding house and if they were not living with a biological, adoptive, or foster parent(s) or other relative.

[83] Percentages not included in tables or figures.

[84] Youth who were age 18 years or older, no longer in high school, and not living with their parents were asked, "Are you happy with this living arrangement, or wouldyou like to change where you live or who you live with?"

[85] Respondents were asked, "Have you [has YOUTH] ever had or fathered any children?"

[86] Calculated from the National Longitudinal Survey of Youth (NLSY), 2005, for out-of-high school 21- to 25-year-olds.

[87] Percentages not included in tables or figures.

[88] Respondents were asked, "[Does this child] or[Do any of these children] live with you now?"

[89] Respondents were asked, "What is your current marital status? Are you [is YOUTH] engaged, single, never married, married, divorced, separated, or widowed?"

[90] Calculated from the National Longitudinal Survey of Youth (NLSY), 2005, for out-of-high school 21- to 25-year-olds. Engaged and divorced/separated/widowed were not available in NLSY.

[91] Respondents were asked, "Do you [does YOUTH] have a savings account?"

[92] Respondents were asked, "Do you [does YOUTH] have a checking account where you write checks?"

[93] Respondents were asked, "Do you [does YOUTH] have a credit card or charge account in your own name?"

[94] Calculated from the National Longitudinal Study of Adolescent Health (Add Health), Wave 3, 2001–02, for out-of-high school 21- to 25-year-olds.

[95] For the 13 percent of young adults who were married, reported annual income included their spouse's income. For all other respondents, independent of their residential status, annual income was based on their individual income. Respondents were asked, "Studies like these often group people according to income. Please tell me which group best describes your [YOUTH's] total income [if spouse included] in the last tax year, including salaries or other earnings, money from public assistance, retirement, and so on, before taxes. Was your income in the past year $25,000 or less or more than $25,000?" Questions with more detailed income categories followed.

[96] Percentages not included in tables or figures.

[97] Regarding young adults who were living independently or semi-independently, respondents were asked if the young adult had "received Food Stamps" at any time in the past 2 years, and young adults who reported having had or had fathered a child were asked if they had received money from "TANF (Temporary Assistance for Needy Families)" and, if so, whether they currently were receiving Food Stamps or TANF. Variables indicating receipt of Food Stamps or TANF since high school were derived from three sets of items: if the young adult had received Food Stamps or TANF in the past 2 years, was currently receiving Food Stamps or TANF, and when he or she had left school.

[98] Protective factors have been defined as "those aspects of the individual and his or her environment that buffer or moderate the effect of risk"(U.S. Department of Health and Human Services 2001, chapter 4, para. 1).

[99] Respondents were asked, "During the past 12 months, about how many days a week [did you/did name of youth] get together with friends (outside of school if youth was in school) and outside of organized activities or groups?" Because the friendship interaction itemrefers to activities in the preceding 12 months findings are reported only for the 98percent of young adults who had been out of secondary school at least a year so as to avoid including secondary school experiences.

[100] Respondents were asked, "How frequently do you [does youth] use e-mail, instant messaging, or take part in chat rooms? Would you say several times a day, once a day, several times a week, once a week, or less often than that?"

[101] Respondents were asked, "During the past 12 months[have you/hasname of youth] taken lessons or classes (outside of school for those in school) in things like art, music, dance, a foreign language, religion, or computer skills?"

[102] Respondents were asked, "During the past 12 months[have you/hasname of youth] done any volunteer or community service activities? This could include community service that is part of a school class or other group activity."

[103] Respondents were asked, if a youth was not enrolled in school, "During the past 12 months[have you/hasname of youth] participated in any school activities outside of class, such as a sports team, band or chorus, a school club, or student government?" All respondents were asked, "During the past 12 months[have you/hasname of youth] participated in any [out-of-high school, for those in school] group activity, such as scouting, church or temple youth group, or nonschool team sports like soccer or softball?"

[104] Ninety-threepercent of young adults included in this report have been out of high school 1 or more years.

[105] Respondents were asked for youth at least 15 years old, "[Do you/does name of youth] have a driver's license or learner's permit?"

[106] Respondents were asked for youth at least 18 years old, "[Are you/is name of youth] registered to vote?"

[107] Youth were asked, "In the past 12 months, have you gotten in a physical fight?"

[108] Youth age 18 or older were asked, "During the past 30days, on how many days did you carry a weapon, such as a gun, knife, or club?"

[109] Youth age 18 or older were asked, "Do you belong to a gang?"

[110] Respondents were asked, "In the past 2 years, [have you/has *name of youth*] been stopped and questioned by police except for a traffic violation?"

[111] Respondents were asked, "[Have you/has*name of youth*] been arrested at any time in the past 2 years?"

[112] Respondents were asked, "In the past 2 years, [have you/has*name of youth*] been in jail overnight?"

[113] Respondents were asked, "In the past 2 years, [have you/has*name of youth*] been on probation or parole?"

[114] LEAs were instructed to include on the roster any student for whom they were administratively responsible, even if the student was not educated within the LEA (e.g., attended school sponsored by an education cooperative or was sent by the LEA to a private school). Despite these instructions, some LEAs may have underreported students served outside the LEA.

[115] Enrollment in grades 7 through 12 was estimated by dividing the total enrollment in all grade levels served by an LEA by the number of grade levels to estimate an enrollment per grade level. This was multiplied by 6 to estimate the enrollment in grades 7 through 12.

[116] "50 percent sampling efficiency" means that a simple random sample of half the size as NLTS2 would have the same standard error as obtained in NLTS2 when the complex sampling design is taken into account. Sampling efficiency is the inverse of the DEFT, where DEFT is the square foot of DEFF (the design effect).

[117] Students who were designated as being in ungraded programs also were sampled if they met the age criteria.

[118] In the process of selecting the student sample, random numbers were generated and the sample universe file was sorted by these numbers. Sample members were selected beginning at the start of the file until the required numberof students had been selected. If two students were selected from the same family, the first student on the list was chosen for the sample (i.e., the one with the smaller random number).

[119] All NLTS2 instruments are available on the NLTS2 website, www.nlts2.org.

[120] Some special schools and school districts reported secondary disabilities for students. For example, a student with visual impairment as his or her primary disability category also could have been reported as having a hearing impairment as a secondary disability.

[121] Parents were asked to use a 4-point scale ranging from "not at all well" to "very well" to evaluate four of their sons' or daughters' skills that often are used in daily activities: reading and understanding common signs, telling time on a clock with hands, counting change, and looking up telephone numbers and using the telephone. These skills are referred to as "functional cognitive skills" because they require the cognitive ability to read, count, and calculate. As such, they suggest much about students' abilities to perform a variety of more complex cognitive tasks. However, they also require sensory and motor skills—to see signs, manipulate a telephone, and so on. Consequently, a high score indicates high functioning in all of these areas, but a low score can result from a deficit in the cognitive, sensory, and/or motor domains. A summative scale of parents' ratings of these functional cognitive skills ranges from 4 (all skills done "not at all well") to 16 (all skills done "very well").

[122] See Wagner et al. (2003)for relationships of demographic factors and disability categories for the full NLTS2 sample.

[123] This includes 19 percent of youth who were reported to have dropped out and 1 percent who reportedly left high school without finishing for other reasons (e.g., permanent expulsion).

[124] General population data computed for 21- to 25-year-olds, using United States Census Bureau 2000 data.

[125] See footnote 4.

[126] See footnote 4.

In: Young Adults with Disabilities
Editors: David F. Morris and Christopher B. Allen

ISBN: 978-1- 61942-159-2
© 2012 Nova Science Publishers, Inc.

Chapter 2

THE POST-HIGH SCHOOL OUTCOMES OF YOUNG ADULTS WITH DISABILITIES UP TO 6 YEARS AFTER HIGH SCHOOL

United States Department of Education

1. INTRODUCTION

Traditional social indicators of adolescents emerging into adulthood include living independently, earning a postsecondary degree, obtaining full-time employment, getting married, or becoming a parent (Haber et al. 2008; Keller, Cusick, and Courtney 2007; Oesterle et al. 2010; Settersten and Ray 2010). Although there has been a shift in the timing and sequence of adult transitions these core indicators have remained the same (Furstenberg 2010). As youth with disabilities leave high school and transition to adulthood, they are increasingly exposed to opportunities for postsecondary education, employment, and independent living (Newman et al. 2010). Current national policy mandates are holding schools and states more accountable for the postschool outcomes of youth with disabilities. The 2004 reauthorization of the Individuals With Disabilities Education Act (IDEA) highlighted the importance of improving the postschool outcomes of youth with disabilities by requiring schools to develop "measurable postschool goals in the areas of employment, education/training, and, if appropriate, independent living" and states to "report student postschool outcome performance" (Morningstar et al. 2010).

The National Longitudinal Transition Study-2 (NLTS2) provides a unique source of information to help in developing an understanding of the experiences of secondary school students with disabilities nationally as they go through their early adult years. NLTS2 addresses questions about youth with disabilities in transition by providing information over a 10-year period about a nationally representative sample of secondary school students with disabilities who were receiving special education services under the Individuals With Disabilities Education Act (IDEA) in the 2000–01 school year.

The NLTS2 Wave 4 overview report describes key postsecondary outcomes for the subset of young adults with disabilities who were out of secondary school up to 6 years and

19 to 23 years old[1] when telephone interviews were conducted in 2007. This report, as all NLTS2 reports are guided by the NLTS2 framework. Specifically, this report addresses questions that reflect critical domains of young adulthood, which are central to the purpose of IDEA as expressed in 20 U.S.C. 1400(d)(1)(A) to "prepare them [children with disabilities] for future education, employment, and independent living." This report focuses on the following research questions:

- What are the postsecondary education, employment, independence, and social outcomes of young adults with disabilities in their first 6 years out of high school?
- How do these outcomes differ for young adults in different disability categories, for those with different school-exit characteristics (high school completion status and length those with different school-exit characteristics (high school completion status and length of time out of high school), and demographic characteristics (young adults' gender, young adults' race/ethnicity, and parents' household income)?[2]
- How do the post-high school outcomes of young adults with disabilities compare with those of similar-age peers in the general population?

As indicated by these research questions, this NLTS2 Wave 4 report focuses on post-high school outcomes, such as postsecondary enrollment rates and employment rates; it does not describe post high-school experiences,such as receipt of accommodations in postsecondary school or job search activities. The NLTS2 Wave 3 and Wave 5 overview reports include full descriptions of both post-high-school outcomes and experiences (Newman et al. 2009; Newman et al. in review).

Study Overview

NLTS2 is a 10-year-long study of the characteristics, experiences, and outcomes of a nationally representative sample of youth with disabilities who were 13 to 16 years old and receiving special education services in grade 7 or above on December 1, 2000. NLTS2 findings generalize to youth with disabilities nationally and to youth in each of the 12 federal special education disability categories in use for students in the NLTS2 age range.[3] (Details of the NLTS2 design, sample, and analysis procedures are presented in appendix A.)[4] The study was designed to collect data on sample members from multiple sources in five waves, beginning in 2001 and ending in 2009. Wave 1 included parent interviews (2001), surveys of school staff (2002), and assessments of the academic abilities of students who were 16 to 18 years old in 2002. Wave 2 involved interviews with both parents and youth (2003), a mail survey of youth whose parents reported they were able to respond to questions but not by phone (2003), school staff surveys for youth still in high school (2004), and assessments of the academic abilities of youth who were 16 to 18 years old in 2004. Wave 3 (2005) repeated the parent telephone interviews as well as the youth interviews and mail surveys. Wave 4 (2007) and Wave 5 (2009) included telephone interviews and mail surveys both of parents and of youth. High school transcripts were collected annually for youth leaving high school each year.

The NLTS2 sample was constructed in two stages, beginning in 2000. The NLTS2 district sample was stratified to increase the precision of estimates, to ensure that low-frequency types of districts (e.g., large urban districts) were adequately represented in the sample, to improve comparisons with the findings of other research, and to make NLTS2 responsive to concerns voiced in policy debate (e.g., differential effects of federal policies in particular regions, districts of different sizes). Three stratifying variables were used: region, size (student enrollment), and community wealth. A stratified random sample of school districts was selected from the universe of approximately 12,000 that served students receiving special education in at least one grade from the 7th through 12th grades. In order to be nationally representative of youth with disabilities who attended the most common types of publicly-supported schools, all known state-supported "special schools"— i.e., those that served primarily students with hearing and visual impairments and multiple disabilities (77 in NLTS2)— also were invited to participate in the studies. These districts and 77 state-supported special schools that served primarily students with hearing and vision impairments and multiple disabilities were invited to participate in the study, with the intention of recruiting approximately 500 districts and as many special schools as possible from which to select a target sample of about 12,000 students. Recruitment efforts resulted in 501 school districts and 38 special schools agreeing to participate and providing rosters of students receiving special education services in the designated age range, from which the student sample was selected.

The roster of all students in the NLTS2 age range who were receiving special education services from each district and special school was stratified by primary disability category, as reported by the districts. Students then were selected randomly from each disability category. Sampling fractions were calculated that would produce enough students in each category so that, in the final study year, findings would generalize to most categories individually with an acceptable level of precision, accounting for attrition and for response rates to the parent/young adult interview. A total of 11,276 students were selected and eligible to participate in NLTS2.

Data Sources for Young Adults with Disabilities

This section presents the multiple data sources used in this report to describe the post-high school experiences of young adults with disabilities at the time of the Wave 4 interview, who were known to be out of secondary school at the time of the Wave 4 data collection. Appendix A includes a description of the overall response rates for each wave of data collection.

Primary sources used in this report were the Wave 4 youth telephone interview and mail survey or the Wave 4 parent telephone interview, conducted in 2007.[5] In addition, those variables that describe young adults' the basis of data from the Waves 2 and 3 (conducted in 2003 and 2005, respectively) youth telephone interviews and mail surveys or from the Waves 2 and Wave 3 parent telephone interviews for young adults who were out of high school at those times. School district rosters, high school transcripts, and the Wave 1 parent interview or mail survey also provided a small amount of the data used in this report. Each data source for young adults with disabilities is described briefly below and discussed in greater detail in appendix A.

Table 1. NLTS2 data sources for post-high school experiences of young adults with disabilities included in this report

Source	Approximate number	Percent of young Adults included in this report
Total number of sample members with responses to Wave 4 survey known to be out of secondary school at the time of the Wave 4 data collection	4,650	100.0
Youth telephone interview	2,300	49.3
Youth mail questionnaire	360	7.8
Parent telephone interview	1,990	42.9
Number in Wave 4 report and out of school in Wave 3, with Wave 3 survey data coming from	2,160	46.5
Youth telephone interview	1,360	29.3
Youth mail questionnaire	160	3.4
Parent telephone interview	640	13.8
Number in Wave 4 report and out of school in Wave 2, with Wave 2 survey data coming from	890	19.0
Youth telephone interview	570	12.2
Youth mail questionnaire	50	<1.0
Parent telephone interview	270	5.8
Number in Wave 4 report with Wave 1 survey data		
Parent interview	4,480	96.0
High school transcript	3,570	77.0
School and school district student rosters	4,650	100.0

The data for young adults with disabilities, the focus of this report, were obtained for approximately 4,650 sample members[6] with responses to the Wave 4 survey who were known to be out of high school at the time of the Wave 4 data collection (table 1).

Parent/Young Adult Data

Wave 4 Data

Information on the outcomes of young adults with disabilities came from young adults themselves in the majority of cases (see table 1), usually from the youth telephone interview. These respondents were young adults with disabilities who were reported by parents to be able to answer questions for themselves by telephone. Young adults who were reported to be able to answer questions for themselves, but not by telephone (e.g., young adults with hearing impairments), were sent a mail questionnaire. For young adults who were reported by parents not to be able to answer questions for themselves (e.g., young adults with significant cognitive impairments), interviews were attempted with parents. Thus, there are three sources of data for Wave 4 of NLTS2. Data from these three sources were combined for the analyses reported here and subsetted to include only data for young adults with disabilities, aged 19 and older.

Youth Telephone Interview

NLTS2 sample members who were eligible for a Wave 4 youth telephone interview were those (1) for whom working telephone numbers or addresses for the youth or their parents were available so that they could be reached by phone (a total of approximately 8,130 young adults) and (2) whose parents or guardians (referred to here as parents) had reported in the Wave 2 parent telephone interview (if interviewed at that time) or the Wave 3 parent interview (if interviewed in Wave 3 for the first time) that the youth could answer questions about his or her experience by phone (a total of approximately 8,130 youth).[7] Wave 4 interview attempts were made directly with youth who were reported in Waves 2 or 3 to be able to participate in a telephone interview, without attempts being made to contact parents in advance. For youth whose parents were not interviewed in Waves 2 or 3 and, therefore, whose ability to participate in a telephone interview or mail survey was unknown, parent interviews were attempted first. At those times, after making the initial telephone contact with the parents of sample members and completing items intended only for parent respondents, parents were asked whether their child was able to respond to questions about their experiences by telephone for themselves. Parents who responded affirmatively and whose sample children were younger than age 18 then were asked to grant permission for their children to be interviewed and told the kinds of questions that would be asked.[8] Parents of young adults 18 or older were informed of the kinds of questions that would be asked, but permission was not requested because the young adults were no longer minors. Interviewers obtained contact information for these young adults and attempted to complete telephone interviews with them. Telephone interviews were completed with approximately 2,490 young adults, 72 percent of the approximately 3,430 young adults who were eligible. If a youth could not be reached by phone or did not return a mailed questionnaire, an attempt was made to recontact the parent and complete the second part of the telephone interview with the parent, which included only items readily answerable by many parents about their adolescent and young adult children with disabilities. Approximately 2,300 telephone interview respondents to the Wave 4 telephone interview were young adults, the focus of this report.

Youth Mail Survey

If parent respondents to the Waves 2, 3, or 4 telephone interviews indicated that youth were not able to respond to questions about their experiences for themselves by telephone, interviewers asked whether youth would be able to complete a mail questionnaire. Parents of approximately 740 Wave 4-eligible youth responded affirmatively, making their children eligible for a mail survey. Permission for youth to be sent a mail questionnaire was not asked of parents because that questionnaire did not contain items considered potentially sensitive and because parents' providing a mailing permission to send it. Mailing addresses were obtained for those sample members, and questionnaires were sent to the youth. Questionnaires were tailored to the circumstances of individual youth. For example, if a parent indicated in the telephone interview that a youth was employed, the questionnaire for that youth contained a section on employment experiences, which was not included in questionnaires for youth reported not to be employed. Questionnaires were returned by approximately 400 young adults, 54 percent of the approximately 740 young adults who were eligible. Approximately 360 mail questionnaire respondents were young adults who are part of the sample that generated the findings reported in this document.[9]

Parent/Guardian Interview

In addition to sample members who completed a telephone interview or mail survey, parents completed a telephone interview for approximately 2,300 sample members who did not respond for themselves, either because they were reported not to be able to do so or because young adults who were reported to be able to respond could not be reached or refused to respond.[10] In the latter case, parents were contacted to complete a subset of interview items that experience demonstrated could readily be answered by many parents (e.g., whether a youth was employed or enrolled in postsecondary education). A total of approximately 1,990 young adults for whom parents were the sole respondents were out of secondary school and are included in the sample that forms the basis of this report. Young adults whose parents responded for them did not differ significantly in their disability category, age identified as having a disability, or functional abilities (appendix B provides detailed information regarding comparisons between these groups).

Wave 2 and Wave 3 Data

Several variables created for this report indicate whether a young adult had had a particular experience "since high school" (e.g., postsecondary enrollment, employment, and parenting and marital status). Fifty-three percent of y respondents (approximately 2,490 young adults) had left high school since the Wave 3 data collection; thus, Wave 4 data are all that are required to generate values for these variables for them. However, the remainder of young adult respondents (approximately 2,160 young adults) were already out of high school in Wave 2 and/or Wave 3. Thus, data from Waves 2 and 3 needed to be taken into account to generate values for variables measuring experiences "since high school." Wave 2 and Wave 3 data also were used to determine whether young adults had completed high school or left without completing and the year in which they left. Waves 2 and 3 data collections mirrored procedures followed for Wave 4. The Wave 3 youth telephone interview produced data for approximately 1,360 young adults included in the sample that forms the basis of this report, the mail questionnaire generated data for approximately 160 young adults, and parent interviews provided data for approximately 640 young adults, for a total of approximately 2,160 sample members. The Wave 2 youth telephone interview produced data for approximately 570 young adults included in the sample that forms the basis of this report, the mail questionnaire generated data for approximately 50 youth, and parent interviews provided data for approximately 270 young adults, for a total of approximately 890 sample members.

Wave 1 Data

The initial wave of NLTS2 data collection involved parent telephone interviews and a mail survey of parents who could not be reached by telephone. Data for two demographic items (gender and race/ethnicity) were drawn from these Wave 1 sources for approximately 4,480 young adults with disabilities that forms the basis of this report.

High School Transcripts

High school completion status and high school leave date were based on data from high school transcripts. High school transcripts were requested for all NLTS2 sample members. Transcript data were collected for approximately 3,570 young adults included in this report.

For those for whom transcript data were not available, school completion status and leave dates were based on information from parent/youth interviews.

School and School District Student Rosters

Information about the primary disability category of NLTS2 sample members came from rosters of students in the NLTS2 age range receiving special education services in the 2000–01 school year under the auspices of participating school districts and state-supported special schools. Additionally, data on the racial/ethnic background of sample members were taken from this source when they were included on rosters. In the absence of roster data on racial/ethnic background, data were taken from the Wave 1 parent interview or mail survey; both sources provide similar racial/ethnic classifications.

Data Sources for Comparisons with Young Adults in the General Population

When similar data items were available, comparisons were made between young adults with disabilities and the same-age young adults in the general population. The analyses approach used for the general population databases mirrors the approach used for NLTS2 data.[11] Comparison data were taken from the following:

- The National Longitudinal Survey of Youth, 1997 (NLSY97). This study includes a nationally representative sample of approximately 9,000 youth who were 12 to 16 years old as of December 31, 1996. Round 1 of the survey took place in 1997. In that round, both the eligible youth and one of each youth's interviews. Youth have continued to be interviewed annually. Comparison data for this report were taken from the 2003 data collection for young adults who were 19 to 23 years old and out of high school at the time, to match the sample of NLTS2 young adults included in this report. Calculations were made from public-use data available at http://www.nlsinfo.org/web-investigator/webgator.php. NLSY data collected in 2003 were the best match for NLTS2 2007 data because of the age of the young adults in both data sets at those time points, however readers should note the 4 year difference between the two data collection periods. Many of the comparisons between data from NLTS2 and NLSY used identical data items and response categories. Any differences in the wording of items and/or response categories are pointed out in footnotes. Readers also should be aware that the population of youth with disabilities in this age range differs from the general population of youth in ways other than disability status (e.g., the population of youth with disabilities is 63 percent male; see appendix B for further description of the populations represented in NLTS2).
- The National Longitudinal Study of Adolescent Health, Wave 3. Comparisons with the general population regarding financial independence, reported in chapter 5, are based on the public-use version of the National Institutes of Health, National Institute of Child Health and Human Development (NICHD), National Longitudinal Study of Adolescent Health (Add Health), Wave 3, a nationally representative study that explores health-related behaviors of adolescents in grades 7 through 12 and their

outcomes in young adulthood. Wave 3 data were collected in 2001–02. Comparisons included a subset of approximately 2,000 respondents who were 18 to 21 years old.

Young Adults Included in the Report

The young adults who are the focus of this report represent only a subset of young adults with disabilities who received special education services in secondary school in 2000–01, not the entire population. The full population to which the NLTS2 sample generalizes is a cohort of youth who were 13 to 16 years old and received special education services in grade 7 or above in participating schools and school districts as of December 1, 2000. Weights for analyses reported in this document were calculated so that all young adults who were out of secondary school and for whom a telephone interview or mail survey was completed or for whom parents responded to the second part of the parent interview generalize to all young adults who were out of high school. Weights were computed adjusting for various youth and school characteristics used as stratifying or poststratifying variables. (See appendix A for additional information related to sample weighting).

Analysis Approaches

Analyses reported in this document involve simple descriptive statistics (e.g., percentages, means) and bivariate relationships (i.e., cross-tabulations). All statistics were weighted to be representative of a larger population of students (as discussed earlier). These analysis approaches excluded cases with missing values; no imputation of missing values was conducted.[12]

Statistical tests examining differences between independent subgroups or between responses to different items given by the same group that involve categorical variables with more than two possible response categories were conducted by treating each of the possible response categories as separate dichotomous items.[13] For example, each of the four possible response categories to a question regarding satisfaction with the amount of services youth received from their postsecondary school ("definitely getting enough," "probably getting enough," "probably not getting enough," and "definitely not getting enough") was treated as a separate dichotomous item. The percentages of young adults who gave each response were then compared across disability or demographic groups or across different questionnaire/interview items. This approach, rather than using scale scores (e.g., the average response for a disability group on a 4-point scale created by assigning values of 1 through 4 to the response categories), was adopted for two reasons: the proper scaling for the response categories was not apparent, and it was felt that reporting differences in percentages responding in each of the response categories would be more meaningful and easier for readers to interpret than reporting differences in mean values. Rather than test for differences between all independent subgroups (e.g., young adults in different disability categories) simultaneously (e.g., using a $k \times 2$ chi-square test of homogeneity of distribution, where k is the number of disability groups), the statistical significance of differences between selected pairs of independent subgroups was tested. This approach was followed because the intent was to identify significant differences between specific groups (e.g., young adults with visual impairments are significantly more likely than those with emotional disturbances to report ever having enrolled in a postsecondary program), rather than to identify a more general "disability effect" (e.g., the observed distribution across disability categories differs significantly from what would be expected from the marginal distributions) for the variable of interest.

The test statistic used to compare Bernoulli-distributed responses (i.e., responses that can be allocated into one of two categories and coded as 0 or 1) for two independent subgroups is analogous to a chi-square test for equality of distribution (Conover 1999) and approximately follows a chi-square distribution with one degree of freedom. However, because a chi-square distribution with one degree of freedom is the same as an F distribution with one degree of freedom in the numerator and infinite degrees of freedom in the denominator (Johnson and Kotz 1995), this statistic can be considered the same as an F value; it also can be considered "chi -squared."[14]

Tests also were conducted to examine differences in the rates at which young adults with disabilities as a whole provided specific kinds of self-representations (for example, the percentage of young adults who reported relying on parents for support "a lot" compared with the percentage who relied on friends "a lot"), using an analogous one-sample statistic based on difference scores.[15] The test statistic follows a chi -square distribution with one degree of freedom for sample sizes 30 or larger and, for similar reasons to those cited above, is considered roughly equivalent to an F (1, infinity) distribution.

Technical Notes

Readers should remember the following issues when interpreting the findings in this report:

- **Purpose of the report.** The purpose of this report is descriptive; as a nonexperimental study, NLTS2 does not provide data that can be used to address causal questions. The descriptions provided in this document concern the post-high school experiences of young adults. No attempt is made to "validate" respondents' reports with information on their understanding of the survey items or with third-party information on their experiences (e.g., from employers or postsecondary education institutions). Further, the report does not attempt to explain why parents or young adults responded as they did or why responses differ for young adults in different subgroups (e.g., disability categories).

- **Subgroups reported.** In each chapter, the descriptive findings are reported for the full sample of young adults; those findings are heavily influenced by information provided by young adults with learning disabilities, who constitute 64 percent of the weighted sample (see appendix B). Young adults with emotional disturbances, mental retardation, other health impairments, and speech/language impairments constitute 13 percent, 10 percent, 5 percent, and 3 percent of the weighted sample, respectively. The other seven categories together make up less than 5 percent of the weighted sample. Findings then are reported separately for young adults in each federal special education disability category in tables that are ordered by disability prevalence, as determined at the beginning of the study. Comparisons also were conducted between groups of young adults who differed with respect to years since leaving high school, school-leaving status, gender, race/ethnicity, and parents' household income. These bivariate analyses should not be interpreted as implying that a factor on which subgroups are differentiated (e.g., disability category) has a causal relationship with the differences reported. Further, readers should be aware that demographic factors (e.g., race/ethnicity and parents' household income) are correlated among young adults with disabilities, as well as being distributed differently across disability categories (e.g., young adults in the category of mental retardation are disproportionately likely to be African American, and those in the other health impairment category are disproportionately likely to be White, relative to the general population; see appendix B table B-4, for percentage of young adults within each disability category, by demographic characteristics).[16] The complex interactions and relationships among subgroups relative to the other variables included in this report (e.g., postsecondary enrollment status) have not been explored.

- **Findings are weighted.** NLTS2 was designed to provide a national picture of the characteristics, experiences, and achievements of youth with disabilities in the NLTS2 age range as they transition to young adulthood. Therefore, all the statistics presented in this report are weighted estimates of the national population of students receiving special education in the NLTS2 age group and of each disability category individually who satisfied the study's eligibility requirement (i.e., who were out of high school).

- **Standard errors.** For each mean and percentage in this report, a standard error is presented that indicates the precision of the estimate. For example, a variable with a weighted estimated value of 50 percent and a standard error of 2.00 means that the value for the total population, if it had been measured, would, with 95 percent confidence, lie between 46 percent and 54 percent (i.e., within plus or minus 1.96 × 2, or 3.92 percentage points of 50 percent). Thus, smaller standard errors allow for greater confidence to be placed in the estimate, whereas larger ones require caution.

- **Combined young adults self-report and parent-report data.** If a Wave 4 youth interview/survey was completed, the young adult's in this report. If a youth interview/survey could not be completed for an eligible young adult or if a young adult was reported by parents not to be able to participate in an interview/survey, parent responses were used. For the subsample of young adults included in this report, the youth interview/survey was the source of data for post-high school outcomes for 84 percent of young adults, and the parent interview was the source for 16 percent of young adults who did not have a youth interview. Combining data across respondents raises the question of whether parent and young adults' responses would concur—that is, would the same findings result if parents' responses were reported instead of young adults' responses. When both parents and young adults were asked whether the young adults belonged to an organized community group, currently worked for pay, and worked for pay in the past 2 years, and wages currently employed young adults earned per hour, their responses agreed from 69 percent to 80 percent of the time (analyses presented in appendix A).

- **Small samples**. Although NLTS2 data are weighted to represent the population, the size of standard errors is influenced heavily by the actual number of young adults in a given group (e.g., a disability category). In fact, findings are not reported separately for groups that do not include at least 30 sample members because groups with very small samples have comparatively large standard errors. For example, because there are relatively few young adults with deaf-blindness, estimates for that group have relatively large standard errors. Therefore, readers should be cautious in interpreting results for this group and others with small sample sizes and large standard errors.

- **Significant differences.** A large number of statistical analyses were conducted and are presented in this report. Because no explicit adjustments were made for multiple comparisons, the likelihood of finding at least one statistically significant difference when no difference exists (i.e., "false positives" or type I errors) in the population is substantially larger than the type I error for each individual analysis. To partially compensate for the number of analyses that were conducted, we have used a relatively conservative p value of $< .01$ in identifying significant differences. The text mentions only differences reaching that level of significance. If no level of significance is reported, the group differences described do not attain at least the $p < .01$ level. Readers also are cautioned that the meaningfulness of differences reported here cannot be inferred from their statistical significance.

Organization of the Report

This report is envisioned as a brief overview of the primary achievements of young adults with disabilities who have been out of high school for up to 6 years, focusing on key outcomes in postsecondary education, employment, residential and financial independence and social and community involvement.[17] Chapter 2 describes two outcomes, the extent to which young adults with disabilities enrolled in postsecondary education and for those who had enrolled, the extent to which they had completed their postsecondary programs. Chapter 3 considers the employment status of young adults and current wages. Chapter 4 addresses the extent to which young adults with disabilities were productively engaged in school, work, or preparation for work after they left high school.

The household circumstances of young adults with disabilities are considered in chapter 5, including the extent to which young adults were living away from home, the prevalence of marriage and parenting, and aspects of their financial independence. Chapter 6 focuses on the social and community involvement in both positive and negative ways of young adults with disabilities, including their participation in organized groups and volunteer activities, and their involvement with the criminal justice system.

Appendix A provides details of the NLTS2 design, sample, measures, and analysis approaches. Appendix B presents data on the characteristics of young adults with disabilities included in the out-of-high school sample.

The following chapters provide the most recent national picture of multiple dimensions of the outcomes of young adults with disabilities who had been out of secondary school up to 6 years. These findings will be augmented in the next few years of NLTS2 as more youth transition to adulthood and have increasing exposure to opportunities for postsecondary education, employment, and independent living.

2. POSTSECONDARY EDUCATION KEY FINDINGS

The potential benefits of attaining a postsecondary degree include increased earnings (Carnevale and Desrochers 2003), improved health (Mirowsky and Ross 2010), and increased job satisfaction (Wolniak and Pascarella 2005); and as the American economy becomes progressively more knowledge based, attaining a postsecondary education becomes more critical (Carnevale and Desrochers 2003). For example, only 20 percent of workers needed at least some college for their jobs in 1959; by 2000, that number had increased to 56 percent (Carnevale and Fry 2000).

Along with their peers in the general population, young adults with disabilities are increasingly focusing on postsecondary education. Postsecondary education is a primary post-high school goal for more than four out of five secondary school students with disabilities who have transition plans (Cameto, Levine, and Wagner 2004). In addition, young adults with disabilities increasingly are taking rigorous academic courses in high school, including college-preparatory courses, such as a foreign language and science (Wagner, Newman, and Cameto 2004).

However, even when their high school programs prepare them for postsecondary education, students with disabilities can encounter a variety of challenges in the transition from secondary to postsecondary school. Postsecondary schools are guided by a legal framework of rights and responsibilities that is different from the framework governing secondary schools. When students leave high school, their education no longer is covered under the IDEA umbrella but instead is under the auspices of two civil rights laws—Section 504 of the Rehabilitation Act and the Americans with Disabilities Act (ADA) (Stodden, Jones, and Chang 2002; Wolanin and Steele 2004).

This chapter describes the postsecondary education enrollment and completion rates of young adults with disabilities who had been out of high school up to 6 years. It focuses on participation in three types of postsecondary institutions—2- year or community colleges; postsecondary vocational, business, or technical schools; and 4-year colleges— and addresses the following questions:

- To what extent do young adults with disabilities enroll in postsecondary schools?
- How does their level of enrollment compare with that of their peers in the general population?
- What are the completion rates for young adults with disabilities who enroll in postsecondary schools?
- How do the postsecondary completion rates of young adults with disabilities compare with those of their peers in the general population?
- How do postsecondary enrollment and completion rates differ for young adults in different disability categories and for those with different school-exit and demographic characteristics?

This chapter presents findings related to postsecondary enrollment and completion for young adults with disabilities as a group as well as differences between young adults who differ in their disability category, high-school leaving status, and demographic characteristics that are significantly different at least at the $p < .01$ level.

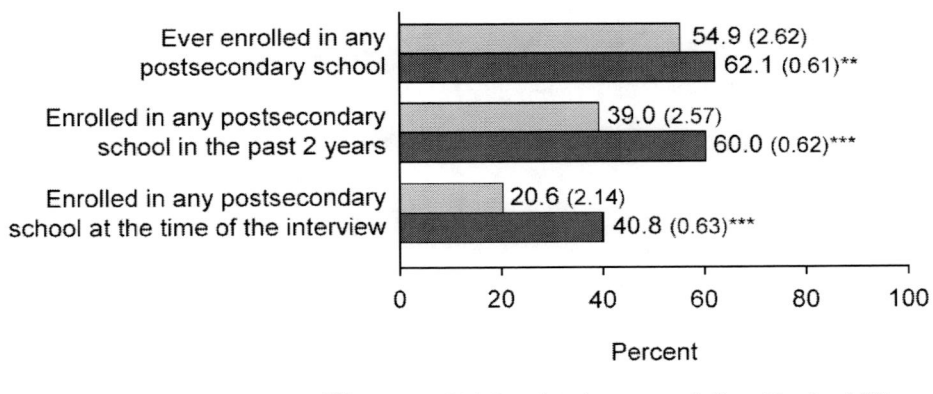

**p < .01; ***p < .001 for difference between young adults with disabilities and young adults in the general population.

Note: Standard errors are in parentheses. Findings are reported for young adults out of high school up to 6 years.NLTS2 percentages are weighted population estimates based on a sample of approximately 3,610 young adults with disabilities.

Source: U.S. Department of Education, Institute of Education Sciences, National Center for Special Education Research, National Longitudinal Transition Study-2 (NLTS2), Wave 4 parent interview and youth interview/survey, 2007; U.S. Department of Labor, Bureau of Labor Statistics, National Longitudinal Survey of Youth 1997 (NLSY97) 2001 youth survey, responses for 19- to 23-year-olds.

Figure 1. Postsecondary school enrollment of young adults with disabilities and those in the general population.

Postsecondary School Enrollment

Ensuring that students with disabilities have "access to and full participation in postsecondary education" has been identified as one of the key challenges in the future of secondary education and transition for such students (National Center on Secondary Education and Transition 2003, p. 1). Postsecondary education has been linked to increased earning potential for young adults who continue their education after high school, even for those who have not earned a degree (Marcotte et al. 2005).

Regarding postsecondary enrollment of young adults with disabilities who had been out of high school up to 6 years:

- Fifty-five percent reported having continued on to postsecondary school since leaving high school (figure 1).[18]
- They were less likely to enroll in postsecondary school than were their same-age peers in the general population, of whom 62 percent ever had attended postsecondary school (p < .01).[19]

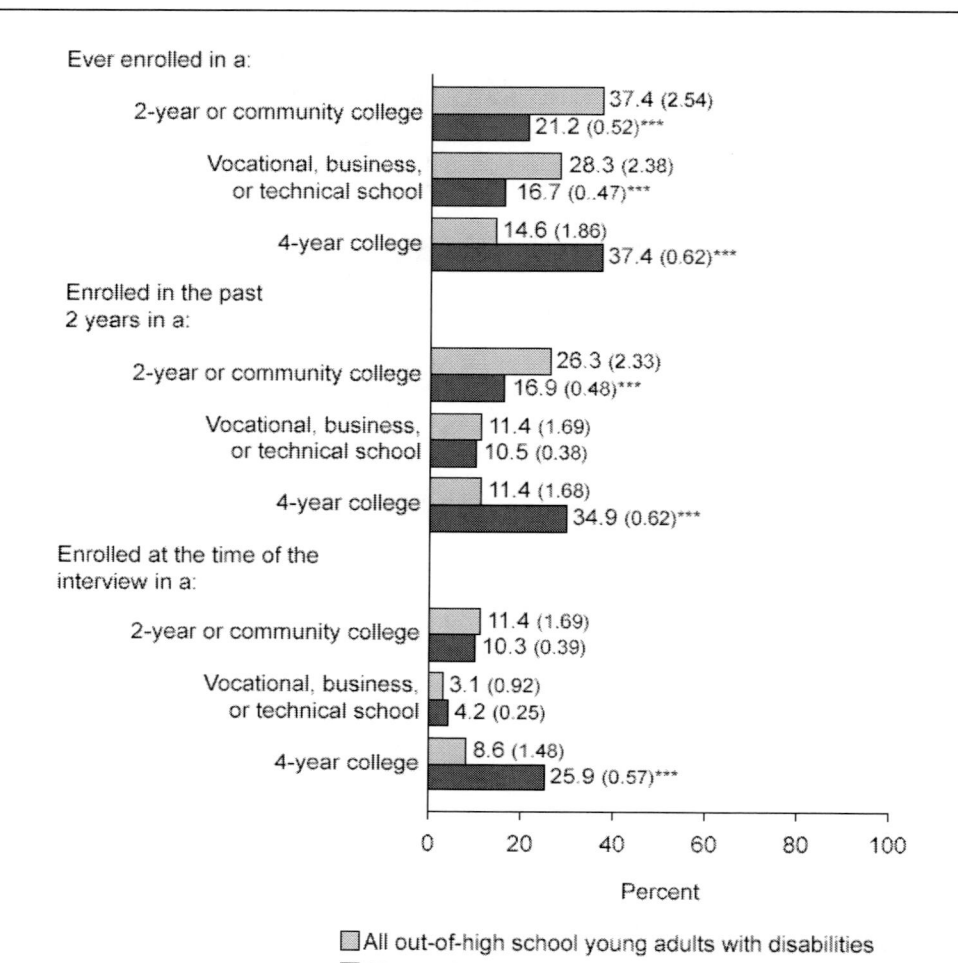

*** $p < .001$ for difference between young adults with disabilities and young adults in the general population.

Note: Young adults who had enrolled in more than one type of postsecondary school were included in each type of school they had attended. Standard errors are in parentheses. Findings are reported for young adults out of high school up to 6 years. NLTS2 percentages are weighted population estimates based on a sample of approximately 3,610 young adults with disabilities. SOURCE: U.S. Department of Education, Institute of Education Sciences, National Center for Special Education Research, National Longitudinal Transition Study-2 (NLTS2), Wave 4 parent interview and youth interview/survey, 2007; U.S. Department of Labor, Bureau of Labor Statistics, National Longitudinal Survey of Youth 1997 (NLSY97) 2001 youth survey, responses for 19- to 23-year-olds.

Figure 2. Postsecondary school enrollment of young adults with disabilities and young adults in the general population, by school type.

- They were less likely to have been enrolled in any postsecondary school in the past 2 years than their same-age peers in the general population (39 percent vs. 60percent, *p* < .001).

- They were less likely to have been enrolled in any postsecondary school at the time of the interview than their same-age peers in the general population (21 percent vs. 41 percent, $p < .001$).
- Young adults with disabilities were more likely to have ever been enrolled in 2-year or community colleges (37 percent) than in vocational, business, or technical schools (28 percent, $p < .01$) or 4-year colleges or universities (15 percent, $p < .001$), and of those options, were least likely to have ever been enrolled in 4-year colleges (figure 2).
- Young adults in the general population were more likely to have ever been enrolled in a 4-year college (37 percent) than were young adults with disabilities (15 percent, $p < .001$). Conversely, young adults with disabilities were more likely to have ever been enrolled in a 2-year or community college (37 percent) or vocational school (28 percent) than were young adults in the general population (21 percent and 17 percent, respectively; $p < .001$ for both comparisons).
- The rate of enrollment of young adults with disabilities in 2-year or community colleges or vocational schools at the time of the interview (11 percent and 3 percent, respectively)[20] did not differ significantly from that of their peers in the general population (10 percent and 4 percent, respectively). This stands in contrast to differences in enrollment rates at 4-year colleges. Similar-age young adults in the general population were about three times as likely as young adults with disabilities to be taking courses at a 4-year college at the time of the interview (26 percent vs. 9 percent, $p < .001$).

Disability Differences in Postsecondary Enrollment

- Overall postsecondary enrollment varied widely by disability category, with attendance since high school ranging from 28 percent to 71 percent (table 2).
- Young adults with hearing impairments or visual impairments were more likely to attend any postsecondary school (71 percent, each) than were those with autism (47 percent, $p < .001$ for comparison with hearing impairments and $p < .01$ for comparison with visual impairments), emotional disturbances (45 percent, $p < .001$ for both comparisons), multiple disabilities (31 percent, $p < .001$ for both comparisons), or mental retardation (28percent , $p < .001$ for both comparisons).
- Enrollment at any postsecondary school was higher for young adults with learning disabilities (61 percent), speech/language impairments (63 percent), orthopedic impairments (60 percent), other health impairments (57 percent), traumatic brain injuries (56 percent), autism (47 percent), or emotional disturbances (45 percent) than for those with mental retardation (28 percent, $p < .01$ for comparison with autism and emotional disturbances, $p < .001$ for other comparisons).
- Similarly, overall postsecondary enrollment was higher for young adults with learning disabilities (61 percent), speech/language impairments (63 percent), orthopedic impairments (60 percent), other health impairments (57 percent), or traumatic brain injuries (56 percent) than for those withmultiple disabilities (31 percent, $p < .01$ for comparison with traumatic brain injuries, $p < .001$ for other comparisons).

Table 2. Postsecondary school enrollment of young adults, by disability category

	Learning disability	Speech/Language Impairment	Mental retardation	Emo-tonal disturbance	Hearing impairment	Visual impairment	Orthopedic impairment	Other health impairment	Autism	Traumatic Brain injury	Multiple disabilities	Deaf-blindness
	Percent											
Any postsecondary school	60.9 (3.88)	63.0 (3.77)	27.6 (3.64)	44.9 (4.36)	70.6 (4.63)	70.8 (5.23)	59.8 (4.59)	56.6 (4.14)	46.6 (5.25)	56.2 (7.49)	31.3 (5.28)	48.8 (6.83)
2-year or community college	41.0 (3.93)	40.9 (3.84)	21.5 (3.35)	29.7 (4.01)	44.9 (5.06)	47.0 (5.74)	45.5 (4.66)	42.9 (4.14)	32.6 (4.93)	33.5 (7.12)	17.2 (4.31)	29.1 (6.21)
Vocational,business, or technical school	31.5 (3.71)	21.3 (3.21)	15.2 (2.92)	28.1 (3.94)	36.8 (4.92)	21.2 (4.70)	21.2 (3.83)	27.7 (3.74)	20.4 (4.26)	33.6 (7.18)	14.8 (4.05)	18.9 (5.35)
4-year college	15.5 (2.89)	29.1 (3.55)	6.3 (1.98)	7.6 (2.32)	31.3 (4.71)	42.7 (5.69)	22.5 (3.91)	19.5 (3.31)	15.5 (3.82)	15.7 (5.49)	8.0 (3.09)	18.2 (5.27)

Note: Young adults who had enrolled in more than one type of postsecondary school were included in each type of school they had attended. Standard errors are in parentheses. Findings are reported for young adults with disabilities out of high school up to 6 years. NLTS2 percentages are weighted population estimates based on a sample of approximately 4,650 young adults with disabilities.

Source: U.S. Department of Education, Institute of Education Sciences, National Center for Special Education Research, National Longitudinal Transition Study-2 (NLTS2), Wave 4 parent interview and youth interview/survey, 2007.

- In addition, young adults with speech/language impairments (63 percent) or learning disabilities (61 percent) were more likely ever to have enrolled in any postsecondary program than were those with emotional disturbances (45 percent, $p < .01$ for all comparisons).
- Young adults with visual (47 percent), orthopedic (46 percent), hearing (45 percent), other health (43 percent), or speech/language impairments (41 percent), or learning disabilities (41 percent) were more likely than those with multiple disabilities ($p < .001$ for all comparisons) or mental retardation ($p < .001$ for all comparisons) to attend a 2-year or community college.
- Young adults with hearing impairments (37 percent) were more likely than those with multiple disabilities (15 percent, $p < .001$), mental retardation (15 percent, $p < .001$), deaf-blindness (19 percent, $p < .01$), speech/language impairments (21 percent, $p < .01$), or orthopedic impairments (21 percent, $p < .01$), to attend a vocational, business, or technical school.
- In addition, young adults with learning disabilities (32 percent) were more likely than those with mental retardation (15 percent $p < .001$) or multiple disabilities (19 percent, $p < .01$) to attend a vocational, business, or technical school.
- Young adults with visual impairments (43 percent) were more likely than those with mental retardation (6 percent), emotional disturbances (8 percent), multiple disabilities (8 percent), learning disabilities (16 percent), autism (16 percent), traumatic brain injuries (16 percent), deaf-blindness (18 percent), other health impairments (20 percent), or orthopedic impairments (23 percent) to attend a 4-year college ($p < .01$ for comparison with deaf-blindness and orthopedic impairments; $p < .001$ for other comparisons).
- Young adults with hearing impairments (31 percent) were more likely than those with mental retardation (6 percent), emotional disturbances (8 percent), multiple disabilities (8 percent), learning disabilities (16 percent), autism (16 percent), or traumatic brain injuries (16 percent) to attend a 4-year college ($p < .01$ for comparison with learning disabilities and autism; $p < .001$ for other comparisons).
- Young adults with orthopedic impairments (23 percent) were more likely than those with mental retardation (6 percent, $p < .001$), emotional disturbances (8 percent, $p < .01$), or multiple disabilities (8 percent, $p < .01$) to attend a 4-year college.
- Young adults with other health impairments (20 percent) were more likely than those with mental retardation (6 percent, $p < .001$) or emotional disturbances (8 percent, $p < .01$) to attend a 4-year college.

- Young adults with learning disabilities (16 percent) were more likely than those with mental retardation (6 percent, $p < .01$) to attend a 4-year college.

Differences in Postsecondary Enrollment by High School-Leaving Characteristics

- High school completers were three times as likely as their peers who did not complete high school to have enrolled in any postsecondary school (59 percent vs. 17 percent, $p < .001$, table 3).

Table 3. Postsecondary school enrollment of young adults with disabilities, by high school-leaving status and years since leaving high school

	Completers	Non-completers	Less than 2 years	2 up to 4 years	4 up to 6 years
	Percent				
Any postsecondary school	59.4 (2.79)	16.9 (5.13)	51.6 (5.06)	52.1 (3.94)	60.4 (4.62)
2-year or community college	40.4 (2.79)	11.6 (4.42)	34.7 (4.83)	32.3 (3.70)	45.5 (4.71)
Vocational, business, or technical school	30.9 (2.62)	6.1 (3.31)	18.8 (3.97)	29.5 (3.61)	31.9 (4.41)
4-year college	16.3 (2.10)	0.2 (0.61)	14.2 (3.54)	11.5 (2.52)	18.9 (3.69)

Note: Young adults who had enrolled in more than one type of postsecondary school were included in each type of school they had attended. Standard errors are in parentheses. Findings are reported for young adults with disabilities out of high school up to 6 years. NLTS2 percentages are weighted population estimates based on a sample of approximately 4,650 young adults with disabilities.

Source: U.S. Department of Education, Institute of Education Sciences, National Center for Special Education Research, National Longitudinal Transition Study-2 (NLTS2), Wave 4 parent interview and youth interview/survey, 2007.

- Completers were more likely than noncompleters to ever have been enrolled in 2-year or community colleges (40 percent vs. 12 percent, $p < .001$); vocational, business, or technical schools (31 percent vs. 6 percent, $p < .001$); and 4-year colleges (16 percent vs. <1 percent, $p < .001$).
- Rates of enrollment in postsecondary schools did not differ significantly by the number of years since leaving high school.

Demographic Differences in Postsecondary Enrollment

- Postsecondary enrollment differences were apparent for families with different income levels. Young adults with disabilities from households with parent incomes of more than $50,000 were more likely to have ever enrolled in any postsecondary school (68 percent, table 4) than were those from households with parent incomes of $25,000 or less (43 percent, $p < .001$) or $25,001 to $50,000 (51 percent, $p < .01$). Young adults with disabilities from households with parent incomes of more than $50,000 were more likely than those from households with parent incomes of $25,000 or less to have enrolled in a 2-year or community college (49 percent vs. 24 percent, $p < .001$) or a 4-year college (22 percent vs. 8 percent, $p < .01$).
- Rates of enrollment in postsecondary schools did not differ significantly by race/ethnicity or gender.

Postsecondary School Completion

For many students in the general population, postsecondary school enrollment does not result in degree attainment or program completion. Fewer than two-thirds of students in the general population who began as full-time freshmen in 4-year universities in 1995 received a bachelor's -year period (Berkner, He, and Cataldi 2002). This section examinesdegree within 6 the postsecondary completion rates of young adults with disabilities who have been out of high school up to 6 years. Postsecondary completion is considered for the 63 percent of young adults who had ever attended postsecondary school but no longer were enrolled at the time of the interview.

- Within 6 years of leaving high school, of the 63 percent of young adults with disabilities who had ever enrolled in postsecondary education, but no longer were attending, 38 percent had graduated or completed their programs (figure 3).[21]
- The postsecondary completion rate of young adults with disabilities was lower than that of their peers in the general population. Fifty-one percent of similar-age peers in the general population had graduated or completed postsecondary programs ($p <$ .01).
- Postsecondary school completion rates for young adults with disabilities ranged from 29 percent at 4-year universities, to 30percent at 2 -year or community college, to 55 percent at postsecondary vocational, business, or technical school. When considering completion rates at 4-year universities it is important to be aware that some young adults had been out of high school for less than 4 years.

Table 4. Postsecondary school enrollment of young adults with disabilities, by parents' household income and young adults' race/ethnicity and gender

	$25,000 or less	$25,001 to $50,000	More than $50,000	White	African American	Hispanic	Male	Female
	Percent							
Any post-secondary school	42.8 (4.73)	50.8 (5.22)	68.0 (3.70)	56.4 (3.14)	50.6 (6.04)	62.5 (7.71)	53.5 (3.27)	57.3 (4.39)
2-year or community college	24.4 (4.12)	36.1 (5.02)	48.9 (3.97)	38.7 (3.09)	30.5 (5.56)	46.0 (8.00)	38.0 (3.19)	36.3 (4.28)
Vocational, business, or technical school	27.9 (4.29)	26.8 (4.64)	30.7 (3.67)	28.8 (2.88)	24.1 (5.17)	35.9 (7.64)	28.5 (2.97)	28.0 (3.99)
4-year college	8.3 (2.64)	10.6 (3.22)	22.0 (3.29)	15.2 (2.28)	14.4 (4.24)	12.0 (5.17)	15.1 (2.34)	14.0 (3.08)

Note: Young adults who had enrolled in more than one type of postsecondary school were included in each type of school they had attended. Standard errors are in parentheses. Findings are reported for young adults with disabilities out of high school up to 6 years. NLTS2 percentages are weighted population estimates based on a sample of approximately 4,650 young adults with disabilities.

Source: U.S. Department of Education, Institute of Education Sciences, National Center for Special Education Research, National Longitudinal Transition Study-2 (NLTS2), Wave 4 parent interview and youth interview/survey, 2007.

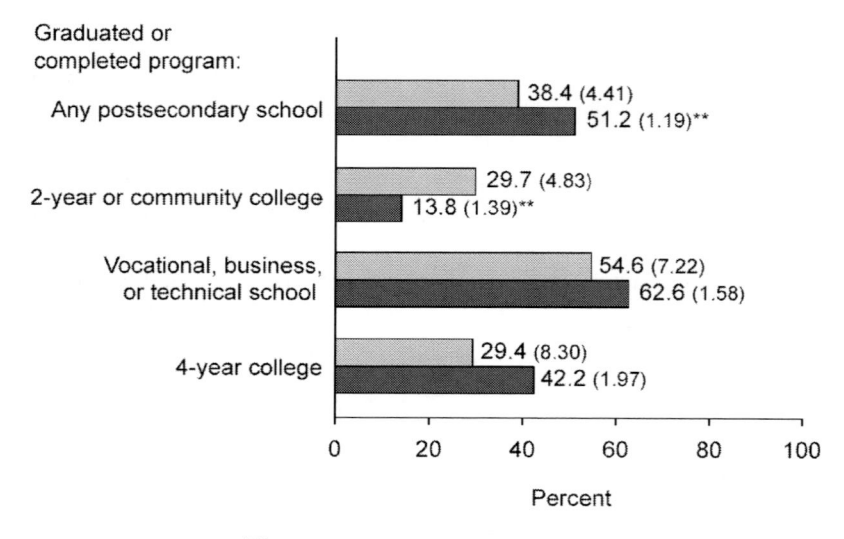

** $p < .01$ for difference between young adults with disabilities and young adults in the general population.

Note: Standard errors are in parentheses. Findings are reported for young adults out of high school up to 6 years.NLTS2 percentages are weighted population estimates based on samples that range from approximately 340 to 1,520 young adults with disabilities.

Source: U.S. Department of Education, Institute of Education Sciences, National Center for Special Education Research, National Longitudinal Transition Study-2 (NLTS2), Wave 4 parent interview and youth interview/survey, 2007.

Figure 3. Postsecondary school completion of young adults with disabilities and young adults in the general population who had ever enrolled in a postsecondary school, by school type.

- Rates of completion did not differ significantly by disability category, secondary-school leaving characteristics, parents' gender (tables 5 through 7).

3. EMPLOYMENT KEY FINDINGS

Employment during the years identified as *emerging adulthood* is associated with differences in psychological well-being (Galambos, Barker, and Krahn 2006) and improved chances for a higher quality of life (Stodden and Mruzek 2010). Full-time employment leads to financial independence and is an important first step on the path to adulthood (Janus 2009). Unemployment not only results in lost wages, but also a reduced quality of life for the individual and diminished growth capacity for society as a whole (Wisman 2010). People with disabilities have a much higher unemployment rate than the overall population (The National Collaborative on Workforce & Disability for Youth and Workforce Strategy Center 2009); and low adult employment is associated with poor quality of life for individuals with disabilities and their families (O'Day and Stapleton 2009).

As young adults with disabilities continue on their path through emerging adulthood, opportunities for employment increase. For those already employed, the opportunity for higher wages increases, as well. This chapter describes the employment of young adults with disabilities who had been out of high school up to 6 years. It focuses on the employment status and wages of post high school young adults and addresses the following questions:

- To what extent do young adults with disabilities have a paid job other than work around the house?
- How does their employment status compare with that of their peers in the general population?
- What is the hourly wage for young adults with disabilities who are currently or who have recently been employed?
- How do the hourly wages of young adults with disabilities compare with those of their peers in the general population?
- How do employment and hourly wage rates differ for young adults in different disability categories and for those with different demographic characteristics?

This chapter presents findings related to employment and hourly wages for young adults with disabilities as a group as well as differences between young adults who differ in their disability category and demographic characteristics. Only differences that are significant at least at the $p < .01$ level are reported.

Employment Status at Time of Interview

Regarding the employment status of young adults with disabilities who were out of secondaryschool at the time of the interview:

- Seventy-one percent were reported to have a paid job at the time of the interview other than work around the house (figure 4).[22]
- They were as likely to have a paid job at the time of the interview as were their same-age peers in the general population, of whom 71 percentreported currently having a paid job.[23]

Disability Differences in Employment Status

- The employment status of young adults with disabilities at the time of the interview varied widely by disability category with employment at the time of the interview ranging from 30 percent to 79 percent (table 8).
- Young adults with learning disabilities (79 percent) were more likely to have a paid job than were those with deaf-blindness (30 percent), orthopedic impairments (38 percent), visual impairments (40 percent), traumatic brain injuries (44 percent),autism (45 percent), mental retardation (46 percent), or multiple disabilities (46 percent, $p < .001$ for all comparisons).

Table 5. Postsecondary school completion of young adults, by disability category

	Learning disability	Speech/language impairment	Mental retardation	Emotional disturbance	Hearing impairment	Visual impairment	Orthopedic impairment	Other health impairment	Autism	Traumatic brain injury	Multiple disabilities	Deaf blindness
	Percent											
Graduation or completion rate of students who had been enrolled in postsecon-dary school but were not enrolled at the time of the interview	37.5 (6.13)	48.4 (6.64)	40.0 (3.65)	41.1 (10.17)	38.9 (8.80)	49.7 (9.35)	35.7 (7.55)	33.8 (6.09)	35.2 (10.35)	50.4 (12.59)	32.1 (10.55)	‡

‡ Responses for items with fewer than 30 respondents are not reported.

Note: Standard errors are in parentheses. Findings are reported for young adults with disabilities out of high school up to 6 years. NLTS2 percentages are weighted population estimates based on a sample of approximately 1,520 young adults with disabilities.

Source: U.S. Department of Education, Institute of Education Sciences, National Center for Special Education Research, National Longitudinal Transition Study-2 (NLTS2), Waves 2, 3, and 4 parent interview and youth interview/survey, 2003, 2005, 2007.

Table 6. Postsecondary school completion of young adults with disabilities, by secondary-school-leaving status and years since leaving high school

	Completers	Non-completers	Less than 2 years	2 up to 4 years	4 up to 6 years
	Percent				
Graduation or completion rate of students who had been enrolled in postsecondary school but were not enrolled at the time of the interview	38.5 (4.50)	34.8 (21.60)	35.0 (11.84)	32.3 (6.35)	45.4 (6.94)

Note: Standard errors are in parentheses. Findings are reported for young adults with disabilities out of high school up to 6 years. NLTS2 percentages are weighted population estimates based on a sample of approximately 1,520 young adults with disabilities.

Source: U.S. Department of Education, Institute of Education Sciences, National Center for Special Education Research, National Longitudinal Transition Study-2 (NLTS2), Waves 2, 3, and 4 parent interview and youth interview/survey, 2003, 2005, 2007.

Table 7. Postsecondary school enrollment of young adults with disabilities, by parents' household income and young adults' race/ethnicity and gender

	$25,000 or less	$25,001 to $50,000	More than $50,000	White	African American	Hispanic	Male	Female
	Percent							
Graduation or completion rate of students who had been enrolled in post-secondary school but were not enrolled at the time of the interview	32.8 (8.75)	39.2 (9.00)	39.9 (6.25)	39.2 (5.25)	29.3 (9.24)	46.3 (13.27)	36.2 (5.22)	41.9 (7.87)

Note: Standard errors are in parentheses. Findings are reported for young adults with disabilities out of high school up to 6 years. NLTS2 percentages are weighted population estimates based on a sample of approximately 1,520 young adults with disabilities.

Source: U.S. Department of Education, Institute of Education Sciences, National Center for Special Education Research, National Longitudinal Transition Study-2 (NLTS2), Waves 2, 3, and 4 parent interview and youth interview/survey, 2003, 2005, 2007.

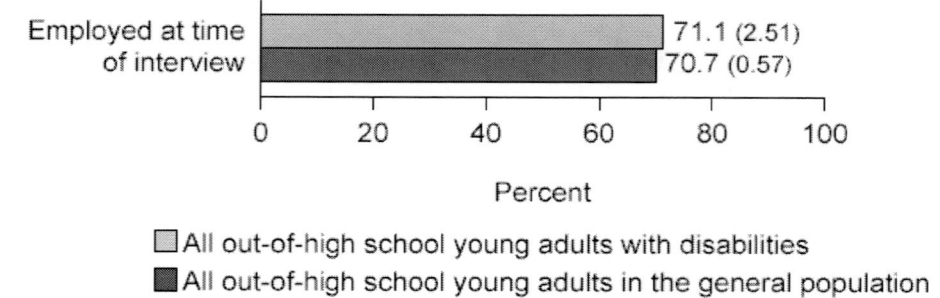

Note: Standard errors are in parentheses. Findings are reported for young adults out of high school up to
    6 years.NLTS2 percentages are weighted population estimates based on a sample of approximately
    4,140 young adults with disabilities.
Source: U.S. Department of Education, Institute of Education Sciences, National Center for Special
    Education Research, National Longitudinal Transition Study-2 (NLTS2), Wave 4 parent interview
    and youth interview/survey, 2007; U.S. Department of Labor, Bureau of Labor Statistics, National
    Longitudinal Survey of Youth 1997 (NLSY97) 2001 youth survey, responses for 19- to 23-year-
    olds.

Figure 4. Employment status of young adults with disabilities and young adults in the general
population.

- Similarly, young adults with other health impairments or speech/language impairments were more likely to have a paid job (68 percent, each) than were those with deaf-blindness (30 percent , $p < .001$ for both comparisons), orthopedic impairments (38 percent, $p < .001$ for both comparisons), visual impairments (40 percent, $p < .001$ for both comparisons), traumatic brain injuries (44 percen t, $p < .01$ for both comparisons), autism (45 percent, $p < .01$ for both comparisons), mental retardation (46 percent, $p < .001$ for both comparisons), or multiple disabilities (46 percent, $p < .01$ for both comparisons).
- Young adults with emotional disturbances were more likely to have a paid job (65 percent) than were those with deaf-blindness (30 percent, $p < .001$), orthopedic impairments (38 percent, $p < .001$), visual impairments (40 percent, $p < .01$), autism (45 percent, $p < .01$), or mental retardation (46 percent , $p < .01$).
- Young adults with hearing impairments were more likely to have a paid job (64 percent) than were those with deaf-blindness (30 percent, $p < .001$), orthopedic impairments (38 percent, $p < .001$), visual impairments (40 percent, $p < .01$), or mental retardation (46 percent, $p < .01$).

Differences in Employment Status by High School-Leaving Characteristics
- High school completers were more likely to have been reported to be employed at the time of the interview thanwere their peers who did not complete high school (73 percent vs. 52 percent, $p < .01$; table 9).
- Employment status at the time of the interview did not differ by the number of years since leaving high school.

Demographic Differences in Employment Status
- Post-high school employment differences were apparent for families with varying income levels. Young adults from households with parent incomes of more than $50,000 were more likely to have a paid job at the time of the interview (79 , table 10) than were those from households with parent incomes of $25,000 or less (58 percent, $p < .001$).
- Employment status did not differ significantly by race or ethnicity or gender.

Hourly Wages at Time of Interview

Earning a livable wage is integral to an acceptable quality of life. As set by the Fair Labor Standards Act (FLSA), the federal minimum wage in 2007 started at $5.15 per hour before being increased to $5.85 per hour effective July 24, 2007 (see *http://www.dol.gov/whd /minwage/coverage.htm*). Although there is some variability in the minimum wages by state, federal minimum wage law supersedes state minimum wage laws where the federal minimum wage is greater than the state minimum wage (see http://www.dol.gov/whd/ minwage/america.html). In those states where the state minimum wage is greater than the federal minimum wage, the state minimum wage prevails. As a result, the minimum wages across the states in 2007 ranged from $5.15 to $7.93 per hour. Young adults with disabilities were asked to report the hourly wage received at their current or most recent job. The average hourly wage is reported here.

Regarding the hourly wages of young adults with disabilities who were out of secondary school at the time of the interview:

- The mean hourly wage was reported to be $9.40 (figure 5).[24]
- They earned less than their same-age peers in the general population, whoearned a mean hourly wage of $13.20 ($p < .001$).

Disability Differences in Hourly Wages
- The average hourly wage did not differ significantly by disability category, with one exception (figure 6). Young adults with learning disabilitieswere reported to earn a higher average hourly wage ($9.60) than those with mental retardation ($7.60, $p < .01$).

Differences in Hourly Wages by High School-Leaving Characteristics
- Average hourly wages did not differ significantly by secondary school-leaving status or the number of years since leaving high school (figure 7).

Table 8. Paid employment outside the home of young adults, by disability category

Employment status	Learning disability	Speech/ Language impairment	Mental retardation	Emotional disturbance	Hearing impairment	Visual impairment	Orthopedic impairment	Other health impairment	Autism	Traumatic brain injury	Multiple disabilities	Deaf blindness
	Percent											
Percentage reported to have been:												
Employed at time of interview	78.6 (3.39)	67.8 (3.81)	46.0 (4.42)	64.5 (4.41)	63.9 (5.24)	40.3 (6.08)	37.7 (4.71)	68.2 (4.06)	45.2 (5.82)	44.1 (7.79)	46.1 (6.24)	29.8 (6.75)

Note: Standard errors are in parentheses. Findings are reported for young adultswith disabilities out of high school up to 6 years. NLTS2 percentages are weighted population estimates based on samples of approximately 4,150 young adults with disabilities.

Source: U.S. Department of Education, Institute of Education Sciences, National Center for Special Education Research, National Longitudinal Transition Study-2 (NLTS2), Wave 4 parent interview and youth interview/survey, 2007.

Table 9. Paid employment outside the home of young adults with disabilities, by high school-leaving status and years since leaving high school

Employment status	Completers	Non-completers	Less than 2 years	2 up to 4 years	4 up to 6 years
	Percent				
Percentage reported to have been:					
Employed at time of interview	73.2 (2.62)	52.3 (7.61)	60.4 (5.30)	72.9 (3.67)	74.4 (4.31)

Note: Standard errors are in parentheses. Findings are reported for young adults with disabilities out of high school up to 6 years. NLTS2 percentages are weighted population estimates based on samples ranging from approximately 3,690 to 4,150 young adults with disabilities.

Source: U.S. Department of Education, Institute of Education Sciences, National Center for Special Education Research, National Longitudinal Transition Study-2 (NLTS2), Wave 4 parent interview and youth interview/survey, 2007.

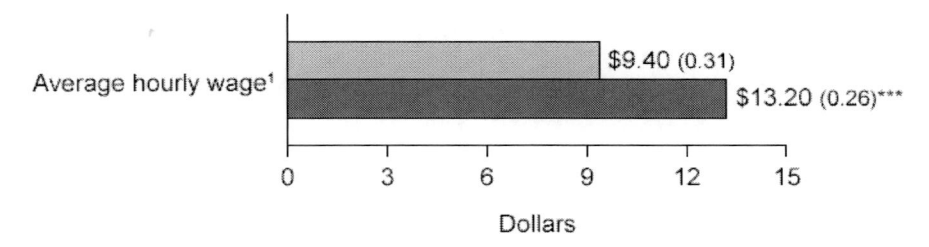

$9.40 (0.31)

$13.20 (0.26)***

Average hourly wage[1]

Dollars

☐ All out-of-high school young adults with disabilities
■ All out-of-high school young adults in the general population

*** $p < .001$ for difference between young adults with disabilities and young adults in the general population.

Note: Standard errors are in parentheses. Findings are reported for young adults out of high school up to 6 years. NLTS2 percentages are weighted population estimates based on a sample of approximately 2,110 young adults with disabilities.

Source: U.S. Department of Education, Institute of Education Sciences, National Center for Special Education Research, National Longitudinal Transition Study-2 (NLTS2), Wave 4 parent interview and youth interview/survey, 2007; U.S. Department of Labor, Bureau of Labor Statistics, National Longitudinal Survey of Youth 1997 (NLSY97) 2001 youth survey, responses for 19- to 23-year-olds.

Figure 5. Average hourly wage of young adults with disabilities and young adults in the general population.

Table 10. Paid employment outside the home of young adults with disabilities, by parents' household income and young adults' race/ethnicity and gender

Employment status	$25,000 or less	$25,001 to $50,000	More than $50,000	White	African American	Hispanic	Male	Female
	Percent							
Percentage reported to have been:								
Employed at time of interview	58.3 (5.08)	74.7 (4.74)	78.9 (3.35)	75.8 (2.82)	59.5 (6.44)	63.6 (8.07)	75.2 (2.96)	63.7 (4.53)

Note: Standard errors are in parentheses. Findings are reported for young adults with disabilities out of high school up to 6 years. NLTS2 percentages are weighted population estimates based on samples ranging from approximately 3,690 to 4,150 young adults with disabilities.

Source: U.S. Department of Education, Institute of Education Sciences, National Center for Special Education Research, National Longitudinal Transition Study-2 (NLTS2), Wave 4 parent interview and youth interview/survey, 2007.

Differences in Hourly Wages by Demographic Characteristics

- Males earned a higher mean hourly wage at their current or most recent job than females ($9.90 vs. $8.40, $p < .01$; figure 8).

- Average hourly wages did not differ significantly by parents' household income or young adults' race/ethnicity.

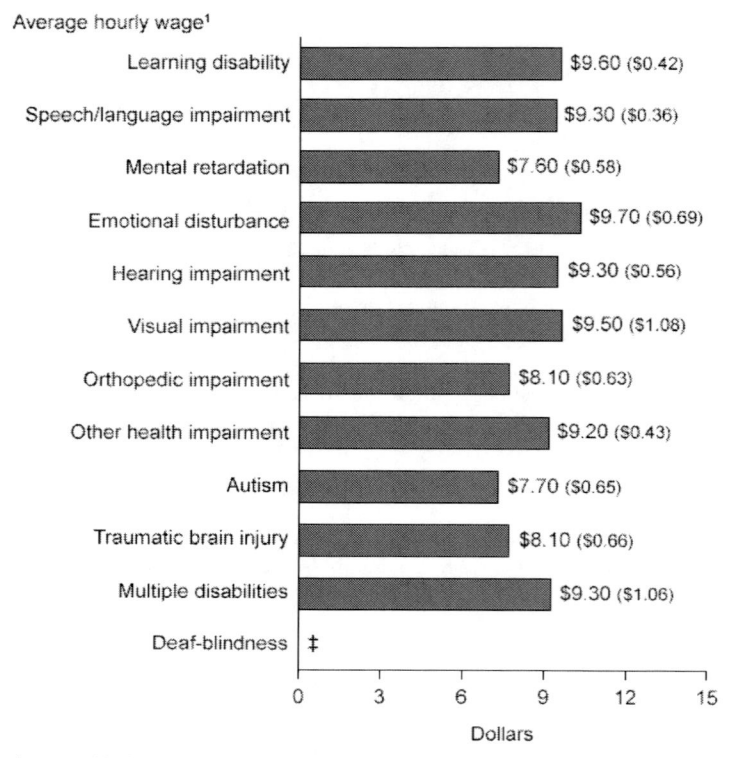

‡ Responses for items with fewer than 30 respondents are not reported.
[1]   Rounded to nearest $0.10.
Note: Standard errors are in parentheses. Findings are reported for young adults with disabilities out of high school up to 6 years. NLTS2 percentages are weighted population estimates based on samples ranging from approximately 3,690 to 4,150 young adults with disabilities.
Source: U.S. Department of Education, Institute of Education Sciences, National Center for Special Education Research, National Longitudinal Transition Study-2 (NLTS2), Wave 4 parent interview and youth interview/survey, 2007.

Figure 6. Average hourly wage of young adults, by disability category.

4. ENGAGEMENT KEY FINDINGS

NLTS2 considered young adults with disabilities as being productively engaged in the community when they had participated in employment, education, and/or job training activities since leaving secondary school. Addressing this broader concept of engagement, rather than considering individual outcomes (employment or postsecondary education) separately, was encouraged by the advisory panel during the design of the initial NLTS; as a result, NLTS was one of the first studies to present a broader perspective on how young adults and young adults with disabilities could be productively engaged in their communities.

The advisory panel for the current study continued to endorse that view of engagement. The importance of this broader view of what constitutes a successful transition is now incorporated in the current federal policy that requires states to collect data on "Indicator 14"—that is, "the percent of young adults who had IEPs, are no longer in secondary school, and who have been competitively employed, enrolled in some type of postsecondary school, or both, within one year of leaving high school" (20 U.S.C. 1416(a)(3)(B)). The NLTS2 operationalization of this concept, as endorsed by the NLTS2 design advisory panel, is somewhat broader than Indicator 14, in that NLTS2 includes all forms of employment, not just competitive employment, and includes job training as a productive form of preparation for work, in addition to enrollment in postsecondary education.

In this chapter, young adults with disabilities are considered productively engaged in the community when they had participated in one or more of the following activities since leaving secondary school:

- Employment—worked for pay, other than work around the house,[25] including supported or sheltered[26]
- Education—attended a vocational, business, or technical school; a 2-year, junior, or community college; or a 4-year college or university. employment.

[1] Rounded to nearest $0.10.

Note: Standard errors are in parentheses. Findings are reported for young adults with disabilities out of high school up to 6 years. NLTS2 percentages are weighted population estimates based on samples ranging from approximately 3,690 to 4,150 young adults with disabilities.

Source: U.S. Department of Education, Institute of Education Sciences, National Center for Special Education Research, National Longitudinal Transition Study-2 (NLTS2), Wave 4 parent interview and youth interview/survey, 2007.

Figure 7. Average wage of young adults with disabilities, by secondary-school-leaving status and years since leaving high school.

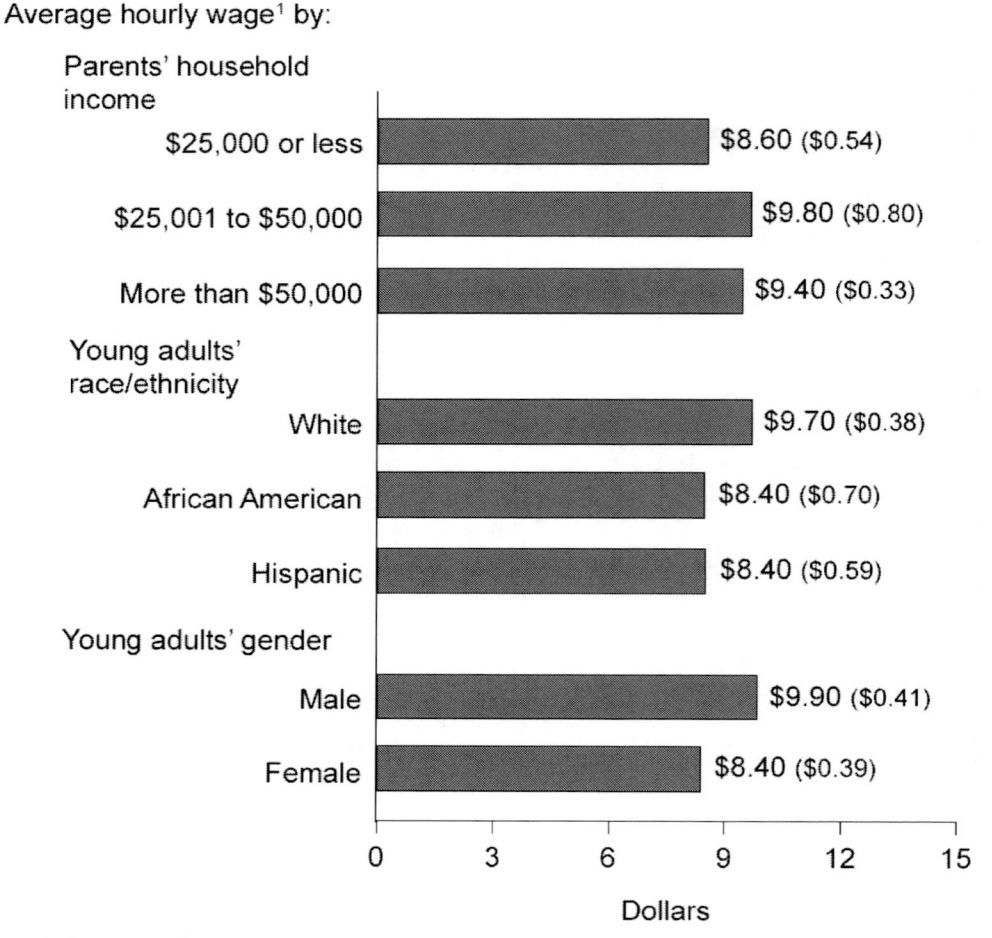

Average hourly wage[1] by:

¹ Rounded to nearest $0.10.

Note: Standard errors are in parentheses. Findings are reported for young adultswith disabilities out of high school up to 6 years. NLTS2 percentages are weighted population estimates based on samples ranging from approximately 3,690 to 4,150 young adults with disabilities.

Source: U.S. Department of Education, Institute of Education Sciences, National Center for Special Education Research, National Longitudinal Transition Study-2 (NLTS2), Wave 4 parent interview and youth interview/survey, 2007.

Figure 8. Average hourly wage of young adults with disabilities, by parents' household income and young adults' race/ethnicity and gender.

- Job training—received training in specific job skills (e.g., car repair, web page design, food service) from someone other than an employer or a family member, such as an agency or a government training program.

This chapter describes the productive engagement in the community of young adults with disabilities who had been out of high school up to 6 years. It focuses on the education, employment, and/or job training of young adults with disabilities since leaving secondary school and addresses the following questions:

- To what extent do young adults with disabilities productively engage in the community?
- How does their engagement in the community compare with that of their peers in the general population?[27]
- How does engagement differ for young adults in different disability categories and for those with different demographic characteristics?

This chapter presents findings related to productive engagement in the community of young adults with disabilities as a group as well as differences between young adults who differ in their disability category and demographic characteristics that are significantly different at the $p < .01$ or $p < .001$ level.

Engagement in Education, Employment, or Training for Employment

Regarding the productive engagement in the community of young adults with disabilities who were out-of secondary school at the time of the interview:

- Eighty-five percent were reported to have engaged in employment, postsecondary education, or job training since leaving high school (figure 9).

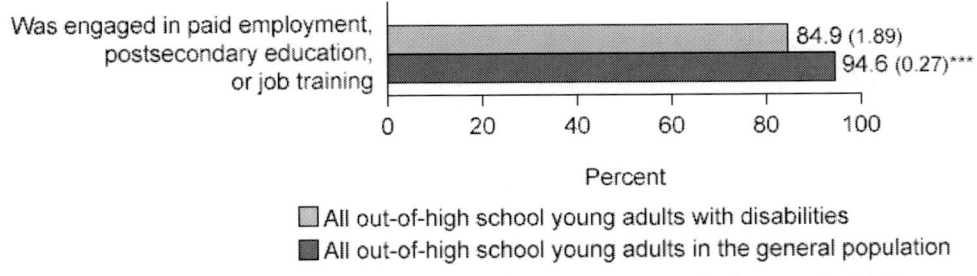

***$p < .001$ for difference between young adults with disabilities and young adults in the general population.

Note: Standard errors are in parentheses. Findings are reported for young adults out of high school up to 6 years. NLTS2 percentages are weighted population estimates based on a sample of approximately 4,650 young adults with disabilities.

Source: U.S. Department of Education, Institute of Education Sciences, National Center for Special Education Research, National Longitudinal Transition Study-2 (NLTS2), Wave 4 parent interview and youth interview/survey, 2007; U.S. Department of Labor, Bureau of Labor Statistics, National Longitudinal Survey of Youth 1997 (NLSY97) 2001 youth survey, responses for 19- to 23-year-olds.

Figure 9. Productive engagement of young adults with disabilities and those in the general population.

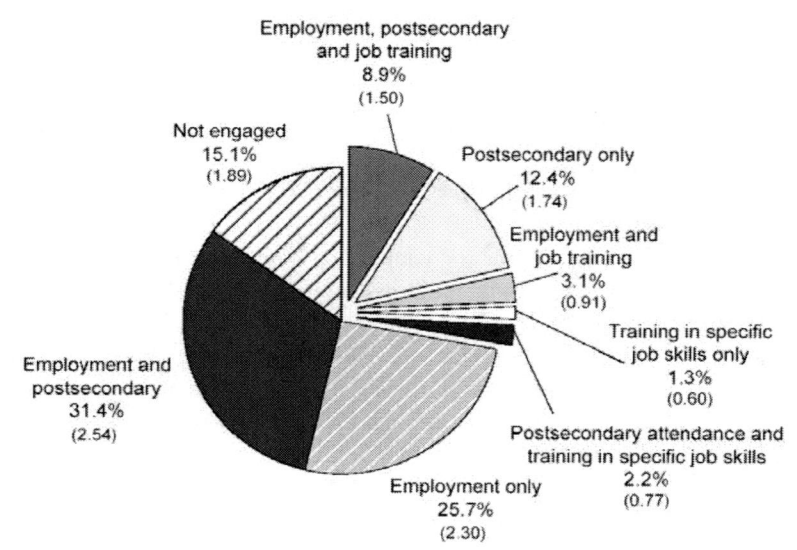

Note: Standard errors are in parentheses. Findings are reported for young adultswith disabilities out of
    high school up to 6 years. NLTS2 percentages are weighted population estimates based on a
    sample of approximately 4,650 young adults with disabilities.
Source: U.S. Department of Education, Institute of Education Sciences, National Center for Special
    Education Research, National Longitudinal Transition Study-2 (NLTS2), Wave 4 parent interview
    and youth interview/survey, 2007.

Figure 10. Modes of engagement of young adults with disabilities.

- They were less likely to engage in these activities than were their same-age peers in
  the general population, of whom 95 percent reported to have been engaged in
  employment, postsecondary education, or job training since leaving high school ($p <$
  .001).
- The productive engagement of young adults with disabilities ranged from training in
  specific job skills (1 percent) to a combination of paid employment and
  postsecondary education (31 percent, figure 10). Except for "paid employment only,"
  young adults with disabilities were more likely to engage in a combination of paid
  employment and postsecondary education than in other modes of engagement ($p <$
  .001 for all comparisons).

Disability Differences in Engagement in Education, Employment, or Training for Employment

- Young adults with hearing impairments (90 percent, figure 11), learning disabilities
  (89 percent), speech/language impairments (86 percent), or other health impairments
  (86 percent) were more likely to have been productively engaged since high school
  than were those with mental retardation (69 percent, $p <$ .001 for all comparisons) or
  autism (69 percent, $p <$ .001 for comparison with hearing impairments and learning
  disabilities; and $p <$ .01 for comparison with speech/language impairments and other
  health impairments).

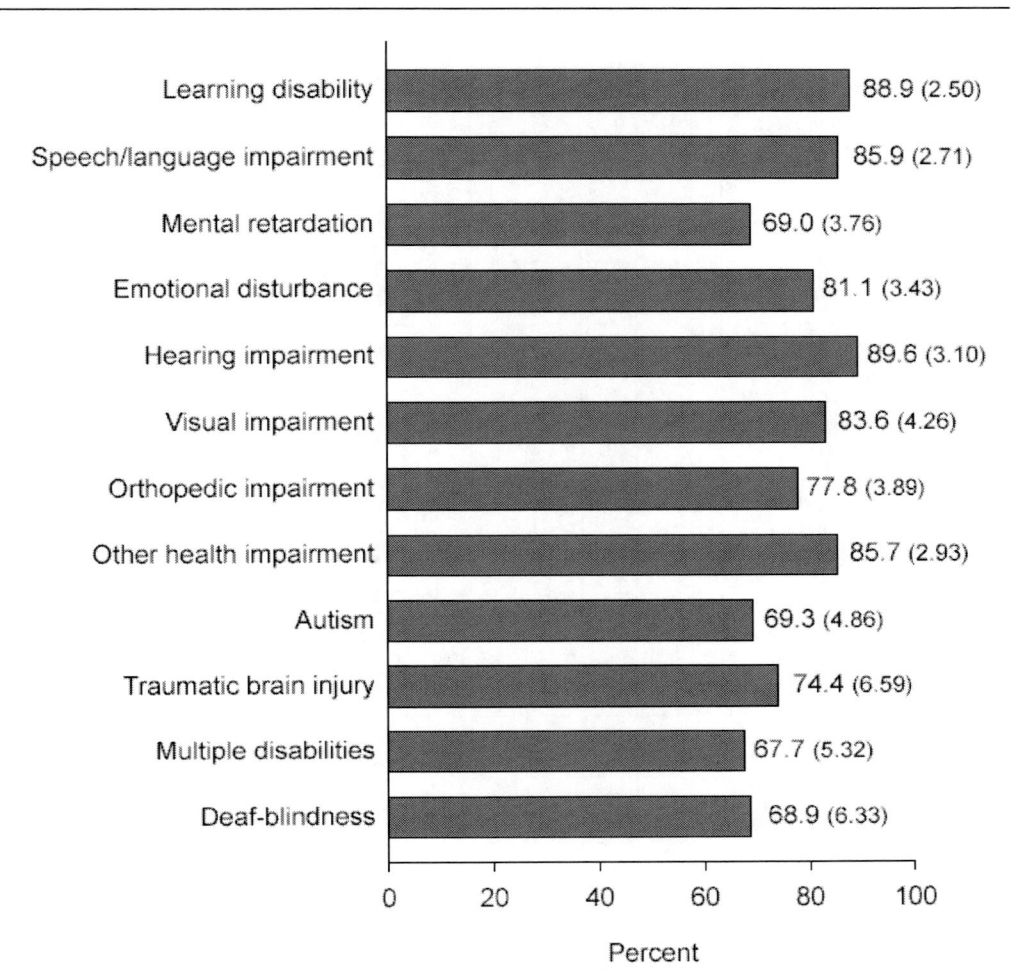

Note: Standard errors are in parentheses. Findings are reported for young adults with disabilities out of high school up to 6 years. NLTS2 percentages are weighted population estimates based on a sample of approximately 4,650 young adults with disabilities.

Source: U.S. Department of Education, Institute of Education Sciences, National Center for Special Education Research, National Longitudinal Transition Study-2 (NLTS2), Wave 4 parent interview and youth interview/survey, 2007.

Figure 11. Productive engagement of young adults with disabilities, by disability category.

- Similarly, young adults with hearing impairments (90 percent), learning disabilities (89 percent), speech/language impairments (86 percent), or other health impairments (86 percent) were more likely to have been productively engaged than were those with multiple disabilities (68 percent, $p < .001$ for comparison with hearing impairments and learning disabilities; and $p < .01$ for comparison with speech/language impairments and other health impairments) or deaf-blindness (69 percent, $p < .01$ for comparison with hearing impairments and learning disabilities).

Table 11. Modes of engagement of young adults, by disability category

	Learning disability	Speech/language impairment	Mental retardation	Emotional disturbance	Hearing impairment	Visual mpairment	Orthopedic Impair ment	Other health impairment	Autism	Traumatic brai injury	Multiple disabilities	Deaf bindness
	Percent											
Employment only	24.2	18.8	33.4	33.4	15.9	10.0	10.8	24.9	15.3	12.5	24.2	14.5
	(3.41)	(3.05)	(3.83)	(4.14)	(3.71)	(3.45)	(2.91)	(3.62)	(3.79)	(4.99)	(4.87)	(4.81)
Postsecondary education only	14.0	14.9	7.2	8.4	15.3	14.8	19.5	8.4	9.3	15.3	10.5	16.2
	(2.76)	(2.78)	(2.10)	(2.43)	(3.66)	(4.09)	(3.71)	(2.32)	(3.06)	(5.43)	(3.49)	(5.04)
Employment and postsecondary education	35.5	41.2	10.8	25.8	34.3	34.8	24.9	38.6	23.2	28.6	10.8	18.9
	(3.81)	(3.84)	(2.52)	(3.84)	(4.82)	(5.48)	(4.05)	(4.07)	(4.44)	(6.82)	(3.53)	(5.35)
Employment, postsecondary education, and job training	9.0	6.3	9.0	8.3	18.7	14.8	10.8	8.7	10.4	12.2	5.0	8.7
	(2.28)	(1.90)	(2.32)	(2.42)	(3.96)	(4.09)	(2.91)	(2.36)	(3.21)	(4.94)	(2.48)	(3.85)
Employment and job training	2.5	3.0	5.2	2.6	2.3	1.9	6.4	3.7	6.0	5.5	9.8	4.6
	(1.24)	(1.33)	(1.80)	(1.40)	(1.52)	(1.57)	(2.29)	(1.58)	(2.50)	(3.44)	(3.38)	(2.86)
Job training only	1.3	1.1	2.3	0.5	0.4	0.9	0.7	0.2	1.5	0.1	2.4	1.1
	(0.90)	(0.81)	(1.22)	(0.62)	(0.64)	(1.09)	(0.78)	(0.37)	(1.28)	(0.48)	(1.74)	(1.43)
Postsecondary and job training	2.5	0.7	1.1	2.0	2.6	6.5	4.5	1.3	3.6	0.1	4.9	4.9
	(1.24)	(0.65)	(0.85)	(1.23)	(1.62)	(2.84)	(1.94)	(0.95)	(1.96)	(0.48)	(2.46)	(2.95)
No engagement	11.1	14.1	31.0	18.9	10.4	16.4	22.2	14.3	30.7	25.6	32.3	31.1
	(2.50)	(2.71)	(3.76)	(3.43)	(3.10)	(4.26)	(3.89)	(2.93)	(4.86)	(6.59)	(5.32)	(6.33)

Note: Standard errors are in parentheses. Findings are reported for young adults with disabilities out of high school up to 6 years. NLTS2 percentages are weighted population estimates based on a sample of approximately 4,650 young adults with disabilities.

Source: U.S. Department of Education, Institute of Education Sciences, National Center for Special Education Research, National Longitudinal Transition Study-2 (NLTS2), Wave 4 parent interview and youth interview/survey, 2007.

- Young adults with speech/language impairments were more likely to have been engaged in a combination of paid employment and postsecondary education since high school (42 percent, table 11) than were those with mental retardation (11 percent, $p < .001$), multiple disabilities (11 percent, $p < .001$), deaf-blindness (19 percent, $p < .001$), autism (23 percent, $p < .01$), orthopedic impairments (25 percent, $p < .01$), or emotional disturbances (26 percent, $p < .01$).
- Young adults with other health impairments (39 percent), visual impairments (35 percent), learning disabilities (36 percent), hearing impairments (34 percent), emotional disturbances (26 percent), or orthopedic impairments (25 percent) were more likely to have been engaged in a combination of paid employment and postsecondary education since high school than were those with mental retardation or multiple disabilities (11 percent, each; $p < .001$ for all comparisons except for emotional disturbances and orthopedic impairments).
- The percentage of young adults with disabilities reported to have been engaged only in paid employment since leaving high school ranged from 10 percent of young adults with visual impairments to 33percent of those with emotional disturbance or mental retardation. Young adults with mental retardation or emotional disturbances were more likely to have been engaged only in paid employment (33 percent, each) than were those with visual impairments (10 percent, $p < .001$ for both comparisons), orthopedic impairments (11 percent, $p < .001$ for both comparisons), traumatic brain injuries (13 percent, $p < .001$ for comparison with mental retardation and $p < .01$ for comparison with emotional disturbance), deaf-blindness (15 percent, $p < .01$ for both comparisons), autism (15 percent , $p < .01$ for comparison with mental retardation and $p < .01$ for comparison with emotional disturbance), hearingimpairments (16 percent, $p < .01$ for both comparisons), or speech/language impairments (19 percent , $p < .01$ for both comparisons).
- The percentage of young adults with disabilities reported to have been engaged only in postsecondary education ranged from 7 percent of young adults with mental retardation to 20 percent of those with orthopedic impairments. Young adults with orthopedic impairments were more likely to have been engaged in postsecondary attendance only than were those with mental retardation (20 percent vs. 7 percent, $p < .01$).
- The percentage of young adults with disabilities reported to have been engaged in a combination of paid employment, postsecondary education, and job training since leaving high school ranged from 5 percent of young adults with multiple disabilities to 19 percentof those with hearing impairments. Young adults with hearing impairments were more likely to be engaged in the combination of these activities (19 percent) than were those with multiple disabilities (5 percent, $p < .01$) or speech/language impairments (6 percent, $p < .01$).
- Engagement in a combination of paid employment and job training ranged from 2 percent of young adults with visual impairments to 10 percent of those with multiple disabilities. Engagement in the combination of these activities did not differ significantly by disability category.
- The percentage of young adults with disabilities reported to have been engaged in a combination of postsecondary education and job training since leaving high school

ranged from less than 1 percent of young adults with traumatic brain injuries to 7 percent of those with visual impairments. Engagement in the combination of these activities did not differ significantly by disability category.

- Two percent or fewer of young adults with disabilities in each disability category were reported to have been engaged only in job training since leaving high school. Engagement in the combination of these activities did not differ significantly by disability category.
- The percentage of young adults with disabilities reported to have not been engaged in paid employment, postsecondary education, or job training since leaving high school ranged from 10 percent of young adults with hearing impairments to 32 percent of those with multiple disabilities. Young adults with mental retardation were more likely to not be engaged in any of these activities than were those in several other disability categories (31 percent), including young adults with hearing impairments (10 percent, $p < .001$), learning disabilities (11 percent, $p < .001$), speech/language impairments (14 percent, $p < .001$), or other health impairments (14 percent, $p < .001$).
- Similarly, young adults with multiple disabilities (32 percent) or autism (31 percent) were more likely to not be engaged than were those in several other disability categories, including young adults with hearing impairments (10 percent, $p < .001$ for both comparisons), learning disabilities (11 percent, $p < .001$ for both comparisons), or other health impairments (14 percent, $p < .01$ for both comparisons).

Table 12. Modes of engagement of young adults with disabilities, by secondary-school-leaving status and years since leaving high school

	Completers	Non-completers	Less than 2 years	2 up to 4 years	4 up to 6 years
	\multicolumn{5}{c}{Percent}				
Employment only	23.5	43.8	23.6	28.0	23.7
	(2.40)	(6.76)	(4.29)	(3.54)	(4.01)
Postsecondary education only	13.4	4.2	14.4	11.6	12.5
	(1.93)	(2.73)	(3.55)	(2.52)	(3.12)
Employment and postsecondary education	33.8	11.5	26.2	32.8	32.4
	(2.68)	(4.35)	(4.44)	(3.70)	(4.42)
Employment, postsecondary education, and job training	9.8	1.2	9.0	5.4	13.4
	(1.69)	(1.48)	(2.89)	(1.78)	(3.21)
Employment and job training	3.2	2.1	1.9	3.5	3.1
	(1.00)	(1.95)	(1.38)	(1.45)	(1.64)
Job training only	1.3	0.6	0.6	0.3	2.9
	(0.64)	(1.05)	(0.78)	(0.43)	(1.58)
Postsecondary and job training	2.4	1.0	1.8	2.3	2.4
	(0.87)	(1.36)	(1.34)	(1.18)	(1.44)

	Completers	Non-completers	Less than 2 years	2 up to 4 years	4 up to 6 years
	Percent				
No engagement	12.6	35.5	22.6	16.1	9.7
	(1.88)	(6.52)	(4.23)	(2.90)	(2.79)

Note: Standard errors are in parentheses. Findings are reported for young adults with disabilities out of high school up to 6 years. NLTS2 percentages are weighted population estimates based on a sample of approximately 4,650 young adults with disabilities.

Source: U.S. Department of Education, Institute of Education Sciences, National Center for Special Education Research, National Longitudinal Transition Study-2 (NLTS2), Wave 4 parent interview and youth interview/survey, 2007.

Table 13. Modes of engagement of young adults with disabilities, by parents' household income and young adults' race/ethnicity and gender

	$25,000 or less	$25,001 to $50,000	More than $50,000	White	African American	Hispanic	Male	Female
	Percent							
Employment only	29.4	32.0	18.2	27.1	20.9	19.9	25.6	25.8
	(4.35)	(4.87)	(3.06)	(2.82)	(4.91)	(6.35)	(2.86)	(3.87)
Postsecondary education only	8.6	14.7	13.4	11.6	8.7	24.2	11.1	14.7
	(2.68)	(3.70)	(2.71)	(2.03)	(3.40)	(6.81)	(2.06)	(3.13)
Employment and postsecondary education	24.4	28.0	40.0	35.6	27.0	23.6	31.1	32.0
	(4.10)	(4.69)	(3.89)	(3.03)	(5.36)	(6.76)	(3.03)	(4.13)
Employment, post-secondary education, and job training	7.8	5.4	12.6	7.9	11.3	12.2	9.3	8.1
	(2.56)	(2.36)	(2.64)	(1.71)	(3.82)	(5.21)	(1.90)	(2.41)
Employment and job training	2.6	3.8	3.2	3.8	1.7	1.6	3.1	3.0
	(1.52)	(2.00)	(1.40)	(1.21)	(1.56)	(2.00)	(1.14)	(1.51)
Job training only	3.4	0.1	0.3	0.3	4.9	0.6	1.6	0.7
	(1.73)	(0.33)	(0.43)	(0.35)	(2.61)	(1.23)	(0.82)	(0.74)
Postsecondary and job training	2.0	2.9	1.9	1.5	3.2	2.5	2.3	2.2
	(1.34)	(1.75)	(1.08)	(0.77)	(2.13)	(2.48)	(0.98)	(1.30)
No engagement	21.8	13.2	10.4	12.2	22.2	15.4	16.0	13.4
	(3.94)	(3.54)	(2.42)	(2.07)	(5.02)	(5.74)	(2.40)	(3.01)

Note: Standard errors are in parentheses. Findings are reported for young adults with disabilities out of high school up to 6 years. NLTS2 percentages are weighted population estimates based on a sample of approximately 4,650 young adults with disabilities.

Source: U.S. Department of Education, Institute of Education Sciences, National Center for Special Education Research, National Longitudinal Transition Study-2 (NLTS2), Wave 4 parent interview and youth interview/survey, 2007.

Differences in Engagement in Education, Employment, or
Training for Employment by High School-Leaving Characteristics

- Young adults with disabilities who completed high school were more likely than those who did not complete high school to have been engaged in a combination of paid employment and postsecondary education (34 percent vs. 12 percent, $p < .001$; table 12); in postsecondary education only (13 percent vs. 4 percent, $p < .01$); or in a combination of paid employment, postsecondary education, and job training (10 percent vs. 1 percent, $p < .001$).
- Young adults with disabilities who did not complete high school were more likely than those who did complete high school to have been engaged be in paid employment only (44 percent vs. 24 percent, $p < .01$) or to not be engaged at all (36 percent vs. 13 percent, $p < .001$).
- Engagement did not vary significantly by the number of years since leaving high school.

Demographic Differences in Engagement in Education, Employment, or
Training for Employment

- Family income differences were apparent in the rate of engagement in paid employment and postsecondary education. Young adults with disabilities from households with incomes of more than $50,000 were more likely to have been engaged in the combination of these activities (40 percent) than were those from households with incomes of $25,000 or less (24 percent, $p < .01$; table 13).
- Engagement did not vary significantly by race or ethnicity or gender.

5. HOUSEHOLD CIRCUMSTANCES KEY FINDINGS

Financial and residential independence have been considered as two important indicators of adult status (Janus 2009). In addition, other identifiers of adulthood include marriage and parenting (Hogan and Astone 1986; Katz-Wise, Priess, and Hyde 2010; Modell 1989; Rindfuss 1991). This chapter describes the household circumstances of young adults with disabilities who had been out of high school up to 6 years. It focuses on the residential independence (rather than residential status), parenting and marriage status, and financial independence of young adults, and addresses the following questions:

- To what extent do young adults with disabilities achieve residential independence, become parents, get married, or use financial management tools?
- How do their experiences compare with those of their peers in the general population?
- How does residential independence, parenting and marriage status, and use of financial management tools vary by disability category and demographic characteristics?

This chapter presents findings related to the household circumstances of young adults with disabilities as a group as well as differences between young adults who differ in their disability category and demographic characteristics that are significantly different at least at the $p < .01$ level.

Residential Independence

Regarding the residential independence of young adults with disabilities who were out-of secondary school at the time of the interview:[28]

- Thirty-six percent were reported to be living independently at the time of the interview (figure 12). Young adults were considered to be living independently if they were living alone or with a spouse, partner, or roommate.
- Three percent were reported to be living semi-independently. Young adults are considered to be living semi-independently if they were living in a college dormitory, military housing, or a group home.[29]
- Young adults with disabilities were less likely to be living independently than were their same-age peers in the general population, of whom 44 percent were reported to be living independently at the time of the interview ($p < .01$).

Disability Differences in Residential Independence
- Young adults with learning disabilities were more likely to be living independently at the time of the interview (41 percent) than were those with multiple disabilities (11 percent, $p < .001$; table 14), autism (12 percent, $p < .001$), deaf-blindness (14 percent, $p < .001$), orthopedic impairments (14 percent, $p < .001$), or mental retardation (21 percent, $p < .001$).
- Young adults with emotional disturbances were more likely to be living independently at the time of the interview (34 percent) than were those with multiple disabilities (11 percent, $p < .001$), autism (12 percent, $p < .001$), deaf-blindness (14 percent, $p < .001$), or orthopedic impairments (14 percent, $p < .001$).
- Similarly, young adults with other health impairments (31 percent) or speech/language impairments (30 percent) were more likely to be living independently than were those with multiple disabilities (11 percent, $p < .001$ for both comparisons), autism (12 percent, $p < .001$ for both comparisons), orthopedic impairments (14 percent, $p < .001$ for both comparisons), or deaf-blindness (14 percent, $p < .01$ for both comparisons).
- In addition, young adults with visual impairments were more likely to be living independently at the time of the interview (31 percent) than were those with multiple disabilities (11 percent, $p < .01$), autism (12 percent, $p < .01$), or orthopedic impairments (14 percent, $p < .01$).
- Young adults in with hearing impairments (29 percent) were more likely to have been living independently at the time of the interview than were those with multiple disabilities (11 percent , $p < .01$) or autism (12 percent, $p < .01$).

Differences in Residential Independence by High School-Leaving Characteristics

- Young adults who had been out of high school 4 to 6 years were more likely to live independently (47 percent) than were those who had been out of high school less than 2 years (21 percent, $p < .001$; table 15).
- Residential independence did not differ significantly by high school-leaving status.

Demographic Differences in Residential Independence

- Race or ethnicity differences were apparent in the residential independence of young adults with disabilities. Young adults who wereWhite were more likely to live independently (39 percent) than were those who wereAfrican America n (21 percent, $p < .01$; table 16).
- Residential independence did not differ significantly by parents'household income; or young adults' gender.

Parenting Status

Regarding the parenting status of young adults with disabilities who were out of secondary school at the time of the interview:

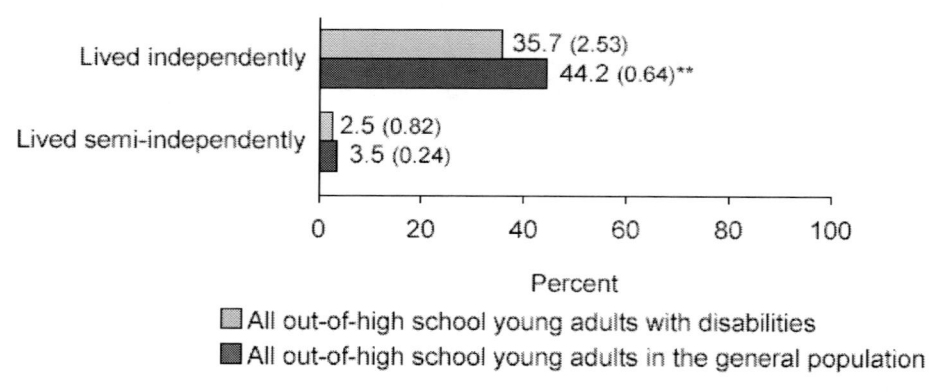

*** $p < .01$ for difference between young adults with disabilities and young adults in the general population.

Note: Standard errors are in parentheses. Findings are reported for young adults out of high school up to 6 years.NLTS2 percentages are weighted population estimates based on a sample of approximately 4,520 young adults with disabilities.

Source: U.S. Department of Education, Institute of Education Sciences, National Center for Special Education Research, National Longitudinal Transition Study-2 (NLTS2), Wave 4 parent interview and youth interview/survey, 2007; U.S. Department of Labor, Bureau of Labor Statistics, National Longitudinal Survey of Youth 1997 (NLSY97) 2001 youth survey, responses for 19- to 23-year-olds.

Figure 12. Residential independence of young adults with disabilities and young adults in the general population at the time of the interview.

Table 14. Residential independence of young adults with disabilities at the time of the interview, by disability category

	Learning disability	Speech/language impairment	Mental retardation	Emotional disturbance	Hearing impairment	Visual impairment	Orthopedic impairment	Other health impairment	Autism	Traumatic brain injury	Multiple disabilities	Deaf blindness
						Percent						
Lived independently	40.6 (3.91)	30.4 (3.60)	21.2 (3.32)	34.4 (4.17)	28.5 (4.60)	31.3 (5.35)	14.0 (3.26)	30.8 (3.86)	11.8 (3.40)	24.8 (6.52)	10.6 (3.50)	13.7 (4.70)
Lived semi-independently	2.9 (1.34)	4.6 (1.64)	0.2 (0.36)	1.3 (0.99)	5.6 (2.34)	3.9 (2.23)	1.6 (1.18)	4.5 (1.73)	1.4 (1.24)	2.6 (2.40)	0.6 (0.88)	3.2 (2.41)

Note: Standard errors are in parentheses. Findings are reported for young adults with disabilities out of high school up to 6 years. NLTS2 percentages are weighted population estimates based on a sample of approximately 4,640 young adults with disabilities.

Source: U.S. Department of Education, Institute of Education Sciences, National Center for Special Education Research, National Longitudinal Transition Study-2 (NLTS2), Wave 4 parent interview and youth interview/survey, 2007.

Table 15. Residential independence of young adults with disabilities, by secondary-school-leaving status and years since leaving high school

	Completers	Non-completers	Less than 2 years	2 up to 4 years	4 up to 6 years
	Percent				
Lived independently	35.0 (2.71)	41.9 (6.74)	21.0 (4.12)	33.5 (3.72)	46.6 (4.71)
Lived semi-independently	3.0 (0.94)	0.0 (0.00)	4.0 (1.98)	3.5 (1.45)	0.5 (0.67)

Note: Standard errors are in parentheses. Findings are reported for young adults with disabilities out of high school up to 6 years. NLTS2 percentages are weighted population estimates based on a sample of approximately 4,640 young adults with disabilities.

Source: U.S. Department of Education, Institute of Education Sciences, National Center for Special Education Research, National Longitudinal Transition Study-2 (NLTS2), Wave 4 parent interview and youth interview/survey, 2007.

Table 16. Residential independence of young adults with disabilities, by parents' household income and young adults' race/ethnicity and gender

	$25,000 or less	$25,001 to $50,000	More than $50,000	White	African American	Hispanic	Male	Female
	Percent							
Lived independently	31.0 (4.42)	41.7 (5.16)	34.6 (3.78)	38.6 (3.09)	21.1 (4.93)	38.2 (7.73)	33.8 (3.10)	39.0 (4.32)
Lived semi-independently	0.4 (0.60)	4.4 (2.14)	2.9 (1.33)	2.9 (1.06)	2.8 (1.99)	0.3 (0.87)	3.1 (1.14)	1.5 (1.08)

Note: Standard errors are in parentheses. Findings are reported for young adults with disabilities out of high school up to 6 years. NLTS2 percentages are weighted population estimates based on a sample of approximately 4,640 young adults with disabilities.

Source: U.S. Department of Education, Institute of Education Sciences, National Center for Special Education Research, National Longitudinal Transition Study-2 (NLTS2), Wave 4 parent interview and youth interview/survey, 2007.

- Twenty-three percent were reported to have ever had or fathered a child (figure 13).[30]
- Young adults with disabilities were just as likely to have ever had or fathered a child as were their same-age peers in the general population, of whom 20 percent reported to have done so since leaving high school.[31]

Marital Status

Regarding the marital status of young adults with disabilities who were out of secondary school at the time of the interview:

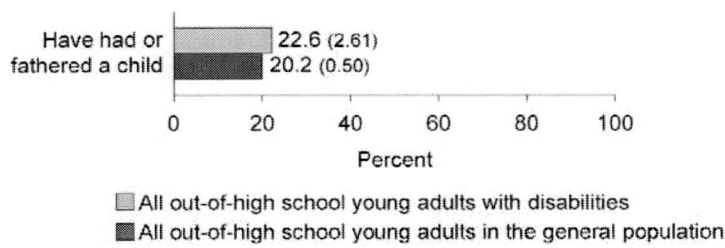

Have had or fathered a child
- 22.6 (2.61)
- 20.2 (0.50)

Percent

☐ All out-of-high school young adults with disabilities
■ All out-of-high school young adults in the general population

Note: Standard errors are in parentheses. Findings are reported for young adults out of high school up to 6 years.NLTS2 percentages are weighted population estimates based on a sample of approximately 3,470 young adults with disabilities.

Source: U.S. Department of Education, Institute of Education Sciences, National Center for Special Education Research, National Longitudinal Transition Study-2 (NLTS2), Wave 4 parent interview and youth interview/survey, 2007; U.S. Department of Labor, Bureau of Labor Statistics, National Longitudinal Survey of Youth 1997 (NLSY97) 2001 youth survey, responses for 19- to 23-year-olds.

Figure 13. Parenting status of young adults with disabilities and young adults in the general population.

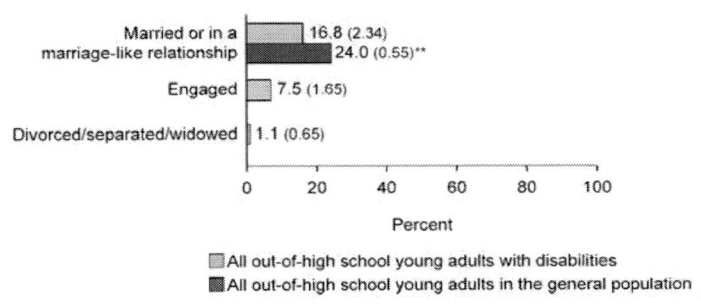

Married or in a marriage-like relationship
- 16.8 (2.34)
- 24.0 (0.55)**

Engaged
- 7.5 (1.65)

Divorced/separated/widowed
- 1.1 (0.65)

Percent

☐ All out-of-high school young adults with disabilities
■ All out-of-high school young adults in the general population

** $p < .01$ for difference between young adults with disabilities and young adults in the general population.

Note: Standard errors are in parentheses. Findings are reported for young adults out of high school up to 6 years. NLTS2 percentages are weighted population estimates based on a sample of approximately 3,520 young adults with disabilities.

Source: U.S. Department of Education, Institute of Education Sciences, National Center for Special Education Research, National Longitudinal Transition Study-2 (NLTS2), Wave 4 parent interview and youth interview/survey, 2007; U.S. Department of Labor, Bureau of Labor Statistics, National Longitudinal Survey of Youth 1997 (NLSY97) 2001 youth survey, responses for 19- to 23-year-olds.

Figure 14. Marital status of young adults with disabilities and young adults in the general population at the time of the interview.

- Seventeen percent were reported to have been married or living in a marriage-like relationship within 6 years of leaving high school (figure 14).[32]
- Young adults with disabilities were less likely to be married or living in a marriage-like relationship than were their same-age peers in the general population, of whom 24 percent reported to have been married or living in a marriage-like relationship within 6 years of leaving high school ($p < .01$).[33]

Disability Differences in Parenting and Marriage

- Young adults with learning disabilities or emotional disturbances were more likely to have ever had or fathered a child (26 percent, each) than were those with deaf-blindness (1 percent, $p < .001$ for both comparisons; table 17), autism (3 percent, $p < .001$ for both comparisons), multiple disabilities (3 percent, $p < .001$ for both comparisons), orthopedic impairments (4 percent, $p < .001$ for both comparisons), visual impairments (8 percent, $p < .01$ for both comparisons), or speech/language impairments (11 percent, $p < .01$ for both comparisons).

- Similarly, young adults with mental retardation or other health impairments were also more likely to have ever had or fathered a child (18 percent, each) than were those with deaf-blindness (1 percent, $p < .001$ for both comparisons), autism (3 percent, $p < .001$ for both comparisons), multiple disabilities (3 percent, $p < .001$ for comparison with mental retardation and $p < .01$ for comparison with other health impairments), or orthopedic impairments (4 percent, $p < .001$ for comparison with mental retardation and $p < .01$ for comparison with other health impairments).

- Young adults with learning disabilities or other health impairments were more likely to be married or living in a marriage-like relationship (19 percent and 17 percent, respectively) than were those with autism (2 percent, $p < .001$ for both comparisons), multiple disabilities (2 percent, $p < .001$ for both comparisons), deaf-blindness (4 percent, $p < .01$ for both comparisons), or orthopedic impairments (4 percent, $p < .001$ for comparison with learning disabilities and $p < .01$ for comparison with other health impairments).

- Similarly, young adults with speech/language impairments were more likely to be married or living in a marriage-like relationship (15 percent) than were those with autism (2 percent, $p < .001$), multiple disabilities (2 percent, $p < .01$), or orthopedic impairments (4 percent, $p < .01$).

- In addition, young adults with emotional disturbances were more likely to be married or living in a marriage-like relationship (14 percent) than were those with autism (2 percent, $p < .01$) or multiple disabilities (2 percent, $p < .01$).

Differences in Parenting and Marriage by High School-Leaving Characteristics

- Parenting and marital status did not differ significantly by school-leaving status or by the number of years since leaving high school (table 18).

Demographic Differences in Parenting and Marriage

Family income differences were apparent in the parenting status of young adults with disabilities. Young adults from households with incomes of between \$25,001 and \$50,000 were more likely to have ever had or fathered a child (31 percent) than were those from households with incomes of more than \$50,000 (13 percent, $p < .01$; table 19).

Table 17. Parenting and marital status of young adults, by disability category

Parenting and marital status	Learning disability	Speech/ language impairment	Mental retardation	Emotional disturbance	Hearing impairment	Visual impairment	Orthopedic impairment	Other Health impairment	Autism	Traumatic brain injury	Multiple disabilities	Deaf blindness
	Percent											
Ever had or fathered a child	25.7 (4.21)	11.4 (2.96)	18.0 (3.66)	25.6 (4.57)	11.2 (4.05)	7.8 (3.42)	4.0 (2.07)	17.5 (3.76)	2.9 (1.96)	10.9 (5.44)	3.4 (2.42)	1.4 (1.84)
Married or living in a marriage-like relationship	19.3 (3.84)	15.2 (3.34)	12.2 (3.08)	13.7 (3.60)	11.0 (3.90)	13.5 (4.41)	4.2 (2.10)	16.9 (3.70)	2.4 (1.73)	14.7 (6.18)	2.4 (2.05)	4.0 (2.97)

Note: Standard errors are in parentheses. Findings are reported for young adults with disabilities out of high school up to 6 years. NLTS2 percentages are weighted population estimates based on samples of approximately 3,480 young adults with disabilities for having or fathering a child to 3,520 young adults with disabilities for marital status.

Source: U.S. Department of Education, Institute of Education Sciences, National Center for Special Education Research, National Longitudinal Transition Study-2 (NLTS2), Wave 4 parent interview and youth interview/survey, 2007.

Table 18. Parenting and marital status of young adults with disabilities, by secondary-school-leaving status and years since leaving high school

	Completers	Non-completers	Less than 2 years	2 up to 4 years	4 up to 6 years
	Percent				
Parenting and marital status Ever had or fathered a child	21.6 (2.69)	39.5 (9.04)	14.9 (4.09)	21.4 (3.87)	28.8 (5.15)
Married or living in a marriage-like relationship	17.9 (2.51)	9.4 (5.40)	12.8 (3.84)	14.8 (3.34)	21.8 (4.76)

Note: Standard errors are in parentheses. Findings are reported for young adults with disabilities out of high school up to 6 years.NLTS2 percentages are weighted population estimates based on samples of approximately 3,480 young adults with disabilities for having or fathering a child to 3,520 young adults with disabilities for marital status.

Source: U.S. Department of Education, Institute of Education Sciences, National Center for Special Education Research, National Longitudinal Transition Study-2 (NLTS2), Wave 4 parent interview and youth interview/survey, 2007.

Table 19. Parenting and marital status of young adults with disabilities, by parents' household income and young adults' race/ethnicity and gender

	$25,000 or less	$25,001 to $50,000	More than $50,000	White	African American	Hispanic	Male	Female
	Percent							
Parenting and marital status								
Ever had or fathered a child	26.9 (4.83)	30.8 (5.86)	13.0 (3.14)	20.1 (3.05)	32.7 (6.21)	22.5 (7.95)	15.0 (2.78)	35.3 (4.97)
Married or living in a marriage-like relationship	16.7 (4.10)	20.8 (5.14)	14.3 (3.27)	20.3 (3.06)	10.5 (4.11)	9.0 (5.47)	16.0 (2.87)	18.0 (3.99)

Note: Standard errors are in parentheses. Findings are reported for young adults with disabilities out of high school up to 6 years. NLTS2 percentages are weighted population estimates based on samples of approximately 3,480 young adults with disabilities for having or fathering a child to 3,520 young adults with disabilities for marital status.

Source: U.S. Department of Education, Institute of Education Sciences, National Center for Special Education Research, National Longitudinal Transition Study-2 (NLTS2), Wave 4 parent interview and youth interview/survey, 2007.

- Gender differences were apparent in the parenting status of young adults with disabilities, as well. Females were more likely to have ever had a child (35 percent) than were males to have fathered a child (15 percent, $p < .001$).
- Parenting status did not differ significantly by race or ethnicity.
- Marital status did not differ significantly by family income, race or ethnicity, or gender.

Financial Independence

Regarding the financial independence of young adults with disabilities who were out of secondary school at the time of the interview:

- Sixty-two percent of young adults with disabilities were reported to have a savings account, 60 percent a checking account and 45 percent a credit card in his or her name, at the time of the interview (figure 15).[34]
- Young adults with disabilitieswere lesslikely to have a checking account or credit card than were their same-age peers in the general population, of whom 71 percent and 55 percent, respectively, reported to have achieved this level of financial independence.

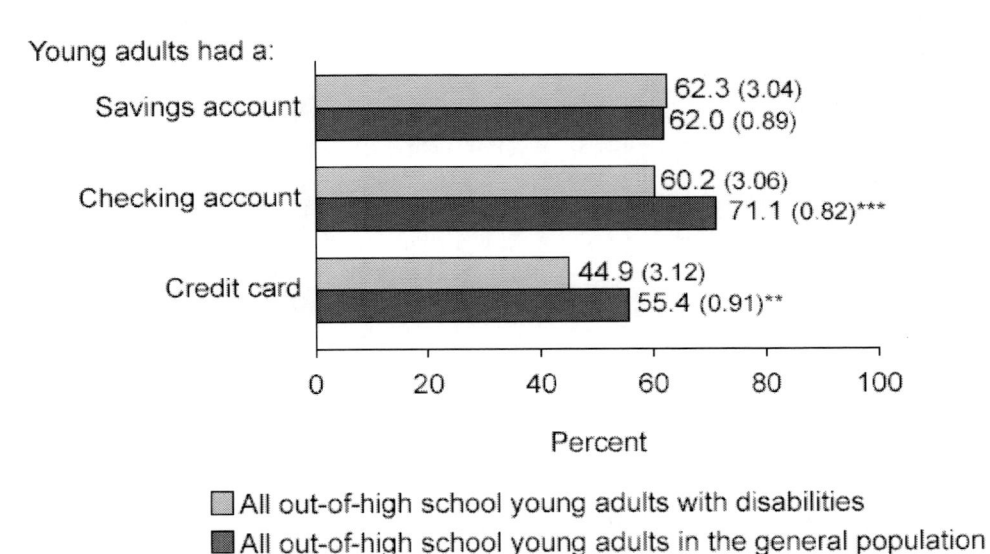

**p < .01; ***p < .001 for difference between young adults with disabilities and young adults in the general population.

Note: Standard errors are in parentheses. Findings are reported for young adults out of high school up to 6 years.NLTS2 percentages are weighted population estimates based on a sample of approximately 3,510 young adults with disabilities.

Source: U.S. Department of Education, Institute of Education Sciences, National Center for Special Education Research, National Longitudinal Transition Study-2 (NLTS2), Wave 4 parent interview and youth interview/survey, 2007; National Institutes of Health, National Institute of Child Health and Human Development (NICHD), The National Longitudinal Study of Adolescent Health (Add Health), Wave 3, 2001–02, responses calculated for 19- to 23-year-olds.

Figure 15. Financial management tools used by young adults with disabilities and young adults in the general population at the time of the interview.

Disability Differences in Financial Independence
- Young adults in several disability categories were more likely to have a savings account at the time of the interview than were those with mental retardation (45

percent; table 20), including young adults with learning disabilities (67 percent, $p <$ .001), speech/language impairments (66 percent, $p < .001$), other health impairments (66 percent, $p < .001$), or hearing impairments (65 percent, $p < .01$).

- Young adults in several disability categories were more likely to have a checking account at the time of the interview than were those with mental retardation (33 percent), including young adults with visual impairments (70 percent, $p < .001$), hearing impairments (69 percent, $p < .001$), learning disabilities (68 percent, $p <$ .001), other health impairments (64 percent, $p < .001$), speech/language impairments (63 percent, $p < .001$), or orthopedic impairments (59 percent, $p < .001$).

- Similarly, young adults in several disability categories were more likely to have a checking account at the time of the interview than were those with multiple disabilities (38 percent), including young adults with visual impairments (70 percent, $p < .001$) hearing impairments (69 percent, $p < .001$), learning disabilities (68 percent, $p < .001$), other health impairments (64 percent, $p < .01$), or speech/language impairments (63 percent, $p < .01$).

- In addition, young adults with visual impairments were more likely to have a checking account at the time of the interview (70 percent) than were those with emotional disturbances (50 percent, $p < .01$).

- Young adults with learning disabilities were more likely to have a credit card in their name (54 percent) than were those with mental retardation (19 percent, $p < .001$), deaf-blindness (19 percent, $p < .001$), autism (21 percent, $p < .001$), multiple disabilities (24 percent, $p < .001$), or emotional disturbances (32 percent, $p < .001$).

- Young adults in several disability categories were more likely to have a credit card than were those with mental retardation (19 percent), deaf -blindness (19 percent), or autism (21 percent), including young adults with learning disabilities (54 percent, $p <$ .001 for all comparisons), visual impairments (49 percent, $p < .001$ for all comparisons), hearing impairments (46 percent, $p < .001$ for comparison with mental retardation and $p < .01$ for comparison with deaf-blindness and autism), orthopedic impairments (44 percent, $p < .001$ for comparison with mental retardation and $p < .01$ for comparison with deaf-blindness and autism), speech/language impairments (42 percent, $p < .001$ for comparison with mental retardation and $p < .01$ for comparison with deaf-blindness and autism), or other health impairments (42 percent, $p < .001$ for comparison with mental retardation and $p < .01$ for comparison with deaf-blindness and autism).

- Eighty-four percent of young adults with disabilities were reported to have annual incomes of $25,000 or less.

- Young adults with deaf-blindness were more likely to have a reported annual income of $25,000 or less (98 percent) than were those with learning disabilities (82 percent, $p < .001$), hearing impairments (84percent, $p < .01$), other health impairments (85 percent, $p < .01$), speech/language impairments (86 percent , $p < .01$), emotional disturbances (86 percent, $p < .01$), or mental retardation (87 percent, $p < .01$).

Table 20. Financial independence of young adults at the time of the interview, by disability category

Financial independence	Learning disability	Speech/Language impairment	Mental retardation	Emotional disturbance	Hearing impairment	Visual impairment	Orthopedic impairment	Other health impairment	Autism	Traumatic brain Injury	Multiple disabilities	Deaf blindness
	Percent											
Young adults had a:												
Savings account	67.0	65.7	44.5	54.5	64.9	63.0	59.1	65.5	61.8	54.4	54.3	51.3
	(4.60)	(4.42)	(4.68)	(5.21)	(6.01)	(6.20)	(5.19)	(4.67)	(5.47)	(8.64)	(6.66)	(7.70)
Checking account	67.7	63.4	32.6	50.1	68.5	70.3	58.8	63.8	49.6	47.4	37.9	47.3
	(4.57)	(4.49)	(4.42)	(5.20)	(5.80)	(5.86)	(5.18)	(4.73)	(5.60)	(8.38)	(6.40)	(7.63)
Credit card	53.7	42.0	19.4	32.1	46.1	48.9	43.8	41.5	21.1	34.3	24.2	19.4
	(4.88)	(4.59)	(3.76)	(4.87)	(6.27)	(6.43)	(5.22)	(4.84)	(4.58)	(8.24)	(5.73)	(6.04)
Young adults' annual income:												
$25,000 or less	82.2	85.6	87.0	85.7	84.1	88.6	94.4	84.7	91.3	95.2	87.7	98.4
	(3.86)	(3.43)	(3.50)	(3.75)	(4.83)	(4.30)	(2.74)	(3.69)	(3.40)	(3.55)	(4.90)	(2.11)
$25,001 to $50,000	15.7	13.1	11.0	12.3	15.5	5.0	4.5	13.9	6.5	3.1	10.5	0.0
	(3.67)	(3.30)	(3.25)	(3.51)	(4.78)	(2.95)	(2.47)	(3.55)	(2.97)	(2.88)	(4.57)	(0.00)
More than $50,000	2.1	1.3	2.0	2.0	0.4	6.4	1.1	1.4	2.2	1.7	1.7	1.6
	(1.45)	(1.11)	(1.46)	(1.50)	(0.83)	(3.31)	(1.24)	(1.11)	(1.77)	(2.15)	(1.93)	(2.11)

Note: Standard errors are in parentheses. Findings are reported for young adults with disabilities out of high school up to 6 years. NLTS2 percentages are weighted population estimates based on samples of approximately 3,520 young adults with disabilities for financial management tools and 3,130 young adults with disabilities for annual income.

Source: U.S. Department of Education, Institute of Education Sciences, National Center for Special Education Research, National Longitudinal Transition Study-2 (NLTS2), Wave 4 parent interview and youth interview/survey, 2007.

Table 21. Financial independence of young adults with disabilities at the time of the interview, by secondary-school-leaving status and years since leaving high school

Financial independence	Completers	Non-completers	Less than 2 years	2 up to 4 years	4 up to 6 years
	Percent				
Young adults had a:					
Savings account	66.3 (3.14)	24.6 (8.05)	63.5 (5.55)	65.2 (4.50)	57.6 (5.69)
Checking account	65.5 (3.17)	19.7 (7.42)	55.3 (5.70)	63.8 (4.52)	58.6 (5.69)
Credit card	48.1 (3.30)	23.2 (7.89)	38.4 (5.63)	40.2 (4.63)	55.2 (5.72)
Young adults' reported annual income:					
$25,000 or less	82.8 (2.59)	88.7 (6.11)	92.2 (3.32)	81.9 (3.76)	81.2 (4.77)
$25,001 to $50,000	14.5 (2.45)	11.2 (6.09)	6.1 (2.96)	17.0 (3.67)	15.4 (4.41)
More than $50,000	2.2 (1.02)	0.1 (0.61)	1.8 (1.65)	1.0 (0.97)	3.4 (2.21)

Note: Standard errors are in parentheses. Findings are reported for young adults with disabilities out of high school up to 6 years. NLTS2 percentages are weighted population estimates based on samples of approximately 3,520 young adults with disabilities for financial management tools and 3,130 young adults with disabilities for annual income.

Source: U.S. Department of Education, Institute of Education Sciences, National Center for Special Education Research, National Longitudinal Transition Study-2 (NLTS2), Wave 4 parent interview and youth interview/survey, 2007.

- In addition, young adults with orthopedic impairments were more likely to have a reported income of $25,000 or less (94 percent) than were those with learning disabilities (82 percent, $p < .01$).

Differences in Financial Independence by High School-Leaving Characteristics

- High school completers were more likely to have a savings or checking account (66 percent for both) than were their peers who did not complete high school (25 percent and 20 percent, respectively, $p < .001$ for both comparisons; table 21).
- High school completers were more likely to have a credit card in their name (48 percent) than were those who did not complete high school (23 percent, $p < .01$).
- The annual incomes of young adults with disabilities did not differ significantly by school completion status or the number of years since leaving high school.

Demographic Differences in Financial Independence

- Family income differences were apparent in the financial independence of young adults with disabilities. Young adults from households with incomes of more than $50,000 were more likely to have a savings (71 percent) or checking account (73 percent), or a credit card (55 percent) than were those from households with incomes of $25,000 or less (49 percent, $p < .01$, 40 percent, $p < .001$, and 31 percent, $p < .001$, respectively; table 22).

- In addition, young adults from households with incomes of \$25,001 to \$50,000 were more likely to have a checking account (65 percent) than were those from households with incomes of \$25,000 or less (40 percent, $p < .01$).
- White young adults with disabilities were more likely to have a checking account (69 percent) than were African American young adults with disabilities (41percent, $p < .001$).
- Financial status did not differ significantly by gender.

6. SOCIAL AND COMMUNITY INVOLVEMENT KEY FINDINGS

Living successfully in their communities has long been considered central to young adults with disabilities' (Halpern 1985). An important aspect of whether a young adult isquality of life living successfully in the community is the "adequacy of his or her social and interpersonal network [which]…is possibly the most important of all" aspects of adjustment for young adults with disabilities (Halpern 1985, p. 485).

This chapter describes the social and community involvement of young adults with disabilities who had been out of high school up to 6 years. It focuses on the friendship interactions, community participation, and involvement with the criminal justice system of these young adults and addresses the following questions:

- To what extent do young adults with disabilities interact with friends; participate in community groups, classes, or volunteer activities; or enter into the criminal justice system?
- How does their social and community involvement status compare with that of their peers in the general population?
- How does social and community involvement status differ for young adults in different disability categories and for those with different demographic characteristics?

This chapter presents findings related to the social and community involvement of young adults with disabilities as a group as well as differences between young adults who differ in their disability category and demographic characteristics. Because the items in this chapter refer to activities in the preceding 12 months (friendship interactions and community participation) or in the preceding 2 years (criminal justice system involvement) and the focus of this report is activities of young adults with disabilities after high school, findings are reported only for young adults who had been out of secondary school at least a year or at least 2 years, respectively, so as to avoid including secondary school experiences.

- Ninety-three percent of young adults included in this report have been out of high school 1 or more years.

Table 22. Financial independence of young adults with disabilities at the time of the interview, by parents' household income and young

Financial independence	$25,000 or less	$25,001 to $50,000	More than $50,000	White	African American	Hispanic	Male	Female
				Percent				
Young adults had a:								
Savings account	49.0 (5.46)	64.9 (6.17)	70.9 (4.23)	65.2 (3.64)	53.1 (6.66)	58.0 (9.36)	65.2 (3.72)	57.2 (5.18)
Checking account	40.4 (5.36)	65.4 (6.11)	72.6 (4.15)	68.9 (3.52)	40.6 (6.59)	50.9 (9.49)	59.8 (3.83)	60.9 (5.09)
Credit card	31.4 (5.09)	45.7 (6.44)	54.7 (4.63)	45.9 (3.81)	36.0 (6.44)	50.9 (9.48)	45.8 (3.89)	43.4 (5.22)
Young adults' annual income:								
$25,000 or less	91.0 (3.44)	79.2 (5.40)	80.8 (3.77)	80.2 (3.17)	87.4 (4.72)	95.0 (4.37)	79.0 (3.30)	91.9 (3.07)
$25,001 to $50,000	7.7 (3.20)	18.1 (5.12)	17.1 (3.61)	17.2 (3.01)	12.0 (4.62)	4.2 (4.03)	19.1 (3.18)	6.0 (2.67)
More than $50,000	1.3 (1.36)	2.7 (2.16)	2.1 (1.37)	2.6 (1.27)	0.6 (1.10)	0.8 (1.79)	1.9 (1.11)	2.1 (1.61)

Note: Standard errors are in parentheses. Findings are reported for young adults with disabilities out of high school up to 6 years. NLTS2 percentages are weighted population estimates based on samples of approximately 3,520 young adults with disabilities for financial management tools and 3,130 young adults with disabilities for annual income.

Source: U.S. Department of Education, Institute of Education Sciences, National Center for Special Education Research, National Longitudinal Transition Study-2 (NLTS2), Wave 4 parent interview and youth interview/survey, 2007.

Friendship Interactions

Unlike adolescence, which is a time for discovering who one is and what world is, the primary developmental task for the young adult is the development of intimate relationships (Erikson 1974). Considerable research has documented the importance of personal relationships as "protective factors"[35] against a variety of adolescent risk behaviors. For example, results regarding factors associated with emotional health, youth violence, substance use, and sexuality from the National Longitudinal Study on Adolescent Health (Add Health), a comprehensive survey of adolescents, provide "consistent evidence that perceived caring and connectedness to others is important in understanding the health of young people today" (Resnick et al. 1997, p. 830). Connectedness with friends has been found to be associated with a variety of youth behaviors in either a prosocial or antisocial direction, depending on the nature of the friendships (e.g., Bearman and Moody 2004; Crosnoe and Needham 2004; Fraser 1997; Rodgers and Rose 2002; Smith et al. 1995).

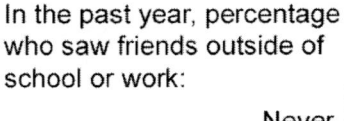

In the past year, percentage who saw friends outside of school or work:

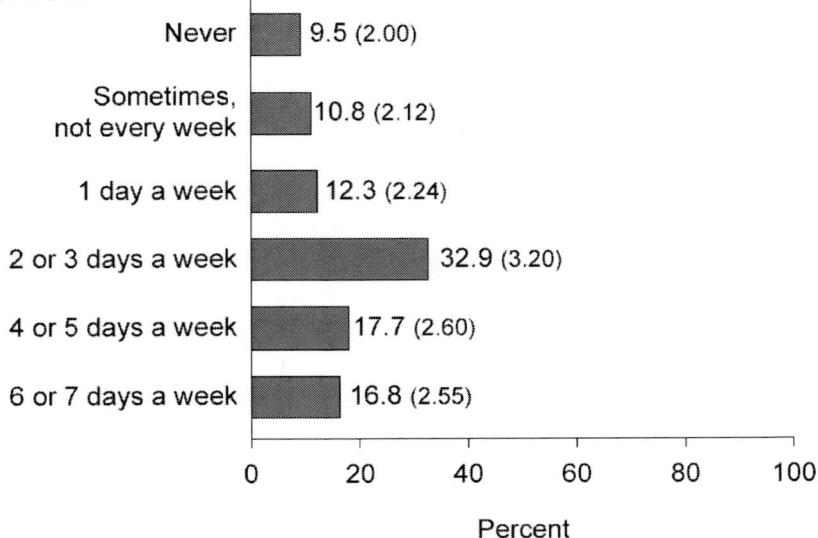

Percent

Note: Standard errors are in parentheses. Findings are reported for young adultswith disabilities out of high school 1 to 6 years. NLTS2 percentages are weighted population estimates based on a sample of approximately 2,930 young adults with disabilities.

Source: U.S. Department of Education, Institute of Education Sciences, National Center for Special Education Research, National Longitudinal Transition Study-2 (NLTS2), Wave 4 parent interview and youth interview/survey, 2007.

Figure 16. Friendship interactions of young adults with disabilities.

- Eighty percent of young adults with disabilities who had been out of high school 1 to 6 years were reported to get together with friends informally at least once a week, compared with the 20 percent who never or only sometimes spent time with friends ($p < .001$; figure 16).[36]

Disability Differences in Friendship Interactions

- Young adults with learning disabilities who had been out of secondary school up to 6 years were more likely to see friends informally at least weekly (85 percent, table 23) than were those with autism (48 percent, $p < .001$), multiple disabilities (58 percent, $p < .01$), mental retardation (62 percent, $p < .001$), or orthopedic impairments (68 percent, $p < .01$).
- Young adults with speech/language impairments (76 percent), emotional disturbances (79 percent), other health impairments (79 percent), and visual impairments (79 percent),were more likely see friends informally at least once a week than were those with autism (48 percent, $p < .001$).

Table 23. Friendship interactions of young adults, by disability category

Friendship interactions	Learning disability	Speech/language impairment	Mental retardation	Emotional disturbance	Hearing impairment	Visual impairment	Orthopedic impairment	Other health impairment	Autism	Traumatic brain injury	Multiple disabilities	Deaf-blindness
	Percent											
In the past year, percentage who saw friends outside of school or work at least weekly	84.9 (3.78)	76.1 (4.28)	61.8 (5.06)	78.7 (4.80)	76.4 (5.91)	78.8 (5.73)	67.6 (5.22)	78.5 (4.32)	47.6 (6.51)	71.5 (8.35)	58.4 (7.61)	63.0 (8.13)

Note: Standard errors are in parentheses. Findings are reported for young adults with disabilities out of high school 1 to 6 years. NLTS2 percentages are weighted population estimates based on a sample of approximately 2,930 young adults with disabilities.

Source: U.S. Department of Education, Institute of Education Sciences, National Center for Special Education Research, National Longitudinal Transition Study-2 (NLTS2), Wave 4 parent interview and youth interview/survey, 2007.

Table 24. Friendship interactions of young adults with disabilities, by secondary-school-leaving status and years since leaving high school

	Completers	Non-completers	Less than 2 years	2 up to 4 years	4 up to 6 years
			Percent		
In the past year, percentage who saw friends outside of school or work at least weekly	80.3 (2.86)	73.2 (9.21)	77.6 (6.07)	77.3 (4.06)	83.9 (4.55)

Note: Standard errors are in parentheses. Findings are reported for young adults with disabilities out of high school 1 to 6 years. NLTS2 percentages are weighted population estimates based on a sample of approximately 2,930 young adults with disabilities.

Source: U.S. Department of Education, Institute of Education Sciences, National Center for Special Education Research, National Longitudinal Transition Study-2 (NLTS2), Wave 4 youth interview/survey, 2007.

Table 25. Friendship interactions of young adults with disabilities, by parents' household income and young adults' race/ethnicity and gender

	$25,000 or less	$25,001 to $50,000	More than $50,000	White	African American	Hispanic	Male	Female
	Percent							
In the past year, percentage who saw friends outside of school or work at least weekly	73.5 (5.31)	79.8 (5.75)	83.7 (3.63)	80.7 (3.28)	73.8 (6.19)	85.6 (7.53)	82.8 (3.22)	74.6 (4.93)

Note: Standard errors are in parentheses. Findings regarding friendships are reported for young adults with disabilities out of high school 1 to 6 years. NLTS2 percentages are weighted population estimates based on a sample of 2,930 young adults with disabilities.

Source: U.S. Department of Education, Institute of Education Sciences, National Center for Special Education Research, National Longitudinal Transition Study-2 (NLTS2), Wave 4 parent interview and youth interview/survey, 2007.

Differences in Friendship Interactions by High School-Leaving Characteristics
- Friendship interactions of young adults with disabilities did not differ significantly by school leaving status or the number of years since leaving high school (table 24).

Demographic Differences in Friendship Interactions
- Friendship interactions of young adults with disabilities did not differ significantly by household income, race or ethnicity, or gender (table 25).

Community Participation

Engaging in activities in the community can provide opportunities for young adults to meet people with like interests, develop new skills, and experience the satisfaction of shared accomplishments and of making a contribution to the community. NLTS2 investigated three forms of community participation in the year preceding the Wave 4 interview/survey by young adults with disabilities:

- taking lessons or classes outside of formal school enrollment;[37]
- participating in a volunteer or community service activity;[38] and
- belonging to an organized community or extracurricular group.[39]
- Forty-one percent of young adults with disabilities who had been out of secondary school from 1 to 6 years were reported to have engaged in some kind of extracurricular activity in the preceding year (figure 17).

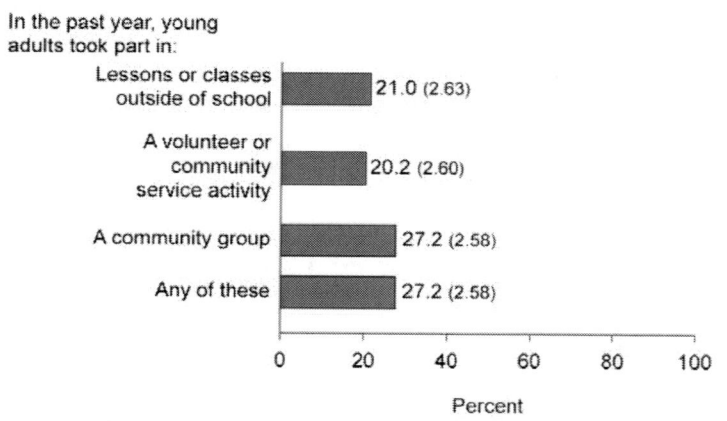

Note: Standard errors are in parentheses. Findings are reported for young adults with disabilities out of high school 1 to 6 years. NLTS2 percentages are weighted population estimates based on samples that range from approximately 3,240 to 3,790 young adults with disabilities across variables.

Source: U.S. Department of Education, Institute of Education Sciences, National Center for Special Education Research, National Longitudinal Transition Study-2 (NLTS2), Wave 4 parent interview and youth interview/survey, 2007.

Figure 17. Community participation of young adults with disabilities.

Table 26. Community participation of young adults, by disability category

Community activities	Learning disability	Speech/language impairment	Mental retardation	Emotional disturbance	Hearing impairment	Visual impairment	Orthopedic impairment	Other health impairment	Autism	Trau matic brain injury	Multiple disabilities	Deaf blindness
	Percent											
In the past year, percentage who took part in:												
Lessons or classes outside of school	22.5 (4.16)	35.8 (4.59)	9.5 (2.87)	16.0 (4.0)	21.8 (5.33)	43.3 (6.61)	31.4 (4.99)	22.6 (4.23)	26.5 (5.43)	24.5 (7.68)	18.9 (5.65)	24.3 (6.71)
A volunteer or community service activity	19.2 (3.94)	30.8 (4.42)	13.4 (3.33)	21.4 (4.48)	31.8 (6.03)	36.0 (6.40)	31.1 (4.97)	24.1 (4.36)	30.1 (5.66)	30.1 (8.19)	30.6 (6.70)	43.1 (7.80)
A community group (e.g., sports team, hobby club, religious group)	26.5 (3.82)	36.5 (4.18)	28.0 (4.11)	22.1 (4.01)	33.9 (5.38)	41.2 (6.11)	28.4 (4.59)	32.8 (4.24)	29.4 (5.40)	21.1 (6.76)	34.0 (6.51)	42.1 (7.49)
Any of these	40.2 (4.25)	56.4 (4.31)	35.1 (4.37)	33.3 (4.55)	52.4 (5.64)	62.8 (6.00)	50.5 (5.09)	48.9 (4.51)	54.2 (5.90)	48.9 (8.28)	53.2 (6.84)	62.8 (7.34)

Note: Standard errors are in parentheses. Findings are reported for young adults with disabilities out of high school 1 to 6 years. NLTS2 percentages are weighted population estimates based on samples that range from approximately (3,240 to 3,790) young adults with disabilities across variables.

Source: U.S. Department of Education, Institute of Education Sciences, National Center for Special Education Research, National Longitudinal Transition Study-2 (NLTS2), Wave 4 parent interview and youth interview/survey, 2007.

- Twenty-one percent of young adults with disabilities took lessons or classes outside of school, 20 percent participated in volunteer or community service activities, and 27 percent participated in a community group.

Disability Differences in Community Participation
- General community involvement of young adults with disabilities ranged from 10 percent to 43 percent for participation in at least one of the activities (table 26).
- Young adults with speech/language impairments were more likely to have participated in at least one of the community activities investigated in NLTS2 (56 percent) than were those with mental retardation and emotional disturbances (35 percent and 33 percent , respectively, $p < .001$ for both comparisons).
- Young adults with visual impairments were likely to have participated in out-of-school lessons or classes (43 percent) than were those with mental retardation (10 percent, $p < .001$), emotional disturbances (16 percent , $p < .001$), other health impairments (23 percent, $p < .01$), multiple disabilities (19 percent, $p < .01$) or learning disabilities (23 percent, $p < .01$).
- Young adults with speech/language impairments (36 percent), orthopedic impairments (31 percent), autism (27 percent), or visual impairments (43 percent), were more likely to have participated in out-of-school lessons or classes than were those with mental retardation (10 percent, $p < .001$ for comparison with speech/language impairments, orthopedic impairments and visual impairments; and $p < .01$ for comparison with autism).
- Young adults with deaf-blindness (43 percent), visual impairments (36 percent), hea ring impairments (32 percent), speech/language impairments (31 percent), or orthopedic impairments (31 percent) were more likely to have participated in volunteer or community services activities than were those with mental retardation (13 percent, $p < .01$ for all comparisons except deaf-blindness, where $p < .001$).
- Participation in community groups by disability category ranged from 21 percent to 42 percent. Young adults with visual impairments (41 percent) were more likely to have participated in community groups than were those with emotional disturbances (22 percent, $p < .01$).

Differences in Community Participation by High School-Leaving Characteristics
- Young adults with disabilities who had completed high school were more likely to have participated in at least one of the community activities investigated by NLTS2 (43 percent, table 27) than were those who had not completed school (16 percent, $p < .001$).
- Young adults with disabilities who completed high school were more likely to have participated in out-of-school lessons or classes (22 percent) or community groups (29 percent) than were those who did not complete school (5 percent and 9percent, respectively, $p < .001$ for both comparisons).

Table 27. Community participation of young adults with disabilities, by secondary-school-leaving status and years since leaving high school

	Completers	Non-completers	Less than 2 years	2 up to 4 years	4 up to 6 years
	Percent				
In the past year, percentage who took part in:					
Lessons or classes outside of school	22.4 (2.86)	5.2 (4.21)	25.4 (6.03)	16.5 (3.47)	24.8 (4.91)
A volunteer or community service activity	21.2 (2.80)	10.0 (5.69)	22.1 (5.76)	18.2 (3.62)	22.0 (4.72)
A community group (e.g., sports team, hobby club, religious group)	29.2 (2.83)	9.3 (4.44)	29.5 (6.02)	22.8 (3.49)	31.9 (4.70)
Any of these	43.3 (3.09)	16.3 (5.66)	43.9 (6.55)	35.9 (3.98)	45.4 (5.02)

Note: Standard errors are in parentheses. Findings are reported for young adults with disabilities out of high school 1 to 6 years. NLTS2 percentages are weighted population estimates based on samples that range from approximately 3240 – 3800 young adults with disabilities across variables.

Source: U.S. Department of Education, Institute of Education Sciences, National Center for Special Education Research, National Longitudinal Transition Study-2 (NLTS2), Wave 4 youth interview/survey, 2007.

- Participation in at least one of the community activities or in volunteer or community service groups did not differ significantly by length of time since leaving high school.

Demographic Differences in Community Participation

- Young adults with disabilities from households with an income of more than $50,000 were more likely to have participated in at least one of the community activities investigated by NLTS2 (51 percent, table 28) than were those from households with an income of $25,000 or less (30 percent, $p < .01$).
- Young adults with disabilities from households with an income of more than $50,000 were more likely to have taken out-of-school lessons or classes (28percent) than were those from households with an income of $25,000 or less (11 percent, $p < .01$).
- White young adults were more likely to have participated in a community group (32 percent) than were Hispanic young adults (13 percent, $p < .01$).
- General participation in the community (i.e., participating in at least one of the community activities) did not differ significantly by race or ethnicity or gender.
- Participation in out-of-school lessons or classes did not differ significantly by race or ethnicity or gender.
- Participation in volunteer or community service groups did not differ significantly by household income, race or ethnicity, or gender.

Table 28. Community participation of young adults with disabilities, by parents' household income and young adults' race/ethnicity and gender

	$25,000 or less	$25,001 to $50,000	More than $50,000	White	African American	Hispanic	Male	Female
	Percent							
In the past year, percentage who took part in:								
Lessons or classes outside of school	10.7 (3.54)	20.7 (5.33)	27.6 (4.28)	22.8 (3.30)	20.4 (5.48)	13.5 (6.94)	21.1 (3.30)	20.7 (4.36)
A volunteer or community service activity	17.2 (4.32)	14.7 (4.66)	27.3 (4.28)	21.9 (3.25)	13.6 (4.66)	24.1 (8.69)	21.4 (3.32)	18.2 (4.16)
A community group (e.g., sports team, hobby club, religious group)	21.6 (4.42)	24.9 (4.96)	32.7 (4.04)	31.9 (3.23)	22.6 (5.45)	12.6 (6.12)	28.0 (3.25)	25.7 (4.26)
Any of these	30.3 (4.93)	38.5 (5.59)	50.6 (4.31)	45.4 (3.45)	33.7 (6.15)	31.6 (8.57)	40.4 (3.55)	41.0 (4.8)

Note: Standard errors are in parentheses. Findings are reported for young adults with disabilities out of high school 1 to 6 years. NLTS2 percentages are weighted population estimates based on samples that range from approximately 3,160 to 3,800 young adults with disabilities across variables.

Source: U.S. Department of Education, Institute of Education Sciences, National Center for Special Education Research, National Longitudinal Transition Study-2 (NLTS2), Wave 4 youth interview/survey, 2007.

- Participation in community groups did not differ significantly by household income or gender.

Criminal Justice System Involvement

Becoming involved with the criminal justice system is a negative aspect of community involvement that is more prevalent among young adults with disabilities than among young adults in the general population. A recent compendium of statistics on the prevalence of juvenile crime among young adults with disabilities indicates that youth with learning, cognitive, behavior, or emotional disabilities are entering the correctional system at rates four to five times those of youth[40] in the general population (Rutherford et al. 2002), and estimated 37 percent of youth in state juvenile corrections facilities are eligible for special education and related services under IDEA (Quinn et al. 2005). A variety of individual and social costs are associated with this criminal justice system involvement, including the disruption to youth's educational programs; 16 percent of youth in short-term youth detention facilities, 52 percent of those in long-term youth corrections facilities, and 71 percent of those in adult corrections facilities were not enrolled in any kind of educational program during their incarceration (Howell and Wolford 2002). Although these statistics are available regarding incarcerated youth with disabilities, less is known nationally about other kinds of criminal justice system involvement for this population or about the characteristics of those who become involved. NLTS2 is helping to fill this information gap by providing information on the percentages of young adults with disabilities who were reported to have

- been stopped by police for other than a traffic violation;[41]
- been arrested;[42]
- spent a night in jail,[43] or
- been on probation or parole.44

Findings are reported for the full sample of young adults with disabilities regarding whether they had ever had each of these experiences.[45] To assess more recent involvement, respondents also were asked to report on these forms of criminal justice system involvement in the 2years preceding Wave 4 data collection.

- At some time in their lives, 47 percent of young adults with disabilities were reported to have been stopped by police for other-than-a-traffic violation (figure 18); 26 percent were reported to have been stopped by police in the preceding 2 years.
- Twenty-three percent of young adults with disabilities reportedly had been arrested at some time, approximately twice the rate for youth in the general population (12 percent, $p < .001$).[46]
- The rate of arrest in the 2 years preceding the interview, for young adults with disabilities was 14 percent.
- Overall, 13 percent of young adults with disabilities had spent a night in jail, and 13 percent had been on probation or parole.

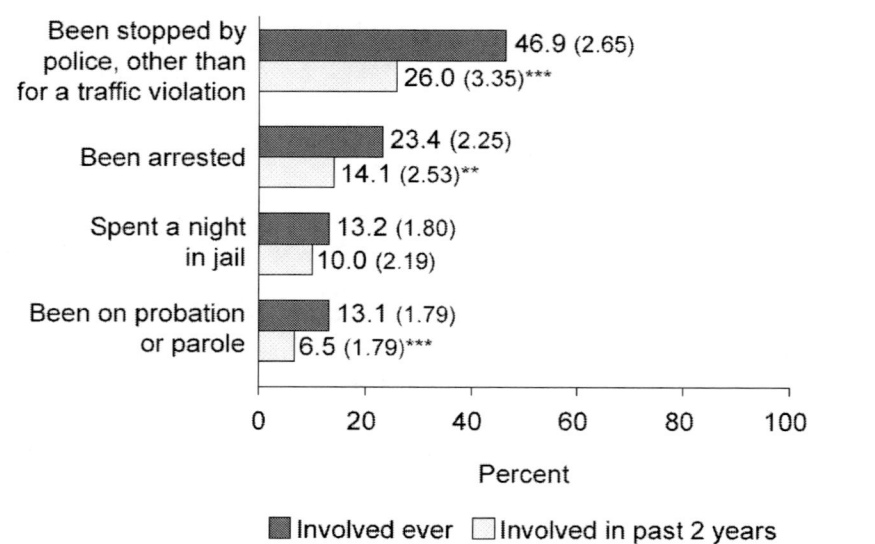

**p < .01; ***p < .001 for difference between young adults with disabilities and young adults in the general population.

Note: Standard errors are in parentheses. Findings regarding involvement in the past 2 years are reported for young adults with disabilities out of high school from 2 to 6 years so as not to include high school experiences; other findings are for young adults with disabilities out of high school up to 6 years NLTS2 percentages are weighted population estimates based on samples that range from approximately 3,350 to 4,600 young adults with disabilities across variables.

Source: U.S. Department of Education, Institute of Education Sciences, National Center for Special Education Research, National Longitudinal Transition Study-2 (NLTS2), Wave 4 youth interview/survey, 2007.

Figure 18. Criminal justice system involvement of young adults with disabilities.

Disability Differences in Criminal Justice System Involvement

- Involvement with the criminal justice system varied by disability category; in particular, students with emotional disturbances had the highest incidence of criminal justice involvement (table 29).
- Young adults with emotional disturbances were more likely ever to have been stopped by police for reasons other than a traffic violation (72 percent) than were young adults in all other disability categories (21 percent to 50 percent, $p < .001$ for all comparisons with emotional disturbances).
- Young adults with emotional disturbances were more likely to have been stopped by police for reasons other than a traffic violation in the past 2 years (50 percent) than were young adults in all other disability categories except traumatic brain injury (6 percent to 25 percent, $p < .001$ for all comparisons except $p < .01$ for young adults with learning disabilities).
- Young adults with emotional disturbances were more likely ever to have been arrested (49 percent) than were young adults in all other disability categories (8 percent to 23 percent, $p < .001$ for all comparisons with young adults with disabilities).

- Young adults with emotional disturbances were more likely to have been arrested in the preceding 2 years (22 percent) than were those with speech/language impairments (6 percent, $p < .01$), hearing impairments (7 percent, $p < .01$), visual impairments (5 percent, $p < .01$), multiple disabilities (5 percent, $p < .01$), orthopedic impairments (4 percent, $p < .001$), or autism (3 percent, $p < .001$).
- Young adults with emotional disturbances were more likely ever to have been in jail overnight (32 percent) than were young adults in all other disability categories (2 percent to 13 percent, $p < .001$ for all comparisons with emotional disturbances, except $p < .01$ for traumatic brain injury).
- Young adults with emotional disturbances were more likely to have spent the night in jail in the preceding 2 years (18 percent) than were those in several disability categories, including young adults with autism (1 percent, $p < .001$), multiple disabilities (2 percent, $p < .01$), orthopedic impairments (2 percent, $p < .01$), hearing impairments (3 percent, $p < .01$), or speech/language impairments (5 percent, $p < .01$).
- Young adults with emotional disturbances were more likely ever to have been on probation or parole (34 percent) than were young adults in all other disability categories except traumatic injury (1 percent to 12 percent, $p < .001$ for all comparisons with emotional disturbances).
- Young adults with other health impairments or learning disabilities were more likely ever to have been stopped by police for reasons other than a traffic violation (50 percent and 47 percent, respectively) than were young adults with deaf-blindness (21 percent, $p < .001$ for both comparisons), orthopedic impairments (22 percent, $p < .001$ for both comparisons), multiple disabilities (22 percent, $p < .001$ for both comparisons), autism (23 percent, $p < .001$ for both comparisons), visual impairments (28 percent, $p < .001$ for comparison with other health impairment and $p < .01$ for comparison with learning disabilities), hearing impairments (30 percent, $p < .01$ for both comparisons), or mental retardation (31 percent, $p < .001$ for comparison with other health impairments and $p < .01$ for comparison with learning disabilities).
- Young adults with other health impairments (23 percent), learning disabilities (25 percent), speech/language impairments (23 percent), or mental retardation (23 percent) were more likely to have been stopped by the police for reasons other than a traffic violation in the past 2 years than were those with autism (7 percent, $p < .01$ for all comparisons.
- Young adults with other health impairments or learning disabilities were more likely to ever have been arrested (22 percent, each) than were young adults in several other disability categories, including those with autism (6 percent, $p < .001$ for both comparisons), orthopedic impairments (8 percent, $p < .001$ for both comparisons), visual impairments (8 percent, $p < .01$ for both comparisons), multiple disabilities (8 percent, $p < .01$ for both comparisons), or hearing impairments (10 percent, $p < .01$ for both comparisons).

Table 29. Criminal justice system involvement of young adults, by disability category

Criminal justice system involvement	Learning disability	Speech/ language impairment	Mental retardation	Emotional disturbance	Hearing impairment	Visual impairment	Orthopedic impairment	Other health impairment	Autism	Traumatic brain injury	Multiple disabilities	Deaf-blindness
	Percent											
Stopped by police other than for a traffic violation												
Ever	47.3	38.8	31.0	71.6	30.4	27.8	21.6	50.0	22.5	42.8	22.1	20.8
	(4.00)	(3.84)	(3.79)	(3.99)	(4.71)	(5.17)	(3.88)	(4.18)	(4.40)	(7.51)	(4.78)	(5.65)
In past 2 years	24.5	22.6	22.5	50.3	13.3	14.7	8.7	22.7	6.8	24.4	17.6	4.0
	(5.03)	(4.81)	(4.81)	(6.42)	(5.04)	(5.53)	(3.28)	(4.78)	(3.53)	(9.15)	(7.02)	(3.73)
Arrested Ever	22.3	16.5	12.5	49.4	10.3	7.9	7.5	22.4	6.2	23.2	8.1	10.5
	(3.34)	(2.92)	(2.71)	(4.41)	(3.12)	(3.12)	(2.48)	(3.49)	(2.54)	(6.41)	(3.14)	(4.27)
In past 2 years	15.2	6.4	8.4	22.3	6.5	4.5	3.8	11.7	2.5	17.8	5.1	0.0
	(3.98)	(2.70)	(3.08)	(4.87)	(3.56)	(3.13)	(2.19)	(3.56)	(2.31)	(7.55)	(4.01)	(0.00)
Spent a night in jail Ever	11.7	6.8	9.5	31.7	5.0	6.7	2.6	12.8	2.4	12.8	2.2	2.5
	(2.58)	(1.98)	(2.40)	(4.11)	(2.23)	(2.89)	(1.50)	(2.79)	(1.61)	(5.07)	(1.69)	(2.17)
In past 2 years	10.7	4.5	5.8	17.5	2.9	4.2	2.1	7.3	1.2	15.5	1.8	0.0‡
	(3.43)	(2.29)	(2.61)	(4.46)	(2.44)	(3.04)	(1.66)	(2.88)	(1.62)	(7.14)	(2.42)	(0.00)
Been on probation or parole												
Ever	11.8	6.3	5.2	34.0	3.0	2.9	3.6	12.4	2.2	19.2	5.0	1.1
	(2.59)	(1.91)	(1.82)	(4.18)	(1.75)	(1.94)	(1.76)	(2.76)	(1.55)	(5.98)	(2.51)	(1.45)
In past 2 years	6.6	2.8	3.6	13.2	0.6	1.1	0.7	4.5	0.8	14.1	3.1	0.0‡
	(2.75)	(1.83)	(2.07)	(3.98)	(1.08)	(1.54)	(0.94)	(2.30)	(1.28)	(6.86)	(3.15)	(0.00)

‡ Responses for items with fewer than 30 respondents are not reported.

Note: Standard errors are in parentheses. Findings regarding involvement in the past 2 years are reported for young adults with disabilities out of high school from 2 to 6 years so as not to include high school experiences; other findings are for young adults with disabilities out of high school up to 6 years. NLTS2 percentages are weighted population estimates based on samples that range from approximately 2,410 to 2,570 young adults with disabilities across variables.

Source: U.S. Department of Education, Institute of Education Sciences, National Center for Special Education Research, National Longitudinal Transition Study-2 (NLTS2), Wave 4 youth interview/survey, 2007.

- Young adults with learning disabilities (15 percent, $p < .01$) were more likely to have been arrested in the past 2 years than those with autism (3 percent).
- Young adults with other health impairments or learning disabilities were more likely ever to have been in jail overnight (13 percent and 12 percent, respectively) than were those with multiple disabilities (2 percent, $p < .01$ for both comparisons); autism 2 percent, $p < .01$ for both comparisons), deaf-blindness (3 percent, $p < .01$ for both comparisons), or orthopedic impairments (3 percent, $p < .01$ for both comparisons).
- Young adults with other health impairments or learning disabilities were more likely ever to have been on probation or parole (12 percent, each) than were young adults with deaf-blindness (1 percent, $p < .001$ for both comparisons); autism (2 percent, $p < .01$ for both comparisons), visual impairments (3 percent, $p < .01$ for both comparisons), hearing impairments (3 percent, $p < .01$ for both comparisons), or orthopedic impairments (4 percent, $p < .01$ for both comparisons).
- Young adults with traumatic brain injuries, were more likely ever to have been on probation or parole (19 percent)than were those with deaf-blindness (1 percent, $p < .01$), autism, (2 percent, $p < .01$), or visual impairments (3 percent $p < .01$).

Differences in Criminal Justice System Involvement by High School-Leaving Characteristics

- High school non-completers were more likely ever to have been stopped by the police for reasons other than a traffic violation (72 percent, table 30) than were those who completed high school (44 percent, $p < .001$).
- Young adults who did not complete high school were more likely ever to have been arrested (48 percent) than were those who completed high school (21 percent, $p < .001$).
- Young adults who did not complete high school were more likely ever to have been in jail overnight or ever to have been on probation or parole (33 percent, each) than were those who completed high school (11 percent, each, $p < .01$ and, $p < .001$, respectively).
- Young adults who had completed high school 4 to 6 years earlier were more likely ever to have been on probation or parole (19 percent) than were those who had completed high school less than 2 years prior to the interview (6 percent, $p < .01$).
- The rates of ever being stopped by the police, arrested, or spending the night in jail did not differ significantly by the number of years since leaving high school.
- The rates of criminal justice system involvement within the preceding 2 years did not differ significantly by school leaving status or the number of years since leaving high school.

Demographic Differences in Criminal Justice System Involvement

- Males were more likely than females ever to have spent the night in jail (16 percent vs. 8 percent, $p < .01$, table 31).
- Rates of young adults with disabilities ever spending the night in jail did not differ significantly by household income or race or ethnicity.

- Rates of ever being stopped by the police, being arrested, or being on probation or parole did not differ significantly by household income, race or ethnicity, or gender.
- In the 2 years preceding the interview , males were more likely than females to have been stopped by police other than for a traffic violation (32 percent vs. 15percent, $p <$ .01), to have been arrested (18 percent vs. 6 percent, $p < .01$), and to have been in jail overnight (14 percent vs. 3 percent, $p < .01$).
- Rates of young adults with disabilities being involved in the criminal justice system within the 2 years preceding the interview did not differ significantly by household income or race or ethnicity.

Table 30. Criminal justice system involvement of young adults with disabilities, by secondary-school-leaving status and years since leaving high school

	Completers	Non-completers	Less than 2 years	2 up to 4 years	4 up to 6 years
			Percent		
Stopped by police for other than a traffic violation					
Ever	43.9	72.2	43.2	46.6	49.3
	(2.84)	(6.21)	(5.05)	(3.96)	(4.78)
In the past 2 years	23.9	51.4	†	25.7	26.5
	(3.43)	(11.84)		(4.32)	(5.32)
Arrested Ever	20.5	47.6	20.1	20.9	28.3
	(2.31)	(6.92)	(4.08)	(3.23)	(4.30)
In the past 2 years	12.1	32.7	†	13.5	14.9
	(2.53)	(9.49)		(3.22)	(4.07)
Spent a night in jail Ever	10.9	32.8	8.2	12.5	16.9
	(1.78)	(6.50)	(2.79)	(2.63)	(3.57)
In the past 2 years	8.0	29.5	†	9.8	10.3
	(2.10)	(9.28)		(2.81)	(3.47)
On probation or parole Ever	10.7	32.9	5.5	11.8	18.8
	(1.77)	(6.51)	(2.32)	(2.56)	(3.73)
In the past 2 years	5.6	14.2	†	5.6	7.6
	(1.79)	(7.11)		(2.16)	(3.03)

† Not applicable. Young adults out of high school less than 2 years not included in these analyses.

Note: Standard errors are in parentheses. Findings regarding involvement in the past 2 years are reported for young adults with disabilities out of high school from 2 to 6 years so as not to include high school experiences; other findings are for young adults with disabilities out of high school up to 6 years. NLTS2 percentages are weighted population estimates based on samples that range from approximately 2,410 to 2,570 young adults with disabilities across variables.

Source: U.S. Department of Education, Institute of Education Sciences, National Center for Special Education Research, National Longitudinal Transition Study-2 (NLTS2), Wave 4 youth interview/survey, 2007.

Table 31. Criminal justice system involvement of young adults with disabilities, by parents' household income and young adults' race/ethnicity and gender

	$25,000 or less	$25,001 to $50,000	More than $50,000	White	African American	Hispanic	Male	Female
				Percent				
Stopped by police for other than a traffic violation								
Ever	44.0 (4.77)	54.3 (5.24)	46.1 (3.97)	46.4 (3.19)	47.3 (6.10)	44.5 (7.93)	51.8 (3.30)	38.5 (4.36)
In the past 2 years	31.7 (6.28)	22.5 (6.83)	25.1 (4.74)	24.4 (4.01)	29.5 (7.36)	29.7 (10.94)	32.2 (4.41)	14.5 (4.59)
Arrested Ever	26.0 (4.21)	23.1 (4.44)	22.5 (3.32)	23.0 (2.69)	22.7 (5.10)	21.6 (6.57)	26.3 (2.91)	18.2 (3.46)
In the past 2 years	16.8 (4.93)	12.4 (4.94)	13.5 (3.59)	13.3 (2.98)	15.8 (5.55)	17.7 (8.85)	18.4 (3.49)	5.8 (2.89)
Spent a night in jail Ever	18.6 (3.74)	11.7 (3.38)	10.3 (2.42)	12.2 (2.09)	16.8 (4.55)	8.9 (4.55)	16.4 (2.45)	7.6 (2.37)
In the past 2 years	15.4 (4.75)	6.7 (3.77)	8.3 (2.90)	8.6 (2.46)	14.1 (5.29)	13.2 (7.84)	13.7 (3.10)	2.9 (2.07)
On probation or parole Ever	16.2 (3.54)	12.5 (3.48)	11.5 (2.54)	14.1 (2.22)	11.0 (3.81)	5.8 (3.73)	15.0 (2.36)	9.7 (2.65)
In the past 2 years	7.2 (3.40)	6.1 (3.60)	6.5 (2.58)	6.2 (2.11)	9.1 (4.37)	5.2 (5.16)	8.4 (2.50)	2.6 (2.98)

Note. Standard errors are in parentheses. Findings regarding involvement in the past 2 years are reported for young adults with disabilities out of high school from 2 to 6 years so as not to include high school experiences; other findings are for young adults with disabilities out of high school up to 6 years. NLTS2 percentages are weighted population estimates based on samples that range from approximately 2,410 to 2,570 young adults with disabilities across variables.

Source: U.S. Department of Education, Institute of Education Sciences, National Center for Special Education Research, National Longitudinal Transition Study-2 (NLTS2), Wave 4 youth interview/survey, 2007.

APPENDIX A. NLTS2 SAMPLING, DATA COLLECTION, AND ANALYSIS PROCEDURES

This appendix describes several aspects of the NLTS2 methodology relevant to the data reported here, including

- sampling local education agencies (LEAs) and students;
- data sources and response rates;
- weighting the data;
- estimation and use of standard errors;
- unweighted and weighted sample sizes;
- calculating statistical significance; and
- measurement and reporting issues.

NLTS2 Sample Overview

The NLTS2 sample was constructed in two stages. A stratified random sample of 3,634 LEAs was selected from the universe of approximately 12,000 LEAs that serve students receiving special education in at least one grade from 7th through 12th grades. These LEAs and 77 state-supported special schools that served primarily students with hearing and vision impairments and multiple disabilities were invited to participate in the study, with the intention of recruiting 497 LEAs and as many special schools as possible from which to select the target sample of about 12,000 students. The target LEA sample was reached; 501 LEAs and 38 special schools agreed to participate and provided rosters of students receiving special education in the designated age range, from which the student sample was selected.

The roster of all students in the NLTS2 age range who were receiving special education from each LEA[47] and special school was stratified by disability category. Students then were selected randomly from each disability category. Sampling fractions were calculated that would produce enough students in each category so that, in the final study year, findings will generalize to most categories individually with an acceptable level of precision, accounting for attrition and for response rates to the parent/youth interview. A total of 11,276 students were selected and eligible to participate in NLTS2.

Details of the LEA and student samples are provided below.

The NLTS2 LEA Sample

Defining the Universe of LEAs

The NLTS2 sample includes only LEAs that have teachers, students, administrators, and operating schools—that is, "operating LEAs." It excludes such units as supervisory unions; Bureau of Indian Affairs schools; public and private agencies (e.g., correctional facilities); LEAs from U.S. territories; and LEAs with 10 or fewer students in the NLTS2 age range, which would be unlikely to have students with disabilities.

The public school universe data file maintained by Quality Education Data (Quality Education Data 1999) was used to construct the sampling frame because it had more recent information than the alternative list maintained by the National Center for Education Statistics. Correcting for errors and duplications resulted in a master list of 12,435 LEAs that met the selection criteria. These comprised the NLTS2 LEA sampling frame.

Stratification

The NLTS2 LEA sample was stratified to increase the precision of estimates, to ensure that low-frequency types of LEAs (e.g., large urban districts) were adequately represented in the sample, to improve comparisons with the findings of other research, and to make NLTS2 responsive to concerns voiced in policy debate (e.g., differential effects of federal policies in particular regions, LEAs of different sizes). Three stratifying variables were used: region, size (student enrollment), and community wealth. The three variables generate a 64-cell grid into which the universe of LEAs was arrayed.

Region

This variable captures essential political differences, as well as subtle differences in the organization of schools, the economic conditions under which they operate, and the character of public concerns. The regional classification variable selected has been used by the Department of Commerce, the Bureau of Economic Analysis, and the National Assessment of Educational Progress (categories are Northeast, Southeast, Midwest, and West).

Size (Student Enrollment)

LEAs vary considerably in size, the most useful available measure of which is student enrollment. A host of organizational and contextual variables are associated with size that exert considerable potential influence over the operations and effects of special education and related programs. In addition, total enrollment serves as an initial proxy for the number of students receiving special education served by an LEA. The QED database provides enrollment data from which LEAs were sorted into four categories serving approximately equal numbers of students:

- very large (estimated[48] enrollment greater than 14,931 in grades 7 through 12);
- large (estimated enrollment from 4,661 to 14,930 in grades 7 through 12);
- medium (estimated enrollment from 1,622 to 4,660 in grades 7 through 12); and
- small (estimated enrollment from 11 to 1,621 in grades 7 through 12).

Community Wealth

As a measure of district wealth, the Orshansky index (the proportion of the student population living below the federal definition of poverty, Employment Policies Institute 2002) is a well-accepted measure. The distribution of Orshansky index scores was organized into four categories of LEA/community wealth, each containing approximately 25 percent of the student population in grades 7 through 12:

- high (0 percent to 13 percent Orshansky);
- medium (14 percent to 24 percent Orshansky);
- low (25 percent to 43 percent Orshansky); and
- very low (more than 43 percent Orshansky).

LEA Sample Size

On the basis of an analysis of LEAs' estimated enrollment across LEA size and estimated sampling fractions for each disability category, 497 LEAs (and as many state-sponsored special schools as would participate)was considered sufficient to generate the student sample. Taking into account the rate at which LEAs were expected to refuse to participate, a sample of 3,635 LEAs was invited to participate, from which 497 participating LEAs might be recruited. A total of 501 LEAs actually provided students for the sample, 101 percent of the target number needed and 14 percent of those invited. Analyses of the region, size, and wealth of the LEA sample, both weighted and unweighted, confirmed that the weighted LEA sample closely resembled the LEA universe with respect to those variables.

In addition to matching the LEA sample to the universe of LEAs on variables used in sampling, it was important to ascertain whether the stratified random sampling approach resulted in skewed distributions on relevant variables not included in the stratification scheme. Several analyses were conducted.

First, three variables from the QED database were chosen to compare the "fit" between the first-stage sample and the population: the LEA's proportion who attended college, and the urban/rural status of the LEA. This analysis revealed that the sample of LEAs somewhat underrepresented African American students and college-bound students and overrepresented Hispanic students and LEAs in rural areas. Thus, in addition to accounting for stratification variables, LEA weights were calculated to achieve a distribution on the urbanicity and racial/ethnic distributions of students that matched the universe.

To determine whether the resulting weights, when applied to the participating NLTS2 LEAs, accurately represented the universe of LEAs serving the specified grade levels, data collected from the universe of LEAs by the U.S. Department of Education's Office of Civil Rights (OCR) and additional items from QED were compared for the weighted NLTS2 LEA sample and the universe. Finally, the NLTS2 participating LEAs and a sample of 1,000 LEAs that represented the universe of LEAs were surveyed to assess a variety of policies and practices known to vary among LEAs and to be relevant to secondary-school-age youth with disabilities. Analyses of both the extant databases and the LEA survey data confirm that the weighted NLTS2 LEA sample accurately represents the universe of LEAs (Javitz and Wagner 2003).

The NLTS2 Student Sample

Determining the size of the NLTS2 student sample took into account the duration of the study, desired levels of precision, and assumptions regarding attrition and response rates. Analyses determined that approximately three students would need to be sampled for each student who would have a parent/youth interview in Wave 5 of NLTS2 data collection.

The NLTS2 sample design called for findings to be generalizable to students receiving special education as a whole and for the 12 special education disability categories currently in use and reported in this document. Standard errors were to be no more than 3.6 percent, except for the low-incidence categories of traumatic brain injury and deaf-blindness. Thus, by sampling 1,250 students per disability category (with the two exceptions noted), 402 students per category were expected to have a parent or youth interview in year 9 (Wave 5). Assuming a 50 percent sampling efficiency[49] (which is likely to be exceeded for most disability categories), 402 students would achieve a standard error of estimate of slightly less than 3.6 percent. All students with traumatic brain injury or with deaf-blindness in participating LEAs and special schools were selected. Students were disproportionately sampled by age to assure that there would be an adequate number of students who would be age 24 or older at the conclusion of the study. Among the eligible students, 40.2 percent will be 24 or older as of the final interview.

LEAs and special schools were contacted to obtain their agreement to participate in the study and request rosters of students receiving special education who were 13 to 16 years old on December 1, 2000, and in at least seventh grade.[50] Requests for rosters specified that they contain the names and addresses of students receiving special education under the jurisdiction of the LEA, the disability category of each student, and the LEAs would provide only identification numbers for students, along with the corresponding birthdates and disability categories. When students were sampled in these LEAs, identification numbers of selected students were provided to the LEA, along with materials to mail to their parents/guardians (without revealing their identity).

After estimating the number of students receiving special education in the NLTS2 age range, the appropriate fraction of students in each category was selected randomly from each LEA and special school. In cases in which more than one child in a family was included on a roster, only one was eligible to be selected.[51] LEAs and special schools were notified of the students selected, and contact information for their parents/guardians was requested.

Data Sources

Data are reported here for the subset of NLTS2 sample members (approximately 4,650) who were out of high school at the time of Wave 4 data collection and who have data from the Wave 4 youth telephone interview or mail survey or the Wave 4 parent telephone interview (2007). In addition to Wave 4 data, several variables that were created for this report indicate whether a young adult had had a particular experience "since high school," (e.g. postsecondary enrollment, employment status, wages, and living arrangements). Fifty-four percent of out-of-high school respondents (approximately 2,500 young adults with disabilities) had left high school since the Wave 4 data collection; thus, Wave4 data are al l that are required to generate values for these variables for them. However, the remainder of the out-of-high school respondents (approximately 2,160 young adults) were already out of school in Waves 2 or 3. Thus, data from prior waves needed to be taken into account to generate values for variables measuring experiences "since high school." Prior wave data also were used to determine whether young adults had completed high school or left without completing and the year in which they left. Wave 2 and 3 data collections mirrored procedures followed for Wave 4.

The Wave 3 youth telephone interview produced data for approximately 1,360 young adults included in the sample that forms the basis of this report, the mail questionnaire generated data for approximately 160 young adults, and parent interviews provided data for approximately 640 young adults, for a total of approximately 2,160 sample members. The Wave 2 youth telephone interview produced data for approximately 570 young adults included in the sample that forms the basis of this report, the mail questionnaire generated data for approximately 50 young adults, and parent interviews provided data for approximately 270 young adults, for a total of approximately 890 sample members.

Wave 1 parent telephone interview or mail survey data are the source for data about youth's gender, race/ethnicity, and household income. Information about the primary disability category of NLTS2 sample members came from rosters of students in the NLTS2 age range receiving special education services in the 2000–01 school year under the auspices of participating school districts and state-supported special schools. High school transcripts provided data on high school completion status and completion date. Each source is described below. Although Wave 4 data have generated the majority of findings reported in this document, parent/youth telephone interviews/mail surveys are described in chronological order because procedures applied in earlier waves of data collection shape the respondent groups for Wave 4.

Wave 1 Parent Interview/Survey[52]

The NLTS2 conceptual framework suggests that a youth's nonschool experiences, such as extracurricular activities and friendships; historical information, such as age when disability was first identified; household characteristics, such as socioeconomic status; and a family's level and type of involvement in school-related areas are crucial to student outcomes. Parents/guardians are the most knowledgeable about these aspects of students' lives. They also are important sources of information on outcomes across domains. Thus, parents/guardians of NLTS2 sample members were interviewed by telephone or surveyed by mail in 2001, as part of Wave 1 data collection.

Matches of names, addresses, and telephone numbers of NLTS2 parents with existing national locator databases were conducted to maximize the completeness and accuracy of contact information and subsequent response rates. A student was required to have a working telephone number and an accurate address to be eligible for the parent interview sample.

Letters were sent to parents to notify them that their child had been selected for NLTS2 and that an interviewer would be attempting to contact them by telephone. The letter included a tollfree telephone number for parents to call to be interviewed if they did not have a telephone number where they could be reached reliably or if they wanted to make an appointment for the interview at a specific time.

Computer-assisted telephone interviewing (CATI) was used for parent interviews, which were conducted between mid-May and late September 2001. Ninety-five percent of interviews were conducted in English and 5 percent in Spanish.

All parents who could not be reached by telephone were mailed a self-administered questionnaire in a survey period that extended from September through December 2001. The questionnaire contained a subset of key items from the telephone interview. Overall, 91 percent of respondents reported that they were parents of sample members (biological, adoptive, or step), and 1 percent were foster parents. Six percent were relatives other than parents, 2 percent were nonrelative legal guardians, and less than 1 percent reported other relationships to sample members.

Wave 2 Parent/Youth Interviews

NLTS2 sample members for whom working telephone numbers and addresses were available were eligible for the Wave 2 parent/youth telephone interview or youth mail survey in 2003. Database matching procedures were used to maximize the eligible sample, as in Wave 1. Contact procedures alerting parents of the interviews also were similar for the two waves. The major distinction between the data collection methods in Waves 1 and 2 is that interviews in Wave 2 were sought both with parents of NLTS2 sample members and with the youth themselves if they were able to respond to questions.

The first interview contact was made with parents of eligible sample members. Those who agreed to participate were interviewed with CATI. Items in this portion of the interview, referred to as Parent Part 1, focused on topics for which the parent was considered the most appropriate respondent (e.g., services received, family expectations, and support). At the end of Parent Part 1, the respondent was asked the following:

> *My next questions are about jobs (YOUTH'S may have gone to, and about (his/her) feelings about (him/herself) and (his/her) life. The questions are similar to those I've answer using scales, like "very well," "pretty well," "not very well," or "not at all*

well." The interview would probably last about 20 to 30 minutes. Do you think that (YOUTH'S NAME) would be able telephone?

If youth could answer questions by phone, they also were told:

I also have some questions about (his/her) involvement in risk behaviors, like smoking, drinking, and sexual activity. Is it all right for me to ask (YOUTH"S NAME) questions like that?

If parents consented, interviewers asked to speak with the youth or asked for contact information to reach the youth in order to complete the youth portion of the interview, referred to as Youth Part 2.

Parents who reported that youth could not answer questions by telephone were asked:
Would (he/she) be able to accurately answer these kinds of questions using a written questionnaire?

If parents indicated that youth could complete a written questionnaire, they were asked for the best address to which to send a questionnaire, and a questionnaire was sent. The questionnaire contained a subset of items from the telephone interview that were considered most important for understanding the experiences and perspectives of youth. Multiple follow-up phone or mail contacts were made to maximize the response rate for the mail survey. Data from the mail survey and Youth Part 2 of the telephone interview were merged for analysis purposes.

If parents reported that youth could not answer questions either by telephone or written questionnaire or declined to have youth asked questions related to risk behaviors, interviewers asked them to continue the interview, referred to as Parent Part 2. If youth were reported to be able to complete a telephone interview or a written questionnaire but did not do so after repeated attempts, parents were contacted again and asked to complete Parent Part 2 in lieu of Youth Part 2.

Wave 3 Parent/Youth Interviews

As in early waves of data collection, NLTS2 sample members for whom working telephone numbers and addresses were available were eligible for the Wave 3 parent/youth telephone interview or youth mail survey (2005). Database matching procedures were used to maximize the eligible sample, as previously. Contact procedures alerting respondents of the interviews also were similar across waves. Wave 3 data collection was similar to Wave 2 in that both parents and youth were sought as respondents, and youth respondents who were reported to be able to respond for themselves but not by telephone were surveyed by mail. The major distinction between the data collection methods in Waves 2 and 3 is that for youth for whom Wave 2 data had been collected, interviews were sought with parents and with youth themselves simultaneously, rather than interviewing parents first, relying on parents' reports in Wave 2 regarding youth's ability to respond for themselves by telephone or mail. For sample members who were eligible for Wave 3 data collection but who could not be reached for data collection in Wave 2, a telephone interview was sought first with parents, and the screening process for the youth interview survey that was described for Wave 2 was repeated when a parent was reached.

Wave 4 Parent/Youth Interviews

Wave 4 data collection (e.g. determining the NLTS2 sample members, matching names and addresses through a database, contacting respondents, conducting interviews) was fielded the same as Wave 3 data collection.

High School Transcripts

High school completion status and high school leave date were based on data from high school transcripts. High school transcripts were requested for all NLTS2 sample members. Transcript data were collected for approximately 3,570 young adults included in this report. For those for whom transcript data were not available, school completion status and leave dates were based on information from parent/youth interviews.

School and School District Student Rosters

Information about the primary disability category of NLTS2 sample members came from rosters of students in the NLTS2 age range receiving special education services in the 2000–01 school year under the auspices of participating school districts and state-supported special schools. Additionally, data on the racial/ethnic background of sample members were taken from this source when they were included on rosters. In the absence of roster data on youth's racial/ethnic background, data were taken from the Wave 1 parent interview or mail survey.

Response Rates

Table A-1 reports response rates for Waves 1 through 4 parent/youth interviews/surveys and for high school transcripts.

Table A-1. Response rates for NLTS2 Waves 1 through 4 parent/youth data collection

Respondents	Number	Percent
Wave 1		
Total sample	11,244	
Respondents		
Completed telephone interview	8,670	76.9
Completed partial telephone interview	300	2.7
Completed mail questionnaire	260	2.3
Total respondents	9,220	81.9
Total nonrespondents	2,046	18.1
Wave 2		
Total sample	11,226	
Respondents		
Completed Parent Part 1 telephone interview	6,860	61.1
Completed Parent Part 2 telephone interview	2,960	26.4
Completed Youth Part 2 telephone interview or mail questionnaire	3,360	30.0
Total respondents with Part 1 and either Parent or Youth Part 2	6,320	56.3

Respondents	Number	Percent
Total nonrespondents (no parent or youth data)	1,350	12.0
Wave 3		
Total sample	11,225	
Respondents		
Completed Parent Part 1 telephone interview	5,190	46.2
Completed Parent Part 2 telephone interview	1,580	14.1
Completed Youth Part 2 telephone interview or mail questionnaire	3,290	29.3
Total respondents with Part 1 and either Parent or Youth Part 2	4,660	41.5
Total respondents with Parent Part 1 or Parent Part 2, or Youth Part 2	5,370	47.8
Total nonrespondents (no parent or youth data)	2,620	23.3
Wave 4		
Total sample	11,128	
Respondents		
Completed Parent Part 1 telephone interview	4,610	41.4
Completed Parent Part 2 telephone interview	1,590	14.3
Completed Youth Part 2 telephone interview or mail questionnaire	2,500	22.5
Total respondents with Part 1 and either Parent or Youth Part 2	3,790	34.1
Total respondents with Parent Part 1 or Parent Part 2, or Youth Part 2	4,900	44.0
Total nonrespondents (no parent or youth data)	3,230	29.0
High School Transcripts		
Total transcript data	9,070	80.5

Note: Deceased youth were eliminated from the pool of sample members.

Combining Parent and Youth Data

If a youth interview/survey was completed, youth's responses were used. If a youth interview/survey could not be completed for an eligible youth or if a youth was reported by parents not to be able to participate in an interview/survey, parents' responses were used. For the subsample of out-of-high school youth included in this report, the youth interview/survey was the source of data for post-high school outcomes for 84 percent of youth, and the parent interview was the source for 16 percent of youth.

Combining data across respondents raises the question of whether parent and youth responses would concur—i.e., would the same findings result if parents' responses were reported instead of youth's responses. Table A-2 shows the level of congruence in parents' and youth's responses to four items related to key outcomes of interest.

When both parents and youth were asked whether the youth belonged to an organized community group, currently worked for pay, worked for pay in the past 2 years, and ever enrolled in a community college since high school, their responses agreed from 74 percent to 88 percent of the time. The greatest congruence are noted regarding youth's enrollment in a community college since high school (88 percent, $K = .74$, $p. < .001$) and current employment status (86 percent, $K = .66$, $p. < .001$). There was 77 percent congruence ($K = .52$, $p. < .001$)

evident regarding employment in the preceding 2 years and 74 percent agreement ($K = .41$, $p. < .001$) regarding whether youth belonged to an organized group in the community.

Table A-2. Congruence of parent and youth responses to key items

	Percentage with			
	Congruent responses	Parent answering yes (higher), youth no (lower)	Parent answering no (lower), youth yes (higher)	Kappa (*K*) score
Youth currently working for pay	86.2	5.9	7.97	.66
Youth worked for pay in past 2 years	77.1	12.5	10.4	.52
Youth belongs to an organized group in the community	73.5	10.5	16.1	.41
Youth ever enrolled in a community college since high school	87.5	8.4	4.1	.74

Source: U.S. Department of Education, Institute of Education Sciences, National Center for Special Education Research, National Longitudinal Transition Study-2 (NLTS2), Wave 4 parent interview and youth interview/survey, 2005.

It is impossible to determine the cause of discrepant responses. Complete congruence would not be expected, even with both respondents answering accurately, because the parent interview and youth interview/survey could have been completed several months apart during the 7-month interview period; the status of youth could have changed in the intervening period. In such cases, both responses would be accurate at the time given. However, discrepancies also could result from one response being inaccurate, either because a respondent gave a socially desirable response (e.g., reported a youth was employed when he or she was not) or because the respondent (usually the parent) had inaccurate information (e.g., a youth no longer living with a parent had not informed the parent regarding a community group he or she had joined, leading to a negative parent response regarding group membership when a positive response was accurate). Although it is not possible to tell which of two discrepant responses is correct, it is noteworthy that with the exception of current employment, discrepant cases are more likely to result from a positive response from youth when parents responded negatively (e.g., youth reported higher wages or a higher rate of group membership than parents). Thus, for some items, youth for whom data were collected through the youth interview/survey may appear to have more positive experiences than those for whom data were collected through a parent interview because of the source of the data, in addition to or instead of actual differences in their experiences. Again, this difference does not necessarily imply inaccuracies in the data, but it does affirm the difference in the knowledge and perspectives of parents and youth.

Weighting the Wave 4 Young Adult/Parent Data

The percentages and means reported in the data tables throughout this report are estimates of the true values for the population of young adults with disabilities in the NLTS2 age range. The response for each sample member is weighted to represent the number of young adults in his or her disability category in the kind of LEA (i.e., region, size, and wealth) or special school from which he or she was selected. Responses also are weighted to represent the best estimate of the number of young adults with disabilities by racial/ethnic category (non-Hispanic White, non-Hispanic Black, non-Hispanic other, and Hispanic).

Table A-3 illustrates the concept of sample weighting and its effect on percentages or means that are calculated for young adults with disabilities as a group. In this example, 10 young adults are included in a sample, 1 from each of 10 disability groups, and each has a hypothetical value regarding whether that youth participated in organized group activities in the community (1 for yes, 0 for no). Six young adults participated in such activities. Summing the hypothetical values for the 10 youth results in an average of 60 percent for the full group. However, this would not accurately represent the national population of young adults with disabilities because many more young adults are classified as having a learning disability than as having orthopedic or other health impairments, for example. Therefore, in calculating a population estimate, weights in the example are applied that correspond to the proportion of young adults in the population who are from each disability category (actual NLTS2 weights account for disability category and several aspects of the districts from which young adults were chosen). The sample weights for this example appear in column C. Using these weights, the weighted population estimate is 88 percent. The percentages in all NLTS2 tables are similarly weighted population estimates, whereas the sample sizes are the actual numbers of cases on which the weighted estimates are based (similar to the 10 cases in column A in table A-3).

Table A-3. Example of weighted percentage calculation

Disability category	A Number in sample	B Participated in group activities	C Example weight for category	D Weighted value for category
Total	10	6	10.0	8.8
Learning disability	1	1	5.0	5.0
Speech/language impairment	1	1	1.9	1.9
Mental retardation	1	1	1.0	1.0
Emotional disturbance	1	0	.8	0
Hearing impairment	1	1	.2	.2
Visual impairment	1	1	.1	.1
Orthopedic impairment	1	0	.1	0
Other health impairment	1	1	.6	.6
Autism	1	0	.2	0
Multiple disabilities	1	0	.1	0
	Unweighted sample percentage = 60 percent (Column B total divided by Column A total)		Weighted population estimate = 88 percent (Column D total divided by Column C total)	

The students in LEAs and state schools with data for each survey were weighted to represent the universe of students in LEAs and state schools by using the following methodology:

- Let i=1, 2, 3, …, 64 index the NLTS2 LEA strata and i = 65 denote the state school stratum.Let $N(i)$ denote the number of LEAs or state schools in the i -thstrata. Let $M(i)$ denote the prespecified sample size of LEAs or state schools in the i-th strata.Within each stratum, all $N(i)$ LEAs and state schools were assigned a uniformly distributed random number and were sorted on the basis of that random number in increasing order. The first $M(i)$ of those LEAs or state schools were selected for the sample in the i-th stratum; consequently the LEA/state school sample in each stratum was drawn with equal probabilities and without replacement. Let $P(i, j)$ denote the probability of selection of the j-th LEA or state school within the i-th stratum.Then $P(i, j) = M(i)/N(i)$.The j-th selected LEA or state school in the i-th stratum was assigned an initial weight of $W(i, j) = 1/P(i, j) = N(i) / M(i)$.

- Let $Q(i)$ denote the number of respondent LEAs or state schools in the i-th stratum.Let $R(i)$ denote the response rate in the i-th stratum.Then $R(i) = Q(i)/M(i)$. The adjusted weight for the j-th selected LEA or state school in the i-th stratum, denoted $W^*(i, j)$, was set to 0 if the j-th selected LEA or state school in the i-th stratum was a nonrespondent and to $W^*(i, j) = W(i, j)/R(i) = N(i)/Q(i)$ if the j-th selected LEA or state school was a respondent. Note that all LEAs in the i-th stratum have the same adjusted weight.

- When rosters were obtained from each respondent LEA or state school, they were separated by disability category and student age groups (13 to 15.99, and 16 to 17.99). Samples were independently selected and weighted for each disability and age category, using the same methodology (with the exception of deaf-blind as discussed later). Without loss of generality, therefore, discussion is restricted to the selection and weighting of students with learning disabilities in the older age category.

- Let (i, j, k) denote the k-th older students with learning disabilities in the j-th LEA/state school in the i-th stratum.Let $Ns(i, j)$ denote the number of older students with learning disabilities in the (i, j)-th LEA/state school.Let $V(i)$ denote the predetermined sampling fraction for older students with learning disabilitiesin the i-th stratum.A uniformly generated random number, denoted $U(i, j, k)$ was generated for each older student with learning disabilities in the (i, j)-th LEA/state school roster. The (i, j, k)-th older student with learning disabilitieswas selected for the study without replacement if $U(i, j, k) < V(i)$.Let $Ws(i, j, k)$ denote the initial weight for the (i, j, k)-th older student with learning disabilities. Then $Ws(i, j, k) = W^*(i, j) / V(i)$.Since $W^*(i, j)$ is a constant for all LEA/state schools in the i-th stratum, note that $Ws(i, j, k)$ is constant for all older students with learning disabilities in the i-th stratum.

- Let $Ms(i, j)$ be the number of sampled older students with learning disabilities in the (i,j)-th LEA/state school and let $Ms(i)$ be the total number of selected older students with learning disabilitiesin the i-th stratum. Let $Qs(i, j)$ be the number of responding older students with learning disabilities in the (i, j)-th LEA/state school and let $Qs(i)$ be the total number of responding older LD students in the i-th stratum.Let $Rs(i)$

denote the older students with learning disabilities response rate in the i -th stratum among selected students. Then Rs(i) = Qs(i) / Ms(i). The adjusted weight for the (i, j, k)-th older student with learning disabilities, denoted Ws*(i, j, k) is defined to be 0 if the student is a nonrespondent and Ws*(i, j, k) = Ws(i, j, k) / R(i) otherwise. Note that Ws*(i, j, k) is a constant for all responding older students with learning disabilities in the i-th stratum.

- Data from Department of Education reports, the Common Core, the rosters of the respondent LEAs and state schools, and the student weights were combined to estimate the following: (1) total number of students in each disability category by age category (for example, the total number of older students with learning disabilities in the universe), (2) the total number of students by disability and race/ethnicity (coded non-hispanic white, non-Hispanic Black, Hispanic, Asian/Pacific Islander, and American Indian/Alaska native), and (3) the total number of students by disability and LEA/state school strata. Deming's raking algorithm was used to adjust the Ws*(i, j, k) weights so that the sum of the adjusted weights in these subgroups (for example, older students with learning disabilities in the universe) approximated their known or estimated national totals.

- Analysis of NLTS2 data after the first wave revealed that respondents to the later waves differed from the Wave 1 respondents with respect to the distribution of their household incomes, whether the parents had volunteered at the school, and whether the student had been held back one or more grade levels. The Wave 1 weights and parental survey responses were used to estimate, by disability and age category, the national number of students in each household income category, each parental volunteering category, and each student advancement category (i.e., whether the student had ever been held back). To reduce nonresponse bias in these later waves, the Deming raking algorithm was extended to modify weights so that their totals also approximate these estimated national totals.

- Recruitment was attempted with all students with deaf-blindness who appeared on the rosters of the responding LEAs and state schools and these students were subject to the same weighting approach as described above (excluding the Deming raking). A few students in the hearing impairment disability category and in the visually impaired disability category with sufficiently severe hearing and vision problems to be classified as deaf-blind were identified. These students were retained in their original disability/age categories for purposes of developing weights for students in those categories, but were classified as deaf-blind for purposes of analysis. The sum of the weights for all students with deaf-blindness (i.e., those originally found in the deaf-blind category and those who were later reclassified as deaf-blind) was equal to 3,196. Due to the small number of students who qualified for the deaf-blind category, SRI and the U.S. Department of Education agreed that the weights for all of these students would be set to a constant, such that the sum of those weights was equal to 3,196.

Estimating Standard Errors

Each estimate reported in the data tables is accompanied by a standard error. A standard error acknowledges that any population estimate that is calculated from a sample will only approximate the true value for the population. The true population value will fall within the range demarcated by the estimate, plus or minus 1.96 times the standard error, 95 percent of the time. For example, if the estimate for young adult's 23.5 percent, with a standard error of 2.67, one can be 95 percent confident that the true current postsecondary enrollment rate for the population is between 18.3 percent and 28.7 percent.

Because the NLTS2 sample is both stratified and clustered, calculating standard errors by formula is not straightforward. Standard errors for means and proportions can, however, be estimated by using pseudoreplication, a procedure that is widely used by the U.S. Census Bureau and other federal agencies involved in fielding complex surveys. To that end, a set of weights was developed for each of 32 balanced half-replicate subsamples. Each half-replicate involved selecting half of the total set of LEAs that provided contact information, using a partial factorial balanced design (resulting in about half of the LEAs being selected within each stratum) and then weighting that half to represent the entire universe. The half-replicates could be used to estimate the variance of a sample mean by (1) calculating the mean of the variable of interest on the full sample and each half-sample, using the appropriate weights; (2) calculating the squares of the deviations of the half-sample estimate from the full-sample estimate; and (3) adding the squared deviations and dividing by (n-1), where n is the number of half-replicates.Since there were 32 replicates, the variance estimates would have 31 degrees of freedom.

Because the method of using replicate weights is computationally intensive and was not easily implemented in the Statistical Analysis System (SAS) during the first years of NLTS2, we sought a simpler formula-based procedure. We selected a variety of categorical and continuous Wave 1 variables and calculated their standard errors using replicate weights. We compared those standard error estimates with those obtained using a formula appropriate for an independent and identically distributed sample with unequal weights. (Under the latter assumptions, the effective sample size can be approximated as

$$N_{\textit{eff}} = N\left(\frac{E^2[W]}{E^2[W] + V[W]} \right)$$

where $N_{\textit{eff}}$ is the effective sample size, $E^2[W]$ is the square of the arithmetic average of the weights, and $V[W]$ is the variance of the weights. For a variable X, the standard error of estimate can typically be approximated by $\sqrt{V[X]/N_{\textit{eff}}}$, where $V[X]$ is the weighted variance of X.) As expected, due to the complex sampling design in NLTS2, the use of the formula given above was not fully adequate. However, we found that if we multiplied these formula-based standard errors by 1.25, this yielded estimates that slightly exceeded the variance estimates via pseudo-replication for approximately 90 percent of the categorical and 90 percent of the continuous variables that were examined. Therefore we modified our formula by including a design factor of 1.25, which accounts for the stratified and clustered nature of the sample.

All standard errors in this report were calculated using formula-based estimates rather than estimates based on the replicate weights. Since our formula-based estimates tend to be slightly larger than the variances using pseudo-replicates, and the cutoff values for t-statistics based on infinite degrees of freedom rather than 31 degrees of freedom are similar, we calculated our p-values based on infinite degrees of freedom.

As a 10-year longitudinal study, NLTS2 has continued to use this formula-based procedure to calculate standard errors rather than use currently available procedures. This decision to maintain consistency in analytical approaches was based on the need to support comparisons of findings across NLTS2 reports. For example, key post-high school outcomes, such as employment rates, postsecondary enrollment rates, and wages, have been reported for NLTS2 data collection waves 2, 3, 4, and 5. Changing the analytic approach would call into question the longitudinal look at such variables. To examine possible differences between the approaches, replicate weights were created for chapter 5 of this report. Findings using the replicate weights were then compared with the findings using formula-based estimate. Of the 623 possible comparisons in the chapter, 19 differences (3percent) were noted: 9 differences that were reported at the $p < .01$ level dropped to $p < .05$; 5 decreased from $p < .001$ to $p < .01$; and 5 increased from either $p < .05$ to $p < .01$ or from $p < .01$ to $p < .001$.

Determining Statistical Significance

The following formula was used to determine the statistical significance of the differences between independent groups.

$$F = \frac{(P_1 - P_2)^2}{SE_1^2 + SE_2^2}$$

For example, this formula could be used to determine whether the difference in the percentages of students who report a particular view among students with learning disabilities and among those with hearing impairments is greater than would be expected to occur by chance. In this formula, P_1 and SE_1 are the first percentage and its standard error and P_2 and SE_2 are the second percentage and its standard error. The squared difference between the two percentages of interest is divided by the sum of the two squared standard errors.

Table A-4. Definitions of disabilities

Autism. A developmental disability significantly affecting verbal and nonverbal communication and social interaction, generally evident before age 3, that adversely affects a child's characteristics often associated with autism are engagement in repetitive activities and stereotyped movements, resistance to environmental change or change in daily routines, and unusual responses to sensory experiences. The term does not apply if a child's educational performance a serious emotional disturbance as defined below.
Deafness. A hearing impairment so severe that the child cannot understand what is being said even with a hearing aid.

Table A-4. (Continued)

Deaf-blindness. A combination of hearing and visual impairments causing such severe communication, developmental, and educational problems that the child cannot be accommodated in either a program specifically for the deaf or a program specifically for the blind.

Emotional disturbance.[1] A condition exhibiting one or more of the following characteristics, displayed over a long period of time and to a marked degree that adversely affects a child's educational performance:
An inability to learn that cannot be explained by intellectual, sensory, or health factors
An inability to build or maintain satisfactory interpersonal relationships with peers or teachers
Inappropriate types of behavior or feelings under normal circumstances
A general pervasive mood of unhappiness or depression
A tendency to develop physical symptoms or fears associated with personal or school problems.
This term includes schizophrenia, but does not include students who are socially maladjusted, unless they have a serious emotional disturbance.

Hearing impairment. An impairment in hearing, whether permanent or fluctuating, that adversely affects a child's educational performance but that is not included under the definition of deafness as listed above.

Mental retardation. Significantly subaverage general intellectual functioning existing concurrently with deficits in adaptive behavior and manifested during the developmental period that adversely affects a performance.

Multiple disabilities. A combination of impairments (such as mental retardation-blindness, or mental retardation-physical disabilities) that causes such severe educational problems that the child cannot be accommodated in a special education program solely for one of the impairments. The term does not include deaf-blindness.

Orthopedic impairment. A severe orthopedic impairment that adversely affects educational performance. The term includes impairments such as amputation, absence of a limb, cerebral palsy, poliomyelitis, and bone tuberculosis.

Other health impairment. Having limited strength, vitality, or alertness due to chronic or acute health problems such as a heart condition, rheumatic fever, asthma, hemophilia, and leukemia, which adversely affect educational performance.[2]

Specific learning disability. A disorder in one or more of the basic psychological processes involved in understanding or in using language, spoken or written, that may manifest itself in an imperfect ability to listen, think, speak, read, write, spell, or do mathematical calculations. This term includes such conditions as perceptual disabilities, brain injury, minimal brain dysfunction, dyslexia, and developmental aphasia. This term does not include children who have learning problems that are primarily the result of visual, hearing, or motor disabilities; mental retardation; or environmental, cultural or economic disadvantage.

Speech or language impairment. A communication disorder such as stuttering, impaired articulation, language impairment, or a voice impairment that adversely affects a child's educational performance.

Traumatic brain injury. An acquired injury to the brain caused by an external physical force, resulting in total or partial functional disability or psychosocial impairment, or both, that adversely affects a child's educational performance. The term applies to open or closed head injuries resulting in impairments in one or more areas, such as cognition; language; memory; attention; reasoning; abstract thinking; judgment; problem solving; sensory, perceptual and motor abilities; psychosocial behavior; physical functions; information processing; and speech. The term does not apply to brain injuries that are congenital or degenerative, or brain injuries induced by birth trauma.

> **Visual impairment, including blindness.** An impairment in vision that, even with correction, adversely affects a child's educational performance. The term includes both partial sight and blindness.

[1] P.L. 105-17, the Individuals with Disabilities Education Act Amendments of 1997, changed "serious emotional disturbance" to "emotional disturbance." The change has no substantive or legal significance. It is intended strictly to eliminate any negative connotation of the term "serious."

[2] OSEP guidelines indicate that "children with ADD, where ADD is a chronic or acute health problem resulting in limited alertness, may be considered disabled under Part B solely on the basis of this disorder under the 'other situations where special education and related services are needed because of the ADD" (Davila, Williams, and MacDonald 1991).

Source: Definitions taken from Knoblauch and Sorenson (1998).

If the product of a calculation is larger than 3.84 (i.e., 1.96^2), the difference is significant at the .05 level—that is, it would occur by chance fewer than 5 times in 100. If the result of the calculation is at least 6.63, the significance level is .01; products of 10.8 or greater are significant at the .001 level (Owen 1962, pp. 12, 51).

Testing for the significance of differences in responses to two survey items for the same individuals involves identifying for each young adult the pattern of response to the two items. Responses to items (e.g., the young adult reported relying "a lot" on parents for support— yes or no—and reported relying on friends "a lot" for support—yes or no) are scored as 0 or 1, producing difference values for individual students of +1 (responded affirmatively to the first item but not the second), 0 (responded affirmatively to both items or neither item), or -1 (responded affirmatively to the second item but not the first). The test statistic is the square of a ratio, where the numerator of the ratio is the weighted mean change score and the denominator is an estimate of the standard error of that mean. Since the ratio approaches a normal distribution by the Central Limit Theorem, for samples of the sizes included in the analyses, this test statistic approximately follows a chi-square distribution with one degree of freedom—i.e., an F (1, infinity) distribution.

Regardless of whether comparisons are for independent or dependent samples, a large number of statistical analyses were conducted and are presented in this report. Since no explicit adjustments were made for multiple comparisons, the likelihood of finding at least one statistically significant difference when no difference exists in the population is substantially larger than the type I error for each individual analysis. This may be particularly true when many of the variables on which the groups are being compared are measures of the same or similar constructs, as is the case in this report. To partially compensate for the number of analyses that were conducted, we used a relatively conservative p value of .01. The text mentions only differences that reach a level of significance of at least $p < .01$. If no level of significance is reported, the group differences described do not attain the $p < .01$ level. Readers also are cautioned that the meaningfulness of differences reported here cannot be inferred from their statistical significance.

Measurement and Reporting Issues

The chapters in this report provide information on specific variables included in analyses. However, several general points about NLTS2 measures that are used repeatedly in analyses should be clear to readers as they consider the findings reported here.

Categorizing Students by Primary Disability

Information about the nature of students' disabilities came from rosters of all students in the NLTS2 age range receiving special education services in the 2000–01 school year under the auspices of participating LEAs and state-supported special schools. In analyses in this report, each student is assigned to a disability category on the basis of the primary disability designated by the student's school or district. Although there are federal guidelines in making category assignments (table A-4), criteria and methods for assigning students to categories vary from state to state and even between districts within states, with the potential for substantial variation in the nature and severity of disabilities included in the categories (see, for example, MacMillan and Siperstein 2002). Therefore, NLTS2 data should not be interpreted as describing students who truly had a particular disability, but rather as describing students who were categorized as having that primary disability.

The exception to reliance on school or district category assignment involves students with deaf-blindness. Because of district variation in assigning students with both hearing and visual impairments to the category of deaf-blindness many students with those dual disabilities are assigned to other primary disability categories, most often hearing impairment, visual impairment, and multiple disabilities. As a result of these classification differences, national estimates suggest that there were 3,196 students with deaf-blindness who were 12 to 17 years old in 1999 (National Technical Assistance Center 1999), whereas the federal child count indicates that 681 were classified with deaf-blindness as their primary disability(Office of Special Education Programs 2001).

To describe the characteristics and experiences of the larger body of young adults with deaf-blindness more precisely, students who were reported by parents or by schools or school districts[53] as having both a hearing and a visual impairment were assigned to the deaf-blindness category for purposes of NLTS2 reporting, regardless of the primary disability category assigned by the school or school district.

Comparisons with the General Population Of Students

In cases in which databases for the general population of young adults are publicly available (e.g., the National Longitudinal Survey of Youth), comparisons have been calculated from those databases for young adults with disabilities who match in age to those included in NLTS2. However, some comparisons have been made by using published data. For some of these comparisons, differences in samples (e.g., ages of young adults) or measurement (e.g., question wording on surveys) reduce the direct comparability of NLTS2 and general population data. Where these limitations affect the comparisons, they are pointed out in the text and the implications for the comparisons are noted.

Reporting Statistics

Statistics are not reported for groups with fewer than 30 members. Statistics with a decimal of .5 are rounded to the next whole number in the text.

APPENDIX A. REFERENCES

[1]   Davila, R. R., Williams, M. L. & MacDonald, J. T. (1991). *Clarification of Policy to Address the Needs of Children with Attention-Deficit Disorders within General and/or Special Education.* Memorandum to Chief State School Officers. Washington, DC: U.S. Department of Education, Office of Special Education and Rehabilitative Services.

[2]   Employment Policies Institute. (2002). *Measuring Poverty in America: Science or Politics?* Available at http://www.epionline.org/studies/epi_poverty_04-2002.pdf.

[3]   Javitz, H. & Wagner, M. (2003). *Analysis of Potential Bias in the Sample of Local Education Agencies (Leas) in the National Longitudinal Transition Study-2 (NLTS2).* Menlo Park, CA: SRI International.

[4]   Knoblauch, B. & Sorenson, B. (1998). Idea's Definition of Disabilities (Eric Ec Digest No. E560). In. Reston, VA: ERIC Clearinghouse on Disabilities and Gifted Education.

[5]   MacMillan, D. L. & Siperstein, G. N. (2002). Learning Disabilities as Operationally Defined by Schools. In R. Bradley, L. Danielson, and D.P. Hallahan (Eds.), *Identification of Learning Disabilities: Research to Practice.* Mahwah, NJ: Lawrence Erlbaum Associates Publishers.

[6]   National Technical Assistance Center. (1999). *National Deaf-Blind Child Count Summary.* Monmouth, OR: Teaching Research Division, Western Oregon University.

[7]   Office of Special Education Programs. (2001). *Table Ad1. Number of Students Age 14 and Older Exiting Special Education, During the 1999-2000 School Year.* Available at http://www.ideadata.org/tables24th/ar_ad1.htm.

[8]   Owen, D. B. (1962). *Handbook of Statistical Tables.* Palo Alto, CA: Addison-Wesley Publishing.

[9]   Quality Education Data. (1999). *State School Guides.* Retrieved August 2, 2004, from http://www.qeddata.com/MarketKno/SchoolGuides/ SchoolGuides.aspx.

APPENDIX B. ADDITIONAL ANALYSES

Characteristics of out-of-High School Young Adults with Disabilities

NLTS2 represents youth with disabilities nationally who were ages 13 through 16, in secondary school, and receiving special education services in grade 7 or above in the 2000–01 school year. This report focuses on young adults no longer in secondary school in 2007. Understanding the characteristics of young adults with disabilities is important for interpreting their after-high school experiences. Tables B-1 through B-3 describe this subsample—young adults with disabilities who were out of high school and for whom data were reported, either by young adult themselves or by their parents, as part of the NLTS2 Wave 4 parent and youth telephone interviews and youth mail survey. They report data for young adults as a group and for those for whom parents and young adults themselves, respectively, were respondents.

**Table B-1. Primary disability category of out-of-high school youth,
overall and by respondent**

Primary disability category	All young adults	Parent respondents	Young adult respondents
	Percent		
Learning disability	63.7 (2.53)	64.1 (3.89)	63.4 (3.34)
Speech/language impairment	4.0 (1.03)	3.2 (1.43)	4.6 (1.45)
Mental retardation	11.0 (1.65)	12.6 (2.69)	9.8 (2.06)
Emotional disturbance	11.4 (1.67)	10.8 (2.52)	11.8 (2.24)
Hearing impairment	1.3 (0.60)	1.5 (0.97)	1.2 (0.76)
Visual impairment	0.5 (0.36)	0.2 (0.40)	0.6 (0.55)
Orthopedic impairment	1.1 (0.55)	0.8 (0.71)	1.3 (0.80)
Other health impairment	4.7 (1.11)	3.7 (1.53)	5.4 (1.57)
Autism	0.5 (0.38)	0.6 (0.64)	0.5 (0.46)
Traumatic brain injury	0.3 (0.28)	0.3 (0.44)	0.3 (0.37)
Multiple disabilities	1.5 (0.63)	2.1 (1.15)	1.0 (0.69)
Deaf-blindness	0.1 (0.19)	0.2 (0.31)	0.1 (0.23)

Note: Standard errors are in parentheses.

Source: U.S. Department of Education, Institute of Education Sciences, National Center for Special Education Research, National Longitudinal Transition Study-2 (NLTS2), Wave 4 parent and youth telephone interview/mail survey, 2007.

The out-of-high school young adult's subsample, like the universe of secondary-school-age young adults with disabilities, is heavily dominated by young adults with learning disabilities; 64 percent of young adults with disabilities were classified for special education services in the learning disability category when they were in high school. At 11 percent for each, the categories of emotional disturbance and mental retardation are the second and third largest categories. All other categories comprise 14 percent of the weighted sample. The disability category distributions of the groups of young adults for whom parents were respondents and those who responded for themselves do not differ significantly.

The majority of young adults (72 percent) were reported by parents to have high functional cognitive skills,[54] from 13 percent to 30 percent had at least some limitation in the functional domains reported in table B-2, and almost one-third (30 percent) had excellent health. Young adults for whom parents responded for them were more likely to be reported as having excellent health than were young adults who responded for themselves (51 percent vs. 23 percent, $p<.01$). There were noother significant differences between respondent groups on these measures.

The majority of young adults with disabilities were identified as having a disability at school entry or in their early years in school (table B-3); 46 percent were reported to have had their disability first identified at ages of 5 to 7, although almost one-third (28 percent) had their disabilities first identified in their infant, toddler, or preschool years. The majority of young adults first began receiving special education services in elementary school, with 47 percent receiving services in their first few years in school and 32 percent healthreceiving services for the first time between ages 8 and 10. No significant differences in the age when a young adult's disability was first identified or when services were first received were apparent between the two respondent groups.

Distribution of Demographic Characteristics across Disability Categories

Findings in this report are presented for young adults with disabilities as a group and then are reported separately for young adults in each federal special education disability category. Findings also are reported for young adults who differ in secondary school-leaving status, gender, race/ethnicity, and household income. These bivariate analyses should not be interpreted as implying that a factor on which subgroups are differentiated (e.g., disability category) has a causal relationship with the differences reported. Further, readers should be aware that demographic factors (e.g., race/ethnicity and household income) are correlated among young adults with disabilities, as well as being distributed differently across disability categories. Table B-4 presents demographic characteristics of young adults with disabilities overall and within each disability category.[55]

This report represents young adults who were in the 19- to 23-year-old age range. Thirty-three percent of young adults were 19- to-20 years old, 20 percent were 21-year-olds, 28 percent who were 22-year-olds, and 19 percent who were 22-year-olds. More young adults with speech/language impairments (45 percent) than youth with disabilities as a group (33 percent) were in the youngest age category (19-to-20 years old, $p < .01$).

Table B-2. Functional characteristics of out-of-high school young adult respondents and those for whom parents responded

Functional characteristics	All young adults	Parent respondents	Young adult respondents
		Percent	
Functional cognitive skills scale score:			
High (13-16)	71.7 (2.67)	70.1 (4.34)	72.9 (3.38)
Medium (8-12)	25.1 (2.57)	24.6 (4.08)	25.5 (3.31)
Low (4-7)	3.2 (1.04)	5.4 (2.14)	1.7 (0.97)
Youth had at least "some trouble":			
Seeing	15.1 (2.15)	16.0 (3.57)	14.5 (2.69)
Speaking	26.7 (2.69)	26.4 (4.32)	26.9 (3.43)

Table B-2. (Continued)

Functional characteristics	All young adults	Parent respondents	Young adult respondents
	Percent		
Understanding speech	30.3 (2.80)	32.2 (4.63)	29.1 (3.50)
Conversing with others	30.3 (2.80)	33.8 (4.66)	28.1 (3.48)
Using one or more appendages	13.3 (2.05)	14.7 (3.46)	12.5 (2.53)
Youth's general was excellent	29.8 (2.59)	40.5 (4.60)	23.0 (2.98)

Note: Standard errors are in parentheses.

Source: U.S. Department of Education, Institute of Education Sciences, National Center for Special Education Research, National Longitudinal Transition Study-2 (NLTS2), Wave 4 parent and youth telephone interview/mail survey, 2007.

Table B-3. Age at identification of and first services for disabilities of out-of-high school young adults respondents and those for whom parents responded

Youth's age	All young adults	Parent respondents	Young adult respondents
	Percent		
Disability first identified at age:			
Birth-1	13.0 (1.86)	14.4 (2.99)	11.8 (2.34)
2-4	15.3 (1.99)	14.1 (2.95)	16.3 (2.68)
5-7	45.6 (2.75)	41.7 (4.19)	48.7 (3.63)
8-10	18.0 (2.12)	19.3 (3.36)	17.0 (2.72)
11 or older	8.2 (1.5)	10.6 (2.61)	6.2 (1.75)
Special education services in school first received at age:			
5-7	46.8 (2.74)	44.2 (4.23)	48.9 (3.57)
8-10	31.5 (2.55)	31.3 (3.95)	31.6 (3.32)
11-13	16.9 (2.06)	19.2 (3.36)	15.1 (2.56)
14 or older	4.8 (1.17)	5.3 (1.91)	4.4 (1.47)

Note: Standard errors are in parentheses.

Source: U.S. Department of Education, Institute of Education Sciences, National Center for Special Education Research, National Longitudinal Transition Study-2 (NLTS2), Wave 4 parent and youth telephone interview/mail survey, 2007.

Table B-4. Demographic characteristics of out-of-high school young adults with disabilities, by disability category

Characteristics	All disabilities	Learning disability	Speech/language impairment	Mental retardation	Emotional disturbance	Hearing impairment	Visual impairment	Orthopedic impairment	Other health impairment	Autism	Traumatic brain injury	Multiple disabilities	Deaf blindness
						Percent							
Age													
19-20	32.5	34.4	44.8	25.4	30.0	26.0	21.1	24.0	29.1	23.9	24.4	20.4	27.8
	(2.47)	(3.78)	(3.88)	(3.53)	(4.02)	(4.45)	(4.70)	(4.00)	(3.80)	(4.49)	(6.48)	(4.58)	(6.12)
21	20.3	18.6	22.8	21.6	24.0	21.6	26.1	21.5	27.8	19.6	20.4	19.2	21.4
	(2.12)	(3.10)	(3.27)	(3.34)	(3.75)	(4.18)	(5.05)	(3.85)	(3.75)	(4.18)	(6.08)	(4.48)	(5.60)
22	28.1	28.8	19.8	30.7	21.9	32.8	29.9	32.4	27.1	33.1	34.7	37.9	25.9
	(2.37	(3.60)	(3.11)	(3.75)	(3.63)	(4.77)	(5.27)	(4.38)	(3.72)	(4.95)	(7.19)	(5.52)	(5.99)
23	19.2	18.2	12.7	22.3	24.1	19.6	23.0	22.1	16.0	23.5	20.6	22.6	24.9
	(2.07)	(3.07)	(2.60)	(3.38)	(3.70)	(4.03)	(4.84)	(3.88)	(3.07)	(4.46)	(6.10)	(4.76)	(5.92)
High school-leaving status													
Completed high school	89.4	90.8	91.8	87.1	80.2	96.2	97.4	95.6	88.4	94.3	95.1	94.9	94.3
	(1.62)	(2.30)	(2.14)	(2.72)	(3.49)	(1.94)	(1.83)	(1.93)	(2.68)	(2.44)	(3.25)	(2.51)	(3.16)
Did not complete high school	10.6	9.2	8.2	12.9	19.8	3.8	2.6	4.5	11.6	5.7	4.9	5.1	5.7
	(1.62)	(2.30)	(2.14)	(2.72)	(3.49)	(1.94)	(1.83)	(1.93)	(2.68)	(2.44)	(3.25)	(2.51)	(3.16)
Gender													
Male	63.1	62.0	62.4	56.4	73.9	52.8	54.0	54.7	71.4	87.3	69.3	61.7	66.9
	(2.54)	(3.86)	(3.78)	(4.03)	(3.85)	(5.07)	(5.74)	(4.66)	(3.78)	(3.51)	(6.96)	(5.53)	(6.43)
Female	36.9	38.0	37.6	43.6	26.1	47.2	46.0	45.3	28.6	12.7	30.7	38.3	33.1
	(2.54)	(3.86)	(3.78)	(4.03)	(3.85)	(5.07)	(5.74)	(4.66)	(3.78)	(3.51)	(6.96)	(5.53)	(6.43)

Characteristics	All disabilities	Learning disability	Speech/language impairment	Mental retardation	Emotional disturbance	Hearing impairment	Visual impairment	Orthopedic impairment	Other health impairment	Autism	Traumatic brain injury	Multiple disabilities	Deaf blindness
							Percent						
Race/ethnicity													
White	64.4	64.7	70.8	56.2	63.5	61.0	64.4	66.6	75.5	72.0	72.1	69.9	59.9
	(2.53)	(3.82)	(3.55)	(4.03)	(4.23)	(4.97)	(5.52)	(4.41)	(3.62)	(4.75)	(6.78)	(5.24)	(6.70)
African American	19.6	17.7	14.0	32.1	23.9	15.5	18.8	16.2	13.8	17.0	15.5	16.2	12.7
	(2.10)	(3.05)	(2.71)	(3.79)	(3.74)	(3.69)	(4.50)	(3.44)	(2.90)	(3.97)	(5.46)	(4.21)	(4.55)
Hispanic	13.3	15.0	12.5	8.6	10.2	18.3	12.9	14.0	9.1	7.2	9.1	10.9	25.3
	(1.79)	(2.85)	(2.58)	(2.28)	(2.65)	(3.94)	(3.86)	(3.24)	(2.41)	(2.73)	(4.35)	(3.55)	(5.94)
Household income													
$25,000 or less	33.0	30.3	22.8	55.2	38.5	28.1	25.8	25.8	18.6	16.8	28.9	31.2	33.9
	(2.50)	(3.70)	(3.31)	(4.10)	(4.31)	(4.61)	(5.10)	(4.15)	(3.28)	(3.97)	(6.86)	(5.34)	(6.51)
$25,001 - $50,000	29.7	31.9	28.5	22.6	27.4	23.4	29.7	29.8	27.4	28.9	28.1	22.7	20.4
	(2.43)	(3.75)	(3.56)	(3.45)	(3.95)	(4.34)	(5.32)	(4.34)	(3.76)	(4.82)	(6.81)	(4.83)	(5.54)
More than $50,000	37.3	37.8	48.8	22.2	34.2	48.6	44.5	44.4	54.1	54.3	43.0	46.1	45.8
	(2.57)	(3.90)	(3.94)	(3.43)	(4.20)	(5.13)	(5.79)	(4.71)	(4.20)	(5.29)	(7.50)	(5.75)	(6.85)

Note: Standard errors are in parentheses.

Source: U.S. Department of Education, Institute of Education Sciences, National Center for Special Education Research, National Longitudinal Transition Study-2 (NLTS2), Wave 5 parent and youth telephone interview/mail survey, 2009.

Eleven percent of young adults with disabilities had left high school without a diploma or a certificate of completion.[56] Fewer young adults with visual impairments (3 percent) or hearing impairments (4 percent) than those with disabilities overall did not complete high school ($p < .001$ for both comparisons).

Whereas about half of young adults in the general population (51 percent) were male,[57] more than two-thirds of out-of-high school young adults with disabilities (63 percent) were male ($p < .001$). Young adults with autism had a higher percentage of males (87percent) compared with young adults with disabilities overall ($p < .001$).

Young adults with disabilities differed from those in the general population in their racial/ethnic backgrounds. They were disproportionately likely to be African American, relative to the general population; African Americans comprised 15 percent of young adults in the general population[58] but 20 percent of young adults with disabilities ($p < .01$). Young adults with mental retardation were more likely to be African American than were young adults with disabilities as a group (32 percent vs. 20percent, $p < .01$).

Young adults with disabilities were more likely than those in the general population to have come from families with lower income level households. One-third of those with disabilities (33 percent) included in this report had families with incomes of $25,000 or less; in comparison, 29 percent[59] of their peers in the general population lived in low-income-level households ($p < .01$). Young adults with mental retardation (55 percent) were more likely and young adults with autism (17percent) or other health impairments (19 percent) were less likely to come from families with incomes of $25,000 or less than were young adults with disabilities as a group (33 percent, $p < .001$).

APPENDIX B. REFERENCE

[1] Wagner, M., Marder, C., Levine, P., Cameto, R., Cadwallader, T.W., Blackorby, J., Cardoso, D. & Newman, L. (2003). *The Individual and Household Characteristics of Youth with Disabilities. A Report from the National Longitudinal Transition Study-2 (NLTS2)*. Menlo Park, CA: SRI International.

REFERENCES

[1]   Bearman, P. S. & Moody, J. (2004). Suicide and Friendships among American Adolescents. *American Journal of Public Health*, *94*, 89-95.

[2]   Berkner, L., He, S. & Cataldi, E. F. (2002). *Descriptive Summary of 1995-1996 Beginning Postsecondary Students: Six Years Later*. Washington, DC: U.S. Department of Education, National Center for Education Statistics.

[3]   Cameto, R., Levine, P. & Wagner, M. (2004). *Transition Planning for Students With Disabilities. A Special Topic Report From the National Longitudinal Transition Study-2 (NLTS2)*. Menlo Park, CA: SRI International.

[4]   Carnevale, A. P. & Desrochers, D. M. (2003). *Standards for What? The Economic Roots of K-16 Reform*. Princeton, NJ: Educational Testing Service.

[5]   Carnevale, A. P. & Fry, R. A. (2000). *Crossing the Great Divide: Can We Achieve*

Equity When Generation Y Goes to College? Princeton, NJ: Educational Testing Service.

[6] Conover, W. J. (1999). *Practical Nonparametric Statistics* (3rd ed.). New York, NY: John Wiley and Sons.

[7] Crosnoe, R. & Needham, B. (2004). Holism, Contextual Variability, and the Study of Friendships in Adolescent Development. *Child Development*, 75(1), 264-279.

[8] Erikson, E. H. (1974). *Dimensions of a New Identity*. New York, NY: Norton.

[9] Fraser, M. W. (1997). *Risk and Resilience in Childhood: An Ecological Perspective.* Washington, DC: National Association of Social Workers Press.

[10] Furstenberg, F., Jr. (2010). On a New Schedule: Transitions to Adulthood and Family Change. *Transition to Adulthood, 20*(1), 67-87.

[11] Galambos, N. L., Barker, E. T. & Krahn, H. J. (2006). Depression, Self-Esteem, and Anger in Emerging Adulthood: Seven-Year Trajectories. *Developmental Psychology, 42(2)*, 350–365.

[12] Haber, M., Karpur, A., Deschenes, N. & Clark, H. (2008). Predicting Improvement of Transitioning Young People in the Partnerships for Youth Transition Initiative: Findings From a Multisite Demonstration. *Journal of Behavioral Health Services and Research, 35(4)*, 488-513.

[13] Halpern, A. S. (1985). Transition: A Look at the Foundation. *Exceptional Children, 51*, 479-486.

[14] Heeringa, S. G., West, B. T. & Berglund, P. A. (2010). *Applied Survey Data Analysis.* Boca Raton, FL: Chapman & Hall/CRC Press.

[15] Hogan, D. P. & Astone, N. M. (1986). The Transition to Adulthood. *Annual Review of Sociology, 12*, 109-130.

[16] Howell, K. W. & Wolford, B. I. (2002). *Corrections and Juvenile Justice: Current Education Practice for Youth With Learning and Other Disabilities. Monograph Series on Education, Disability and Juvenile Justice.* College Park, MD: University of Maryland.

[17] Janus, A. L. (2009). Disability and the Transition to Adulthood. *Social Forces, 88(1)*, 99-120.

[18] Johnson, N. & Kotz, S. (1995). *Distributions in Statistics: Continuous Distributions* (Vol. 2). New York, NY: John Wiley and Sons.

[19] Katz-Wise, S. L., Priess, H. A. & Hyde, J. S. (2010). Gender-Role Attitudes and Behavior across the Transition to Parenthood. *Developmental Psychology, 46(1)*, 18–28.

[20] Keller, T. E., Cusick, G. R. & Courtney, M. E. (2007). Approaching the Transition to Adulthood: Distinctive Profiles of Adolescents Aging out of the Child Welfare System. *Social Service Review, 81(3)*, 453-484.

[21] Marcotte, D. E., Bailey, T., Borkoski, C. & Kienzel, G. S. (2005). The Returns of a Community College Education: Evidence From the National Education Longitudinal Survey. *Educational Evaluation and Policy Analysis, 27(2)*, 157-175.

[22] Mirowsky, J. & Ross, C. E. (2010). Well Being across the Life Course. In T.L. Scheid (Ed.), *A Handbook for the Study of Mental Health: Social Contexts, Theories, and Systems* (2nd ed., pp. 361-383). New York, NY: Cambridge University Press.

[23] Modell, J. (1989). *Into One's Own: From Youth to Adulthood in the United States 1920-1975.* Berkeley and Los Angeles: University of California Press.

[24] Morningstar, M. E., Frey, B. B., Noonan, P. M., Ng, J., Clavenna-Deane, B., Graves, P., Kellems, R., McCall, Z., Pearson, M., Bjorkman Wade, D. & Williams-Diehm, K. (2010). A Preliminary Investigation of Transition Preparation and Self-Determination for Students With Disabilities in Postsecondary Education Settings. *Career Development for Exceptional Individuals, 33(2)*, 80-94.

[25] National Center on Secondary Education and Transition. (2003). *A National Leadership Summit on Improving Results for Youth: State Priorities and Needs for Assistance.* Retrieved July 19, 2004, From http://www.ncset.org/summit03/NCSETSummit 03findings.pdf.

[26] The National Collaborative on Workforce & Disability for Youth and Workforce Strategy Center. (2009). *Career-Focused Services for Students With Disabilities at Community Colleges.* Washington, DC: Institute for Educational Leadership.

[27] Newman, L., Wagner, M., Cameto, R. & Knokey, A. M. (2009). *The Post-High School Outcomes of Youth With Disabilities up to 4 Years after High School. A Report From the National Longitudinal Transition Study-2 (NLTS2)* (NCSER 2009-3017). Menlo Park, CA: SRI International.

[28] Newman, L., Wagner, M., Cameto, R., Knokey, A. M. & Shaver, D. (2010). *Comparisons across Time of the Outcomes of Youth With Disabilities up to 4 Years after High School. A Report of Findings From the National Longitudinal Transition Study (NLTS) and the National Longitudinal Transition Study-2 (NLTS2)* (NCSER 2010-3008). Menlo Park, CA: SRI International.

[29] Newman, L., Wagner, M., Knokey, A. M., Marder, C., Nagle, K., Shaver, D., Wei, X., (with Cameto, R., Contreras, E., Ferguson, K., Greene, S. & Schwarting, M. (2011). *The Post-High School Outcomes of Young Adults With Disabilities up to 8 Years after High School: A Report From the National Longitudinal Transition Study-2 (NLTS2)* (NCSER 2011-3005). Menlo Park, CA: SRI International.

[30] O'Day, B. & Stapleton, D. (2009). *Transforming Disability Policy for Youth and Young Adults With Disabilities* (Research Brief 09-01). Washington, DC: Center for Studying Disability Policy.

[31] Oesterle, S., Hawkins, D., Hill, K. & Bailey, J. (2010). Men's and Women's Pathways to Adulthood and Their Adolescent Precursors. *Journal of Marriage and Family, 72(5)*, 1436-1453.

[32] Quinn, M. M., Rutherford, R. B., Leone, P. E., Osher, D. M. & Poirier, J. M. (2005). Youth With Disabilities in Juvenile Corrections: A National Survey. *Exceptional Children, 71*, 339-345.

[33] Resnick, M. D., Bearman, P. S., Blum, R. W., Bauman, K. E., Harris, K. M., Jones, J., Tabor, J., Beuhring, T., Sieving, R. E., Shew, M., Ireland, M., Bearinger, L. H. & Udry, J. R. (1997). Protecting Adolescents From Harm: Findings From the National Longitudinal Study on Adolescent Health. *Journal of the American Medical Association, 278(10)*, 823-832.

[34] Rindfuss, R. R. (1991). The Young Adult Years: Diversity, Structural Change and Fertility. Population Association of America Presidential Address. *Demography, 28*, 493-512.

[35] Rodgers, K. B. & Rose, H. A. (2002). Risk and Resiliency Factors among Adolescents Who Experience Marital Transitions. *Journal of Marriage and the Family, 64(4)*, 1024-1037.

[36] Rutherford, R. B., Bullis, M., Anderson, C. & Griller-Clark, H. (2002). Youth With Disabilities in Juvenile Corrections: A National Survey. *Exceptional Children, 71(3)*, 339-345.

[37] Settersten, R. A., Jr. & Ray, B. (2010). What's Going on With Young People Today? The Long and Twisting Path to Adulthood. *Transition to Adulthood, 20(1)*.

[38] Smith, C., Lizotte, A. J., Thornberry, T. P. & Krohn, M. D. (1995). Resilient Youth: Identifying Factors That Prevent High-Risk Youth From Engaging in Delinquency and Drug Use. In J. Hagan (Ed.), *Delinquency and Disrepute in the Life Course* (pp. 217-247). Greenwich, CT: JAI Press.

[39] Stodden, R. A. & Mruzek, D. W. (2010). An Introduction to Postsecondary Education and Employment of Persons With Autism and Developmental Disabilities. *Focus and Autism and Other Developmental Disabilities, 25(3)*, 131-133.

End Notes

[1] The age of young adults with disabilities in 2007 was based on birthdates provided by parents during interviews and the date of the Wave 4 interview.

[2] Findings are reported for White, African American, and Hispanic youth; other racial/ethnic categories are too small (less than 3 percent of the population of youth with disabilities) to report findings separately. Parent's household income is reported using the three income categories included in the data collection instrument (i.e., $25,000 or less, $25,001 to $50,000, and more than $50,000. NLTS2 household income item categories were based on a review of general population statistics to ensure that the household income response categories fairly evenly divided the population. In NLTS2 Wave 1, the income breakdown was 35 percent for the category of $25,000 or less, 31 percent for $25,001 to $50,000, and 34 percent for more than $50,000. For consistency across the report, all comparisons are presented for all variables unless otherwise noted in a section (i.e., by length of time out of high school, high school completion status, disability category, age, gender, household income, and race/ethnicity.)

[3] The definitions of the 12 primary disability categories used in this report are specified by law and presented in table A-4, appendix A.

[4] Additional information about NLTS2 is available at www.nlts2.org.

[5] NLTS2 instruments are available at www.nlts2.org.

[6] All unweighted sample sizes included in the text, figures, and tables of this report are rounded to the nearest 10, per IES Disclosure Review Board requirements.

[7] See appendix A for more information on sample eligibility.

[8] Parents of youth age 18 or older were told that interview questions would pertain to "school or work and social activities, as well as a few questions about things like [his/her] attitudes and experiences, including smoking, drinking, and ever having been arrested"; items related to these kinds of risk behaviors were asked only of youth age 18 or older. A total of 164 parents reported that their children could respond to the telephone interview but did not give permission for their children to be interviewed (4 percent of those reportedly able to respond); the interview then continued with the parents and obtained additional information on subjects such as employment and postsecondary education. Analyses of the disability category distribution and demographic factors of youth who were able to respond and given permission to do so and those who were not permitted to be interviewed revealed no significant or sizable differences between the two groups.

[9] Readers should be aware of the potential for differences in reports across modes of data collection (i.e., mail questionnaire vs. telephone interview). Differences between modes of data collection were explored and most were minor and did not support further examination, The one exception was that more young adults with hearing impairments responded to the mail rather than the telephone survey.

[10] Youth respondents were informed that the study would contact parents and that the youth could ask that their parent not be contacted; 20 percent of parent part 2 interviews were completed by parents after young adult could not be reached.

[11] Young adults with disabilities are included in the general population comparison sample because excluding them would require using self-reported disability data, which frequently are not an accurate indicator of disability, resulting in both over- and underestimations of disability. For example, a large proportion of self-identified disabilities in postsecondary are visual impairments because of confusion by students who wear glasses. In addition, NLTS2 findings indicate that less than one-third (32 percent) of youth who were identified by their

secondary school as having a disability consider themselves to have a disability by the time they are age 17 or older.

[12] Given that interview/survey respondents were weighted to represent the universe and individuals who failed to respond to the survey as a whole were assigned a weight of zero, imputing missing values for nonrespondents would not affect analysis results. In addition, for those who responded to the interview/survey, item nonresponse was relatively low— item nonresponse ranged from less than 1 percent to less than 3 percent for the key outcome variables.

[13] All standard errors in this report were calculated using formula-based estimates rather than estimates based on replicate weights. See Appendix A for description of estimating standard errors. As a 10-year longitudinal study, NLTS2 has used this formula-based procedure to calculate standard errors throughout the duration of the study, rather than use currently available procedures. This decision to maintain consistency in analytical approaches was based on the need to support comparisons of findings across NLTS2 reports. To examine possible differences between approaches, replicate weights were created for chapter 5 of this report. Findings using the replicate weights were then compared with the findings using formula-based estimate. Of the 623 possible comparisons in the chapter, 19 differences (3 percent) were noted, supporting the decision to maintain the use of formula-based estimates.

[14] In the case of unweighted data, two percentages are usually compared by using nonparametric statistics, such as the Fisher exact test. In the case of NLTS2, the data were weighted, and the usual nonparametric tests would yield significance levels that are too small (Heeringa, West, and Berglund 2010) because the NLTS2 effective sample size is less than the nominal sample size. Instead, to test for the equality between the mean values of the responses to a single survey item in two disjoint subpopulations, we began by computing a ratio where the numerator was the difference of the sample means for those subpopulations. (In the case of Bernoulli variables, each mean was a weighted percentage.) The denominator for the ratio was the estimated standard error of the numerator, where the standard errors were adjusted to take into account clustering, stratification, and unequal weights. The adjustment to the variances was determined in a design effect study that compared traditionally calculated variances with those calculated using 32 balanced repeated replicate weights. Sample sizes (and consequently degrees of freedom) for Student t types of ratios were typically reasonably large (i.e., never fewer than 30 in each group), so the ratio follows, by the Central Limit Theorem, an approximately normal distribution. For a two-tailed test, the test statistic is the square of the ratio, which then follows an approximate chi-square distribution with one degree of freedom. Because a chi-square distribution with one degree of freedom is the same as an F distribution with one degree of freedom in the numerator and an infinite number of degrees in the denominator, the test statistic approximately follows an $F(1, infinity)$ distribution. Since the application of adjustments from the design effect study tended to slightly overestimate the standard errors from balanced repeated replicates, the use of infinite degrees of freedom, rather than 31 degrees of freedom, nevertheless resulted in actual p values that were slightly lower than nominal p values.

[15] Testing for the significance of differences in responses to two survey items for the same individuals involves identifying for each youth the pattern of response to the two items. The response to each item (e.g., the youth reported relying "a lot" on parents for support— yes or no— and reported relying on friends "a lot" for support—yes or no) is scored as 0 or 1, producing difference values for individual students of +1 (responded affirmatively to the first item but not the second), 0 (responded affirmatively to both or neither item), or -1 (responded affirmatively to the second item but not the first). The test statistic is the square of a ratio, where the numerator of the ratio is the weighted mean change score and the denominator is an estimate of the standard error of that mean. Since the ratio approaches a normal distribution by the Central Limit Theorem, this test statistic approximately follows a chi-square distribution with one degree of freedom, that is, an $F(1, infinity)$ distribution.

[16] See Wagner et al. (2003) for relationships of demographic factors and disability categories for the full NLTS2 sample.

[17] The final NLTS2 overview report, (Newman et al., 2011), based on 2009 data, when young adults with disabilities had been out of high school up to 8 years will include a description of outcomes (e.g. employment status) as well as experiences (e.g. type of job, number of hours worked).

[18] Respondents were asked, "Since leaving high school have you taken any classes from a [postsecondary school]?"

[19] U.S. Department of Labor, Bureau of Labor Statistics, National Longitudinal Survey of Youth 1997 (NLSY97) 2001 youth survey, responses for 19- to 23-year-olds.

[20] Respondents were asked, "Are you [YOUTH] going to a [postsecondary school] now?" Those who had been enrolled in a postsecondary school but were not currently enrolled, were asked, "Are you [YOUTH] not going to a [postsecondary school] now because you: are on school vacation, graduated or completed the program, or some other reason?" Young adults who were on school vacation were recoded as being currently enrolled in postsecondary school.

[21] Respondents who had been in a postsecondary program earlier but were not currently enrolled were asked, "Are you [YOUTH] not going to a [postsecondary school] now because you are on school vacation, graduated or completed the program, or some other reason?"

[22] Respondents were asked, "Do you [YOUTH] have a paid job now, other than work around the house?"

[23] Respondents to the general population NLSY97 2001 survey were asked, "Are you currently working for an employer?"

[24] Respondents were asked, "About how much are you [YOUTH] paid at this job?" Weekly, yearly, and monthly wages were converted to hourly wages by dividing the wage by the number of hours worked per week, and then multiplying by 4.3 for monthly-reported wages or by 52 for yearly-reported wages.

[25] This chapter focuses on involvement in any type of paid employment (other than work around the house), mirroring much of what is presented in this report's employment chapter.

[26] Sheltered employment is employment provided for individuals with disabilities in a protected environment under an institutional program.

[27] Young adults in the general population were considered to have been positively engaged if they were employed or had a job since turning 18; or had ever attended a postsecondary school.

[28] Respondents were asked where youth had lived in the past 2 years and where youth lived "now." A variable measuring the degree of residential independence since high school was derived from three items: if the young adult had lived independently or semi-independently in the past 2 years, was currently living independently or semi-independently, and when he or she had left school.

[29] This section has focused on young adults who lived independently or semi-independently at the time of the interview. Young adults not included in figure 9 are those who lived with a parent or family member or guardian (62 percent at the time of the interview), in an institution (1 percent at the time of the interview), or in a group home (1 percent at the time of the interview).

[30] Respondents were asked, "Have you [Has youth] ever had or fathered any children?"

[31] Calculated from the National Longitudinal Survey of Youth (NLSY), 2001, for out-of-high school 19- to 23-year-olds.

[32] Respondents were asked, "Are you [Is youth] engaged, single, never married, married, in a marriage-like relationship, divorced, separated, or widowed?"

[33] Calculated from the National Longitudinal Survey of Youth (NLSY), 2001, for out-of-high school 19- to 23-year-olds. Engaged and divorced/separated/widowed were not available in NLSY.

[34] Respondents were asked, "Do you have [a savings account], [a checking account where you write checks], and [a credit card or charge account in your own name]?"

[35] Protective factors have been defined as "those aspects of the individual and his or her environment that buffer or moderate the effect of risk" (U.S. Department of Health and Human Services 2001, chapter 4, paragraph 1).

[36] Respondents were asked, "During the past 12 months, about how many days a week [did you/did name of youth] get together with friends (outside of school if youth was in school) and outside of organized activities or groups?"

[37] Respondents were asked, "During the past 12 months [have you/has name of youth] taken lessons or classes (outside of school for those in school) in things like art, music, dance, a foreign language, religion, or computer skills?"

[38] Respondents were asked, "During the past 12 months [have you/has name of youth] done any volunteer or community service activities? This could include community service that is part of a school class or other group activity."

[39] Respondents were asked, if a youth was not enrolled in school, "During the past 12 months [have you/has name of youth] participated in any school activities outside of class, such as a sports team, band or chorus, a school club, or student government?" All respondents were asked, "During the past 12 months [have you/has name of youth] participated in any [out-of-high school, for those in school] group activity, such as scouting, church or temple youth group, or nonschool team sports like soccer or softball?"

[40] Youth are those less than 18 years old.

[41] Respondents were asked, "In the past 2 years, [have you/has name of youth] been stopped and questioned by police except for a traffic violation?"

[42] Respondents were asked, "[Have you/has name of youth] been arrested at any time in the past 2 years?"

[43] Respondents were asked, "In the past 2 years, [have you/has name of youth] been in jail overnight?"

[44] Respondents were asked, "In the past 2 years, [have you/has name of youth] been on probation or parole?"

[45] Data on criminal justice system involvement in the preceding 2 years that were collected in Wave 4 were combined with reports of involvement in Waves 1, 2, and 3 to construct variables measuring whether youth had ever experienced each form of involvement.

[46] Calculated from the National Longitudinal Study of Adolescent Health (Add Health), Wave 3, 2001–02, for out-of-high school 19- to 23-year-olds.

[47] LEAs were instructed to include on the roster any student for whom they were administratively responsible, even if the student was not educated within the LEA (e.g., attended school sponsored by an education cooperative or was sent by the LEA to a private school). Despite these instructions, some LEAs may have underreported students served outside the LEA.

[48] Enrollment in grades 7 through 12 was estimated by dividing the total enrollment in all grade levels served by an LEA by the number of grade levels to estimate an enrollment per grade level. This was multiplied by 6 to estimate the enrollment in grades 7 through 12.

[49] The "50 percent sampling efficiency" indicated in the above text means that a simple random sample of half the size as NLTS2 would have the same standard error as obtained in NLTS2 when the complex sampling design is taken into account. Sampling efficiency is the inverse of the DEFT, where DEFT is the square foot of DEFF (the design effect).

[50] Students who were designated as being in ungraded programs also were sampled if they met the age criteria.

[51] As part of the process of selecting the student sample, random numbers were generated and the sample universe file was sorted by these numbers. Sample members were selected beginning at the start of the file until the required number of students had been selected. If two students were selected from the same family, the first student on the list was chosen for the sample (i.e., the one with the smaller random number).

[52] All NLTS2 instruments are available on the NLTS2 website, www.nlts2.org.

[53] Some special schools and school districts reported secondary disabilities for students. For example, a student with visual impairment as his or her primary disability category also could have been reported as having a hearing impairment as a secondary disability.

[54] Parents were asked to use a 4-point scale ranging from "not at all well" to "very well" to evaluate four of their sons' or daughters' skills that often are used in daily activities: reading and understanding common signs, telling time on a clock with hands, counting change, and looking up telephone numbers and using the telephone. These skills are referred to as "functional cognitive skills" because they require the cognitive ability to read, count, and calculate. As such, they suggest much about students' abilities to perform a variety of more complex cognitive tasks. However, they also require sensory and motor skills—to see signs, manipulate a telephone, and so on. Consequently, a high score indicates high functioning in all of these areas, but a low score can result from a deficit in the cognitive, sensory, and/or motor domains. A summative scale of parents' ratings of these functional cognitive skills ranges from 4 (all skills done "not at all well") to 16 (all skills done "very well").

[55] See Wagner et al. (2003) for relationships of demographic factors and disability categories for the full NLTS2 sample.

[56] This includes 10 percent of young adults who were reported to have dropped out and 1 percent who reportedly left high school without finishing for other reasons (e.g., permanent expulsion). Approximately 8 percent had not completed high school in an earlier wave of NLTS2 data collection, but had since earned their GED or high school equivalency. These young adults are included in this report's analyses as being high school completers.

[57] General population data computed for 19- to 23-year-olds, using United States Census Bureau 2000 data.

[58] See footnote 4.

[59] See footnote 4.

CHAPTER SOURCES

The following chapters have been previously published:

Chapter 1 - This is an edited, reformatted and augmented version of a United States Department of Education publication, report NCSER 2011-3005, dated September 2011.

Chapter 2 - This is an edited, reformatted and augmented version of a United States Department of Education publication, report NCSER 2011-3004, dated September 2011.

INDEX

D

E

F

symptoms, 186, 290

T

target, 18, 171, 173, 211, 276, 277
target number, 173, 277
taxes, 206
taxonomy, 43
teachers, 172, 186, 276, 290
team sports, 207, 304
technology, 47, 95
telephone, 2, 18, 19, 20, 21, 22, 24, 174, 175, 176, 177, 178, 179, 189, 190, 191, 193, 194, 202, 207, 210, 211, 212, 213, 214, 216, 279, 280, 281, 282, 283, 294, 296, 298, 302, 305
telephone numbers, 20, 175, 176, 177, 207, 213, 280, 281, 305
test statistic, 16, 25, 185, 203, 217, 291, 303
testing, 47
trade, 27
training, 5, 6, 12, 13, 17, 67, 76, 79, 81, 82, 83, 96, 100, 101, 102, 103, 104, 105, 119, 120, 121, 122, 124, 125, 126, 195, 205, 237, 238, 240, 242, 244, 245
transcripts, 20, 22, 175, 177, 202, 210, 211, 214, 279, 282
transition to adulthood, vii, 209
transportation, 76
trauma, 186, 291
traumatic brain injury, 9, 33, 34, 77, 86, 96, 146, 165, 174, 270, 271, 278
tuberculosis, 186, 290
tutoring, 49

U

U.S. Department of Commerce, 3, 28, 200
U.S. Department of Labor, 30, 31, 63, 72, 84, 91, 128, 133, 203, 221, 222, 232, 235, 239, 248, 251, 303
U.S. economy, 3, 28
UK, 198
unemployment rate, 228
unhappiness, 186, 290

unions, 172, 276
United, 24, 207, 300, 305
United States, 24, 207, 300, 305
universe, 18, 171, 172, 173, 181, 182, 184, 189, 203, 207, 211, 276, 277, 278, 286, 287, 288, 295, 303, 305
universities, 3, 8, 30, 47, 49, 51, 61, 223, 227
urban, 18, 172, 173, 211, 276, 278
urbanicity, 173, 278

V

variations, 96
violence, 13, 14, 28, 145, 146, 158, 159, 160, 161, 162, 260
vision, 18, 171, 183, 186, 211, 276, 288, 291
vote, 7, 12, 151, 153, 154, 155, 156, 157, 207

W

wages, 67, 88, 94, 95, 174, 180, 185, 205, 218, 219, 228, 229, 233, 279, 284, 289, 304
Washington, 188, 197, 198, 199, 200, 201, 293, 299, 300, 301
wealth, 18, 172, 173, 180, 211, 277, 285
weapons, 160
wear, 202, 302
web, 23, 119, 215, 238
welfare, 139
workers, 3, 28, 85, 86, 87, 88, 90, 220
working conditions, 67, 101, 102, 103, 104, 105

Y

yield, 203, 303
young people, 146, 260
young women, 13, 82, 88
youth transition, 27, 219
youth with disabilities, vii, 2, 5, 17, 18, 26, 28, 67, 78, 80, 81, 82, 83, 127, 189, 201, 209, 210, 211, 215, 218, 269, 278, 294, 295, 302